A JOURNEY THROUGH TIME IN AFRICA

By Peter Peeters:

The Elephant Within Us, Book Guild Publishing, 2011
Wherever You Are I Will Find You, Book Guild Publishing, 2013

A Journey Through Time in Africa

Peter Peeters

Claire van Velsen

Book Guild Publishing

First published in Great Britain in 2015 by
The Book Guild Ltd
9 Priory Business Park
Wistow Road, Kibworth
Leics, LE8 0RX

Typesetting in Baskerville

Printed and bound in Malta by Gutenberg Press Ltd

A catalogue record for this book is available from
The British Library.

ISBN 978 1 910508 50 3

CONTENTS

When we think of Africa today, chaos and misery come to mind. This is not a book about that kind of Africa. For there exists another Africa, one of hope and expectations, of beauty and smiles – a world akin to the dreams of our forgotten youth where adventure beckons; where things can happen that are so unexpected, sometimes so surreal, that they happen nowhere else; where nothing can be taken for granted; but where you feel truly alive.

ACKNOWLEDGEMENTS

We wish to thank Bernard Stroobant for his care in getting the Land Rover ready for the journey, and both him, Aziz and Philippe De Cordier for helping to restore the roof of Claire's house after the fire.

We are particularly grateful to all those people – some mentioned in this book, others not – who kindly invited us into their homes throughout the journey, giving us unstinting help; and to Jean-Paul Jesse for allowing us to discover Kenya and the nomadic Turkana tribe.

Our heartfelt thanks to all the people of Africa we met along our journey for making us feel welcome in their villages, for their smiling friendliness and for generously sharing the little they had with us.

Our thanks also go to Ms Voogt of the Belgian Ministry for Cooperation and Development, and Pierre Cros of the European Commission, for convincing their respective services to buy our films on development in Africa.

Robert Poole, a great Land Rover specialist, made sure we used the right mechanical terms, and his wife, Caroline, who read some chapters, corrected a number of mistakes.

And last but not least, the authors wish to thank Catherine Meakins for her unfailing dedication. We found in her someone who applied her great sense of the English written word to weeding out many inadequate expressions, Gallicisms and unbalanced sentences. She also pointed out a number of abrupt transitions in the story. She has given her thoughts and time unsparingly aiming to create a perfect text.

PART 1

Preparing for the Journey

We can but try ...

CHAPTER 1
Planning and Reality

How dull life would be if we didn't have dreams …

When we are young, everything seems possible. Each moment is lived intensely, days are long, a year feels interminable and the future lies far away, almost beyond the horizon, but that future is sure to be exciting. Think of what we will do once our studies are over – the moment we are free! We know nothing yet of the years of toil ahead, or of the money we will have to earn to pay the bills. No … we dream. We are going to do fantastic things …

Then we are thrown onto the treadmill of working society … and as if that wasn't enough, we set up house. We are busy from morning till night, we have no time to let our minds wander; we have to carry on. And maybe this is all for the best because otherwise we might begin to think about the meaning of the life we're leading. We might even look back and wonder where all our dreams have gone …

After ten years of working life, my dreams should have been ground down, too, but they weren't. I suppose that some people are incurable and I must have been one of them. I had been doing research in High Energy Physics, coming up with one idea after another, the grander the better. Then, as I returned to Brussels after a year in the USA, I met Claire – a dreamer if ever there was one. She went through life light-heartedly, moving about as if she were surrounded by a sparkling bubble. And being with her, I just lived for the day.

Unfortunately this happy state of innocence was not to last. So far I had been unaware of much of what was going on in the wider world, but in 1975 I came across reports containing dire predictions about the future, and this set me thinking. Was it true that 'mankind was at a turning point'? Were we really heading for a planetary crisis?

As I have always had an independent turn of mind, I decided to find out for myself what was going on. I began to collect data on anything that seemed connected to human activities and population, and to write computer programs to analyse these. My analysis suggested that the great wave of planetary problems was not going to happen until the twenty-first century, and that the origin of future crises would lie in the lack of development of the poorer two-thirds of the human population.

I continued to do my work at the University of Brussels as best I could, but gradually the world's future began to take centre stage in my preoccupations. The more I thought about it, the more I became convinced that only the rapid development of its poorer parts could avert a future planetary crisis. But what was stopping the then-called 'Third World', in particular Africa and India, from developing rapidly?

I started to read whatever I found on development and its problems, but none of the dozens of opinions I encountered really satisfied me. By now I was worrying about the planet as if it were a personal matter. I felt I had to do something. Maybe I should go to the Third World to study the problems of development at first-hand?

Had I lived with someone who had her two feet squarely planted on the earth, this phase of deep involvement might have passed without any lasting consequences, but I lived with Claire and when I told her about my preoccupations, she overflowed with enthusiasm. Going to the Third World was the right thing to do; being on the spot I could discover what was going wrong and, she was sure, I would come back with the answers I was seeking. Why not set off together in a four-wheel-drive vehicle and head for faraway places?

It was music to my ears. When you are in your late thirties, you still believe that your work is important and your contribution will make a difference. I was convinced that once I had understood the problems I would be able to suggest solutions. And so was born the idea of an expedition through the developing world. As Claire would have said, 'Of course there is a place for dreamers in the world.'

Planning …

You do not improvise an expedition like the one we were about to undertake. If you want to be successful, you have to start preparations well in advance. And you do not take chances; you plan everything very carefully, down to the smallest details. You want to be sure that things will run smoothly, like clockwork …

I had applied for a sabbatical year well in advance and the University of Brussels had given me a year's leave without salary, beginning 1 October 1981. And I had found a second-hand four-wheel-drive vehicle that seemed exactly right for the trip: a long-wheelbase Land Rover with a diesel engine that would be our home on wheels for a whole year. Opening the back gave access to the 'sleeping compartment', which was conveniently separated from the front by a thick plywood enclosure. But in an emergency it was possible to access the steering cabin from the sleeping compartment. You had to be a snake man, though, to wriggle through the narrow central opening in the plywood.

'This Land Rover is just what you need,' said the man who sold it to us. 'And look, it even has a mesh security grill over the rear windows for safety! You won't find anything better.' The price he asked – 200,000 Belgian francs (about £2,900 at the time) – seemed a bit high for a fifteen-year-old vehicle, but he assured me that it was in top condition. He had driven it a couple of times back and forth to Iran where he'd been working and was full of praise for its performance. When I pointed out that it already had 120,000 miles on the clock, he waved away my objections and boasted that it could easily do as many miles again without any problem. 'These engines go on forever,' he said. I finally agreed to the price, reasoning that I was lucky to have found a second-hand, four-wheel-drive vehicle that suited my purpose. Anyway, a new, unequipped one would have cost at least three times as much and we simply didn't have the funds for that.

A photograph taken in front of our home for one of the newspapers. The Land Rover is still as we bought it. Note the boots to make us look like adventurers.

By mid-June journalists had come to take photographs and interview Claire and me, and articles were appearing in newspapers and magazines. The precise itinerary had been established: through Africa, then crossing to India, Southeast Asia, Indonesia, Latin America and back to Europe – around the world, no less. We were going to drive most of the way, shipping by sea only where land travel was impossible. Even the date of departure had been fixed: the morning of 1 October, the first day of my sabbatical year. Nothing was left to fate …

… and Reality

There was a problem, however. Money wasn't coming in as I had hoped. We had contacted a number of magazines and Claire had secured a commitment from a women's magazine. During our trip she would send them articles and photographs, and if they thought the material suitable, they would pay for it. I had also contacted lots of organisations, ministries, the European Commission … you name it. At the European Commission (the EEC as it was then called) I had found an enthusiastic backer.

'Africa is where you should go,' he told me, and he gave me a list of EEC projects south of the Sahara. Some of these were in very out-of-the-way places, but he assured me that I would have no problem getting there by Land Rover. He also suggested that I make a documentary about African development. Could I write a scenario for him to submit to the Commission?

I did all that was asked, but all he was eventually able to offer was logistical support in certain

African countries where he personally knew the EEC people.

'And the documentary?' I asked.

Well … he promised that he would look at it on my return and show it to people in the relevant departments. If they found it of interest, he would do his best to persuade the Commission to buy my films.

I had high hopes of the Belgian Ministry for Cooperation and Development, and submitted a proposal that, I was certain, would please them. I also included an outline of the estimated costs of the expedition. Taking into account the cost of our Land Rover and all the rest of the equipment still to buy, and adding minimal travel expenses (which meant sleeping inside the vehicle most of the time), it came to 1,200,000 Belgian francs (about £17,000 at the time). The minister received me personally and, yes, he liked what I proposed and promised to do what he could to support my project. A month later, I got a letter telling me that they had decided to offer me financial backing. Inside the letter, I found a cheque for 60,000 Belgian francs (£850)!

However, not everyone was quite as enthusiastic about a trip to Africa as the EEC man and the Belgian Minister. I had to take the Land Rover to the national distributor to have a new number hammered into the chassis in order to pass the MOT test – the previous owner had been unable to tell me why the old number had rusted away. When the mechanic asked me why I'd bought this old banger, I told him rather proudly that in less than four months' time I would be driving it through Africa.

He seemed shocked. 'Africa!' he exclaimed. 'What'd you want to go there for?'

'Wouldn't you like to travel through Africa?' I stammered, taken aback.

'Go over there and risk my life?' he retorted vehemently. 'Never! Not if they paid me a fortune!' And he stared at me with horror in his eyes.

By the time June was drawing to an end, it was clear that our funds were as low as our hopes had been high. We had spared no effort trying to raise money for our expedition; we had spent as little as possible for months, and Claire and I had also turned to restoring and selling some of her antique furniture. But after buying the Land Rover we had no more than 400,000 Belgian francs (£5,700) left. And I had yet to find a second-hand 16mm cine camera and buy film reels! Our situation was beginning to look pretty desperate.

Then, one day when I returned from the university, I found Claire bubbling with excitement.

'You know what?' she said. 'I've been thinking about our predicament and I've found the solution.'

I told her that I didn't see what solution there could possibly be.

'I've discovered a way of bringing in money while we're travelling.' She looked at me excitedly. 'I'm going to let the house!'

'What? Our home!' I had never before lived in a house that felt so much like home and found the idea of someone else living there and taking over everything, even our own bedroom, repulsive. 'How can you let the house when Papé and Philippe are living here?' I objected, trying to put forward an argument that wouldn't sound too personal. 'Are you planning to let out your father and your son with the house?'

'I've thought of that! We can easily transform the garage into a studio for Papé, and Philippe can move in with school friends for a year. He says he doesn't mind.'

I kept bringing up arguments to put her off the idea. 'Do you think we can transform the garage into a studio overnight? And do you really imagine that people will start queuing at the door the moment you put up a "To Let" sign? Forget it. They'll just take one look at the house and never come back.'

'But it's a lovely house!'

She was right, of course. It was a six-bedroom house with garage in a select part of Brussels and it was surrounded by a nice garden. What's more, it had that indefinable feeling of happiness, and I had loved every moment I had spent there since moving into Claire's house five years before. But letting it was a different matter altogether. I began to argue that it needed a thorough overhaul before people would even look at it, when Claire interrupted me.

'I think you're too pessimistic. All the house needs is a fresh coat of paint.'

'What about the gutter at the top?' I countered. 'The paint is peeling off, it's in very bad condition and we don't have the funds to pay a qualified painter to do the job.'

'Don't worry,' said Claire. 'I'll find someone.'

On the first Sunday in July, we went to the boot fair in Woluwe on the east side of Brussels. I was just strolling around, not very interested because we were due to leave within three months, when I noticed Claire coming towards me, carrying an old fruitwood set of shelves with four small drawers.

'What do you want that for?' I asked in an offhand voice. 'We shouldn't be buying anything. We should be selling things!'

'That's neither here nor there,' she replied. 'It's a rather complicated story. You see, I met a charming young man who was trying to sell a few odds and ends, and when we began to talk he turned out to be extremely interesting. He's just back from Morocco where he did his civil service – he spent two years teaching mathematics in a secondary school. And guess what? Over there he had a Land Rover, and he has been to the outskirts of the Sahara. Isn't that amazing! I told him we were going to drive to Africa in a Land Rover and then we got on really well. Poor Bernard – that's his name; he hadn't sold anything and I felt I had to do something. He needed luck and so I bought this from him.'

'I see,' I said with a long face, but Claire was not to be stopped. Her eyes shone with excitement.

'And that's not all. He hasn't got anything to do for the moment and when I mentioned that our house needed some painting, he replied, "No problem. I can do anything you like." He'll drop by next Wednesday to discuss terms with you. Isn't that wonderful?'

I had my doubts. 'Do you think he'll be able to paint the gutter? It's very high and he doesn't seem to have any experience. It's a dangerous job.'

Claire put her hand on her heart. 'I can feel it when something is right,' she declared. 'Don't you worry; just trust me.'

Bernard duly arrived on Wednesday evening. He was going to start a job in Germany in two months' time but he was free until then, and was willing to take on the painting of the gutter and other odd jobs around the house.

'Basically there's no problem,' he said after we had discussed everything, 'but there's a slight complication.'

When he was in Morocco he had been lauding up Belgium to counter the idea his pupils had that nothing could beat Moroccan hospitality. To give an example of the great sense of hospitality of the Belgians, he had stated grandiloquently that if ever one of his pupils came to Brussels, there would always be a place for him in his parents' home – not that he ever expected anyone to turn up, of course. But then, two days ago, the unexpected had happened. One of the pupils from his school in Fez had arrived in Brussels and was counting on his hospitality as promised. His parents weren't very happy with it, but Bernard had no choice but to give him his own bedroom. As he didn't want to leave the Moroccan alone in his parents' house all day long, he asked me if he could bring him along. That was fine with me, provided he did his share of the work.

'Well,' replied Bernard, 'I'll tell him.'

He was eager to begin the next day but I told him that Claire would have to go shopping for paint, brushes and a paint burner. And so, finally, he and his Moroccan lodger started work on Friday morning …

Friday 10 July 1981

Tout va très bien, Madame la Marquise …
Tout va très bien, tout va très bien.

It was a quarter to three and I was just ready to leave my office in one of the buildings of the University of Brussels when the phone rang.

'Hello, darling, it's me.' It was Claire.

Knowing how much she liked talking on the phone – at home she sometimes spent over an hour chatting with one or another of her friends – I thought it wise to say, 'I'm just about to go to an important meeting. Is everything all right?'

'Oh yes. Everything's all right. Don't worry …'

'Why should I worry?'

'Well, you know … Bernard is here …'

'I know, I know …' I replied impatiently.

That morning Bernard and his lodger had turned up as planned and I had helped them to get the old three-part, wooden ladder out of the cellar. When fully extended it just reached up to the gutter, 30-feet high. It was a bright, sunny day and I imagined that Bernard would enjoy his work, but when I left him with a paint burner and scraper up there he appeared to be much less self-assured. Unfortunately I wasn't able to stay any longer, as this was a particularly busy day at the university. I had to attend the meeting where the professors and lecturers of the science department were going to decide which students would pass their year and which would have to resit their exams in September. I hadn't given the matter of how Bernard might be getting on a single thought since, but now I heard Claire say, 'Well … you see … there's been a small accident…'

'An accident! Bernard hasn't fallen off the ladder?'

'Oh no, nothing as terrible as that! He was burning the paint off the gutter and … well … it caught fire.'

'What! It's not bad I hope!'

'No, no! There's nothing to worry about.'

'Oh, that's all right then. Can you take care of it please? I really have to rush now.' I was about to say, 'Bye,' and hang up when I heard Claire's voice calling, 'Hello, hello!'

'Yes?'

'There's one more thing …'

'Please tell me quickly. It's getting on towards three … I can't be late for the meeting.'

'What do you want me to save in our bedroom?'

I stood there for a few seconds holding the receiver in my hand, unable to grasp the meaning of her words.

'In our bedroom?'

'Well, you see … the fire spread a bit … and … and the corner of our room burned.'

'What!' I began to feel panicky. 'Our room has burned?'

'No, no. Don't be silly! But just in case … tell me what you want me to take out of there.'

I couldn't think clearly. I would never be in time for the meeting. 'Well … I … I don't know … Take whatever you see. My books and … Edna's paintings … and … oh yes, the moneybox of course.'

'All right, I'll do that. Now tell me … what do you want me to save in the study next to our bedroom?'

'What!' Suddenly a nameless fear filled me. 'I'm coming!' I shouted, slamming down the receiver. I ran out of the building to where the Land Rover was parked, jumped in, started and drove off at top speed. When I got to within 100 yards of the house I found the road blocked by a policeman who was diverting the traffic. I tried to pass but he held up his arm and came over to me.

'You can't go that way,' he said sternly. 'There's a house on fire down there.'

'But I live there!' I exclaimed.

'Oh. In that case …' and he waved me on.

A great commotion was going on at the crossing below. A police car was blocking the street and a big, red fire engine was parked in front of Claire's house. A group of onlookers were watching from a safe distance – I vaguely noticed Bernard amongst them. I parked the Land Rover and ran to the gate but was unable to go inside. A rain of tiles was coming down and it would have been suicidal to try to cross the short distance between the gate and the front porch. A hose ran from the fire engine through the open front door and the firemen must have run it all the way up to the top of the house because one of them was blasting tiles off the roof from inside the attic, water spouting skywards like the jet of a fountain. Other men were hacking away with their axes at tiles and supporting wood alike, and chucking down the debris all around the garden. They looked like beings from a sinister world, their heads first disappearing and then popping up again through the devastated roof like black birds of prey in a ritual dance, moved by an irresistible urge to destroy.

Suddenly the destruction mob moved to the back of the roof, allowing me to run to the front door. I called out for Claire but she was nowhere to be seen. The ground floor seemed all right but as I followed the big, rubber hose, curling up the stairs like a fat serpent, things began to get worse; water was leaking down the walls of the first floor and the carpet on the stairs seemed in a terrible state. The real mess was on the second floor. The door of our bedroom was wide open and as I looked in, I was not prepared for the shock of what I saw.

This had been our refuge; up there we had been away from the rest of the family, living just above the tops of the trees – it felt so close to the sky. We had painted the walls, waxed the wooden floorboards and bought a new mattress, which we had laid upon the floor. We had decorated the room with photographs of places we had been to, jewels and objects brought back from our journeys, a poem I had written … No one came into this room but Claire and I. No one else belonged here. This was our very private world.

The first thing that struck me was the big hole. The room looked as if it had been bombed. A third of the ceiling and the roof above had gone, and some charred beams stuck out against the blue of the sky around the edges of the hole. Everything had been sullied, the walls were blackened with soot, and the mattress was lying on the floorboards in a dirty puddle. And in their haste to get to the roof, the firemen had literally thrown our clothes cupboard to the other side of the room where it was lying half open. Our clothes had fallen out and lay scattered all over the floor in the dirty water.

I stood there for a few seconds, unable to move, trying to take in the scene, shocked by the desecration of what was dear to me. Then, almost like an automaton, I stepped forward and began picking up my suit, Claire's skirts and blouses.

Suddenly a sharp voice came from behind. 'Hey, what are you doing in here!'

I turned around and stared at an unexpected apparition: one of the firemen was blocking the doorway with his great bulk. Before I had time to react, he grabbed my arm, pulled me out of the room shouting, 'You're not allowed up here! It's too dangerous!' and without further ado, he pushed me down the stairs.

When I got back to the university, I sneaked through a side door into the conference room where the professors and lecturers were meeting, and tried to sit down as inconspicuously as possible, but of course the head of my department had seen me and motioned to me to come and sit next to him.

'You're late,' he hissed accusingly under his breath. 'This is intolerable! The session began at 3.00 p.m. and –' he gazed at his watch with a disapproving look on his face – 'it's 3.45 already!'

I showed him my hands, black with soot, whispering, 'I'm sorry but I was called unexpectedly to the house where I live. The roof's just burned down.'

He looked at my hands without as much as a hint of sympathy and finally replied, 'Oh, well … I suppose that's all right,' implying that a burned roof was probably a valid reason for being late and that he might consider letting me off the hook. And at that, he turned towards the other professors and took no further notice of me.

By the time the meeting was over and I got back home, peace had returned to the house. There was a huge hole in the roof, the garden was covered in broken tiles and pieces of charred wood, but otherwise all was quiet. I found Claire in the kitchen preparing something to eat.

'Are you all right?' I inquired anxiously. 'When I rushed over here at three o'clock I didn't see you.'

'Oh … I must have been somewhere around. It was extremely busy with all the firemen in the house. Maybe I was up in the attic?'

'In the attic!' I shook my head. 'And why were the firemen jumping all over the roof? I would have expected them to spray water from the outside over the house.

'That's what they usually do, and apparently this causes enormous damage. All the water runs down into the house, ceilings collapse and the whole inside gets black from top to bottom. But the chief officer explained that there was another way, which firemen don't like because it's much more laborious and dangerous. They could pull the big hose upstairs all the way to the attic, blast the tiles away from the inside and hack away any wood left smouldering. "Please," I asked the chief, "would you tell your men to do that? Please, save my house. I love it." And so this is what he did. He was such a nice man. The firemen protested, of course, but finally they did as their chief told them.'

I sighed. 'And what's happened to Bernard and his friend? What's his name again?'

'You mean Aziz. He's been so good; couldn't have been more perfect.'

'Did he help?'

'No …'

'Then, why do you say he's been perfect?'

'Well, he might have lost his head and got in everybody's way, but no! For three whole hours he lay hidden behind a bush at the back of the garden. Didn't as much as move a limb. Nobody noticed him.'

'But why did he hide?'

Claire laughed. 'Apparently it was because of the men in uniforms storming into the house. At least, that's what he told me afterwards.'

'Men in uniforms?'

'Well, yes, the firemen. He thought they were local policemen who had come to throw him into prison.'

'But that's ridiculous!'

'Apparently not for someone used to the ways of the Moroccan police.'

Suddenly I remembered something important. The moneybox! It contained all the money we had saved over the last months from the sale of our antique furniture – more than 300,000 Belgian francs in cash plus some cheques we hadn't yet cashed.

'Hey!' I exclaimed. 'What's happened to the moneybox? Where is it?'

'Oh! Yes … the moneybox … it's all right,' said Claire in a soothing voice.

'Yes, but where is it?'

'Well, that's a long story. When I phoned you earlier you told me to save it, didn't you? So I quickly ran upstairs, found it and ran down again, all the while thinking of a good place in which to hide it. And you know what happened?'

'No …' Looking at the apologetic expression on Claire's face, I feared the worst.

'The firemen were just dragging a long hose up the stairs and I tripped over it!'

'You didn't!' I held my breath.

'Yes, I did. And as I grabbed the banister trying to steady myself, the box escaped from my hands and bounced down the steps. You should have seen the faces of the firemen downstairs when a cloud of 1,000-franc notes descended on them!' She giggled.

'What!' I nearly had a fit.

'But the firemen were extremely nice. They helped me collect the banknotes and cheques and I stuffed everything safely back into the box.'

I put a hand over my eyes and sighed. 'And the box? What did you do with it?'

'Well … you know … with all the people rushing in and out of the house, I thought it best to hide the box somewhere outside and as I walked out I noticed the trailer in front of our garage. Now, that's an ideal hiding place, I thought. I lifted up the groundsheet that covers the trailer and pushed the box underneath. Wasn't that clever?' Claire turned a beaming face towards me.

'I don't believe this!' I exclaimed. 'In a trailer in front of the garage! Out in the street …' I began to panic. 'Have you checked the trailer since? Is the box still there?'

'Well … no. It's not there any more.'

'My God!' I felt faint and sank down on a chair. First the roof gone. And now the moneybox! This was the end of our round-the-world trip.

'Wait, wait,' came Claire's voice. 'Let me continue. Sometime later, as I went into the hall, I bumped into Theirquin.'

I was feeling more dazed than ever. 'Their quin? What's a quin?'

'Not what – *who*! You know … Mr Theirquin.'

'Mr Theirquin?' I groaned. 'Who is he?'

'He lives three houses further down.'

'I don't know him.'

'Nor did I until today, but he's a very nice man. It was his son Jean-Luc who saw smoke coming out of the roof while he was playing in his garden. Mr Theirquin immediately phoned the fire brigade and then sent his son running to our house to tell us that the roof was burning. I didn't believe him at first. I thought it was a joke, but the boy insisted and begged me to come outside to have a look. And he was right!'

'But how did it catch fire?'

'It all happened while we were having tea. Poor Bernard! He had been working the whole morning. Just imagine him standing on that ladder thirty-feet high, straining his neck! I thought he really deserved a nice cup of tea and a piece of cake, and called him down. Afterwards we reconstructed what must have happened. Bernard was burning the paint off the gutter outside our bedroom. It wasn't in very good condition …'

I knew. I had checked that particular spot in the morning. The paint was peeling everywhere and there were big cracks in the wooden boards; there was even a hole through which birds flew in and out.

'… and the flames of the burner must have got inside and set the birds' nests on fire just as I called Bernard down. He didn't notice anything of course since we were having tea. By the way, do you realise that he drove all the way to India through Iran and Afghanistan? So interesting! But he couldn't tell me any more details because just as we were having a nice chat, the neighbour's son rang the bell. And then the firemen arrived. They were not far from here when they got an order to drive directly to our house. And they arrived within minutes. Wasn't that fortunate?'

'That's all very well but the moneybox? What's happened to it?'

'Oh yes … I was just coming to that. I told you I bumped into Mr Theirquin in the hall and he expressed his sincere regrets at what had occurred and asked me if there was anything he could do to help. Now, what can he possibly do? I thought. And then I remembered the moneybox. So I went to the trailer, lifted up the ground sheet, took out the box and handed it to him, asking him to put it in a safe place. And he went off with it.'

'What! And you haven't seen him or heard from him since?'

'Well, to tell you the truth, I completely forgot about him. You see …'

I didn't wait any longer but rushed out into the street and rang the bell three houses further down. A man, whom I presumed to be Mr Theirquin, opened the door and I asked straightaway about the box.

'Oh yes, yes … do come in,' he said, leading me into his living room. And there, sitting on the mantelpiece, was the box. As I ran forward and picked it up I noticed that the corners of several banknotes were sticking out from under the lid. I couldn't possibly begin to check the cash in front of Mr Theirquin and anyway, I had no idea of the exact amount of money that was supposed to be in the box. So I hoped for the best and thanked the man profusely, but he just waved his hand saying, 'At your service. And do come to me when you hear from the insurance company. I'm an architect and I will arrange for a builder to be present and protect your interests when the insurance people arrive to assess the damage.'

When I got back home with the moneybox, I felt so tired I had to sit down. The strain was beginning to tell on me, but apparently not on Claire. I could have sworn that she was enjoying everything tremendously.

'See!' she said when she saw the box. 'I told you there was nothing to worry about. I knew Mr Theirquin was to be trusted. I hope we'll see more of him. He's such a considerate man.'

'I suppose so. He said he wanted to help us when the people from the insurance company arrive to assess the damage.' Suddenly I was assailed by misgivings. 'Tell me,' I asked, barely able to hide my concern. 'The house is insured against fire, isn't it?' Although I had been living in the house for several years now, I had never given the matter a single thought since it was Claire's house.

'Well … yes.'

'Phew! That's a great relief.'

'Oh … but …' Claire put a hand in front of her mouth.

Knowing Claire, I felt alarmed. 'What is it?'

'The annual renewal of the fire insurance! You see … the letter came some time ago and what with the excitement of preparing for the journey, I forgot all about it. Where's that letter?'

'What! You haven't paid the fire insurance!' I hit my forehead, slumped in my chair and closed my eyes. This was well and truly the end.

'You didn't see that letter by any chance?' asked Claire, looking at me. 'No? I must have put it somewhere.' And she disappeared into the drawing room where I heard her rummage in the drawers of a bureau.

She reappeared a few minutes later, triumphantly holding up the letter. 'I found it!' She tore the envelope and began to read. Then she asked, 'What date are we today?'

'The tenth of July.'

'Oh God … it says here that I have to pay on the tenth at the latest.' She looked at the clock. 'And it's 6.00 p.m. The banks are closed by now.'

'And it's a Friday,' I added glumly.

'But we're still the tenth,' said Claire with a determined expression on her face. 'I'm going to sign the transfer straightaway, pre-date it, put it in an envelope and drop it through the letterbox of the local branch of my bank. I'll phone the bank manager first thing on Monday morning. I know him personally; it'll be all right.'

'I hope so,' I replied despondently. Suddenly I thought of Bernard. 'By the way, what's happened to our first-class painter and his assistant? Have they gone home?'

'Oh!' exclaimed Claire. 'I forgot about them. They must still be up on the roof checking if there's anything left smouldering.' She rushed upstairs and I heard her call, 'Bernard! Aziz! Are you there?'

Minutes later, Bernard came down. I didn't feel too pleased about the disaster he had caused but when I saw him standing there with his head hanging down, looking totally dejected, my anger evaporated.

'Never mind,' I told him. 'It could have happened to anyone. Just a bit of bad luck.'

'Of all the days ...' Bernard sighed deeply. 'Why did this have to happen today?'

'What's so special about today?'

'It's my birthday,' he replied in a voice like an undertaker's.

I was about to say, 'Well, you celebrated it in style!' but held back. There was no point in rubbing it in. What was done could not be undone. Then I remembered that there was a bottle of champagne in the fridge and got it out. Claire brought some glasses and after everyone had gathered around, I poured the champagne and lifted my glass to Bernard, saying, 'A birthday is always a special day, but this one is very, very special. I'm sure it's going to live on in our memories. So, let's celebrate: to friendship and many happy returns.'

That night, after Bernard and Aziz had left and Claire had returned from the bank, we were finishing an improvised supper.

'Well, I'm sure the insurance company won't pay,' I sat pondering, 'but at least we've got the moneybox back. And we've still got some money in the bank, too. With luck we'll just be able to repair the roof. That is, if we do everything ourselves ... and we've never done such a thing; we have no experience whatever. I wouldn't even know where to begin.' I stopped for a while, looking gloomily around me. 'Anyway, we can say goodbye to our world trip, that's for sure. And I don't know what we're going to live off from October onwards, as I won't be drawing a salary for a whole year.'

'Oh, stop worrying about the future!' interrupted Claire. 'Let's go to bed.'

'And where do you suggest we sleep tonight? There's a big hole in our bedroom.'

'We'll sleep in the guestroom, in the four-poster bed. That'll be a nice change.'

Moments later, in the guestroom, I looked out at the sky and noticed threatening clouds blowing in from the west. 'I hope it's not going to rain tonight,' I said, overcome by dark misgivings. 'That would be a total disaster.'

'Darling,' replied Claire as she resolutely slid under the bedcovers, 'let's go to sleep. No more talk about what might go wrong, please. We've had enough disasters for a single day.'

CHAPTER 2
A Delayed Departure

A Visit from the Insurance Man

Within days, Claire got a phone call from the insurance company and I went at once to Mr Theirquin to let him know that they would send one of their inspectors the following morning.

'I'll come,' he said, sounding very pleased.

He turned up early the next day with his builder in tow. 'You'd better leave it all to us,' he declared with an air of authority. 'That way we'll get the best possible price for you.' I was relieved to have some competent people around. I didn't have the faintest idea of how much it would cost to rebuild the roof and turned to the builder – a stocky man in hobnailed shoes – to ask him. He stared at me as if I had committed a grave breach of etiquette but when I insisted, he reluctantly began to climb the stairs. A quarter of an hour later, he was down again, looking as if all the problems of the world were weighing on his shoulders.

'So what's the verdict?' I asked anxiously.

He made a vague gesture. 'There's a lot of damage …'

'We know that,' intervened Claire, 'but how much is it going to cost to have everything repaired?'

The builder stared at us, looking like someone who had a painful duty to perform. 'This job is going to cost at least …' he nodded a couple of times to give himself courage, '… at least two million francs.' He sighed deeply as if to show us that all this wasn't his fault.

'But that's wonderful!' exclaimed Claire. 'We're going to get two million francs!'

'I don't know about *you* getting anything,' corrected the man with a sour face. 'The figure I quoted is what it will cost you if you contract an experienced builder such as myself to repair the damage.'

Just then a car stopped in front of the house and an impeccably dressed, clean-shaven man got out carrying an attaché case. When Claire saw him giving the house a good look-over from the other side of the street, she exclaimed, 'The inspector from the insurance company!' and rushed up to the bathroom; I suppose she wanted to look her very best. A minute later the insurance man made his way through the broken tiles and rubble in the front garden, stepped into the hall, introduced himself, demanded to see the top of the house and went up without further ado.

Claire still hadn't appeared when the inspector came down again – doing her face seemed to take a long time.

'There's a lot of damage, isn't there,' I began, trying to sound as amiable as possible, but the insurance man ignored my attempt at small talk.

'Can I see the owner of this property?' he demanded in a businesslike voice. 'A Ms …' he looked at his papers, '… a Ms Claire van Velsen.'

'She'll be here any minute now,' I replied, taken aback. 'Is there a problem?'

'Yes. There's a big problem with the insurance.'

That's it, I thought. They're refusing to accept the late payment of the fire insurance. This is the end!

At that moment, Claire came down the stairs, all charm and smiles. The man now turned to her, his face taking on a stern expression.

'Are you Ms Claire van Velsen, the owner of this property?' When she nodded affirmatively he said disapprovingly, 'Do you realise that your house is not insured for its full value?'

'I don't really understand what you mean,' replied Claire, looking puzzled.

'This property is insured for just three million francs,' explained the man, 'when its market value is probably more like five to six million.'

'And why is that important?'

'Well, according to my estimates, about one-third of the house is damaged. So, all we can pay is a third of the value you've insured it for, or one million francs.' He fiddled for a while with the papers in his attaché case, produced a document and held it up to Claire saying, 'I'll fill in the amount. All you've got to do is sign here.'

'But no one will ever repair the damage for that price!' I protested. 'The builder here estimates that it will cost at least two million.' I turned around for support and just saw the backs of Mr Theirquin and his builder as they vanished through the front door; they'd left the house without so much as uttering a word! I was about to rush after them when I heard the inspector retort, 'That can't be helped! Madame here should have thought of that when she drew up her insurance policy. You can't pay low premiums and then expect us to cover the full damage.'

Claire suddenly gave the man an eager look. 'I'm willing to accept your proposal …'

'Aha!' The inspector seemed relieved. 'I hoped that you would see reason.'

' …but as no builder will do the repairs for that price,' she continued, 'I must ask you to allow us to repair everything ourselves. Would your company agree to that and pay the money into my account?'

The insurance man seemed to have been caught completely unawares. 'I don't know about that,' he replied evasively. 'This is unusual.' He rubbed his forehead repeating, 'this is highly unusual,' looking at Claire in surprise. 'I don't know what to say … I've never in my career encountered a case like this …' He stood there pondering deeply while Claire continued to smile at him, nodding encouragingly. 'OK!' he said finally. 'I don't think there's a rule forbidding the owner to do the repairs but –' he stared hard at Claire – 'don't expect more from us than a million francs.' Then he corrected himself. 'Well … that's not quite true. If you do the work yourself, you can submit the invoices for the materials you buy. Our company can reclaim the VAT, so, obviously, we'll be delighted to reimburse the VAT on the invoices for the materials.'

'Wonderful!' exclaimed Claire enthusiastically.

'So you're going to do it all yourself.' The inspector stood there shaking his head as if he found this hard to believe. Then he turned to me. 'Have you ever done any building work?'

Before I had time to say anything, Claire blurted out, 'Oh yes! We're experienced. Matter of fact, we've done quite a lot of restoration work.'

The man looked impressed. 'And how long do you think it will take you to repair the roof? A month?'

'Probably,' said Claire without even blushing, 'or maybe a little longer.'

'That's all settled then, Ms van Velsen,' said the man with a flicker of admiration in his eyes. 'We'll leave it all to you. Just call us when you're ready and we'll send you an inspector. If he's satisfied that the roof has been properly repaired, you'll need to come in person to our head office and bring us all your invoices. We will then add the VAT you paid on the materials to the 1,000,000 francs we have agreed on, and pay the total amount into your bank account.'

The insurance man filled in all the figures and conditions agreed upon, signed first and handed the documents to Claire who signed in her turn. Then he left, looking pleased with himself. He had barely got into his car when I turned to Claire. 'How could you tell such lies? We've never done any building work in our lives! That's a job for specialists!'

'I haven't been telling lies!' retorted Claire. 'It's just that you sometimes have to stretch the truth somewhat. And we *have* done restoration work!'

'Yeah! We've restored furniture, not houses.'

Claire waved away my objections. 'What's the difference? If you can do one, you can do the other.'

'But I can't rebuild a roof!'

'Two years ago you told me that you had never done any woodwork in your life, that you were an intellectual, incapable of doing any manual work. And now look! It goes to show that you must never underestimate your potential. That's just what people do all their lives. They'd be surprised at what they're capable of doing if they really set themselves to it.'

'All right, all right! I'll give it a try. But how are we going to pay for the repairs?'

'We've still got the moneybox and some money in the bank, haven't we?'

'Do you really think we'll be able to repair everything for four hundred thousand francs? The builder said that it would cost at least two million.'

'Well, for the moment we're just going to buy materials, and four hundred thousand francs will have to do. We'll think about the rest when the insurance pays up,' carried on Claire, brushing my objections aside.

Just then I heard a polite cough behind my back. It was Mr Theirquin.

'I've got good news for you,' he said, beaming. 'My builder has agreed to restore your roof for 1,500,000 francs. He said it wasn't really sufficient but I talked him into it because I wanted to do you a favour. Mind you, that's just for the roof and won't include repairing anything else. But the main thing is to have a roof over your head, isn't it?'

I stood there, gaping, unable to utter a word, but Claire showed more presence of mind.

'Thank you so much for your kind offer, Mr Theirquin,' she replied suavely, 'but unfortunately we've just made other arrangements with the insurance company. We have agreed to repair everything ourselves.' She looked at him apologetically as she saw his face fall. 'A shame you went away so suddenly. I have signed the documents and cannot possibly go back on the commitment. I'm sure you understand. I'm really sorry. Another time, perhaps?'

Repairing the Roof

We were in luck; the weather, which usually does its utmost to be as unreliable as possible the moment the summer holidays start, remained dry and steady. Day after day we woke up to see the sun shine and hear the birds sing. I, who had always had the greatest difficulty in getting up early for work, was now down for breakfast by 7.00 a.m. every day. By 8.00 a.m., I was already up on the roof, carrying on till the evening with only short breaks for lunch and tea.

Claire's son, Philippe, had joined the work team, too. The moment he woke up – which might be any time between 9.00 a.m. and 11.00 a.m. – and had wolfed down his breakfast, he would phone his classmate Pierre to come over. They had originally planned to spend their summer holidays on a farm in Brittany, but in view of the emergency that had arisen they had changed their plans and were helping us to rebuild the roof instead. Not that Pierre was very efficient; we often lost sight of him, only to discover him sometime later, hidden in a corner, fast asleep. Fortunately he didn't turn up very often and Philippe more than compensated by working for two.

Bernard and Aziz made up the core of our team, arriving every morning from the other side of Brussels. And finally there was Claire who, in between making meals and serving teas, didn't want to miss any of the excitement. We saw her head pop up between the charred beams at the most unexpected moments. If we didn't give her something to do straightaway she would begin to carry up materials, but as she was the only woman in the team we didn't want to tax her too much. Aziz in particular was very deferential to her, and if he noticed her lugging up something heavy he would rush down at once, wring it from her hands and carry it up himself.

Aziz had been expecting us to shout orders at him and make him do everything. That's the way it was in Morocco where no one of any consequence would have so much as lifted a finger and where labourers were treated with disdain. He was convinced that it would be just the same in Belgium and was determined not to accept this. But when he saw Claire and me joining in all the tasks without sparing our efforts, his attitude changed.

He was only eighteen, but he'd had plenty of time for muscle-building at his father's grocery shop where from a young age he had been made to carry all the crates. We were indeed very fortunate to have him. When a big dustbin was filled with rubble in the attic and had to be carried down, he invariably volunteered for the job. Two of us would lift the heavy bin onto his shoulders and, bent nearly double, he would then walk down the stairs with it.

We did our very best to keep costs down but found that building materials were prohibitively expensive when we bought them in do-it-yourself shops. This was particularly the case for new beams cut to exact size; paying for them seemed beyond our means until we discovered a company selling standard length, rough, wooden beams in bulk. We calculated the number of beams we needed, ordered the lot and a huge lorry arrived one day and dumped everything in the garage entrance.

Some friends of Claire, who had just finished building stables for their horses, owned a professional circular saw fixed on a heavy table. They were happy to lend it to us, installed it in our front garden and showed me how to operate it. I had never done this kind of work in my life, but this was a case of dire necessity. I somehow had to manage and I soon mastered the art of cutting beams to size, just as Claire had predicted. We would measure the charred remains of the old beams on the roof before knocking them down and I used these measurements to cut new beams to exactly the same size, with the ends finished off at 45 degrees if needed. As this was a dangerous job, I forbade the others to touch the saw, but I did enlist my daughter, Natasja, as help. She was over for her summer holidays and was only eleven, but she would bravely hold up the far end of the beam on her shoulder, making sure that the side I was working on was lying flat on the table.

When a beam was ready, the others would attach long ropes to it, pull it up to the top of the house and then hammer it in with 8-inch-long nails. Day after day the new wooden structure, which was to support the roof, grew until at last everything was in place and we were ready to put on second-hand tiles, which we had bought for less than a quarter of the price of new ones – although of course we'd had to go and take them down from an old hangar ourselves.

By the middle of August, the roof was back on the house. Toiling six days a week, ten hours a day, we had managed to get the job done! Claire immediately called the insurance company and as the inspector arrived, we held our breath. He went up to the attics, had a good look around and, to our relief, pronounced himself satisfied with the job. That night we celebrated. We bought champagne for the roof team and Claire surpassed herself by producing a dinner which, for once, was not burnt or out of a tin.

Claire spent the next morning hunting all round the house for the invoices she had collected over the last weeks, stuck them in a folder and added up the total amount of VAT paid on the materials.

'Look,' she said, proudly showing me the neatly classified invoices and the sums she had calculated. 'This is sure to impress the insurance people.' Then she left the house, impeccably dressed in skirt, frilly blouse and jacket, the folder pressed under her arm, calling out, 'Wish me luck!'

I'd not even had time to turn around when she reappeared, saying, 'I forgot the car keys.' She was out of the house again in a minute, got into the car and drove off.

At last, I thought, that's the end of all our troubles. The insurance company will pay us and we'll be saved!

About a quarter of an hour later, I was sitting in the kitchen sipping a glass of water. I had just taken off my dirty shoes and was feeling very relaxed when I heard a car pull up in front of the house. Seconds later, Claire walked in, a puzzled expression on her face.

'You haven't by any chance seen the folder with the invoices?' she asked. 'You didn't put it away, did you?' She sounded slightly vexed.

'Don't be ridiculous! You took it with you.'

'Well, I thought I did and was well on my way when I noticed it wasn't in the car.'

'But you had it with you when you left the house!'

'I can't have had it! It's nowhere in the car.'

'I'm sure you had it under your arm.' I closed my eyes trying to visualise the scene. 'Yes … I can clearly see you go out of the house with the folder. Then, a few seconds later, you rushed back into the house for the car keys and … and you were no longer carrying the folder! So you must have put it … Oh my God!'

It was a very hot day; I was wearing a dirty old T-shirt and ripped trousers and was sweating profusely; my hands were black and so was my face where I'd wiped it, but there was no time to wash or change. I took Claire by the hand, rushed her to the car, pushed her behind the wheel and then plonked myself down next to her.

'Be quick!' I urged her. 'Drive back the exact way you went when you left the house.'

'I don't see why you're making me do this,' protested Claire. 'I want to find the folder.'

'Just do as I say. There's not a second to lose.'

She started the car unwillingly and as we began to drive slowly down the avenue, she kept questioning me. 'If you say you didn't take the folder, then I must have put it somewhere. Where do you think I put it?'

'On the bonnet,' I groaned.

'On which bonnet?'

'The car bonnet of course! And you drove off with it lying there.'

She stared at me as if I were demented. 'Do you really think me capable of putting the folder on the bonnet of the car and then driving off without noticing it?'

'Yes.'

She looked offended. 'And I thought that you loved me.'

'You're everything to me,' I said, trying to appease her. 'You know that I would run to the end of the world for you …' It was then that I noticed I was barefooted. I had rushed out of the house without putting my shoes on!

We had covered just over half a mile when we came to a point where Claire had taken a sharp turn to the left. And there, in front of our wheels, we saw the folder. It was lying open on the tarmac, a car had driven over it, most of the invoices were scattered around and a fair breeze was carrying the sheets of paper away; I even noticed some floating far down the avenue.

'Stop!' I yelled.

Claire stopped the car abruptly, swerving towards the other side of the avenue to avoid the folder. I flung the door open, rushed out, picked up the folder, threw it inside the car and then I hurriedly began to pick up the invoices before they were lost forever. Some were lying on the tarmac, others on the pavement and some had been blown into the front gardens of houses further along.

I started diving in and out of the small gardens to salvage our invoices, running frantically from one side of the avenue to the other while picking up any sheets of paper I saw and adding them to the pile I was clutching in my hand. I'd already covered some 50 yards when I looked back and saw two policemen arrive on motorbikes. They pulled up next to our car and dismounted.

Oh damn, I thought; when you need them they're never there, but when you absolutely don't want to see them they turn up! But there were still too many invoices floating down the avenue, so I ran on. It was only when I had grabbed the last invoice I saw lying around that I looked up; the car had turned and was moving off with the two policemen in tow!

'Hey!' I yelled. 'Wait for me!' And I began to run after them, shouting and gesticulating, but to no avail. I was unable to catch up and I finally stopped, panting; Claire had abandoned me half a mile from the house! There was nothing else to do but walk home barefooted, carrying a pile of crumpled papers in my hands. Fortunately there were hardly any people about at this time of the day, but the few pedestrians I did meet looked at me with unconcealed distrust. One woman even crossed over to the other side. Then, suddenly, I saw our car reappear.

'Get in!' Claire called out.

'Why did you drive away?' I protested, not too pleased.

'It's those policemen. They said I was blocking the traffic and kept pestering me. As I began arguing one of them even shouted, "Will you remove this dustbin immediately!"'

'A dustbin? We haven't got a dustbin in the car.'

'That's what I told the policeman, whereupon he nearly exploded and aggressively jabbed his finger at our car!'

'Well,' I laughed, 'it does look dirty.'

'That's no reason for being so rude!' retorted Claire. 'But what worried me most was that they might have noticed you. You looked, well …' She seemed to hesitate, '… slightly demented, and I was afraid that they would arrest you. So you understand that I had to draw them away from you. That's why I turned the car around, and it worked! They followed me all the way to the house and only when I parked and went inside did they drive off.'

As we got home and Claire spread the crumpled invoices out on the dining table, an expression of doubt crept over her face.

'My nice folder,' she sighed. 'And now look! I'm not sure how pleased the insurance people will be when they see this lot. I've got to do something.'

She spent an hour washing the dirt off the invoices and repairing those that had been torn with sticky tape; she even ironed some. When she was satisfied with the result she put the lot into a new folder, and this time I saw to it that it was lying next to her on the passenger's seat when she drove off to the insurance company.

She returned two hours later, all smiles.

'It went all right?' I asked.

'No problem.'

'But they must have noticed the state of the invoices?'

'Well …' said Claire, 'the insurance man did seem surprised when he opened the folder, but then I explained what had happened. "I almost didn't dare come and show them to you," I said, looking very distraught. He smiled encouragingly at me. "You did well to come, Madame. After all, invoices are invoices."

'"So you think it's all right?"

'"Don't you worry," he reassured me as we shook hands. "Just leave it to me. I will arrange everything for you."'

To our great relief, the insurance company paid up a few days later; we now had the money we needed for our expedition! We carried on for another week, cleaning out the remaining dirt and removing all debris from the garden. Then, by the end of the third week in August, the worst was over and, anyway, everyone seemed to have had enough. Aziz went back to Morocco; Philippe and Pierre boarded a train to France, and Bernard went off to Germany where he had secured a job. And Claire and I spent a well-deserved week in Deal, Kent, with Claire's Aunt Mary who touched us deeply by giving us £1,000 from her precious savings as a contribution towards our trip.

In one way our situation had taken a very positive turn. Repairing the roof had not even cost half a million francs, less than a third of the price for which Mr Theirquin and his builder had been willing to do it as a 'very special favour'. We still needed to repaint the house and transform the garage but even so, we would be able to buy all the sound equipment and the films I needed, equip the Land Rover and still have enough money left for our trip. As Bernard had proudly declared before setting off for Germany, 'Wasn't it lucky I set fire to your roof? You may thank me for it. I saved your expedition!'

But in another way, we were worse off. Up till now we had been concentrating on rebuilding the roof and had stopped trying to find sponsors or thinking about our trip. But now, back from our holiday, it was clear that we would never be able to start on 1 October. This would have left us a mere four weeks in which to apply for visas, finish the work on the house and prepare everything for the expedition, which was impossible, especially since Aziz and Bernard had gone, and Philippe and his classmate were returning to school. Furthermore, I would have to spend most of September at the university.

The fire and subsequent rebuilding of the roof had totally upset my travel schedule. Even under the best of circumstances, it would have been extremely difficult to complete a round-the-world trip in one year. This was out of the question now. We would have to revise our plans drastically and work flat out to be able to leave by November.

Further Delays

I was staring at the Land Rover, wondering where to begin – the fact was that I didn't know anything about car mechanics – when Claire came out of the house calling, 'Guess who's coming round?'

I told her that I didn't have the slightest idea; it might have been any of her friends and she had a good many.

'Bernard,' she said, nodding her head in approval.

I was surprised. 'But it's Tuesday! What about his job?' He should have been working; in fact, he should have been miles away from Belgium. 'He isn't going to come back from Germany just to say hello, is he?'

'No, no, silly one. He's in Brussels.'

And indeed, half an hour later, a car drew up in front of the house and out climbed Bernard. We shook hands and then, without further ado, he came to the point. 'I'm sure there are many tasks that need doing here,' he said, 'and I have time now. I'm willing to help you out.' He looked at me eagerly.

'You have time? But didn't you tell me you were going to work in Germany? Don't you have a job?'

'Well … yes, I had a job but … well … I happen to be free just at the moment.' He turned his head sideways, looking embarrassed.

'Don't tell me you've already lost your job! How did that happen?'

'Well … you see … there was a small accident …'

'Another small accident! You didn't set fire to a roof in Germany, did you?'

'No, nothing of the sort.' He hesitated a few seconds. 'A week ago they sent me to do the maintenance of a large mainframe computer. I was getting on very well when suddenly, as I plugged in a cable, there was an explosion. All the lights went out and then the computer went up in flames. I still don't understand how it could have happened.' Bernard stood there, visibly thinking hard. Then he turned to me. 'So I'm free now, and if you could employ me until I find a new job, I'm willing to help you.'

'Well, I don't really know …'

'Take the electrical system of the house, for example,' he interrupted. 'I know the wires are old. When was this house built?'

I looked at Claire. 'Around 1910?'

'That's right,' she confirmed.

'See! Things have evolved a lot since then. They obviously had no idea what they were doing seventy years ago. From what I remember when we redid the roof, the whole circuit is a mess; it's totally illogical.' Seeing me hesitate, he pressed his point. 'The job needs doing urgently. Anything could happen to those old circuits. There was no time to renew it all before, but as I have time now, I can easily rewire the lot …' He looked at me hopefully.

'Well, I don't know about redoing the wiring. Wouldn't that take a long time?'

'Oh no! It's not difficult. It'll go in a flash.'

That was exactly what I didn't want to happen and I realised that I had to stop Bernard before he started to fiddle with the electrics.

'I *am* qualified you know,' he insisted. 'I'm an engineer.'

'I know, but there's a problem.' I looked him straight in the eye. 'We need to keep all our funds for the journey and for equipping the Land Rover. We couldn't possibly pay for work on the house.'

'The Land Rover, you say. I know a lot about car mechanics.' He went over to the Land Rover and began walking around it with an air of 'one who knows'. He opened the bonnet, looked underneath then switched on the engine and listened carefully. 'Poor old car,' he finally said. 'It needs a thorough overhaul.' He nodded a couple of times. 'There's a lot of work to be done … but I can easily take care of that. You just leave everything to me.'

And that's how Bernard became a daily fixture again.

'I've got our visas for Algeria,' I announced proudly, coming home one day towards the end of September. 'At last, things are beginning to move.'

Claire didn't seem very enthusiastic. 'What do you want to go to Algeria for? I'm not interested in Algeria.'

'Oh! Well … I don't plan to stay there. We can't anyway. All they were willing to give me were two-week transit visas, would you believe it? I hope two weeks are sufficient to cross the Sahara.'

'What! You want to cross the Sahara?'

'I don't see any other way if we're to reach black Africa,' I mumbled evasively.

'But you promised me we would drive around the Sahara!'

'Well, that was when we still had lots of time. But we'll have to hurry now and the shortest way is through the Sahara.' This sounded very convincing, at least to me, and I thought it settled the argument. 'Anyway,' I added, 'what have you got against the Sahara?'

I saw Claire hesitate. 'Well … if you really want to know … I've often dreamt that I was lying in the desert dying of thirst. And all around me vultures were sitting on big cacti watching me, waiting for me to die to devour me. So please, do understand that I don't want to go there.'

'But there are no cacti in the Sahara and no vultures! I think you're mixing things up. You must have been dreaming about Arizona.'

'You can say what you like,' retorted Claire stubbornly, 'but I believe in premonitions. Those dreams warned me not to go into the desert. If I do, I'll die, and if you really care for me you won't want that to happen, will you?' She looked at me pleadingly.

I tried one last argument. 'But I always thought you wanted to see black Africa.'

'Yes, but not if we have to drive through the Sahara! I'd rather go to India instead.'

Over the next few weeks I tried to work out a way to reach India without having to drive through the Sahara. I went to the embassies of Iraq and Iran, but both countries were at war and wouldn't let us cross. Driving through Afghanistan, then under Soviet occupation, was out of the question, too. So, finally, I decided that we would have to board a ship from Italy to Alexandria and drive south through Egypt into the Sudan. This still meant crossing the Sahara and I was worried about Claire's reaction, but she said this was totally different. As we would be following the Nile, there would be water nearby all the time and anyway, she had always longed to see Egypt. From the Sudan we would be able to get into Kenya, enter Tanzania and sail to India from Dar es Salaam.

Claire, meanwhile, was concentrating on establishing contacts with India. She had invited several people from the Indian Embassy to supper, we had been invited to an embassy dinner in return, and the most cordial relationship had been established. Driving through India was not a problem, although it seemed that you had to watch out for cows lying down on the roads. But there were some administrative hurdles. Apparently, if you imported a vehicle into India, high import taxes would have to be paid. And if you exported it again later, you had to pay export taxes! The greatest problem, however, was filming. I was requested to present a complete scenario of the documentary I wanted to make, including what I was going to film and where. I also had to sign a declaration that, upon completion of the movie, I would submit it to the Indian authorities and accept that they had the right to veto any images or any comments they didn't like. Furthermore, a liaison officer would have to accompany us for the whole of our time in India and I would be expected to provide adequate lodgings for the man during our stay, pay his wages and cover any extra expenses he might incur.

'How can I tell you what I want to film before I've seen anything?' I protested, but there was nothing to be done. I improvised a scenario, submitted it, signed all the documents and hoped for the best. Next the Indian Embassy sent everything to New Delhi for approval.

'This may take a few months,' our Indian friends warned us. 'It's unlikely we'll have a reply before you leave, so we've arranged for your permits to be sent to the Indian Embassy in Dar es Salaam.'

However, I soon discovered that getting to Tanzania from Egypt would not be as straightforward as I had believed. Trouble had broken out in southern Sudan and, furthermore, it appeared that vehicles were not allowed to cross the border between Kenya and Tanzania without special permission. I therefore kept working on an alternative route through the Sahara in spite of Claire's premonitions, but I was careful not to tell her.

Applying for visas turned out to be a frustrating, time-consuming and costly experience. Some African embassies wanted me to give a very good reason why I absolutely had to drive through their country; others required an incredible number of personal details, including the names of father and mother, religious affiliation, credit-worthiness and so on.

Worst of all was the Embassy of Zaire (now the Democratic Republic of Congo). They didn't seem to find time to process my request for visas in spite of being over-staffed and when I kept pressing them they became frankly rude. I suppose it was their way of paying the Belgians back for seventy-odd years of colonial occupation, but still, why should I be punished for what other people had done?

I wanted to enter Zaire from the Central African Republic in the north and leave the country at the border with Rwanda in the east, a journey that might take three weeks. And all the Embassy finally gave me, after making me wait ten days, were one-week visas with entrance at Kinshasa, the capital in the west of the country. When I protested they told me that it was that or nothing, and almost threw our passports at me.

Meanwhile, Bernard was working full-time on the Land Rover. He had driven it around for a couple of days and then came to me proposing a number of improvements.

'Now that we have the money,' he said, 'I can at last equip the Land Rover properly.'

I was pleased that someone was willing to take on a job far beyond my capacity and gave him carte blanche.

Soon the Land Rover was permanently stationed in the garage entrance while Bernard began to explore what was hidden underneath the bonnet, undoing part after part of the vehicle's innards; some he put back again before nightfall while others were shoved inside the garage after Bernard had slammed down the bonnet. The following morning he would retrieve the parts and look attentively at one or another of them while scratching his head. Next he would dive under the bonnet to undo some more of what was underneath. Day after day the scene repeated itself as if it were part of a ritual; after a week or two I began to wonder whether he would ever be able to put the vehicle together again.

But not all days were the same; sometimes Bernard would ask for money, hop into his own car and drive off to a dealer for spare parts, leaving behind a total mess of bits and pieces, tools and what-not around the Land Rover while the bonnet remained wide open. Then, an hour or two later, he would return with a broad smile on his face, holding up the new, carefully wrapped spare part as if he had found a treasure.

The inner workings of a car had always been a mystery to me and this mystery had only deepened after seeing Bernard in action. It was obvious, though, that I would have to learn about repairing the vehicle before setting off on the expedition. We were well into October now – my sabbatical year had begun and I was at home every day painting the house – and I thought that, maybe, it was time to start my apprenticeship in car mechanics. As I went out to look for our car specialist, I found the Land Rover bonnet wide open, but I didn't see Bernard. I drew nearer and began to look doubtfully at some of the parts that were lying about; I had no idea of their use. And this was nothing compared to the cables and other odds and ends that still remained under the open bonnet.

Suddenly I noticed a pair of legs sticking out from underneath the chassis and as I called out, 'Bernard!' the legs began to move, knocking over a pile of neatly stacked-up pieces in the process. Finally, after a lot of huffing and puffing, the rest of Bernard appeared. He seemed very upset when he noticed what had happened.

'I spent a whole hour stacking everything in the right order and then you come, upsetting it all! How do you expect me to fix this vehicle?' This was obviously not the right moment to ask questions and I returned to my painting, hoping there would be a more propitious opportunity later.

I had thought the work on the Land Rover would be over by the end of October, but I was sorely mistaken. This was the time when Bernard started on major improvements such as having two extra fuel tanks welded underneath the chassis and removing the old roof rack, installing in its place a solid new one made from welded hollow steel bars, bolted onto the vehicle's body. When I asked him what was wrong with the old roof rack, he snorted derisively.

'That was an amateur roof rack! It would collapse in no time on any unmade road. Trust me. I've driven to India.'

'But this Land Rover has been to Iran and back several times!' I protested.

He shrugged his shoulders. 'You'll see, this new, strong roof rack will allow you to take a large number of jerry cans; and there'll also be room for a big metal box to store all your tools and spare parts, and for loads of other things, all fixed safely up there.' He held his head to one side, which was a sign that he was pondering everything carefully. 'And I think it's essential to carry two spare wheels and several spare tyres.'

'Is that really necessary?'

Bernard cut me short at once. 'You won't find spare tyres in Africa, you know. So you will need to carry everything with you. When you have your third or fourth blow-out in the middle of nowhere you will understand and thank me for this.'

I thought of the roof rack and all it was supposed to hold. The whole proposition sounded terribly heavy to me; I couldn't help feeling worried about total weight, especially since Bernard was also thinking of installing an electric winch, but I thought it best not to object.

'So, when will you be ready?'

Bernard scratched his head. 'Give me a few more weeks,' he said.

By mid-November I had most of the visas we required for the first few months. I had also found a second-hand 16mm cine camera, bought eight hours of movie film, a second-hand professional sound recorder and audiotapes, and loads of other equipment I thought we would need during the journey.

The transformation of the garage into an apartment was progressing, too; we had fitted a shower and kitchenette inside, and put in a skylight and a large window towards the garden. And the painting of the house was nearly finished. Another week or two, maybe, and we would be ready to leave. And Bernard had even found time to give me a course on car maintenance! Unfortunately it was all over in an hour, but I was not to worry. He handed me a thick book on Land Rover repair, saying, 'You'll find everything in here,' while tapping it with his finger. 'Do I really have to read all this?' I asked, looking at it with deep misgiving. 'And what if we break down and I can't repair it?'

'Well …' Bernard started, hopping from one leg to the other. 'In that case, you'd better break down in front of a repair garage.'

That night, as we were going to bed, I said to Claire, 'I just hope that there are plenty of repair garages in Africa.'

'Why?'

'To break down in front of them.'

For a moment Claire looked at me as if she were wondering if the day's work had affected my brain. Then she shrugged her shoulders, saying, 'We'll see tomorrow,' turned over and switched off the light after a 'Good night darling'. And that was that.

Off at Last

Leaving is often the most difficult part of a journey. It was now 8 December, we were well behind schedule and would have to hurry and cross the Sahara via Algeria in spite of Claire's misgivings. The problem was that we had to enter Algeria before 16 December or else start the process of applying for visas all over again. This would have been an administrative nightmare for which we lacked the time if we wanted to complete even a part of the travel schedule we had so enthusiastically shown reporters.

Somehow we had to get going, even though we hadn't managed to let the house.

'Don't worry,' said Papé, Claire's father. 'You just leave. I'll look after the house for you; I'm sure to let it.'

Bernard and Philippe set about collecting all the equipment, blankets, pots and pans and so on – all we might need during the trip – while Claire brought down our clothes and shoes, and I began to search for maps and documents.

To make sure we would leave I phoned Claudine, a good friend of ours who lived near the motorway ten miles south of Brussels. I felt that if we committed ourselves to get to her that night, we would at last have started our journey. It was already late afternoon and I apologised, 'but,' I asked, 'would you be kind enough to put us up overnight?'

Claudine was surprised but she said, 'Of course you can come along. I'll be delighted to have you.' And, being a very hospitable person and an excellent cook, she added, 'I'll prepare you a nice supper.'

When I walked into the living room with my maps and documents, I had a shock: a mountain of things a few feet high had appeared in the middle of the carpet.

'What's this?' I stammered.

'It's what you need for your journey,' said Philippe, looking as if he had done us a great service.

'How on earth do you expect us to take all that?' I exclaimed. 'It won't fit into the Land Rover!'

'Then you had better choose,' suggested Bernard.

Claire and I had just started the difficult process of selecting what we might need when the doorbell rang.

'I'll go!' shouted Philippe. 'It'll be François. I'm expecting him.' He was back in a second, looking flustered. 'You'd better go, Mum,' he whispered.

In the doorway stood a short, strongly built, dark-faced man with a very broad nose and curly hair, dressed in an impeccable suit. He announced himself as the First Secretary of the Embassy of Papua New Guinea. Driving along our avenue he had seen the 'To Let' sign in front of the house and had taken the liberty of ringing the bell in order to enquire whether the house was still free.

When Claire said, 'Yes,' the man brightened up and asked whether she would be kind enough to show him the house. Claire began by showing him the ground floor. The kitchen and dining room seemed all right but as he entered the living room a puzzled expression passed over the man's face.

'Hmm …' he said, pointing a finger towards the mountain of things in the centre of the room. 'Is one allowed to remove this? Or is it part of the scene?' He hesitated a second and then ventured, 'Or maybe it is a local custom?'

Claire hastily explained that it was to be removed that same evening, which reassured the First Secretary no end, and then she quickly took him upstairs. He particularly liked the bookcases along the landing.

'Lots to read here, nice, nice,' he said.

But most of all he appreciated the big guestroom with the four-poster bed. He sat down upon it and then tried out the solidity of the springs by bouncing up and down on the mattress while exclaiming all the time, 'Nice, nice.'

When he had finished the tour of all the rooms and came down again, he asked for the monthly rent and then said, 'OK, I take it.'

This was a really wonderful last-minute surprise! We had been working for months towards getting the house ready for this, our funds were dwindling, and letting the house would assure us of an income we very much needed.

'Nice house,' repeated the diplomat. 'Very nice house. Three years then, OK?'

'But … but …' Claire looked apologetically at the man. 'We can't do that. We can let it for a year at most. We'll be back by that time.' Then doubt clouded her face and she added, 'At least, I hope so.'

'I'm appointed for three years!' the diplomat argued. 'I must have it for three years.' When he realised that he wouldn't get his way, he became visibly upset. 'Why didn't you tell me from the start?' he grumbled, then turned abruptly and left.

By the time he had gone, it was already 7.30 p.m. and we rushed into the living room to sort out the pile of things lying there, picking out anything that seemed useful for the journey. As we opened the front door to dump our choice items into the back of the Land Rover, a wintry blast entered the house: the weather had suddenly turned icy cold and we had to put on our thickest clothes. By 8.30 p.m., when we were ready to go, it began to snow and we slowly drove off while everyone waved goodbye.

This was it then. Our dream journey had started at last; we were off to tropical Africa. As we turned round the corner of the avenue the snow began to come down in sheets and we had barely covered a mile when the windscreen wiper on the driver's side broke off under the weight of the piled-up snow. I had to stick my head out of the side window to be able to see anything. The snow nearly blinded me and froze on my beard but I was determined to carry on. If we turned back now we would never leave our cosy home! And we had something to look forward to: Claudine was waiting for us with a nice supper.

We got onto the motorway to Paris, crawling forward at a snail's pace, and finally made it to Halle where Claudine lived. We had just passed the church and only had another 300 yards to go when a loud rattling became audible. It sounded as if the bottom had fallen out of the Land Rover.

'Damn, damn!' I shouted. This was just too much. There are limits to what one can take in a single evening, and the idea of the vehicle's bottom lying on the cobblestones surpassed those limits. As I got out in the falling snow to inspect the damage, everything seemed normal. Then I noticed a long metal wire trailing behind the Land Rover with lots of empty metal tea tins attached to it. I stood there, gaping, and then burst out laughing. I realised who had played this prank, but I didn't know that Bernard and Philippe were watching us. They had followed us along the motorway at a safe distance, had stopped close by and were having a good laugh, hiding behind their car. A year later they told me how they had done the trick; the wire had been held up by a thin cotton thread attached to the exhaust pipe, and when the thread had burnt through, the metal wire with the tins had crashed down, making a terrific din.

That night, as we lay in bed in an unfamiliar room after a friendly welcome and a delicious meal, thoughts kept whirling through my head. I had just turned forty; this was going to be the greatest adventure of our lives; and I had no idea what was awaiting us in Africa or how we were going to cope with the many problems that were sure to crop up.

The next day dawned bright and sunny and we managed to find a Land Rover garage and had the windscreen wipers replaced. The rest of the journey to the Mediterranean passed uneventfully, apart from a moment of panic when I tried to switch gears on the motorway between Dijon and Lyon: the gearbox didn't respond; the gears seemed to be stuck. I struggled for quite a while with the big gear stick while we began to slow down. Then, to my relief, the gears moved and we shot forward again. I hoped that this was just a freak occurrence and that the gearbox, and the rest of the mechanics, would behave and get us safely through our journey. Little did I know then that our old gearbox would give us no end of trouble until we finally managed to have it repaired in a proper Land Rover garage halfway across Africa.

When I say that we shot forward, this is meant in a relative sense, of course. Bernard had added so many features to the Land Rover, which he thought were absolutely necessary, that the old engine struggled visibly to pull all that weight along. The best we could get out of it was a steady 50 miles per hour on the flat, smooth motorways of France. It made me wonder what kind of speed it would be able to sustain in the Sahara.

It was quite warm in France for the time of the year and we made good headway. I was worried every evening, though, about finding a secure place to park, and even then I would take out our 16mm camera and several of our most precious belongings and keep them with us in our hotel room. I managed to rent a locked garage for our second night in a small provincial town in the Rhône Valley, and congratulated myself for having done so the next morning when other guests in the hotel found that their brand new car, which they had parked in the market square only 50 yards away, had been stolen during the night.

We reached the Mediterranean, 700 miles further south, in three days and stopped at several cheap hotels, asking where we could park. The people invariably pointed at the road and when I inquired whether they thought it safe out there, some shrugged their shoulders; one man replied that this was not his responsibility and, when pressed, another one admitted that there was a fair chance that the vehicle would be gone by the morning. Then he eyed the old Land Rover with a condescending look in his eyes and corrected himself. 'Well, maybe not the vehicle, but certainly its contents.' At last we discovered a small motel in an isolated spot away from the road near the edge of a cliff. We parked on the cliff side between the door to our motel room and some pine trees; the Land Rover was totally invisible from the road and I felt it was safe for the night.

On 13 December, we drove to Marseilles and found that a ferry was sailing the next morning and would reach Algiers on 15 December, the last day our visas permitted us to enter Algeria. We were in luck! We booked our passage, drove back to the motel and spent the afternoon unloading the pile of things that clogged up the Land Rover's back compartment where we were planning to sleep. As we unloaded more and more of the stuff onto the grass and the pile became substantial, I wondered how we would ever be able to arrange it all inside. I had no idea where to start but Claire, who had been raised on puzzles, set to it with gusto, stowing the least useful and heaviest items first and gradually building up from there.

A couple of hours later, the bottom of the compartment had been turned into a base upon which a wooden board and our foam mattress were laid out, and she had even made our bed with sheets and a blanket. It seemed like a miracle: we now had a proper sleeping compartment! The back did not have a door like most Land Rovers, but consisted of a top half with handle and key, and a bottom half. When we raised the top half we could easily crawl upon the mattress and when we lowered the bottom half, the cooking equipment underneath the mattress became immediately accessible. Claire had done her stacking very cleverly and I now felt ready to face the long journey.

The next morning, the ship left Marseilles harbour and, leaning against the railings, holding hands, we saw Europe recede. A feeling of elation swept over us. This was it at last! This was the life we had so often dreamed of, sailing to adventure and unknown destinations over a smooth blue sea. It was just wonderful!

Towards the south, the Mediterranean stretched endlessly under an azure sky, but we knew that, far beyond the horizon, lay the Africa of our dreams. As I looked out over the silky waters, whitecaps began to appear. Within an hour, the sea became choppy and by late afternoon, a strong gale was blowing and the ship started heaving and rolling. When it was time for supper, Claire said she couldn't face eating and preferred to stay put on her bunk.

'Do as you like,' I replied with cool determination, 'but *I* am hungry and I'm going to have my supper.' I worked my way through empty corridors, holding on first to the rail on one side and then to the one on the other. Where had all the passengers gone? I found no more than three or four intrepid diners in the vast dining room and had just sat down when a waiter brought in a steaming dish of chicken kebab. As the rich smell struck my nostrils, I suddenly felt my stomach turn. I walked slowly out of the dining room, trying to remain dignified, and then rushed along on unsteady legs holding a hand over my mouth. Just as I thought I would no longer be able to hold back, I reached our cabin, swayed inside, sank down on my knees and started retching helplessly.

I remember the following night as possibly the worst in my entire life. Giant waves were constantly slamming into the hull and the ship vibrated as if it were going to fall apart. There were sinister creaking noises, doors banging shut and the loud clanging of chains, and all the time our luggage kept sliding back and forth over the floor of the cabin. For endless hours we lay on our bunks moaning, as our prostrate bodies seemed to fall into a void, to rise brusquely upwards and next to fall again. Sometimes the downward movement appeared to go on forever as if we were sinking, and I could hear Claire's wailing voice in the darkness. 'I don't want to die …' I just prayed for this nightmare to be over.

By late morning next day, as we approached the North African coast, the storm had blown itself out. I stumbled onto the deck together with some other passengers who were slowly emerging from their cabins; some were white-faced and shaky, others ashen-grey. As the ship drew steadily nearer to the coast, I stared at the dirty-looking jumble of buildings spreading into the hills under a dull grey sky. Was this the famous Alger la Blanche (White Algiers)? Only the day before I had imagined the excitement I was going to feel when I saw sunny, happy Africa for the first time in my life. Was this Africa?

PART 2

Africa from the North to the Equator

The Age of Innocence

The political and social conditions described in this book reflect the situation as it was at the time. They have changed since – for better, or more often for worse.

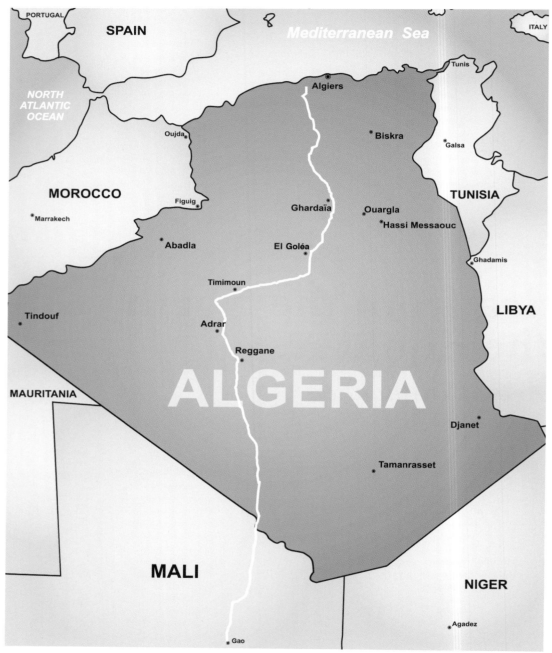

Map 1: Algeria and the Sahara

From Algiers to Ghardaïa, to El-Goléa and Timimoun, to Reggane and Gao

CHAPTER 3
Algeria: A Different World

You don't have to be naïve to embark upon a wild adventure …
but it helps

Algiers

Going through immigration was an unpleasant experience: there wasn't a smile to be seen on anyone's face and the customs officers brought in a mechanic who set about working on the Land Rover with spanners and screw drivers. He took the floor panels to pieces and began to look meticulously under the bonnet and inspect all the nooks and crannies underneath the vehicle. I had no idea what he was searching for and he was unwilling to elucidate. Did we look suspicious or was it just a routine search?

We had to declare all the foreign currency we had brought into Algeria. This, as I learned later, was to make sure we would only exchange at official banks. We had 200,000 Belgian francs in travellers cheques, hidden inside the vehicle, and another 200,000 francs in cash, which we carried inside our belts. From the outside these looked just like ordinary belts but they had a zip on the inside which, when opened, revealed neat rows of tightly folded banknotes. Those 400,000 francs (about £5,700 at the time) would have to get us through the journey as far as India and back home, and we knew we would have to be very careful to make our money last.

Inexperienced as I was, I declared all the foreign currency we had with us, dutifully writing down the total amount on a form which was then attached to our passports. We were told that the border police would check everything when we left Algeria.

By the time all inspections and formalities were over and we were allowed to enter the country, it was already mid-afternoon. We found a bank just before closing time, bought some Algerian dinars and drove out of town along the western coastal road without having the slightest idea where we were going. We were dead-tired and hungry and could think only of having something to eat and then finding a quiet spot to camp and sleep.

On the outskirts of Algiers, we came upon a park and noticed a sign pointing to a restaurant down a lane between scattered pine trees. The restaurant was open but strangely enough, we were the only customers. As we sat down on heavy metal chairs, we had visions of a copious meal but one look at the price list sufficed to suppress our appetite: the cheapest item on the menu, a salad for two, and a small bottle of water shared between us, came to 800 francs (£11.00)! At that rate our funds were going to melt like butter in the African sun.

It was pitch dark by the time we had finished our frugal meal. I just couldn't face having to drive any further and asked the two men in the restaurant whether they had any objections to us sleeping in our vehicle just outside.

'Do as you please,' they replied as they began pulling down heavy iron shutters and disappeared in a hurry, leaving us alone in the darkness of the park. This was our first night camping out but we were too tired to think. We just crept inside the back of the Land Rover and were asleep within minutes.

We returned to the centre of Algiers the following morning to call on the Belgian Embassy; I wanted to find out if there were any Belgian projects we could visit in Algeria. We were ushered into the office of a low-ranking civil servant who asked in an offhand way to see my introductory letter from the Belgian Ministry of Foreign Affairs.

I was taken aback. 'I … I thought that the Ministry was going to notify all the embassies of the countries on our itinerary,' I stammered. 'At least … that's what they promised …'

'Well, I'll have a look.' The man disappeared with a sullen face and when he returned sometime later I could see from his manner what the answer was going to be. 'We have not received any letter authorising us to lend you our assistance,' he said in an indifferent, official voice. 'I'm afraid the Embassy cannot do anything for you.'

'What a flying start!' I whispered under my breath to Claire as we left the Embassy. 'You come full of good intentions but they can't even give you an address of a project because they haven't received a letter. Great, isn't it?'

'Never mind,' said Claire. 'We'll find plenty of interesting projects to visit and film during our journey. For the moment, let's start by doing a few easy things; that'll cheer us up. What I'd like right now is to complete our equipment. We need a new teapot and that shouldn't be too difficult to find in a country where everyone drinks tea.'

We had an aluminium teapot but Claire didn't like it because the handle was broken.

'And we might as well look around for two light, folding chairs so we can eat out in comfort,' she added.

We went to shop after shop but they only had big clumsy chairs made of heavy welded steel tubes that didn't fold, and ornate ceramic teapots which wouldn't have survived very long. At last we met a dealer who told us that he might be able to find us a cheap metal teapot.

'Come back later in the afternoon,' he said, 'and we shall see, Inshallah.'

When we returned a few hours later, he showed us his prize purchase: a small, ornate copper teapot. It cost the equivalent of £10.00 and the smile on his face was as large as the price he asked! When he realised that the deal was not going through, his smile disappeared at once.

'You don't want it!' he barked. 'You don't want it! You foreign dogs!' And suddenly he began to shout at us in Arabic. Other men now appeared from nearby shops and as we hastened to our Land Rover and made off, they shook their fists and began to hurl abuse at us.

As we drove out of town in a hurry, I turned to Claire. 'We'd better start looking for a place to camp while it's still light.'

'Why don't we go back to that park where we slept last night?' she proposed. 'It's peaceful and very pretty – and it seems a safe place.'

'All right, but I don't want to go to that restaurant again. We simply can't afford it.'

By the time we reached the park, darkness was beginning to set in. We drove up the lane very quietly, parked well away from the restaurant, had a sober meal of bread, water and sardines, climbed into the Land Rover's sleeping area and lay down without even undressing.

The next day we stopped further along the coast for diesel fuel and when the pump attendant saw our Belgian licence plates he told us there was a Belgian family living just around the corner. 'Come along,' he motioned. 'I'll take you to them.'

The door was opened by a dark-haired woman of generous proportions who was visibly moved when she heard that we were Belgians. 'What a wonderful surprise!' she exclaimed, pressing us to her ample bosom. 'Don't just stand there on the doorstep. Do come in. I'm Martine.' She called out to her husband, 'Alain, come and see what I've got here! Compatriots!'

She wanted to know all about us, what we were doing in Algeria, where we were going and where we had slept so far.

'We camped in a park just outside Algiers,' said Claire, describing the place.

'You didn't!' she exclaimed. 'And nothing happened?'

'No,' replied Claire, surprised. 'It was such a nice spot with all those trees that we spent two nights there. We were so tired that we slept like logs and wouldn't have heard anything anyway. What could have happened? Are there wild animals?'

'Animals!' Martine shook her head in disbelief. 'You must have good guardian angels! God does protect the innocent.'

'But why?'

'That park where you so foolishly spent two nights is one of the most dangerous places in the whole of Algiers! They cut people's throats there all the time. Only last week they found a foreigner lying dead under a tree. You don't realise how lucky you are to still be alive!'

'You're exaggerating, surely,' objected Claire. 'I never felt any danger.'

'Look here, I can't have any more of this,' said Martine. 'You're going to spend the night here in our house. Then, at least, I'll be sure you won't do any more foolish things. And I'll tell you which hotels to stop at on your way south.'

As it happened, our stay turned out to be so interesting that we spent not one, but two nights with Martine. Everything went smoothly but for one incident: for some mysterious reason, Claire, who has always had a tendency to mix up names, kept calling our hostess Monique. The first time I saw her wince and the second time she nearly exploded.

'Will you stop calling me that awful name!' she snapped.

'I don't know what you mean, Monique,' replied Claire, taken aback.

'That's not my name!' She nearly shouted. 'That's the name of my husband's mistress! I'm Martine.'

'Oh! I am sorry.'

Martine was an outspoken woman and she told us that her husband, who was working here for a Belgian project, saw his mistress every time he went back to Belgium, which happened all too frequently for our hostess's liking. 'It's very upsetting,' she said, giving her husband a sharp look. But she was not one to take such an insult lying down. She was paying him back in kind and had started an affair with the local police commander. 'Here, at least, they appreciate women like me,' she boasted.

'What do you mean, Mon … er, Martine?'

Thrusting her bosom forward and towering over Claire, she explained, 'The police commander says that I'm worth at least ten camels!'

I was about to comment that this showed that they preferred bulk down here, but I wisely abstained.

'Is ten camels a high price for a woman?' asked Claire, very interested.

'A high price?' Martine snorted. 'That's a top price!'

'And me?' Claire wanted to know, looking eagerly at Martine. 'How much do you think I would be worth?'

She gave Claire a good looking-over and then said derisively, 'Pff … they wouldn't pay more than a few goats for you. That's all *you* would fetch. You're much too skinny.'

'And how much is that in camels?'

'That's not even a camel. There are ten to fifteen goats to a camel, depending on whether the goats are skinny or fat. You see,' she explained, 'men here like value for their money. They like to get their hands onto something.'

'Gosh … er, Martine, you are very valuable, then.'

'Yes I am,' agreed Martine without the slightest hint of modesty.

It turned out that it wasn't just the local police commander who benefited from the relationship. Apparently Martine was free to do whatever she liked. She sold her woven goods on the black market and the police never bothered her. Her activities had brought her loads of Algerian dinars but there was a slight drawback: she said she was unable to exchange her Algerian cash for hard currency.

'But can't you go to a bank?' I asked.

'Banks don't change dinars,' she retorted.

'How can that be? I've just changed money in a bank in Algiers.'

'You didn't!' she exclaimed. 'At the official rate! That's just plain stupid!' And then she asked if I needed more money. When I nodded affirmatively she ran upstairs and came back with a wad of dinars, which she pressed into my hands. 'Look here,' she said, 'I can give you a much better rate than banks.'

Communist regimes all over the world were known for their indifference towards the customer, and we were to find out that Algeria was no exception. But communism – or socialism as it was called here – had its compensation for foreigners: as so many Algerians wanted to get out of the country and were unable to change enough money, there was a thriving black market. You had to be careful, though, with whom you changed. I was therefore overjoyed when Martine offered me dinars at the black market rate – which turned out to be five times the official rate! – because we would now be able to get through Algeria without ruining our budget. In exchange I wrote her a cheque in Belgian francs, which she would cash when she returned home for her holidays.

When I asked how the country survived under socialism, Martine's husband commented, 'Well, some people get a lot out of the system. Didn't you notice all those rich villas along the coast when you drove out of Algiers?'

'Yes. I wondered about them. They looked like walled cities.'

'That's where the families of members of the government and the top military live – those who won the revolution and divided up the cake. And no privations or Islamic restrictions for them and their children! There are bars and discotheques within those walled compounds.'

'What about the others? What kind of future do they have?' I had noticed that many young men just seemed to be hanging about, looking bored. 'Maybe they're dreaming of emigrating to Europe,' I ventured.

'They do want to emigrate,' confirmed Alain, 'but then, they don't realise that they wouldn't have much of a future in Europe either if they got there because they have little or inadequate education. The problem seems insoluble. There are too many children in this male-dominated society, few jobs and a growing resentment against a government and a ruling party whose members keep filling their pockets and flaunting their riches ostentatiously in the faces of the poorer ninety-five percent. And so the poor build their hopes on religious movements. And you know what the government did to appease the imams?'

'I have no idea.'

'They've given them control over education!' He shook his head. 'I'll bet you that education will soon be reduced to religion, Arab literature and history! You wait. That's going to cause no end of a problem when the children who are now young boys grow up to become fanatical, unemployed, young adults!'

Martine employed a young woman to clean her house and in no time Claire was plying her with questions, trying to find out all she could about local customs for her women's magazine. Claire was eager to see how she lived and in the end, Aisha, the young woman, promised that she would ask her mother if we could visit the house.

So, the next morning, instead of carrying on southwards, we followed Aisha through a jumble of streets bustling with activity. We came to an open-air basin where small girls were standing in the water up to their knees, washing clothes.

'How come these children have to work?' asked Claire.

'Oh, they're girls. They go to school for no more than a few years and then have to help with the household.'

'Did you have to do that, too?'

'No, I've been lucky. My parents left me in school till I was fifteen. That's how I managed to learn French and got a good job with Madame Martine. It's a really wonderful opportunity!' Aisha looked very pleased. 'And my parents don't even make me wear the veil when I go out. They don't object as I work for foreigners and pay my father all the money I earn.'

'Will you continue to work when you marry?'

'That depends on my husband. I pray that he will be nice to me.'

'But can't you choose?'

'Oh no! My parents will find me a husband.'

'How awful!'

Aisha shrugged her shoulders. 'That's the way it is. I will have to obey my husband and accept my future mother-in-law's authority in the house.'

'Why would you have to live with your mother-in-law?' asked Claire, surprised. 'Don't married couples have a place of their own?'

'If you're rich you may be able to get an apartment, but usually sons have to carry on living with their parents after they marry.' She looked sideways at Claire. 'You'll see when we get to the house: my married brothers have their own sleeping quarters with their wives and children, but everything else is shared.'

'But daughters move out?'

'As long as they're not married they live with their parents and help in the house but, yes, once they marry they move in with their husband's family.'

'What happens if you don't get on with your mother-in-law?' asked Claire, curious to know.

'That would be a disaster for the bride because the husband will side with his mother. It's best not to think about such things,' whispered Aisha.

At that moment, we entered the house, which was really a large compound with small rooms giving on to a central yard. I noticed that all the men were absent, which was probably why we were allowed in. The women were there, but when they saw me they quickly disappeared inside the rooms.

'I'd better leave you alone,' I said to Claire and turned around. I had almost shut the door behind me when I quietly peeped through the crack; the women were slowly coming out of hiding and beginning to surround Claire. Then they started touching her, all the while making excited sounds.

When she had satisfied her curiosity about me, Aisha's mother signalled to me to follow her and led me into one of the low, white rooms that opened onto the inner yard; it turned out to be the kitchen. Inside, the light was dim and it was quite stifling but all the same, everyone came in behind us and pressed around while the mother sat me down on a cushion. One of her daughters immediately prepared strong, sugary tea flavoured with mint leaves and as I sat sipping the sweet brew, the old lady, who was dressed in a flowery outfit and wearing a large silver necklace, kept talking in Arabic and pulling my sleeve to attract my attention. All the younger women were talking, too, and after a while it became very confusing. Aisha was trying to translate a sentence here and there, but her French was limited and I didn't understand any Arabic.

'Doesn't anyone speak French?' I asked, feeling lost.

Finally her mother spoke while Aisha translated. 'Yes, I have a daughter-in-law who speaks French fluently, but she is no good. She is not strong like my own daughters. She's always ill and has to lie down.'

'May I see her?'

An embarrassed silence followed but when I insisted, saying I would like to meet her just to wish her luck, the mother finally made a sign.

'Come,' Aisha beckoned. She led me to a small room at the back of the compound and then retreated. On a hard bed, in the semi-darkness, lay Fatima with her small son. She received me with a sweet smile but seemed very shy. Then, as I sat down and took her hand in mine, she hesitantly began to talk.

She came from a town in the south where she had gone to school till she was eighteen; she had had the freedom to go out, have friends and read books, and had very much hoped that she would be allowed to continue her studies. Then, out of the blue, her parents had married her off to the son of a family they knew. The shock had been great; she had been separated from her friends and family, and had to live in the house of her husband's family where they demanded that she do her part of the work, and expected her to bear a child every year. She pined away. She had to live with a stranger with whom she had nothing in common and the trauma was impossible for her to overcome. Every evening she dreaded the return of her husband, an uneducated, strong, demanding man who was displeased with all she did and often beat her. He wanted a second child and she was pregnant again, but she weighed only ninety pounds and feared she would die.

'I'm so worried about my little son,' she confided. 'He is weak and no one will protect him once I'm gone.'

As she spoke a great hopelessness invaded me. She looked so frail and terrified that my eyes filled with tears. There was no way to save this young woman, too gentle and weak to bear the hardships of this sort of life, and I was filled with rage when I left her.

Claire returned to Martine's house an hour or two later, looking very upset.

'What is it?' I asked.

She didn't want to speak at first but then, suddenly, she blurted out the whole story. 'How can life be so unjust?' she kept saying. 'But at least, I'm going to do something to give her a happy moment.'

'You're not going to do anything silly?'

'I'm going to do it,' she retorted, 'and I don't care whether it's silly or not. You see, Fatima comes from the south of the country where there's nothing but barren soil and sand, and one of her great wishes was to see the sea. And imagine: here she is, having lived less than half a mile from the Mediterranean for the last two years, and she's never seen it! So I have arranged to take her to the sea this afternoon after the men have eaten and have all gone out again.'

'How did you manage that?'

'I talked to Aisha's mother. I was very firm and she didn't dare refuse.'

'But what if the husband finds out?'

'He won't. The women all know about it of course, but I'm sure they'll keep quiet. I think that, privately, they all enjoy the idea of fooling the men and disobeying them.'

A few hours later, I went to fetch Fatima. She put her arm through mine and we went down to the sea, walking very slowly because she was so weak, and I sat her down on a flat rock. Below our feet the Mediterranean broke with thundering noise.

'The sea, the sea,' whispered Fatima, looking out towards the waves with eyes wide with astonishment. 'They told me about it in the oasis where I lived, but I didn't believe there could be so much water.' She pulled down the veil that covered her face and breathed in the fresh sea air; it brought colour to her pale cheeks. Then she dug out a small brightly coloured handkerchief from between the folds of the long garment she wore and held it up hesitantly. I looked at her.

'What are you going to do, Fatima?'

She seemed embarrassed. 'When I was a young girl, I was told that, when you see the sea for the first time, you have to throw a treasured possession into the water and make a wish.' And she dropped her handkerchief.

'Yes, make a wish, Fatima!'

The handkerchief fluttered like a coloured bird in the wind, fell into the waves and slowly drifted away while she followed it with her eyes till it had become a tiny speck.

'What did you wish?'

'That, I cannot tell you.'

May the heavens hear you, I thought, holding her small hand tightly in mine. We sat there for a long while, so close together, yet so many worlds apart.

Heading South

We left the coast the next morning and began to pass through one small town after another with a well-defined aim: we were looking for petrol stations. A few months before, back in Brussels, we had been trying to buy cooking equipment. We wanted a small, cheap cooker that functioned on gas canisters, but in the posh shop to which we had gone, the staff had advised against this.

'You won't find gas canisters anywhere in Africa,' they had warned us. What we needed, they said, was a different kind of cooker: one that was unbreakable and easy to operate. And we were lucky! They happened to have a model that exactly fitted the bill, a small stove that functioned on unrefined oil – the cheapest of all fuels!

'But they don't sell unrefined oil in Belgium,' I had objected.

'Well,' they had replied, 'you say you're going to Algeria? You'll have no trouble finding unrefined oil there. Remember that Algeria is an oil producer. Just ask at any petrol station. You'll even find unrefined oil in shops.'

It had all sounded very reassuring. The oil stove was small but it was top of the range, we were told; we wouldn't find anything better or easier to operate. It was expensive, but that was the price you pay for quality. The little stove was made of shiny brass and looked very attractive indeed. It even had a name. It was called the Little Bee and had bee images stamped in relief around its rim. 'Anyone seeing this in Africa will want it,' they had said, 'so you'd better buy two. And anyway, you'll need two as each stove has only got one hob.' They'd been very convincing and we were now the proud owners of two Little Bee stoves.

So far we had already stopped at five petrol stations but no one seemed to have heard of unrefined oil; they all wanted us to buy gasoline instead. It was no good explaining that we needed the fuel for cooking and that we could not cook with gasoline because the stove would blow up. When they realised that we were not going to buy their gasoline they just turned away and ignored us. I had almost given up hope when in the next petrol station they did have unrefined oil, and they were willing to fill up one of our jerry cans with it!

We didn't feel at ease, though, in the mountains south of Algiers. It was not only the petrol station attendants who were uncooperative; people seemed generally unfriendly, even quite offhand, and I felt relieved when we left the coastal mountain range behind and entered the vast expanse leading to the Sahara.

We were driving on the road to Laghouat, it was 5.00 p.m. and we still had 30 miles to go when suddenly, without the slightest warning, the wind grew in intensity; it was startling to see sand rush along the ground like a fast-flowing river!

Nomads and their camels generally do not mind crossing patches of loose sand – they will even work their way through dunes where no vehicle would risk going – but there is one thing that makes them stop: a sandstorm. When it blows hard and the air becomes so saturated with sand that it stings their faces, even camels lie down. They turn their hind parts towards the wind and keep their heads low, while humans huddle behind their recumbent camels, draw their burnouses over their heads and wait for the storm to blow over.

This isn't the case for modern, motorised people. They have no time to lie down; they want to get to their destination, storm or no storm. I, too, tried to carry on because I wanted to reach a hotel in Laghouat before nightfall, but within minutes the sunlight was dimmed and the air became thick like dirty milk. Nothing seemed to be able to stop the sand. It penetrated the cabin through the smallest gaps, whirled around our heads and got into our ears, noses and throats. We seemed to be floating in spinning, fine dust and began to feel suffocated.

This is the time to switch on our extra-strong headlights, I thought. When he'd installed them, Bernard had declared proudly, 'With these you'll be able to see anything anywhere,' but the strong beams of light just bounced off the thick, surreal mist of twirling sand and blinded us. The road seemed to have been obliterated.

Finally I gave up and followed the advice people had given us: if you run into a sandstorm, turn the back of the vehicle towards the wind to protect the engine and wait for the storm to blow itself out. After an hour, the worst was over and by the time we reached Laghouat, bright stars had begun to sparkle in the dark, velvety sky.

Around Ghardaïa, an oasis further south, the land had a soft pink and red hue. This was the home-town of the Mozabites, a tribe famous for its traders. We drove through narrow streets lined with shops displaying their wares in crates outside. When Claire saw these, she made me stop and rushed out, looking at what each stall had for sale. She was particularly interested in women's makeup, and when she began asking how they used the black kohl-lining for the eyes and what they did with the henna, the vendors swarmed around her like flies and began pressing all sorts of articles into her hands; it took me a long time to extract her and pull her back into the Land Rover. She was bubbling with enthusiasm and as I drove off, she was saying, 'This will make such an interesting article for my women's magazine.'

A few streets further on, Claire noticed quite a grown-up girl who wasn't yet veiled. She immediately jumped out and when the girl told her that her elder sisters were weaving an oriental rug on a large handloom in one of the houses further along, Claire followed her without a second's hesitation. A moment later they disappeared inside a house and I was left alone. Just then a nearby school finished and suddenly the street swarmed with boys. When they noticed the Land Rover, they rushed towards it with whoops of joy and took it by assault, climbing all over it until it seemed to be covered by layers of children.

By the time Claire reappeared half an hour later, the children had gone. Their enthusiasm must have cooled off – or did they have to return home to eat?

'Well, how was it?' I asked.

'What a fascinating experience,' replied Claire. 'There were three girls inside the house, but as they were of marriageable age, they were all veiled and refused to be photographed. But then I let them touch my clothes and soon they wanted to show me their best dresses. In the end they seemed to have forgotten all about their veils; they were demanding to be photographed and posed like film stars! I had to be quick though because they were afraid their father might return.

The Mozabites were indeed a very traditional people. In the streets you saw only men and young children, who ran barefoot in the dust. Women were severely restricted in their freedom. You rarely saw them go out for shopping, and when they did they slipped along the walls like shadows. Those you met were probably older women, but it was hard to tell because they were covered from head to foot.

We saw such a woman. She wore black-leather, low-heeled shoes which stuck out from underneath her long, dirty-white gown, and she carried a leather handbag. We couldn't see the hand, though; it was hidden somewhere inside the garment. Most striking was the top of the gown, entirely covering head and face. A small hole was left free for one eye to look out. The eye must have been there, but could not be seen in the darkness of the small hole. That hole was all the contact the woman was allowed to have with the outside world. I wondered about stereoscopic vision. Not content with severely curtailing the freedom of women, tradition here obliged these unfortunate beings to cut down their vision from three to two dimensions.

It was near El-Goléa that Charles de Foucauld, a famous French mystic of the early twentieth century, founded a church. Better known as le Père de Foucauld, he then withdrew into the Hoggar Mountains near Tamanrasset where he lived as a hermit until he was found murdered some years later. The mystery surrounding his death has never been fully solved.

We decided to visit his little church, which stood alone on the edge of the desert a few miles away from the town. It was supposed to be a museum, and we met the kind old guardian who was pleased to have some visitors to talk to. He had been with the church all his life and was half blind now, while his camel, which was tethered next to him, was so old and tattered that it seemed as if it might fall to pieces any moment. The guardian unlocked the door to let us have a look inside the church; there was nothing left. The benches, the altar, the ornaments … everything had gone. Even most of the stained glass windows were smashed, the desert wind blew freely through the little church and sand lay in piles on the floor and in the corners. It seemed symbolic. Was this all that was left of more than a century of French presence here?

We spent the night in a small hotel in El-Goléa. Its oriental charm was magical: the rooms were on the first floor and all led onto a large inner patio with flowers and a fountain; it felt like a tale from *A Thousand and One Nights*. We would willingly have stayed here longer, but had to move on: we were obliged to leave Algeria in less than a week. To do so we would have to cross the Sahara and we were not looking forward to that journey.

In Brussels, I had planned to drive straight to Niger where we had friends and from there cross into Nigeria. The route to Niger, via In Salah, was not only the most direct way to Central Africa; it was also the most popular and the most spectacular, leading to Tamanrasset and the Hoggar Mountains. But I had heard that the asphalted road, which apparently had been built without any regard to surfacing and drainage, had been destroyed by heavy traffic. It was full of potholes and strewn with stones and bits of old tarmac, and many vehicles were reported to have broken down on it. I didn't know whether this was true or not but it scared me, and that night, on the spur of the moment, I opted for the safer crossing via the western route, driving to Mali instead. This decision, taken so lightly, would turn out to change our journey radically and, although I had no inkling of it at the time, it was to affect my life deeply.

So far, the road south had been a two-lane road in good condition but now, as we headed west towards the oasis of Timimoun, we found ourselves on a single strip of tarmac on a level plain, a straight line carrying on seemingly endlessly towards a point far on the horizon. Nothing seemed to change; hour after hour we kept moving under the burning sun and there was no feature of interest either to the left or right, just a vast expanse of stony waste.

The only excitement was meeting a car, which happened every quarter of an hour or so. As this was a single-track road, the rule was that both cars moved partly off the tarmac. Being slow, we made sure that we got out of the way well in time, but Algerian drivers seemed to look upon these encounters as sporting events. They invariably drove extremely fast, swerving to move away from us only at the very last moment. Every time we saw a car appear on the horizon and race towards us, we felt our nerves tense. As we moved our right wheels off the tarmac and they hit the unmade side of the road with a bump, the Land Rover would rattle and shake. Then, when the other vehicle had rushed by in a cloud of dust, we had to get back onto the asphalted surface, which was about 4 inches higher than the unmade side.

When a lorry came towards us, however, the rules were different. In this case, the law of the strongest applied, and the lorry was definitely the strongest. On our first encounter we had not yet understood this new rule. We had moved our outer wheels off the road, but when the wildly hooting lorry kept coming closer without budging, we finally realised that it intended to keep the tarmac all to itself and only managed to get out of the way in the last split second. After that hair-raising experience, we no longer pushed our luck but swerved completely off the tarmac and onto the rough, dusty side every time we saw a lorry rush headlong towards us.

We had got to within 30 miles of Timimoun and Claire was driving when I noticed a light flashing red on the dashboard.

'Cut the engine!' I shouted and I jumped out, intending to open the bonnet to find out what had gone wrong, but there was no need for that: a stream of black oil was flowing out from underneath the Land Rover. I stood there for a while, dumbfounded, unable to utter a word. I feared the worst and suddenly felt very vulnerable. We had been driving on and off the one-lane road; maybe we had hit a big stone and somehow cracked the sump? How was I ever going to repair this kind of damage? This was surely the end of our journey before we had so much as left the tarmac and entered the no man's land of the Sahara? What a let-down!

I crawled underneath the Land Rover and noticed that the oil was leaking out of a hole in the middle of the sump. After a while, the stream of oil became a drip and that, too, finally stopped; all the oil must have run out. I now stuck my finger into the hole. The first thing I realised was that I had burned my finger; the second was that inside the hole there was a thread. This set me thinking. Although I didn't know much about car mechanics, it was obvious that a bolt had gone missing here. I also understood its use. It was the oil drain plug, which you unscrewed when you wanted to change the engine's oil every 3,000 miles or so, to let the used oil run out.

I felt much better after that. This was just a case of finding another bolt and screwing it in, something even I could handle. I climbed onto the roof rack and rummaged in the spare-parts chest, got out an assortment of bolts and tried them all; nothing fitted. This was obviously a very special bolt, and I had no spare!

There was nothing to do but try and hunt for the lost plug. A line of black oil led from under the Land Rover some 50 yards back; that was where the leak had started and where the oil drainage plug, probably shaken loose by all the moving off and on to the road, had fallen out. I went to the beginning of the black line but there was nothing to be seen anywhere. The plug must have bounced off the tarmac and disappeared into the stony waste. Good heavens, I thought, this is like looking for a needle in a haystack.

Just then, a car appeared from the other direction, stopped, and out came a couple with two teenage children. They were Hungarians working on an engineering project – a socialist country helping another socialist country. We explained our predicament as best we could in a mixture of French and German, and when they understood what had happened, the Hungarians were eager to help. We formed two search parties of three on each side of the road and began scanning every square foot, starting well before the beginning of the trail of black oil and proceeding slowly, bending towards the ground. We didn't leave a stone unmoved, kneeling down every now and then to inspect the terrain more closely. Fifteen minutes had passed and I was about to give up hope when suddenly the Hungarian woman let out a loud yell. She held up something: it was a big bolt. It seemed too long to be right, but we ran back to the Land Rover and it fitted! We all clapped our hands, dancing around the heroine who had found the missing piece. Her husband, who was a tall, strong man, now went down on his back under the Land Rover and set about screwing the oil drain plug into position and tightening it with all his might.

There remained the problem of filling up with new oil. We only had two litres of spare engine oil with us, but the Hungarian went to his car and with a smile, handed me a tin containing another two litres. The engine really needed six, but with four litres we would be able to make it to Timimoun if we drove carefully so as not to overheat the engine. We thanked him profusely, asking what we could do for him.

'Nothing,' he said. 'It's been a pleasure meeting you. Drive safely.' And off they went.

There was a large petrol station at the entrance of Timimoun and as we explained our problem, we were ushered into the office of the boss, a pleasant man in his late twenties who spoke French fluently. He advised us to go to the hotel at the edge of the oasis and invited us to tea the following day.

The next morning, we visited the little town. It was still early and the great heat that comes in the afternoon had not yet descended upon us. Children were playing about, people were hammering at things, discussing the prices of the wares on display or carrying heavy loads on their backs, while ramshackle cars were trying to negotiate the narrow streets without squashing anyone.

As we entered the oasis, we stepped back in time; there were no cars, only donkeys and mules. No space was wasted; in between the date palms, people cultivated vegetables and even wheat. Sowing was done by hand and so was weeding and collecting firewood.

The irrigation system, which was the lifeline of the oasis, came straight out of Moorish, or maybe Roman times; the water from the *seguia* entered through a comb-like system that split it into channels distributing it to different sectors. When one sector of the palm grove had had the allocated quantity, the passage was simply blocked, impeding the water from flowing into that sector.

A man came along leading his mule, and Claire, who enjoys riding any animal she can get up on, motioned to him that she would like to ride the mule. The man was willing, helped her onto the animal's back and did not even notice that I took a photograph.

'He looked pleased,' I said after Claire had got down and we walked on.

'I should think so,' she replied. 'He was pinching my bottom!'

'He'll have a day to remember then,' I commented dryly.

In the afternoon, we went to have tea with the boss of the petrol station. We had brought some cakes and as we sat down on cushions in the sparsely furnished living-dining room, I enquired how business was going. The man seemed surprised.

'I don't quite know what you mean,' he answered. 'I'm just doing my job.'

'But isn't this your business? *Your* petrol station? Who's the owner, then?'

'The state petrol company, naturally. I'm the director of this station.'

'How did you become director, then?'

'I studied at the university,' he explained, 'and afterwards the government gave me this job.'

I was slightly taken aback. Of course, Algeria was a socialist country, but one tends to forget. Just at that moment, his wife brought in the tea and then retreated into a corner of the room where she crouched down on the floor with their little son.

'Won't she join us?' asked Claire.

'She is not going to sit with us.' Our host's voice was polite but firm. 'Anyway, she doesn't speak any French. My sister will come later. She teaches French, and you will enjoy talking to her.'

'Where did you study?' I asked, trying to change the subject.

'In Algiers.'

'And did you like it?'

He paused for a while, as if speaking about it were painful. At last he said, 'Yes, very much.' He turned around, looking furtively at his wife before carrying on, somewhat lowering his voice. 'When I was at the university, I met someone. She was a modern girl, very intelligent and open-minded … She was the wife I would have liked. I was certain I was going to marry her and …' He hesitated, '… and our love was consummated.' He stopped a moment while his eyes seemed to look inward. Then he carried on. 'When I finished my studies, I told my parents that I wanted to marry her. They wouldn't hear of it! My father made it clear that he had already arranged marriage for me with the daughter of a family he was well acquainted with. I pleaded with him but there was no changing his mind. He gave me a lecture on family honour and obedience. There wasn't a thing I could do about it.'

'Did you know the girl they wanted you to marry?'

'No. I met her and her family only a week before the wedding. The families discussed the dowry and all the practical matters such as marriage arrangements and who should pay for what. The girl was sitting on the other side of the room with her own family. Her hair was covered and the bottom of her face veiled. She was looking down at the floor all the time.'

'And you had to marry her shortly after!'

'Yes. There was a big wedding celebration a week later.'

'At least they left you in peace afterwards,' said Claire.

The man hesitated, not sure whether to speak or not. Then he made up his mind. 'It is not like that. By the end of the evening, the bridegroom has to take the newly-wed bride to a room upstairs, specially prepared for the occasion. He has to consummate the marriage and then appear to show the blood-stained sheet, which proves that the bride was a virgin.'

'Good heavens!' exclaimed Claire. 'Does he really have to do that?'

'Yes. It's not easy. The young man is nervous and the young woman frightened, but it's got to be done. Both families want proof of virginity. The blood on the sheet is the proof that the bride was worth the price the groom's family paid. If on the other hand it turns out that she's not a virgin, the groom's family will annul the marriage, and the bride's family will be dishonoured and have to leave in shame.'

'I don't dare think what they do to the poor girl in that case,' whispered Claire.

'But what with all the din going on downstairs, can't they at least put off the showing of the sheet till the next day?' I ventured. 'Leave the two young people a little time to get to know each other?'

Our host shrugged his shoulders. 'One has to do it. If the groom does not appear with the sheet within a quarter of an hour, men of both families will start banging on the door, shouting, "Get on with it. We're all waiting. Are you a man or what?"'

I felt shocked. 'So that's how marriage begins?'

'Yes, that's how...'

'What happened to the girl you loved when you were at the university?' Claire wanted to know.

Our host paused for a long while before answering; then he murmured, 'When she heard about my marriage, she took her life.' He looked away but I could see the sadness in his eyes. Finally he said, 'But I have my little son. He is my pride, the light of my days; he is all I have in life now.'

At that moment the sister came in. She had just finished her classes in a primary school in Timimoun and as she entered, the atmosphere, which had become ever more sombre as the man told his story, suddenly gave way before her sunny nature. She was extremely pleased to meet us, especially Claire who explained that a few years ago she had been teaching English at home to some private pupils. The young woman gave her a large smile, feeling that she was in the presence of a soul sister, and began to show Claire her French textbooks. They were odd, to say the least. They must have dated back to long before independence and testified to the French way of seeing the world in those days: the colonies were the periphery, while France was the centre. All the rules came from the metropolis and what was good for France was considered good enough for the rest. We read some of the stories that had been spoon-fed to generations of Algerian children (and probably black African children, Tahitian children and many others). The first story was about *Nos ancêtres les Gaulois* (Our ancestors the Gauls). Another story told the children about winter: the fields were hidden under a thick layer of snow; the ponds were frozen; ducks were flying high overhead and little children were skating over the ice with wooden clogs on their feet, imagine! This was the end of December – wintertime in Timimoun – but there were no snow-covered fields, no ponds, no ice, no ducks flying overhead and no rows of bare poplars, only sand and palm trees. I wondered how children over here could relate to what they had to read. What's more, children no longer had clogs on their feet in rural France and parents no longer allowed their children such simple amusements as having fun on frozen ponds without any supervision. But twenty years after independence, Algerian children here at the edge of the Sahara were still supposed to learn all about their ancestors the Gauls, and were still getting a 'good' idea of what a 'typical' winter in the French countryside was like!

'What a nice young woman,' Claire remarked after the sister had left.

The man sighed. 'Yes, but there's a problem. We'll have to find her a suitable husband and that won't be easy.'

I stared at him. 'I don't understand.'

'Well, my father is no longer so young and I have to act for him as head of the family. I'm the eldest son, you see.'

'But why can't your sister find a man on her own?' interrupted Claire.

Our host was firm. 'That's not possible,' he said. 'We'll have to find her a man befitting her education. And his reputation has to be impeccable; the honour of the family demands it.'

That evening, we climbed onto the flat roof of the hotel. The oasis stretched below us, a jumble of date palms and scattered patches of vegetable plots from which came the sound of voices dimmed by the distance and the palm fronds. It was the moment just before sunset; several small fires glowed like jewels in between the palm trees; the sunlight had begun to lose its blinding brightness; colours turned to pastel and then to a deeper shade of orange, and the birdsong in the trees gradually quietened down. The oasis felt like a sheltered, intimate world surrounded by a vast expanse of sand dunes that turned red in the rays of the setting sun. As the light faded from the sky, bright stars lit up one after the other, peace descended into our hearts and everything was perfect.

Above: Claire and young girls at a local 'launderette.' The girls are standing with their feet in the water

Below: Ghardaïa at nightfall

Above: El-Goléa: the church of Père de Foucauld

Middle: On the road to Timimoun: losing all our engine oil

Above: Oasis of Timimoun: the irrigation system

Below: Oasis of Timimoun: Claire on a mule

Below: The Sahara around Timimoun

CHAPTER 4
The Sahara: The Purity of Complete Emptiness

Into the Tanezrouft

Some people imagine the Sahara to be a vast expanse of sand. In fact, sand is only part of it, and a small part at that. The Sahara is like any other geographical area on earth. Several mountain ranges run through it – some with peaks around 10,000-feet high – and there are also vast plains. But here and there you come across sand dunes. There is something impermanent about these. When the wind blows, rivers of sand run up their slopes and plumes of fine sand particles stream off their razor-edged crests, making the dunes come alive and moving them slowly towards the lee side. Sometimes, when it blows hard, the Sahara becomes a dustbowl and whole dunes are on the march. But when there is no wind the dunes can take you back to childhood – on a grand scale.

When we came upon our first giant dunes, all the inhibitions that had grown around us during adult life fell away. Claire and I ran up the slopes, the loose sand slipping away from under our feet as we tried to climb up to a steep crest. Then we let ourselves roll down, seeming to take half the dune with us in a whirlwind of sand. It was magic – a gigantic playground for grown-ups with more warm, soft sand than any child could ever dream of.

We ran up again and when I got to the top, my heart was pounding so hard and my legs felt so shaky that I had to sit down. An incredible view stretched below our feet: we seemed to be engulfed in an immense expanse of sand, a vast landscape of crests upon crests of dunes that appeared to go on forever. My eyes were dazed by their sheer splendour and my heart was full of wonder at the unknown vastness that surrounded us. We sat there very still, marvelling at the majestic beauty of the dunes around us, our eyes following the swirling lines of their crests curving against the blueness of the sky, the purity of their contours accentuated by the golden colour of the sand. I just wanted to become one with this land, touch its golden beauty, let the fine grains slip away through my fingers … I buried my feet in the warm sand and became oblivious of time.

There was not the slightest breeze – we had stepped into a world of silence. I had never known absolute silence before and dared not speak for fear of breaking its purity. We just sat there, immobile, filled with deep awe. This was perfect beauty and the peace of eternity.

Slowly the colour of the sand changed from orange-yellow to red as the sun began to set. I could have sat there forever …

I wanted to return to the dunes the next morning, but I heard Peter say, 'No, we have to go,' and I was suddenly hit by what was to come: we were going to venture into the Sahara! Of course, I had known that Peter wanted to cross the desert, but somehow I had managed to push the thought away to the back of my mind. I had been unwilling to think about the future and had just lived each day as it came. Now Peter's words made me come down to earth and as I realised what was awaiting us, it filled me with fear …

Months before at the Algerian embassy in Brussels, they had given us two-week transit visas and made it clear that this was all we could expect. The Algerian authorities did not seem to understand the meaning – or maybe didn't even know the existence – of the word 'flexibility'. There was no joking at their embassy and no joking with the authorities when we landed in Algiers either. All official contacts so far had left the impression that our presence was tolerated rather than desired. Algeria was a 'socialist' country and rules and regulations were to be taken seriously. We had entered the country on 15 December, so we would have to be out of it on 29 December at the latest. And today was 26 December! With luck, if we didn't break down or get lost, we would be able to reach Mali before our visas ran out.

Looking at a map, you might well be under the impression that there are roads across the Sahara. It's true that asphalted roads continue deep into the Algerian south, but when we reached Reggane, the tarmac finished. It wasn't the border yet, but this was where the easy bit came to an end and where the real endurance test began.

If it hadn't been on the direct route south, I doubt whether anyone would ever have bothered to visit Reggane. It certainly wasn't worth the detour. It consisted of an open square surrounded by some indifferent, low buildings, a few dusty streets, a couple of shops, a post office and a police station. What made it special, though, was that you could buy petrol here; and that the next petrol station was in Gao, Mali, more than 800 miles further south on the other side of the Sahara.

The Land Rover's petrol tanks and jerry cans could hold 320 litres. That seemed plenty for the crossing, and yet I hesitated. I had brought twelve collapsible 20-litre containers, and finally decided to fill four of these with diesel fuel as well. The fuel would attack the plastic and would ruin the containers forever but I thought, better safe than sorry. The total amounted to no less than 400 litres, but petrol was heavily subsidised in Algeria (as in most oil-producing countries), and since I had exchanged my dinars at the black-market rate, I would have to pay no more than 2.5 pence per litre (or about 10p per gallon)!

'Fill it all up,' I told the petrol station attendant, making a royal gesture as I went to the water tap with the remaining collapsible containers. It took the pump attendant a long time to fill all the tanks, jerry cans and containers. At one point he stopped and looked at me in disbelief, but I motioned him to carry on. When he had finally finished I fished a wad of dirty dinars out of my pocket and paid him the equivalent of £10.00 (1981 value)!

As I heaved the heavy jerry cans and plastic containers onto the roof rack and began to secure the lot, I thought I'd better write a letter to my parents. It was not very inspired:

Dear Mum and Dad,

Everything is going well. We have had a very interesting journey so far and are now in the last oasis in the south of Algeria and ready to cross the Sahara. This will take several days if all goes well and I hope we'll make it. I cannot write much as the post office is about to close and we must set off before darkness falls. We'll write when we get to the other side to keep you informed.

Much love from
Peter and Claire

When I returned from the post office I found Claire in rebellious mood. My absence had made her think and given her the courage to speak up.

'Why don't we stay in Algeria?' she began, looking at me with hope in her eyes. 'It has everything I ever wanted to see: oases, colourful life, the secret world of women behind closed gates.'

When she realised that I wasn't going to give in, she blurted out, 'I … well … I don't want to go into the Sahara. If we do we'll die, I can feel it. You know that I've often dreamed that I lay dying in the desert while the vultures were watching.'

'But I've told you before that there are no vultures in the Sahara.'

'I don't care,' Claire retorted vehemently. 'I want to stay in Algeria. If you decide to carry on, you know I will go with you, but I tell you that the journey will be finished for me. I will no longer be interested.'

These were strong words and I felt deeply for Claire, but there was nothing I could do about it since we had to be out of the country within three days. I also argued that, if we were about to leave civilization behind – however little the term 'civilization' befitted Reggane – we were certainly not the first ones to do so. Many people had crossed the Sahara before us and many would do it after us. I even knew someone who had done it: Luc, a young engineer who, after finishing his studies, had preferred enlisting in a civil service project for two years rather than doing the usual one-year military service. He had been sent to a secondary school in Zaire to teach maths, and when his two-year contract came to an end, he thought, Why not drive back to Belgium instead of boarding a plane like everyone else? That'll be much more fun. As luck would have it, Roger, one of his colleagues, was finishing at exactly the same time and Luc managed to convince him to come, too, telling him that this was a unique opportunity to visit some interesting, remote places. And so they bought a small second-hand, open, army jeep, boarded the steamer that took them up the Congo River, drove northwards and finally entered the Sahara.

Luc told me about his crossing:

'I had no idea what it was going to be like. I had imagined that there were roads – at least, the map indicated roads – but there was nothing. We were completely alone in a vast landscape. It was a shock but there was no way back, and Roger and I carried on hoping for the best.

'It was the most surreal trip I have ever made. We had some truly weird experiences. One day we were driving as fast as we could over a flat expanse, it was hot and I was steering, nearly asleep, when suddenly from the corner of my eye I noticed that something was moving alongside our car and overtaking us: it was a wheel! I thought I was hallucinating!

'For a few seconds, I just couldn't figure out what that wheel was doing there, crossing the Sahara all on its own, and how it could have overtaken us, but then I became aware of a loud scraping noise, the car slowed down and we came to a standstill. It was our own rear wheel that had come off! Eventually the wheel decided to call it a day and fell on its side. We got out to recover it and then we retraced our way on foot, following the tracks of our car and searching everywhere until we had retrieved a few wheel nuts and, adding the spares we had with us, we were able to fix the wheel again.

'But that wasn't the worst. On the third day, the engine spluttered and then it went dead in the middle of nowhere. I checked all the connections but couldn't find anything wrong, yet there didn't seem to be a spark of life left in the stupid car. It was mid-afternoon, the sun hung like a heavy ball of fire in a leaden sky and the heat had become unbearable – you cannot begin to think what it's like when you haven't been in that furnace. What with the heat, the thirst and the panic that took hold of us, nerves were beginning to get frayed. Roger, who had been looking on with growing displeasure, suddenly exploded. "It's all your fault! Driving home was your bright idea! I should never have listened to you! Look what you've got me into now, you stupid idiot! If this is what you call interesting tourism, you can have it! I've had enough of your tourism and of you, too!" And as he picked up his bag, he shouted, "Goodbye! I never want to see you again!" Little by little, as he walked away in a northerly direction, his figure became smaller until he disappeared beyond a slight elevation.

'I felt stunned – abandoned by fate. Suddenly I became mad and started screaming, "What have I done to deserve this? What have I done to deserve this?" all the while kicking the jeep and banging my fists on the bonnet. Gradually I quietened down, went inside and sat behind the wheel while waves of despair flowed through my body. Then, without thinking, almost like an automaton, I turned the key in the ignition and the engine started! Banging the car must have re-established an electric contact somewhere. It was like a miracle; I could have wept with joy and as I set off, the purring of the engine was music to my ears. By the time I caught up with Roger a mile or two further on, his quick stride had slowed down to a tedious plodding.

"Want a lift to Europe?" I shouted as I stopped by his side.

'He stared at me in disbelief, his face dripping with sweat, grabbed a water bottle from the back of the jeep and poured the contents into his mouth. Then he got in and simply said, "Thanks, mate. I thought I'd had it this time".'

And now, we in turn were going to cross the Sahara and maybe risk our lives. I suddenly had an attack of fear. Ahead lay hundreds upon hundreds of miles of a flat, uninhabited expanse, the Tanezrouft, which was said to be a desert within the desert. Why was I going there? What if the Land Rover broke down? Then I thought again of our visas, which didn't allow us to stay any longer. I suppose most people are fatalistic and come up with any kind of argument to justify their actions. 'I can't do anything about it anyway,' they argue or, 'It's better not to go against fate; you'll see, everything will turn out all right.' I was no different. It's too late to turn back now, I reasoned, and slowly I proceeded to Emigration with Claire trailing unwillingly behind. The authorities stamped our passports and told us that we had to form a convoy with four Frenchmen. They were driving ordinary Peugeots, which they hoped to sell on the other side, and they hadn't been allowed to leave unless accompanied by a four-wheel-drive vehicle. The Frenchmen had already been waiting for some hours, getting more impatient as time went by. They were eager to set off and wanted to rush ahead to calm their nerves; if we couldn't keep up with them we were not to worry, they said. They would wait for us twenty miles further on. And they promised to prepare a supper we would remember – a very special treat.

As we left the last houses behind and the tarmac ended, I felt apprehensive. The Peugeots were much lighter than our Land Rover and however much I tried to push the engine, I had to let them go; soon they disappeared in a cloud of dust. We were alone now, but the tyre marks made by other vehicles in the bumpy, irregular surface guided us. Then, after some ten miles, I noticed that the marks began to fan out as if the cars had wanted to get away from the centre of the dirt road. I soon found out why. Ploughing straight on, I hit a patch of soft sand. I revved up the engine trying to get through, but all I managed was to bury the Land Rover in the sand up to the axles. Then the engine stalled, emitting a low groan as if conceding defeat, and we were firmly stuck. This was my first test of desert travelling and I had failed it ignominiously! How were we ever going to cross 800 miles of desert if we were already stuck after a mere 10?

There are people who pretend that they crossed the Sahara just like that; that they never had a moment of doubt. I felt nothing but doubt. Why am I doing this? I thought. Risk Claire's life and mine! And even if we make it to the other side of the Sahara, how am I ever going to get through Africa in an old Land Rover without knowing even the basics of car mechanics? This is sheer madness! I was so scared that I just wanted to turn back to Reggane and to safety. But first I had to get out of this patch of soft sand.

I took down the spade and the aluminium sand ladders, and began to dig. After a while, I had removed enough sand to shove the ladders in front of the wheels, climbed behind the steering wheel, switched to low-gear, four-wheel-drive mode and let in the clutch very carefully. And yes! The Land Rover began to move, slowly at first and then more rapidly.

'Keep it going until you hit firm soil,' I encouraged myself. I got out of the sandy patch some twenty yards further on, stopped and waited for Claire who came running along, dragging the sand ladders behind her. It was our first victory in the long battle against defeatism and cowardice, and it gave me such a boost that I carried on southwards, forgetting all about turning back to Reggane.

As we moved along as fast as we could, scanning the horizon because the French were waiting for us somewhere out there, the sun began to sink down really fast. Then we came to a large dune and saw small human figures waving at us from the top: the French! We stopped, climbed the sand dune and joined them just in time to see our glorious sun set in a sea of flames. Everything turned pinkish-yellow while we looked out over the vastness of the desert. There was nothing but undisturbed space as far as the eye could see and the silence was absolute. As we slid down the still warm, but now dark sand, a few stars began to twinkle and we started preparations for our first camp.

The French immediately shot into action. They began to prepare supper as they had promised us, and for an hour or so they fiddled with small jars, food packets and wrapped-up objects. Three of the men were quite young, maybe in their twenties, but the fourth, a tall, strong fellow, looked about ten years older.

While the French were busy, Claire just sat there, gazing at a sky purer than anything she had ever seen.

'What's that star just above the moon?' she asked. 'It's so bright.'

'That's not a star; it's Venus.'

'Well, anyway … it's pure magic.' She looked at me with a fairy-tale face.

I took her hand in mine. 'Glad you came after all?'

'Yes.' She pressed my hand.

We both sat there in awe, our minds and hearts far away, when suddenly the French called out, 'Supper's ready!' They had placed a few fuel containers together to form a table and spread a cloth over them, and as we sat in the sand around our improvised table, they proceeded to bring out plastic plates on which they had artistically arranged a variety of food delicacies.

Alain, the eldest one, now made a little speech. 'Before leaving we decided to celebrate our first night out in the Sahara in style,' he said, almost beaming, 'so we brought all this especially from France. I'm sure you will enjoy it.'

Each of the plates on the table contained a different delicacy. On the first they had placed six square, buttered pieces of toast coated with *paté de foie gras* – one for each of us – and on the second, six small crackers with caviar; next came a dish with olives stuffed with anchovies; and finally there was a plate on which a flat round of camembert cheese sat proudly. The meal was rounded off with two long French baguettes and a bottle of wine.

It was quite delicious, but I saw Claire glance at me with a quizzical expression as if to ask, 'Do they really believe this is going to fill them up?'

When the French delicacies were finished, Claire brought out bread and sardines, just in case. Our companions fell upon this like hungry wolves and when everything was gone, they looked at us expectantly. Fortunately we had bought an enormous bunch of fresh dates in Ghardaïa. After devouring a large number of these, they finally seemed sated and we all turned in for our first night under the starry sky.

Temperature contrasts are enormous in the Sahara. From early morning till late afternoon the rocks and naked earth absorb more heat than they radiate out. The temperature goes up rapidly and by 2.00 p.m. it has risen to almost 40°C (in wintertime). By 5.00 p.m., the sun has lost most of its strength and just after sunset the temperature becomes very pleasant. Throughout the night the rocks and earth give off their heat and as there is no cloud cover and little humidity in the atmosphere, most of the heat is radiated back into space and the temperature starts falling rapidly. Just before sunrise it drops to near zero.

Bernard had given us a thick blanket made from coarse camel hair, which he had brought back from Morocco. We had laughed at him, saying, 'You're not serious. You don't really believe we'll need this in Africa, do you?' Now we were glad to have heeded his advice. We slept inside our Land Rover with the back flap open and when it became too cold at night we pulled the blanket over us and were comfortably warm underneath.

Our French companions were not as lucky. Their Peugeots were saloons and they were unable to sleep inside, as the back seats were stacked with containers holding the fuel to get them across the Sahara. So they had to sleep outside, but they didn't mind; they had in fact been looking forward to it. During supper they were talking excitedly about the great adventure awaiting them, about *dormir à la belle étoile* (sleeping under the starry sky). When bedtime came they stretched themselves out on top of their sleeping bags next to their cars and fell asleep happily. Then, some time after midnight, they crawled inside their sleeping bags and zipped them up. And by 4.00 a.m., it was getting so cold that they began to shiver and were forced to seek refuge in the front seats of their cars, covering themselves in any piece of clothing they possessed, waiting in misery for the sun to rise.

It took us time to get organised that first morning and it was nearly 8.00 a.m. before everybody was ready to set off southwards. I tried to speed up the Land Rover, going high in third gear and then switching to fourth, but I felt the engine struggle and then slow down and I was obliged to switch back to third gear; it was unable to do more than 35 miles per hour, however hard I pushed it. The heavy roof rack, spare wheels and other equipment, the 400 litres of diesel fuel and 160 litres of water, the food and all the rest had brought the total weight to almost 3 tons! It was just too much for the old engine.

Our slowness annoyed the French. They decided to speed ahead and wait for us every two hours, and soon the two Peugeots began to move away from us. After a quarter of an hour, we saw no more than the dust thrown up by their wheels far ahead, and after half an hour, even that had gone and they had totally disappeared from view. It didn't really matter since they were going to wait for us, but it accentuated our feeling of being left behind in an inhospitable world.

We were completely alone now on a vast, flat expanse of empty space stretching endlessly in every direction. There were no landmarks anywhere, not a single mountain, not even a hillock, nothing against which to measure progress. When you fixed your gaze on the horizon, movement seemed an illusion, but the bumpy movement of our wheels certainly wasn't.

The 'road' through the Tanezrouft from Reggane to the border of Mali is relatively easy as African roads go. Millions of years ago, the Tanezrouft was an inland sea and when it dried out it left a hard, monotonous, flat surface with few sandy patches – ideal for crossing. Before the advent of motorised traffic, the surface must have been relatively smooth; however, as elsewhere in Africa, generations of lorries had transformed this flat surface into a driver's nightmare.

The road, if you could call it such, consisted of dozens of tracks made by southbound traffic. Sometimes they ran close together and the whole set of tracks was no more than a hundred yards wide; sometimes they spread out over hundreds of yards. The centre was the worst part to drive on. Too many heavy vehicles had transformed that part into a corrugated, undulating surface. At times it was so bumpy that the whole Land Rover began to vibrate and everything rattled.

I remembered losing the plug of the sump on the road to Timimoun. I didn't want to repeat that experience and therefore decided to drive outside the tracks. There was a pair of deep wheel marks on our right, probably made by a heavy lorry a few days before; as long as I kept those in view I felt sure that we would be safe.

We were now well away from the tracks made by heavy vehicles. Driving on the undisturbed surface became a pleasure and I began to relax. In fact, I could have blocked the steering wheel and even have closed my eyes: not only was the surface almost as flat as that of a motorway, but this was a motorway ten, twenty miles wide and there wasn't the slightest danger of colliding with another vehicle – you were lucky if you met one a day.

We had been driving for about two hours using the wheel marks as a guide and expected to see the French waiting for us any moment now, but there wasn't a single car anywhere on the horizon. And there was something else that didn't seem normal. Instead of heading south, the marks we were following were going in a south-south-easterly direction. This was strange! I swerved to the wheel marks made by the lorry and crossed them to look for the other tracks, but there were none, just flat desert. The southbound road had vanished! How could this have happened? Then I realised that the marks I had used as a guide must have been made by a lorry that had split off from the main road, and we had been following them for God knows how many miles.

What were we to do? Turn back on our tracks, follow them to where they connected with the main road and then turn south, hoping to join up with the French? That would take three to four hours and, impatient as they were, the French might not wait that long. Also, a light wind had begun to blow, gradually filling in our tracks. We might not even be able to get back to where we came from!

As I turned off the engine, the soft sound of sand hitting the Land Rover was all that was audible. The awareness that we were well and truly lost suddenly hit me and I felt panic rise. Every year people got lost and perished in the Sahara. Had Claire's premonition been right? Was it our turn?

'Why not drive west and look for the other tracks?' I heard Claire suggest.

'And get lost?' I objected. But I had to do something. Maybe if I took out the binoculars and climbed up on the roof rack I would be able to see the French.

I began to scan the horizon but there was only empty space out there as far as the eye could see. The flat, barren terrain stretched for miles in all directions, with only the merest hint of low hills towards the south-east. We were utterly and devastatingly alone. It was a desolate feeling; we seemed to be shipwrecked in a sea of shimmering shale.

'Can you see anything?' came Claire's voice from below. Her face was full of apprehension.

I was just about to reply, 'No,' when all of a sudden, far away in a westerly direction, I noticed something unusual: a bright point, sparkling like a diamond. I was puzzled. What could possibly sparkle so brightly in the desert? There was nothing I could think of unless … of course, that must be it!

'I can see the French!' I shouted. 'There's a bright sparkling point in the far distance. It must be the sun reflecting in the windscreen of one of their cars!'

'That's impossible,' objected Claire. 'Are you sure?'

I wasn't. There could be no more than a chance in a million that one of the Peugeots was parked in such a position that the sunlight just reflected off the windscreen towards us, but still … I turned the Land Rover in the direction of the bright point and pushed the engine for all it was worth. The bright light, which gleamed like a beacon, was our only lifeline and I hoped that the French, if it was them, wouldn't move the car.

After some time, we vaguely began to discern the shape of the two Peugeots and as Claire threw her arms around my neck with relief, I nearly lost control of the steering wheel. When at last we pulled up next to them, the French were at a loss as to how we could possibly have come upon them from the east. They wisely agreed to reduce their speed from then on, and to stay together as one convoy.

Noon sun blinding the vision. The air is quivering. Suddenly to the left, far away along the horizon, I perceive a gleaming patch, shining like liquid metal: water! Long waves of silvery water wherein blue-grey undulating shapes seem to rise!

'Look, look!' I exclaim. 'An oasis. There are even palm trees. How wonderful!'

Peter just shakes his head. 'The map doesn't indicate any water,' he tells me. 'It must be a mirage.' And as he carries on driving, the shimmer begins to fade into the lonely distance.

I suddenly understand the dreadful rage of men who have lost their way, when they see this vision of heaven vanish and then lie down in despair on the scorching sand.

I shut my eyes and when I look again the dry line between land and sky is all that remains. But the enchanting, luminous illusion lingers in my mind's eye.

By early afternoon, the heat became difficult to bear; the fierce sun bleached all colours from the land, making the world blank and empty, and burning the blue out of the sky. Driving was torture: the engines seemed to be boiling and we decided that it was time to stop and give them, and ourselves, a rest. We were all lying in the shade of our cars when we heard one of the Frenchmen complain that he felt thirsty. The French had foolishly imagined that they were going to cross the Sahara in two days at most. They had brought very little food and had just finished their last bottle of water. Alain, the eldest of the group, now came over to ask us if we could spare any water.

We had, of course, a large quantity of water, but drinking it straight from the plastic containers was not safe. Everything you drank had to be sterilised, a vital precaution if you were to avoid the many water-borne diseases which abound in Africa. We did have a filter system: you filled up the top half in the evening, the water dripped slowly through a ceramic filter into the bottom half during the night and you had two gallons of pure water by the morning. Unfortunately we had forgotten to fill up the filter the previous evening. What were we to do? Europeans living in Africa sterilised their water through boiling it for at least ten minutes, but this was totally impractical on the road. The French were not willing to boil water and wait for it to cool down, and with the temperature so high, no one was keen to drink hot tea in the afternoon either.

Fortunately, we had also brought a small hand-held filter; pumping water through it removed any impurities and bacteria it contained. Bernard, who had lent us this utensil, had told us that it would be the ideal solution. 'It will allow you to filter rapidly any water you find anywhere without having to bother about its quality,' he had said, 'and to drink your fill in no time.' The filter had the look of a compact bicycle pump and was worked exactly the same way. You dipped a tube coming out of the top end into the water and as you pushed with all your might on the pump, drop after drop of water was pressed through the filter and squirted out through a tube on the other side. This was independence and safety combined. What more could one ask for?

When Alain saw me taking the filter out of its holder, he nearly wrenched it from my hands. 'I'll do this!' he exclaimed. 'I'll prepare the water.' And he started pumping straightaway. After a minute he began to perspire heavily; after two minutes sweat started to drip from his brow every time he pressed the pump; after five minutes of hard labour the first glass was finally filled with precious filtered water, but before anyone had time to pick it up, Alain grabbed it and downed it himself. Thenceforth, he just stuck the loose tube at the end of the filter into his mouth and pumped the droplets straight into himself, leaving out the intermediate stage of the glass. In fact, he just about replaced the liquid he lost through perspiration!

'Why don't you let me drive?' I offered after we set off again. 'You're dead tired.' Peter had been steering the whole day and he was showing signs of extreme fatigue.

'This is not an ordinary road,' he mumbled evasively.

'What difference does that make?'

'If you bang into a hole and the Land Rover breaks down I can't repair it …' And he just continued to concentrate on the surface in front of the wheels.

His reaction annoyed me profoundly. 'So you prefer me to sit here and be totally useless!'

There was an expression of exasperation on his face, but he carried on stubbornly. Then, suddenly, it happened: the front wheels clanked ominously as they hit a deep rut, Peter's hands tightened around the steering wheel and his face was distorted by a strained grimace.

I flared up. 'That's really enough! If you don't trust me to drive, you should have taken a man with you – not me!'

Peter looked at me dumbfounded, stopped, opened the door, stammering, 'All right,' and got out.

I walked around the Land Rover ready to take over when, in the last split second, he changed his mind and hopped back behind the wheel. This was just too much. Before I had time to think I yelled, 'You … you bastard!' The words had hardly left my mouth when I bit my lip. I would never have dreamt that one day I would call Peter such names.

As I saw him stare at me in a state of shock, I whispered, 'I'm sorry,' my face red with shame. 'I didn't mean what I said, but I'm so worried about you.'

'No, you're right,' replied Peter as he got out. 'I *am* a bastard, not letting you drive. I should trust you … always.' And I felt his arms tighten around me as I buried my head in his shoulder.

I climbed behind the wheel, slightly shaky, and set off driving very carefully to show that I deserved his trust. Peter soon relaxed and from then on let me take turns; in fact, he seemed rather relieved that I was doing my share of the hard work.

We were about to stop for the day when the three cars ran into a large sandy patch and we all got stuck. After half an hour, I managed to get the Land Rover out with the help of the metal sand-ladders, but the French were still struggling without much success. As the sun sank below the horizon and the flat plain began to turn into an inky-black expanse, we heard the sound of engines: two pairs of headlights were zigzagging through the desert, coming towards us at high speed. Within minutes, two open lorries appeared, stopped outside the sandy patch and a dozen men jumped out, all wearing turbans and dressed in loose desert gowns. I immediately told Claire to hide inside the Land Rover. I didn't want them to find out that there was a woman with us!

The men turned to the two Peugeots and ordered, 'Unload your cars!'

The French did as they were told and then one of the Berbers got behind the steering wheel while the others pushed. The car began to move slowly, skidding through the sand until some hundred yards further it reached firm soil. They freed the second Peugeot in exactly the same manner and then returned to their open lorries, clambering back in and setting off into the dark night at right angles from the tracks.

We were left speechless. What we had feared to be an attack had turned out to be a rescue operation! But what really amazed me was how these men knew their way in a desert that appeared totally featureless to us. They didn't stick to the tracks made by other vehicles, as we were obliged to do; what's more, those expert Berber drivers skirted around any patch of soft sand, darting back and forth like dragonflies. They seemed to know the desert just as thoroughly as we knew the part of the country in which we lived. Still, I wondered, how did they dare drive through the pitch-dark of the night? Did they navigate by the stars?

The French had finished their last perishables from the Algerian oases that day, and since they had prepared supper the previous night – a very special supper – they were looking at Claire to see if she was going to return the favour.

When I saw the four Frenchmen looking at me eagerly, I knew there was nothing else for me to do but cook. This was the moment to inaugurate one of the special Little Bee stoves we had bought in Brussels. I fetched the little thing and felt lost; it just looked to me like a shiny, round container on a narrow base, and I had no idea how to operate it. Of course, they had explained everything in Brussels but that seemed eons ago. All I remembered was that it had to be filled with unrefined oil.

I called for help and Peter immediately dropped what he was doing and came to the rescue. He filled the container with oil but when I wanted to light it he told me I couldn't do that straightaway. It seemed that the unrefined oil had to be pre-heated by pouring methyl alcohol into a rim around the Little Bee and first lighting this. When the oil had been heated sufficiently for vapours to come out through the holes in the hob, I would finally be able to light it and put my pot with water and whatever I was going to cook on top of it.

That wasn't all. There was a small pump at the side, which had to be activated frequently to keep up the oil pressure and prevent the flames from going out. The whole setup looked like a small tower and was highly unstable in the uneven sand; it emitted a faintly sinister hissing sound like a snake and as I was soon to find out, it blackened all my pots and pans. Anyway, I did manage to produce a large pot of spaghetti with corned beef and tomato sauce. The French didn't seem very keen at first, but ended up devouring everything and then claiming they were still hungry.

Later that night, we ate a supplement of sardines, biscuits and dates by the flickering flames of two petrol lamps under the vastness of the star-spangled sky. Some crumbs fell onto the sand, small bits of food seemingly lost forever. After a while, though, I saw something moving close to my feet in the faint light of the lamps: a small mouse, the colour of the sand, was nibbling the crumbs! There was no vegetation around for dozens of miles, no water, nothing, and yet, here was this mouse – a desert gerbil – cleaning up fallen crumbs in the middle of the Sahara! When I told the French they said they had a gerbil, too; so there was a pair around and maybe more. It seemed a miracle that they managed to stay alive at all in this Godforsaken spot.

The desert is indeed a forbidding place. It is hard to believe that life can possibly survive its extremes of temperature and lack of humidity, but it does. The tenacity of life, the determination to survive in the desert, is a source of sheer wonder. You find lots of tracks if you care to look for them, especially in the sand dunes. The black beetle, rushing about on its crooked legs, leaves tiny imprints. You can see the footprints of the lizard left and right of a continuous line where its tail trailed. However inhospitable the desert appears to humans, plenty of little creatures feel perfectly at home in it.

The camel (or more correctly, the dromedary) is the only large animal truly adapted to the dryness of the Sahara. We humans need to drink regularly. Not so the camel. It's a tough and resistant animal, built for the desert like no other beast of burden. It goes where its master leads it and needs no roads, nor man-made shelter.

The following day we saw our first caravan appear on the horizon. It is surprising how everything stands out in the vast landscape of the Sahara – a vehicle, a man, or a camel: they can all be seen at huge distances. The French hurried over to the caravan, led by a man and his two young sons, and started taking photographs. Claire too got very excited. She had always wanted to ride a camel and started patting the one nearest to her, motioning to the owner that she wanted to get up on it. The man's face expressed great pleasure and he immediately pulled the camel down.

Camels are stoical beasts but they are very contrary. They can be nasty and are known to bite. Some moan and groan when they are pulled down, folding the lower half of the front legs first, then the back ones and finally the upper part of the front legs. They emit grumbling sounds while someone clambers up on them and again when they have to get up. This camel was no exception. It began to make protesting noises, but once it was up on its legs with Claire on its back, it quietened down.

As the man began to pull the camel along, Claire seemed to be fully enjoying her ride.

'Up there,' she told me later, 'your perception of the world changes.'

Everything appeared to be going well when, to our surprise, the man led the camel away with Claire perched on top of it, motioning to us to continue in the opposite direction! Then I realised what was going on. The man believed he had found a willing woman in the middle of the Sahara and was wasting no more time: he was carrying off his precious find to where he was going to camp that night. No wonder he looked so satisfied! But he had gone no more than twenty yards when we all ran after him, blocking his way and making signs that he had to release Claire immediately. When he understood that his hopes were shattered, he grudgingly pulled down his camel and let Claire get off. Then he climbed onto the animal and removed himself at a rapid pace, muttering under his breath.

There are no natural landmarks in the Sahara. Each mile looks exactly like the last one and when the wind blows hard, it obliterates all tracks. You can easily get lost and when your car breaks down, there is a fair chance that you won't survive. Death is never far away in the Sahara. Every year there are stories of people who ran into trouble and perished of thirst.

When a vehicle is abandoned, the wheels and anything that can be carried off will disappear within a week or two. The vehicles do not keep their vivid colours very long either. The zillions of fine sand particles, carried by the wind when it blows, act like sandpaper. Sand storms will wear the bright paint away and expose the naked metal, and within months the sand blast and the little humidity the air contains, turn the leftovers into rusty wrecks. The way south is strewn with them. Every 30 or 40 miles we passed one of those dull-brown carcasses, stripped of all its essentials, terrifying reminders of dramas that had occurred months, or maybe years ago, putting an end to dreams and often to lives. These wrecks acted as landmarks in the flat expanse, indicating that we were still on the right track to the south. At the same time, they made us shudder because they served as a warning that we too were at risk. We were insufficiently prepared for the adventure upon which we had embarked so light-heartedly and could easily end up like those travellers who had lost their all.

We pushed on to Bordj-Mokhtar, the Algerian border garrison, and got there by the late afternoon of 28 December without overstaying our visas. We entered the place through a gate and our little convoy came to a halt in a small square surrounded by barracks where a detachment of the Algerian Army was stationed. Our passports were stamped and next they checked our money forms, which had been stapled to the passports. As I had duly reported all the money we had brought into the country, I had to count all our cash and traveller's cheques in front of the customs officers and account for any difference from the amount written down on the money forms by showing bank receipts. I now know better and would never again disclose that we were carrying an amount of cash and cheques equivalent to several years of local income. Doing so was sheer madness. Caution dictates that you never show the money you're carrying on you so as not to attract covetousness. Even the military – especially the military – are not to be trusted in Africa. But according to Claire, innocents probably have special guardian angels because they need them very much.

We were all tired out after a hard day's driving and decided to stop early. The evening was approaching as we set up camp and the glow of the sun, sinking towards the horizon, began to infuse the land-scape with soft colours. We would have loved to just sit down and gaze at the western sky where the colours were changing continuously, but there were numerous jobs to be done before total darkness enveloped us. I began to check the oil and water levels and slid under the Land Rover to tighten nuts and bolts, while Claire set about preparing a meal. Cooking for six was an effort, especially on the Little Bee stove, but Claire again managed to produce a dish of spaghetti supplemented with tomato sauce and corned beef.

By the time supper was ready, it was dark and the French lit their petrol lamps. They no longer seemed as choosy and had resigned themselves to eating whatever Claire could provide. Unfortunately, when she handed Alain his plate, he was so tired that he dropped it and the spaghetti fell onto the sand. We were all extremely hungry but one look at Alain's desolate face was sufficient to make up our minds. We all chipped in part of our food, while Claire generously gave half of her own plateful. Within just a few days, camping out in the desert with people who had been strangers at the start, a comradeship had developed that I hadn't felt for many years. There was a simplicity of contact and the respect that springs up among those travelling together in circumstances where trust has to be complete and where helping each other is vital to maximise the chances of survival for all.

Once we had finished our frugal supper, we didn't turn in straightaway. The starry sky was so beautiful that we just sat there, staring in awe at the vast expanse above us, talking very little and quietly, almost unwilling to break the deep silence of the desert. The moment we forgot about ourselves and became one with the environment, everything felt right; everything was timeless.

It was here that feelings which had remained just beneath the surface of consciousness for many years became crystal clear. I had been in forests and fields, on beaches and in mountains, and had thought that I was close to nature, but here, for the first time, I was surrounded by nature in its harshest, most elemental form, and the austere majesty of the desert – its stark contrast to life – was exerting a strange attraction. Maybe it was simply the peace, the perfect, undisturbed solitude and absolute silence that impressed me; perhaps it was the sudden awareness of my insignificance in this infinite space.

Those who have never experienced it may find it difficult to understand how pure complete emp-tiness can be. In the desert, life is stripped down to its bare essentials. There are no superfluities in the desert – the superfluous is of no value here; all the clutter of modern life, all the artificial glitter behind which people hide, drop away to leave only the really vital.

In our cities we lull ourselves into believing that humans are the centre of everything, that we are in control. Not so in the desert. Here space is so vast as to be beyond comprehension; we are no more than a grain of sand in the infinity of the universe. Here we do not control; this is far beyond man's limited power; here we undergo.

You cannot escape being affected by the desert, by its immensity, its majestic grandeur, its purity. All human endeavour is reduced to its proper dimension and the futility of most of what we do, of what we say, becomes apparent. As you sit there, staring at the seemingly unending expanse, slowly but surely, the spirit of the desert takes possession of your soul.

Is it surprising that the bare rocks and lifeless land, the very sterility of the great deserts, have fashioned the character of those who live there? They stop being critical or sceptical; they accept. The harshness of their world and insecurity of their lives impose deep respect for higher powers. In the endless expanse around them, contemplation of the infinite comes naturally, and the immeasurable cosmos above invites them to unify with something higher. The desert has always been a land of mystics and believers. No wonder it was the birthplace of the great monotheistic religions.

Just before sunrise, as everyone begins to wake up, the temperature is at its lowest. You are reluctant to come out of your shelter; the eyes are still filled with slumber and the mind is numbed by the cold, which makes you shiver. Your body is almost unwilling to move and you look towards the east where the sun is about to rise and fill you with warmth. Suddenly the first rays of the rising sun set the morning alight; streaks of orange flame through the sky and the dark-grey colour of the sand turns into a light pink. The body soaks up the sun's warmth and slowly, as the hue of the sand changes to a pale yellow, your muscles relax and you begin to function.

Together with the evening hours, the first hours of the day are the best. Water is boiling on the little oil stove. Soon breakfast will be ready and we will all sit together around a cloth spread out on the sand, drinking cups of piping-hot tea and eating biscuits and dates while looking at some nearby dunes, seeing their shadows shorten and noticing how the colour of the sand turns a warm yellow. There is no hurry; all tasks are done slowly, with economy of movement, but thoroughly. Everyone is doing his or her own part of the smaller or bigger chores that are to be done in the morning. In the few days since we left the last oasis, we are all settled into our travel routine.

Our Land Rover and the two Peugeots are parked away from each other in order to leave a certain degree of privacy. For 'calls of nature', an important part of the morning ritual, we walk away into the desert.

Before setting off on our journey, one of our friends took us to see a couple who had twice made the overland trip to India before the overthrow of the Shah of Iran in 1979. The man, a plumber by profession and very jovial, showed us a slide of his wife setting off for a call of nature in the desert in the morning. She wanted absolute privacy and went a long way, always towards the east, probably because anyone looking in that direction would be blinded by the rising sun and not see her as she crouched down on the flat expanse.

'Look,' said the man, 'this is my wife going to Mecca,' and he laughed heartily at his own joke while his embarrassed wife urged him to move to the next slide.

Claire never went as far as that but she did search for slight depressions where she would be out of sight, being the only woman amongst five men. I walked some distance away, not out of a sense of timidity but because the feeling of being alone in the immense space of the desert was so extraordinary. Being out there made me realise that the way we live in our modern cities is far removed from our deepest nature, and nothing is more so than when it comes to letting the natural functions of the body perform their daily routine. This is shrouded in all forms of euphemisms. In America they do not even go to the loo but to the 'rest room'. I would never have expected to discover that crouching down, not within the confines of a small cubicle but in the vastness of the open space around me, would bring about such a feeling of peace, of unity with my surroundings. I returned to nature what came from nature. It felt right, felt good. I was part of the great cosmic cycle of birth, maturing and death; I no longer asked questions; I just belonged.

The Sahel

Although the Malian border post was still half a day's drive away, we were now officially in Mali and the landscape seemed to know it. Within a few hours there was a definite change from the monotonous, empty expanse through which we had been travelling. Scattered thorn bushes and patches of dry vegetation began to appear, indicating that the Sahara was coming to an end. Life was returning, however hesitantly, and it made our spirits soar.

That morning, as we were picking our way between the low vegetation, we noticed what looked like a tent and headed for it. When we got close, we saw that it was the tent of a Tuareg family. A man was there with his young wife and their little son, and goats and camels were grazing nearby.

Claire had told me that she regretted being the only woman travelling with five men, and when she saw the woman she brightened up and went over to her with exclamations of joy. The young woman seemed overjoyed too and though they had no language in common, they started an animated conversation. They seemed to have a natural way of expressing their feelings through little gestures, signs and sounds, as if these formed a universal language between women. Claire pointed at herself, saying her name, and then, her face one big question, she looked at the young woman, who pointed at herself answering in turn, 'Leila.'

Within no time they had formed a close bond: Claire was admiring Leila's ornaments while Leila was touching Claire's clothes. Soon Claire took her by the hand and led her to our Land Rover, opened it and began pulling out different clothes.

All the exotic stories of my childhood, all the imaginary adventures evoked by reading throughout my youth, suddenly became reality when I saw Leila. To me she was the personification of the desert beauty. I thought her so absolutely captivating that I felt stunned. All her features were perfect: her heart-shaped face, her lovely curly mouth showing shining white teeth as she smiled, her soft, rounded nose and her golden-brown skin. But what fascinated me above all were her eyes; they were two deep pools of gentleness, but shy like a fawn's.

I would never have imagined there could be a link between two women of such different backgrounds. I was so unlike her in appearance, yet as we held each other's hand, something passed between us. The touch of Leila's hand revealed this singular bond between women, however many miles separated their lands of birth. There was a feeling of deep sameness as we stood there gazing at each other. In Leila's silent smile, mirroring the greater silence around us, lay the gentle acceptance of the other and the shared experience of being alive.

I took Leila to the Land Rover and began to show her my clothes. When she saw my black cashmere pullover she took it and held it against her chest for a long time, stroking its softness with longing in her eyes. I made a sign that it was for her and she folded her arms around it with exclamations of delight; I felt happy that she would be warm during the cold desert nights. I also gave her a pair of leather sandals from Greece as she was barefooted, and a tube of cream for her hands. I had become aware of the coarseness of her skin when I had taken her hand: the wind and sand had roughened it, and the contact with the icy water in the morning had left several painful cracks.

When we returned together, Leila's husband – a proud, tall man with piercing dark eyes and an aquiline nose – gestured to me to come and sit down on a large coloured carpet in front of their tent, while Leila went to fetch her little son from inside and put him on my lap. The boy wasn't frightened and sat there quietly, gazing at me with curiosity; he could feel that I loved him.

Suddenly the man put his hand on my knee and made a sign to indicate that I could stay if I wished. I looked at Leila and we both shook our heads in a firm 'no' gesture.

Nomads possess little, yet they are extremely hospitable. Tuaregs welcome you by touching the inside of the fingers of your right hand with theirs and then putting their hand on their heart while bending slightly forward. You sit down with them and they offer you tea. There is a natural slowness and gentleness about their movements, a total absence of hurry.

We, city people, rush about from daybreak till nightfall, trying to be efficient. Not so the nomads of the desert. They will camp in one place as long as the grazing is good, go about their daily chores and then sit contentedly in front of their tents. When the grazing diminishes, they pack up, load their tents and few belongings onto their camels, and walk slowly with their herds of camels and goats to another water point and new grazing lands. In fact, time has no value for them. Tomorrow will be like today. The sun will rise, reach its zenith and then sink down to disappear below the horizon in a sea of fire. This is followed by a bright starry night and yet another day. Is it this that has created the difference between the contemplative culture of the desert people and us, restless Westerners? We are impatient; we move about in speedy cars, isolated in a world of our own, and we find reason to grumble. But if you are a nomad of the desert, you walk – a few miles or a few hundred miles – it doesn't make a difference. And you are pleased to meet other nomads; you stay together for a while before going your way, because meeting someone is important; because you know that nothing can be taken for granted; that, depending on the vagaries of travel and life, you will not run into each other again for several months, for a year or maybe never …

Back in Belgium, friends had warned us against the many dangers we might encounter in Africa. 'Have you thought about snakebites?' they had asked us. 'Or of fatal scorpion stings? You've got to protect yourselves.'

I had left Brussels in black leather boots – it was winter – and had continued to wear them in Algeria. They had strong soles and I always zipped them up to the knee. I wasn't going to take any risks. Nothing was going to bite its way through the thick leather. By the time we got to Timimoun, the boots had become unbearably hot and there came a time when I couldn't stand them any longer. So I finally stowed them away underneath our luggage and dug out the special, thick, canvas shoes with rubber soles we had bought in the exclusive shop in Brussels that had also sold us the Little Bees. They had thought it their duty to advise us also on footwear for Africa. Peter had innocently confessed that we would just be wearing sandals but, 'Oh no,' they had said, 'that would be wholly inappropriate.' It seemed there were lots of dangers besides snakes or scorpions: there were poisonous spiders just waiting to bite you wherever you put down an unprotected foot and 'had we thought about cuts that would get infected and would never heal in the heat and dirt?' Then they came up with these canvas shoes, which went up to well above the ankle, saying, 'This is what the French Foreign Legion is wearing in the Sahara. The very best!' The price they asked seemed to be the very best, too, but 'it was money well spent,' they had affirmed. 'Your security requires it.'

Right from the start, my feet seemed to be stifling in those thick canvas shoes. What with the sweltering heat and burning sun, they felt as if they were caught in a prison. I hated the moment when, in the morning, I had to pull on those awful shoes and lace them up tightly!

When I saw Leila walking barefooted, I envied her the freedom. And after I had given her one pair of sandals and saw her put them on with a happy smile, I thought, why shouldn't I do like her? We're no different!

So I put on the other pair of sandals I had and from then on, my feet felt light and free. And I was never once bitten or stung during the rest of our travels.

As we penetrated further into Mali, the vegetation became denser; there were low bushes everywhere and scattered thorn trees. Then we began to pass alongside round straw huts and even small hamlets. The Sahara was clearly behind us. However, driving didn't become any easier. The track had narrowed between hills and low mountains, making it impossible to swerve left or right to avoid the worst corrugated parts; at times we ran straight into a bad patch and then the Land Rover vibrated so strongly that it seemed as if it was going to fall apart. It was hotter, too: the air above the hills was vibrant as the sun reached its zenith. But at least I didn't have to concern myself with where we were going; we had a well-established dirt road to guide us and I was content just to follow the French cars, although they churned up a cloud of thick, yellow dust.

We had been bumping along like this for quite some time and Claire was writing her notes, her feet on the dashboard, when suddenly she remarked, 'Isn't it strange? Some time ago I had the sun in my face and now I'm in the shade. How do you explain that?'

I hadn't even noticed that the position of the sun had changed but when I heard Claire's voice, reality caught up with a jerk. If she was in the shade, it could only mean one thing: that we were driving due west instead of south! Sweat broke out at once. 'How long have you been in the shade?' I asked anxiously.

'Well, I don't really know. Maybe an hour or so …'

I began hooting till the French heard me and stopped. A lively discussion now ensued. 'We're on the wrong track,' I said.

'No we're not!' they retorted, and to prove their point they brought out a detailed Ordnance Survey map of the area. As we consulted it, everything became clear. There had been a fork in the road maybe some 30 miles back and we had gone the wrong way. The track we had been following carried on due west through the Sahara towards Taoudenni, some 900 miles further! Taoudenni was a prison camp and the prisoners' punishment was to dig for salt under the blazing sun, standing with their feet in the corrosive brine. The camp was surrounded by hundreds of miles of wasteland and considered so safe that there were neither walls nor barbed wire to stop the prisoners from escaping. Running away into the desert would have meant dying of thirst.

The moment they realised their mistake, the French wanted to take a shortcut and drive due east. 'Sooner or later we're bound to hit the road to Gao,' they argued, but I was unwilling to do that because it meant driving through a trackless hilly landscape.

'We'll just get lost or be stuck in the sand,' I objected, 'and then we've all had it. We must go back the way we've come.'

The problem was that the fuel reserves of the French were already dangerously low. They were worried about not making it to Gao if they had to turn back on their tracks, and only after I offered them diesel fuel did they agree to do so. We finally found the junction and the track to Gao, but the error prolonged our trip by 60 miles and several hours!

I soon discovered that there was another big problem. The French had been living off our food and water for several days and were now using our fuel too but the real calamity, from their point of view, was that they had run out of cigarettes, and here we couldn't help them! Not eating or even drinking for a day would have been difficult but tolerable, but they hadn't smoked since yesterday morning and were becoming extremely tense. They could no longer stand it and were determined to push on, not wishing to spend another day without smoking. A general rule for desert travellers is not to drive at night; it was nearly 6.00 p.m. and we still had a long way to go, but there was no holding the French back. So we kept driving through the pitch dark and on the evening of 31 December, we finally entered the dusty streets of Gao. It had taken us five days to cover the 800 miles since Reggane, and the terrible conditions of the tracks had taken their toll; we had less than 50 litres of diesel fuel left out of the 400 we had set off with. But we had made it!

I had entered the Sahara full of apprehension, even fear. Then, gradually, I had fallen under the spell of the desert. When we arrived in Gao, I felt a sense of relief of course, and yet deep down I was sad the journey was over. Crossing the desert had been strenuous. It had produced extreme fatigue and discomfort, yet it had created an intense feeling of being alive. My vitality had soared, my senses sharpened and I felt like a reborn being. Over the years, thousands of Europeans have made the trip – crossed the Sahara and gone into black Africa – and I'm only one of them, but I'm glad I did it because it changed my life. For the first time ever I realised how ephemeral our existence is and how insignificant we really are. And I couldn't help wondering whether life as it was lived in the West was really the extraordinary adventure it pretended to be.

We humans have been given the incredible privilege of spending some seventy or eighty years on our planet and what are we making of it? Of course, society cannot consist solely of desert-lovers. It needs all sorts to make a world: active, efficient people and practical minds who forge ahead, as well as contemplative spirits who think of the Earth as a living, breathing entity and would rather leave everything in peace, live in harmony with their environment and not take too much from it. But I have the impression that today there are far too many people in the first category and not enough in the second. And I cannot rid myself of the foreboding that the planet, and we humans, will end up paying very dearly for this.

Above: Camping in the Sahara with the Moon and Venus in the sky

Below: A meeting before the sun sets

Above: Claire on a camel

Below: Meeting Tuaregs: Claire with Leila

Above: Northern Mali: we passed alongside clusters of straw huts…

Below: …and the people came out to look at us

CHAPTER 5
The Enchantment of Mali

The road to Mopti

There we were then, in sub-Saharan Africa where I was hoping to learn all about the problems of development. I was soon to find out that reality was very different from what I had expected.

We had no idea where to go for the night, but the French led us to a campsite on the outskirts of Gao where we found travellers who, like ourselves, had just crossed the Tanezrouft; other Europeans had come from the south and were staying here before heading north into the Sahara. As it was 31 December, the owner of the campsite, a French woman, had decided to throw a grand party for the guests. There was a stall with food and drinks, she had hired a small local orchestra and the atmosphere was festive. Everyone was looking forward to celebrating New Year's Eve by dancing under the starry sky.

Celebrations were in full swing when an hour or so before midnight a few Africans turned up, seemingly from nowhere, and began to mingle unobtrusively with the revellers. Suddenly, for no apparent reason, they started pushing each other, shouting ensued and then one of the Africans slapped another in the face. To my surprise, the man fell flat on the ground and seemed to be knocked out! I stared at the scene in astonishment: it looked like a badly enacted, third-rate slapstick comedy. Within seconds, whistles blew and half a dozen Africans in uniforms charged in shouting, 'Police!' They immediately rounded up the intruders who didn't put up the slightest resistance. I wondered what they were going to do with the man who'd been floored, but he just got up and joined the rest! The Africans were all led away by a single policeman and not one made any attempt to escape!

The other policemen now began bellowing, 'This establishment is a cause of disorder! The owners are unable to guarantee the safety of the guests! We are forced to close it down!' The police stood firm and slowly, dragging their feet, the European revellers returned to their vehicles and tents and turned in for the night. Then the police ordered the lights to be switched off and that was that.

The next day, I listened to the rumour mill. Apparently the French campsite was going to be closed down for not being able to keep order. I also heard that some campers had been 'encouraged' to move to another campsite in town which, it was whispered, belonged to a well-connected Malian. We went to have a look later in the day and found the site unclean, the service poor and prices high.

Our French companions hadn't had enough to eat for the last few days and were ravenous when they woke up late next morning. They were eager to have an early lunch in town and pressed us to accompany them to a local restaurant where they ordered a meat dish with huge fresh salads. When their food was brought in they fell upon it like hungry wolves and emptied several glasses of iced drinks to wash everything down. We thought it safer not to eat anything uncooked and had toast and omelette with bottled water.

After lunch we went looking for a petrol station. Crossing the Sahara and helping out the French had left us with too little diesel fuel to reach Mopti, the next town where it was for sale; I would need to buy at least an additional 20 to 30 litres. We located the only petrol station in town but as I pulled up and told the assistant to fill our tanks, we were in for a shock: he refused to do it! It appeared that the Paris-Dakar Rally was due to go through within a few days and all available diesel fuel was reserved for its participants. We would have to wait till they had gone and a fresh supply of fuel had been ferried up the River Niger.

'And how long will that take?' I asked warily.

The man just made a vague gesture as if to show that this was way beyond his responsibility. 'And if you don't like it,' he added with a grin, 'you can always file a complaint with the chief of police.'

I didn't want to hang around in Gao for an indefinite period of time and although there seemed little hope of success, I decided to go to the police station. Unfortunately, the chief of police was not there. Apparently he was engaged elsewhere and when I asked when he would return, they shrugged their shoulders and suggested, 'Maybe come back tomorrow.'

I was not going to give up, though, and after asking around we finally tracked the man down at his home. It appeared that his eldest son had a high fever, he had been desperately trying to find medicine since early that morning and he was about to go out again. When Claire told him that we had anti-fever tablets, he was overjoyed and immediately invited us to have lunch with him. I wasn't very keen; his wife and other children were all sitting on the floor eating out of a communal bowl, sticking their hands into it and licking them clean afterwards. So I politely declined, saying we had just eaten, but would he be able to do something else for us? And I explained that they had refused to sell us diesel fuel.

'Oh!' exclaimed the chief of police. 'You want diesel fuel. That *is* a problem.' Then he looked at the anti-fever tablets in his hand and said, 'But it can be arranged. Would 50 litres do?'

A quarter of an hour later, we were back at the petrol station and when I showed the pump assistant the permit allowing me to buy 50 litres, he beamed at me. 'With official permission, no problem,' he said, moving towards the pump. 'Now you can buy fuel.'

Back in the campsite, we turned in early, but were woken around midnight by moans and groans. We jumped out of our Land Rover fearing something terrible had happened, only to find one of our French companions doubled up with cramps and vomiting. The other three were lying behind their Peugeots in not much better condition. They complained that the contents of their copious lunch were burning like fires inside them, so we gave them some of our precious medicine to help relieve their discomfort. The next morning, they seemed to have recovered. I thought they would have learned their lesson, but we found them talking animatedly about what they were going to eat! We left them to it, wishing them, 'Bon voyage!'

As we set off from Gao, we hesitated. Should we drive to Timbuktu? For centuries the town had been a major centre of commercial exchange. Here local merchants unloaded trans-Saharan caravans, shipped the goods onward down the River Niger and reloaded the caravans with supplies from the south to be transported to destinations north of the Sahara. However, when boats began to sail around West Africa, the fabled city of Timbuktu lost much of its importance. Then, during the twentieth century, as the camel was gradually superseded by the lorry, the town lost even more of its lustre and was rumoured to be no more than a shadow of its former self.

All the same, it was only 250 miles away. Having got so close we would have liked to visit it, but we were told that the track between Gao and Timbuktu, which followed the north bank of the River Niger, consisted of nothing but loose sand for most of the way. After our experiences with sandy patches so far, we thought it wiser not to go. Anyway, as we had left Brussels two months late, I felt we should keep to a strict schedule. So I opted for driving directly south to Bamako, the capital of Mali, with a quick detour to the famous Dogon area in the east of the country. I was sure that, within two to three weeks at most, we would be in the south of the Ivory Coast, ready to head for Nigeria and Central Africa. Little did I know then that fate had something quite different in store for us.

Mali is a beautiful, culturally rich country full of wonderful sights, and no destination in Mali is more popular than the Dogon area. The Dogons are the only people in the Sahel to have resisted conversion to Islam; they had clung to their animistic rites and were now famous for their unique culture and also for their beautiful carvings. Many tourists have visited the Dogon area, but this tourist traffic has its downside. In the campsite in Gao, some travellers told us that you could never sit down or stop anywhere along a route frequented by Western tourists without immediately being surrounded by Africans who would molest you with their incessant begging. Children in particular could be very annoying, as we found out. When we stopped they would slowly draw nearer while making a tour around the Land Rover, looking at it with interest. Then they would come forward, approaching us with a 'Bonjour Monsieur! Bonjour Madame! Where are you from?' as if they just wanted to seek friendly contact. But once those preliminaries were over, they would push closer, calling out, '*Cadeau! Cadeau!*' (A present! A present!) with outstretched hands. 'Give me shoes, give me money, food, clothes, a ball to play with, a pen, a toy...'

However, the moment we were away from the tourist routes and big towns, we found that people were invariably friendly. They were curious, of course, because we represented the faraway world for them, but they had a natural dignity and always approached us with great courtesy. In fact we fell in love with Mali's cheerful people and with the soft colours and beauty of its landscapes.

When camping out, we would get up with the first light and start busying ourselves. Breakfast was usually one of the most enjoyable moments of the day. Claire would be making semolina pancakes and begin to boil water for our morning tea on her Little Bee, while I would be pouring fuel from the jerry cans into the reservoirs and topping up oil levels while listening to the pleasant hissing of the stove.

After breakfast we would put everything away and clean up the sleeping compartment. There was no rush but it was better not to start too late: the first hours of the day were the best for driving as it was still cool and the sand, hard and crusty after the cold of the night, would be firm. So the moment all the morning chores were over, I would start up the engine and we would set off through the wide-open Malian landscape.

We were driving along a sandy track through a magnificent area of scattered bushes and thorn trees, and I was thoroughly enjoying myself when suddenly the Land Rover got stuck, the engine stalled and I heard Peter swear, 'Damn, damn! Not again!'

It was maybe the third or fourth time we'd been stuck in the sand that day and the last time the engine had refused to start for two long, anxious minutes. I didn't know anything about cars – I left that side of things entirely to Peter – but by now I knew very well the part I had to play in the routine of getting the car unstuck. I sighed, got out, dug some of the sand from underneath the front wheels, climbed to the top of the Land Rover, threw down the sand ladders and pushed them underneath the front tyres.

We were in luck. By the time I had completed all the tasks allotted to me, Peter had managed to restart the engine; he revved up and slowly the tyres got a grip on the sand ladders, the Land Rover began to move and Peter kept it going till it was on firmer soil some fifty yards further on.

I now started the next phase of the task assigned to me. I pulled with all my might to get the ladders, which the wheels had pushed down hard, out of the sand and then dragged them along, one in each hand, running as fast as I could. I had nearly reached the Land Rover when I felt an excruciating pain in my right foot: I had inadvertently stepped on a thick thorn! It went straight through the sole of my sandal, pierced my foot through the web between the big and second toe, and emerged on the top.

'Help!' I screamed, but Peter was not to be moved.

'Come on!' he yelled. 'What are you waiting for? I've got to keep the engine going or it'll stall again. Hurry up!'

There was nothing else to do but hop along on my left foot and right heel. I managed to throw the ladders onto the roof rack and got in, nearly in tears. 'Peter, please, stop a minute,' I pleaded, but we were already moving.

'What is it?'

'I've got a thorn in my foot,' I groaned. 'Can you help me pull it out?'

'Can't you pull it out yourself?'

'But it's a very long one … from an acacia tree … They're poisonous …'

'Can't stop now,' Peter said, keeping his eyes riveted on the track. 'Sorry.'

I clenched my teeth, wrenched up my right leg and managed to extract the thorn by pulling off the sandal. Blood was dripping over the floor and the pain had become unbearable by now. 'Can't you stop please,' I pleaded again. 'I have to disinfect it.'

The track was just going up a low dune and Peter was concentrating fully on manoeuvring uphill. Finally I heard him say, 'Disinfect what?'

'My foot!'

'Oh, you need disinfectant! Well, you know where it is: inside the back compartment.' And he repeated, 'Can't stop.'

I resigned myself to climbing through the narrow opening while the Land Rover was moving unsteadily, found some Dettol, grabbed a bucket and a bottle of water and emerged with the lot into the steering cabin where I dropped down on my seat. I poured some Dettol and water into the bucket and stuck my foot firmly into it while we kept bumping along.

After a while the track became firmer and we were going downhill, Peter relaxed and as he finally looked my way, he exclaimed, 'But there's blood all over the place! Why didn't you ask me to stop?'

'Oh, don't bother,' I replied, feeling braver now. 'It's nothing, really.'

An hour later, when it was time to set up camp, my foot came out of the bucket all wrinkled but the bleeding had stopped and the wound was perfectly disinfected.

That night, instead of discarding it, I decided to keep the three-inch long thorn as a souvenir. I put it in a bag with seeds and flowers I had collected, stowed it away underneath our beds and forgot all about it.

In the African countryside, the daily rhythm is ruled by the sun. Mornings are pleasant, but as the sun rises in the sky and passes its zenith, it turns into an unbearable ball of fire high overhead, and moving about becomes an effort. By late afternoon, finally, the furnace-like heat makes room for more gentle warmth, the sun begins to lean towards the west and slowly, the light changes from the brilliant, angry white of noon to the pale yellow of early evening. Then, quite suddenly, the sky turns amber and pink, and the giant globe of the sun drops almost visibly towards the horizon, to disappear in a sky reddened by its last flames. Within ten minutes, the light fades and you find yourself surrounded by the deep darkness of the night. We, therefore, always began to look for a suitable place to camp well before sunset, as there were so many tasks we had to do before turning in. I would start the daily maintenance of the Land Rover and slide underneath it to tighten nuts and bolts while Claire would busy herself a few paces away, boiling water for our supper.

Our meals tended to be rather monotonous. We ate little fresh food as it went off very rapidly in the great heat. We did have a small fridge inside the Land Rover's back compartment, but that was used exclusively for preserving our exposed films and slides. Sometimes, when we passed through a small town and found a bakery, we managed to buy a loaf of fresh bread. That was a real treat but, basically, we had to survive on the tinned and dry food we had with us. This usually meant rice and sardines or, alternatively, spaghetti and corned beef, the lot enlivened with concentrated tomato sauce from a tin.

Cooking on the Little Bee was quite a feat and I admired Claire for stoically carrying on with it day after day, but one evening, as I was lying on my back under the Land Rover, I heard her scream. This was so unusual that I feared something dreadful had happened: she must have been bitten by a snake or at least been stung by a scorpion! In my haste to crawl from underneath the chassis, I hit my head hard on the boiling-hot sump, nearly knocking myself out. When I finally emerged, I saw her hopping about in a state of great agitation.

'What's the matter with you?' I asked anxiously.

'There's nothing the matter with *me*!' she yelled.

'What is it then?'

'It's that hateful Little Bee!'

'Hey! Careful!' I shouted as I saw our cooking pot lying in the sand. But it was too late to be careful.

I had lit the flame of the Little Bee for the fifth time that evening when suddenly the highly unstable stove fell over, the cooking pot slipped off and our spaghetti spilled into the sand just as it was ready. I had put up with the whims of the Little Bee horror so far, but this was just too much and I screamed.

Evening after evening, ever since we had set out into the Sahara, my frustration had grown. I dreaded having to make supper. You just couldn't take your eyes off the capricious Little Bee for a second! You had to pump it up at regular intervals because the pressure had the nasty habit of dropping the moment you had your back turned, and then the flame went out and you had to start the whole process of lighting alcohol, etc. all over again. As if that weren't enough, the stove had to be shielded from the wind because the slightest gust would blow out the flame. This was not regular cooking; it was cooking in small instalments! And even if the flame kept burning, it blackened all my pots and pans. I hated that Little Bee stove intensely! How the idiot who had invented this instrument of torture could ever have imagined that it was possible to cook properly on it was beyond me.

But tonight topped it all. To see our evening meal lie in the sand after half an hour of uninterrupted effort was more than I could cope with. I was raving mad and when Peter shouted, 'Hey! Careful!' I screamed and gave the shiny brass stove a good kick.

Peter was stunned when he saw my cross face, clenched teeth and matted curls, which I was shaking from side to side. He stood there, his hair full of sand and prickly grass, and was rubbing his head with a painful expression on his face, which was streaked with oil and dust. Suddenly his eyes twinkled and he burst out laughing, saying, 'You're so attractive.' My anger disappeared at once; I rushed into his arms and laughed, too, and all was well.

After this, Claire refused to have anything more to do with cooking unless I promised to buy her a camping gas stove the moment we reached a big town. Then she set about salvaging the spaghetti, which was lying in the sand. She washed it as well as she could and turned it out on a plate with the usual tomato sauce and sardines. I had got used to being pleased with whatever was served, but the spaghetti was lukewarm and chewing it 'with added sand' made a crunching sound. However, I thought it wiser not to make any comments and managed to finish my supper with a satisfied expression on my face.

When supper was over, we would sit outside and on evenings when there was no moon, look for a while at the bright stars, which one after the other would become visible in the vast expanse of the sky overhead. In our urbanised societies we are so used to switching on electric lights when it gets dark that we no longer bother about the moon, but in those parts of the world not yet transformed by modern ways of living, the moon is still extremely important.

At the beginning of its cycle, it is no more than a tiny sliver which, seen from Mali, is lying on its back with the points uppermost, a strange sight when you have never seen it so before. It is stunningly beautiful, but doesn't give much light and disappears below the horizon an hour or so after sunset. Then, evening after evening, as it moves away from the position of the sun in the sky, the moon grows in size until it is bright enough to bathe the landscape in a soft glow. Towards full moon, its brilliant light is so strong that it throws ethereal moon shadows, and the silvery moonlight is very reassuring in its soothing brightness, but as the lunar cycle continues past full moon, there is no light in the sky after the sun has disappeared. Within minutes, ink-black darkness envelops you, making you feel very lonely in a frightening, mysterious world. This is how people must have felt in Babylon or Ancient Greece, I couldn't help thinking.

When you sit there in the African night with nothing much to do, you start wondering about the meaning of things and strange questions enter your mind. Why, I thought, are there seven days in a week? It seemed odd, given that we do not have seven fingers on each hand. And then I was sure I had found the answer. The seven-day week, which has been with us for thousands of years, must obviously have to do with the central place the moon occupied in ancient civilizations.

A year is a very long time, and lunar cycles were a straightforward way of dividing it up into more manageable bits, which were called months. Dividing these in turn into quarters of the lunar cycle, from new moon to first quarter, from first quarter to full moon, etc. – each of which took about seven days – was even more suited to the purpose of celebrating recurrent religious rites in ancient cultures. So, the moon gave us the seven-day week, which still modulates our work rhythm, even though we now live in cities where we rarely notice the moon and hardly ever think about it.

We arrived in Mopti just after the sun had set and began to drive around, looking for a place to park and sleep. After searching for a while, we came upon a wide-open space at the edge of the town. There was no one around and it seemed to be the best place we'd be able to find. We stopped, set up camp and spent the night there.

Imagine our surprise the next morning to be woken up by loud chatter and great merriment. When we stuck our heads out of the Land Rover, we found ourselves in the middle of a lot of activity: stalls were being set up all around us. We hadn't realised that we were camping in the middle of the area where the weekly market was being erected!

It made me think of a story my friend Luc had told me. He and Roger, his travelling companion, had arrived late in a large town and they thought themselves lucky when they found a nice flat, quiet space. They put out their foam mattresses and crept into their sleeping bags. The next morning, when they woke up, people were stepping over them: it was Sunday morning and they were lying in front of the steps of a church!

After a hasty breakfast, we set out for the town hall hoping to obtain forms permitting us to film, because unauthorised filming is forbidden by Malian law. And the misery doesn't end there; you have to obtain a separate permit in each province. After asking around for quite a time and being sent from one place to another, we ended up at police headquarters. It seemed that the chief of police was the one who had to stamp the forms.

Claire subscribed to the notion that you need to be important to get anything done in Africa. Since I have a PhD, she was determined to make the most of this and as we entered the police station, she stepped in front of me saying, 'Let me introduce you.' Then she turned to the chief of police, a tall, hefty man, and waving an arm towards me she said in French, 'This is Doctor Peeters.'

I stood there, feeling embarrassed that she was using such blunt means to reach our goal and certain that it would have the contrary effect, but to my surprise I saw the man get up and come to me with a broad smile and outstretched arm. It seemed to have worked! Then, to my horror, I heard him say, 'How lucky that you're here, Doctor. I've got such a terrible headache!'

'Now what?' I said to Claire in English so that the man wouldn't understand. 'How am I going to get out of this?'

'We have some medicine for headaches,' she replied calmly. 'There's a box full of suppositories in the Land Rover.'

I remembered how we had got them. Back in Belgium, we had contacted several pharmaceutical companies, asking if they would be willing to give us free medicine to take to Africa. One company had donated a large box full of suppositories to relieve headaches in young children. We didn't think that this would be of any use in Africa, but it is difficult to reject a gift.

'I can't give him suppositories to treat his headache,' I protested. 'He's probably never heard of such a thing.'

'Well, that's all there is,' said Claire with an even face. 'And since you're the doctor, you'll have to get us out of this. You'd better treat him.' And she rushed off to the Land Rover to hunt for the suppositories.

I closed my eyes, sighed and turned reluctantly to the chief of police. 'Well, ahem, I've got some strong medicine …'

'Yes?' The man beamed at me.

'But you see … this medicine is very special. You … you must not swallow it. Ah, here it is,' I said as Claire returned with a handful of suppositories.

'I must not swallow it?' The man stared in puzzlement at the little wrapped-up stick I pressed into his hand. 'Then what am I to do?'

'Well … you see … you stick it up here …' I made a gesture that showed clearly where it was supposed to go. 'That's what you do.'

'What! Stick it up my …' He shook his head while looking at the suppository with unconcealed distrust. 'Please,' he said suddenly, 'you wouldn't have something I can put into my mouth?'

I tried to be as authoritative as possible. 'No. You must stick it up there. This is how this very special medicine works.'

'But this will never work!' The chief of police wagged a fleshy finger at me.

'Why not?' I asked, completely bewildered.

'Because of the distance!' He indicated the distance between his head and his anus and looked sternly at me. 'If I put medicine into my mouth it will work because that's close to the headache, but if I do as you say, it won't because the distance is much too great!'

As I was to find out so often during our travels through Africa, events had suddenly taken on a course of their own. I was just wondering how we would ever get out of this when the chief of police unexpectedly burst out laughing.

'Stick it up there … Ha ha!' I heard him roar. 'That's a good one! What will doctors tell us next? Ha ha ha!' He shouted to the subordinates who had been hanging around outside and as they came running in he at once began to tell them the story of the suppositories, exploding in gasps of laughter when he illustrated his words with gestures that left nothing to the imagination. The subordinates in turn repeated the story to any newcomers and soon everyone in and around the office was rocking with mirth. Never before had I seen people so completely convulsed with laughter.

'Stick it up there!' one policeman cried, laughing so much that he had to hold onto the commander's desk for support. Another man was shaking like a jelly until he could no longer stand and had to sit on the floor.

I must do something, I thought. I need this permit. I went to the chief of police, put the official document in front of him and asked politely whether he would stamp it.

'Yes, yes, no problem,' replied the man between hiccoughs of laughter and put official stamps all over the paper. Then, as I handed him some more suppositories, he nearly went into hysterics and collapsed into his chair.

As we rushed to our Land Rover, shouts of laughter kept coming from inside the police station. More people were running towards it to find out what was happening while we saw others stumble out, bent double, holding their sides. For days they would probably go off into fits of laughter whenever they told the story.

As we drove off I felt relieved that we didn't have to repeat such a weird experience until we got to the next province. The important thing was that we had our permit and I kept it at the ready whenever we brought out our cameras – only to find that no one ever asked to see it. I never again applied for a permit to film.

The Dogon Area

After camping in the middle of the weekly market, we wisely decided to spend the following night in a hotel, especially because this would allow us for once to have a proper wash. We were soon to find out that there were drawbacks to staying in a hotel, too. Tourism had not only given rise to children begging for 'presents', but also spawned a cottage industry to supply those items tourists are looking for: souvenirs. And some of those souvenirs were fakes sold as authentic antiques by peddlers all the way from Mopti, the gate to the Dogon area, to its capital, Bandiagara. Gullible people end up paying the bill, as I did next morning.

I called to Claire to come outside, bubbling with enthusiasm. 'There's a man in front of the hotel who sells antiques. He has a few very special seventeenth-century bronze pieces which have been dug up recently!' There was a ring with a small lizard on top, a pendant representing the sun and a curved staff about eight-inches long which, the vendor claimed, had belonged to a powerful chief of the Telem period (which preceded the Dogon period).

Claire didn't seem very impressed. 'They're small,' she said, but my enthusiasm was not to be quenched.

'That's perfect,' I commented. 'We need small pieces since we have to transport them all the way through Africa.'

The peddler must have noticed my excitement because he asked no less than 100,000 Malian francs (about £90.00, 1982 value: the annual income of a Malian at the time) for these 'authentic' Telem antiques.

Claire was more interested in the man's blue and silver embroidered *boubou*, a traditional, wide-sleeved robe. She thought this particular one a fantastic piece of clothing and kept pestering the man to sell it to her. He wasn't very keen on selling the clothes he stood in, but as Claire made it clear that it was either his 'antiques' *and* the *boubou* or nothing, he finally consented to part with it for another 100,000 Malian francs. Then, having been paid, he rapidly disappeared around the corner with no more on him than his baggy underpants.

Having started collecting Dogon antiques, I was not to be stopped and found out the whereabouts of a local antiques dealer. The man had a fever and didn't want to see us, but when I let it be known that we would give him medicine, he finally received us. I proudly showed him the antiques I had just bought, asking whether he had any bronzes of the same period for sale. He looked at the pieces for no more than a second or two and then said with contempt, 'Those aren't antiques. They're fakes.'

'How come then that they have such an authentic patina,' I countered, upset.

'When they come hot out of the kiln the artisans bury them in ashes for a while,' explained the man. 'That's how they make them look old.' And he explained that there were very few authentic bronzes left, and that European antiques dealers had even bought up most of the carved wooden granary doors for which the Dogons are so famous.

When he saw the disappointment on my face, the man got up, went to the back of his house and reappeared a minute later, holding a small bronze horse, saying, '*This* is a real antique.'

Claire was thrilled when she saw the little horse. It held its head high, wore a saddle and stood proudly on straight legs. Unfortunately, one of the back legs was missing.

'I've got the broken leg somewhere,' continued the man and he began rummaging in several boxes until he found it. He now turned to Claire. 'I see that you like the horse.'

'I do,' she admitted. Suddenly I heard her ask, 'How much do you want for it?'

Oh no, I thought, we can't afford this. I held my breath while the antiques dealer was pondering the question. Then, to my utter surprise, he replied, 'Nothing. You have been good to me and given me medicine. Allow me in turn to be good to you.' And as he handed the horse to Claire, he added, 'Be so kind as to accept my gift. I know that the horse will be happy with you.' We left almost with tears in our eyes.

We still have the horse. Back in Brussels we had its leg repaired and it is now standing proudly on a kneehole desk, a joy to behold. The fake antiques are there, too. As for the pendant representing the sun, Claire came to love it and often wore it around her neck during our further travels through Africa.

We did not have the means to sleep in a hotel very often, especially after our encounter with the 'antiques' peddler, and so, most of the time, we camped out. I have to admit that I sometimes felt insecure listening to the strange whispering noises emanating from the bush that crept into my ears in the darkness of the night. Claire had no such qualms. She had what she called a magic drawing and always put this up at night. The first time this happened I wasn't prepared for it. We were setting up camp when I saw Claire fiddling amongst our belongings.

'What are you looking for?' I asked.

'Oh nothing,' she replied and carried on searching. Then, finally, with a sigh of relief, she pulled out a thick sheet of paper on which a strange drawing had been made consisting of black and deep-red circles and lines. It looked vaguely like a mask.

'What's that?' I asked.

Claire hesitated for a moment and then said in a firm voice, 'It's to protect us.'

'To protect us against what?'

'Against anything. This will ward off evil powers.'

I shook my head. 'You can't be serious!'

'But we need protection! I had this specially made in Brussels by someone who's often been to Africa.' She looked rather pleased with herself.

I had imagined that I knew all about Claire by now, but this opened up a totally unexpected side of her personality. 'You don't believe in magic, do you?' I asked, surprised.

'Well …' She thought for a while and then said, 'It's always better to be on the safe side. After all, we're in Africa, the land of witchcraft.'

'But there's no longer any witchcraft in Africa! That was all a long time ago.'

'I wouldn't be so sure,' countered Claire. 'They told me that witchcraft is still very much alive in the bush.'

'Who told you so?'

'People who know,' she said evasively, and resolutely stuck the 'magic' drawing against the window. 'That'll protect us for the night,' she stated in a firm voice.

Next she began to pull a decorated Tuareg sword, which we had bought in Gao, from underneath our bedding where it was hidden.

'Why are you taking the sword out?' I wanted to know.

She didn't reply but went outside, looked at the Land Rover from a distance in the light of the setting sun, and then returned and put the sword against the vehicle in such a position that it would be clearly visible to anyone approaching us.

'Hey! What are you doing that for?'

'Well, this is an extra precaution against attackers – this is sure to keep them away. I've been told that you've got to show that you're well armed.' She spoke with great self-assurance.

'But it's the only weapon we've got!'

'Yes, but they wouldn't know that, would they? Putting the sword outside just shows them how confident we are. Anyway, there's nothing to worry about.' She pointed at the drawing. 'We've got special protection.'

I shook my head at such a piece of female illogicality and resigned myself to what fate would bring. I don't know whether it was the combination of the magic drawing and the sword leaning against the Land Rover that did the trick, or driving off the track just before sunset when no one was in sight and finding a sheltered spot in the bush, but we were lucky: we were never molested.

When we arrived in Bandiagara, we found out that there was a school run by a Belgian missionary. I was delighted to meet someone from my country and as he began to talk about the good works he was doing, I gave him a box full of penicillin and some medicine. We seemed to be getting on well until I told the missionary that I was lecturing at the University of Brussels. Suddenly his attitude changed. He had studied at Louvain, the Catholic university, and considered those from Brussels University godless heathens. He told us abruptly that he didn't want us to camp within the perimeter of the mission, turned around and walked away, taking the medicine box with him.

Fortunately there were two other men in the mission who didn't seem to have such hang-ups, and they were very happy to talk to us. One of them was a young man who was due to fly back to Belgium within two weeks. He kindly suggested that if there was anything we no longer needed, he was willing to take it with him. It was an extremely generous offer and I handed him my heavy winter coat and a thick sweater. He never told us that his baggage allowance was limited, so he wore the thick sweater and the winter coat over all the rest of his clothes when he boarded the plane in Bamako. Poor man! Ten months later, he told us he had been sweating all the way, but he kept his promise and dutifully hung onto the clothes until we reclaimed them.

We were disappointed that the Belgian missionary hadn't allowed us to sleep within the perimeter of the mission, which forced us to camp several hundred yards outside the little town, but after the first night out we realised how lucky we were to be woken up by the sound of braying donkeys and the distant voices of people setting about their daily chores. Camping in the bush near Bandiagara left us with a sense of belonging to this world, to the natural cycle of life.

After breakfast, we returned to the mission to see the other man, Brother Henri, a French Canadian. He was extremely kind and was overjoyed to be able to talk to people who were interested in his life and work. He spoke enthusiastically about the school he ran and, around noon, took us to see the boys' dormitory. This was where the boarders slept – those who lived more than 10-15 miles away, too far to walk to school and back home every day.

All the children were having lunch outside – boys and girls apart – sitting on the floor around a few big communal cauldrons. The parents of the boarders had to provide the food and a few sturdy mothers took turns to cook the meals. There was no cutlery. The children simply dipped a hand into the cauldron and drew it up full of steaming millet porridge; then they stuck the hand into a smaller pot filled with a green slimy substance, which turned out to be a sauce of baobab leaves. Next they shoved the lot into their mouths, licked their fingers clean and started all over again with great gusto till the cauldron was empty. I found the smell sickening but the children seemed to enjoy their food, which was lucky since they had millet porridge for breakfast, millet porridge for lunch and millet porridge for supper. The only variation was the sauce, which was nearly always made with green onions.

Those who lived very far away only went home for a week at Christmas and Easter, and for longer during the summer holidays. We made friends with a boy, Sanélou, who lived no less than 60 miles from the school. When he went home, all those living in the same direction would set off together on foot and walk day and night. The group would gradually thin out as some of the boys and girls split off to their own villages. After two days, Sanélou would finally arrive home with a few remaining children, spend some happy days with his family and then had to return to Bandiagara. That was the price to be paid for the chance of being able to go to school. Parents contributed food and also some money, and as they were poor they often only sent their brightest child to school – usually a boy. Nobody was spoiled here and nobody complained. Going to school was a privilege, not the compulsory affair it has become in the West.

We wanted to visit Sanélou's village and asked if we could drive him there on Saturday morning.

'No problem,' replied Brother Henri, 'as long as you bring him back by Sunday evening at the latest.'

We set off and drove for a while along green onion fields, which the farmers irrigated by hand. They filled big calabashes with water from a nearby stream, walked with these on their shoulders to their plot and then sprinkled the water over their crops, repeating the process all day long. After a while, we left the onion fields behind and soon found that the further we went, the more impossible the track became. It was fine for walking, but driving was a different matter. Sometimes the track disappeared completely and we simply had to carry on through the bush or over a rocky expanse. But there was a positive side to all this: access by car was so difficult that no tourists ever came here.

The people in Sanélou's village were astonished to see the boy; they hadn't expected him for another two months. They were even more surprised to see foreigners arrive and led us in a procession to Sanélou's parents. Their house consisted of a single space that seemed to be a combination of living room, dormitory, kitchen, goat shed and chicken coop. The father, a hunter, wore a typical peaked Dogon cap and carried an impressive, old-fashioned rifle. We found the mother, who was pregnant with her fourth child, bent over a log fire. Fate condemned her, like most African women, to work in the fields, fetch water, prepare meals, bear children and take care of them. When she turned to welcome us we saw that her teeth were filed into sharp points – a sign of beauty here, but it gave her a rather diabolical air.

The villagers were very poor, yet they were extremely welcoming, and Sanélou was beaming with pride as he took us along narrow alleyways between small houses and granaries. Women were pounding millet in front of their homes and young boys stared at us in surprise as if we had come from another planet. Many were scantily dressed and suffered from kwashiorkor – inflated tummies due to protein deficiency – a sorry sight.

Sanélou wanted to show us his father's granary. He climbed up a typical Dogon ladder made of a single log, which had deep notches cut down its length to form steps, opened the door and before our astonished eyes he disappeared head first into the granary. I was about to rescue him when suddenly his smiling face reappeared in the narrow opening.

We were struck by the beauty of the few remaining authentic granary doors. They were real works of art, finely sculptured in great detail and covered with mythical figures. There was a carved lizard on some of the wooden locks – a special Dogon symbol.

As we looked out over the village, numerous granaries like the one Sanélou had shown us dominated the skyline; they looked like a collection of mediaeval watchtowers. The mud and stone houses were small, some were square and others perfectly round. And the cliff wall behind, in which the dead were buried in holes dug out by millions of years of erosion, was shimmering in the heat. We were sad to leave this fairy tale world.

We went to say goodbye to Brother Henri on Monday morning and were ready to drive off when he held us back. 'There's something I must warn you about,' he said. 'A few weeks ago I was drinking a pint of beer in town when several policemen came along and ordered me to open my bag. I couldn't understand why and protested that I had nothing to hide, but I had to open it all the same. Then they turned to an African who was sitting next to me. I had been talking to him and he seemed quite an ordinary fellow, but when he opened his bag there was a woman's head inside!'

Apparently, every seventh year, the corpses of big chiefs were dug up and buried again on a bed of women's heads. Lighter-skinned women were preferred. A man would come along on a bicycle and when he found a suitable young woman alone in a field, he would pretend there was a problem with one of the tyres and ask the woman to have a look at it. Then, as she bent down, he would swing his machete and chop her head off.

'It's the seventh year,' continued Brother Henri. 'The year of the head cutters. Be wary of men on a bicycle who carry a machete!'

The story made a great impression on Claire. She seemed very agitated and kept talking about it as we drove off. 'They shouldn't be cutting women's heads!' I heard her mutter. 'That shouldn't be allowed. It's highly illegal!'

We had left the main road an hour or so before sunset and had just begun to set up camp in the bush, when an African appeared on a bicycle. He stopped some fifty yards away, got hold of his machete and went towards a low tree. The machete made a ringing sound as it cut into the tree and a branch broke with a sharp snap.

'A head cutter!' exclaimed Claire, panicking. 'I'm not going to stay here.'

We packed up and set off. Within half an hour we reached the main north-south trunk road, which was asphalted all the way to the capital, and turned southwards. It was almost dark by the time we finally found a place where it was easy to leave the road: there was a narrow track which led into a small wood some hundred yards away.

'At least we're safe here,' I said.

We unpacked again, ate and were just ready to turn in when we heard a 'Tcheep! Tcheep!' sound. To our utter amazement, a man on a bicycle came pedalling along between the trees and passed by in the darkness within a few feet of the Land Rover!

This really upset Claire. 'I don't want to end up with my head chopped off!' she exclaimed, her eyes wide with fear. It was 8.00 p.m. by now but she immediately made me get behind the wheel and start up; there was no way she was going to stay in this spot after seeing that man on a bicycle. 'We must get as far away from that head cutter as possible,' she said firmly.

So we set off again in the pitch dark, Claire in her light-blue nightdress and I in pyjamas. There was no moon, no light at all, except for the long beam of our headlights. We had already travelled a considerable distance when the engine began to cough and then stalled.

'What is it?' Claire asked anxiously.

I grunted. 'It's surely another airlock.' I got out, opened the bonnet, bled the fuel system and pressed the starter, but nothing happened. I tried again but the engine stubbornly refused to start. There was nothing I was able to do about it and after a while I gave up. 'Of all the places to break down,' I groaned. We had entered a kind of valley, the road surface had been raised and ran well above the land around and the unmade edge along the tarmac was no more than a foot wide!

Claire wanted to go to sleep right there, but I refused. 'We can't stay here,' I objected.

'Why? There's no traffic.'

'There's very little traffic, but this is the main north-south trunk road and lorries use it.'

'At this time of the night?'

'Certainly. And African drivers have a reputation of not paying much attention at night. They're sure to bang straight into us and knock us off the road. We'll just have to push until we come to the end of this raised part.'

'All right,' sighed Claire, seeming resigned.

We put our shoulders against the Land Rover, me on the driver's side with the door open to control the steering wheel and Claire behind in her long nightdress. It was hard work and we had been pushing for a while, advancing slowly, when I heard Claire complain, 'I'm fed up. First those head cutters and now this! You do what you like, but I'm tired and I'm going to sleep.' By the time I had walked round she had opened the back compartment and I saw her disappear inside! Whether I liked it or not, I had to carry on alone.

I finally came to a part where the unmade side was somewhat wider and managed to put the two outer wheels on the very edge. This still left the two inner wheels on the tarmac, but I was exhausted by now and turned in.

Claire slept like a log through the night but I was unable to close an eye. I kept straining my ears, waiting for the sound of an approaching lorry, worrying myself to death. Every hour or so, when I heard a heavy lorry come rumbling along, I feared that this time we were going to get it. I was lying there, sweating, my nerves tense as the sound grew louder, but each time the lorry seemed to swerve in the last split second and miss us by a couple of inches, leaving the Land Rover shaking. We seemed to be lucky. Was it the elevation of the road that made the drivers look out more carefully?

It was nearly daybreak when I finally dozed off. Minutes later, I was woken up by singing: a group of Africans, mostly women, were going to the market of a small town 10 miles further on, carrying large baskets on their heads; one man was even pushing a bicycle on which a sheep was tied. They greeted us cheerfully and then carried on at a good pace. It is a scene you can see all over Africa: women carrying goods to a market. They get up very early to reach the market place in plenty of time and there they will sit patiently all day long with their goods spread out in front of them, waiting for customers. Then they will walk back home before darkness sets in.

During breakfast, I was pondering how we would ever be able to start the engine.

'Why don't you try to bleed the fuel circuit again,' suggested Claire. 'Maybe it'll start this time.'

'I tried all that last night,' I protested, feeling tired and utterly dispirited. 'If it didn't start then, why would it now?'

'You never know.' Claire smiled encouragingly. 'Just give it one more try?'

I did and to my utter surprise the engine started without the slightest hesitation. 'Damned engine!' I fumed. 'Why does it start now? Had it started last night it would have saved us all this trouble!'

'There's probably a reason for it,' said Claire enigmatically.

As we drove off, we came to the end of the elevated part of the road and a little further on, a wide track split off. Had the engine not stalled, we would certainly have left the road there and followed that track into the bush. To our horror, we saw that there had been a fire: as far as the eye could see, the earth was black and still smouldering. Had we camped out there, we would have been burnt to death during the night!

Claire drew in her breath when she saw the scorched earth and charred trees. 'So that's why our engine wouldn't start,' she murmured, nodding to herself. Then she turned to me. 'Maybe you'll believe me now when I say that we're protected?'

Later in the day, I disconnected the extra fuel tanks, suspecting the connections Bernard had installed to be the cause of our trouble, but there was a downside. There was still a lot of fuel left in the extra tanks and only one way to empty them: I would have to siphon the fuel out and that wasn't a pleasant task.

Bernard had explained the theory of siphoning and it sounded easy. First you prepare a jerry can into which you are going to transfer the fuel. Then you stick a flexible tube into the tank, put the other end into your mouth and lie down on your back so as to be lower than the tank. You breathe out till your lungs are empty, start sucking with all your might and when you can suck no longer you pinch the tube at your mouth. You have now begun to lift the fuel out of the tank, but you will have to repeat the process till the fuel reaches your mouth. The art of siphoning consists in pinching the tube just before the diesel fuel flows into your mouth. At that point, you transfer the end of the tube from your mouth into the waiting jerry can, unclench your fingers and the fuel will then flow into it. You wait for the can to fill up, pull the flexible tube out of the tank and, hey presto, the job is finished.

I must admit, though, that I never mastered the art of siphoning. Time and again, I received a mouthwash of fuel before I managed to pinch the tube and stop the flow and most of the time I even swallowed the foul stuff. I can testify that diesel fuel has an awful taste and that it doesn't digest easily. After I had swallowed some, I would burp for a day or two and each time this would bring back the ghastly taste. Still, I was soon about to witness worse than swallowing diesel fuel.

Ségou

When we got to Ségou, we found a garage and I thought I might as well have the oil changed after the gruelling sandy conditions of the Sahara and northern Mali. Changing the engine oil was straight-forward. The technician just had to unscrew the oil drain plug underneath the sump (the one we had lost on the road to Timimoun) and let the used oil run out. Changing the gearbox oil, however, was a different matter; it meant siphoning out the heavy oil. So I showed the African garage assistant how to do it and told him that, the moment the oil came, he had to let it run away. He seemed to understand and I left him to it and climbed onto the roof rack to get some spare gearbox oil.

When I came down, I had a shock. I found the African lying flat on his back with the end of the tube stuck in his mouth, swallowing the heavy oil as it came out!

'Stop!' I shouted, pulling the tube out of his mouth.

The man sat up, wondering what he had done wrong as I flared up.

'You shouldn't have swallowed the oil. It's horrible!'

'Oh,' he replied, looking surprised. 'No problem. Tastes good.'

Good Lord, I thought. I hope he's got an iron stomach.

We liked Ségou, a pleasant town along the River Niger. Children were running about naked, small wooden boats were being punted quietly past and no one appeared to have a care in the world. We met Amadou, a young boy, and he offered to be our guide. He took us to the river and called out to a man who was sitting there in his dugout – a hollowed-out tree trunk. We all got inside and set off for some islands and to what they called 'the floating gardens'. Although we slid gracefully over the calm surface of the river, there was a problem: water kept seeping in through cracks in the wood of the dugout and Amadou took upon himself the task of scooping it out with a calabash.

We passed another dugout with a man who was in the process of making tea and struck up a conversation while he carried on with what he was doing. He washed his teapot, filled it up with water from the river and put it on a small charcoal fire inside his dugout. When the water came to the boil, he added tea and sugar, and when all was ready he poured the tea into a couple of glasses and held one out to me. I politely declined, having noticed a number of unidentified objects floating in the river, and having seen people washing at the river's edge and even crouching down to relieve themselves.

After our trip on the river, Amadou took us to meet his family. We walked through a brightly coloured doorway to emerge into a large inner courtyard, which was surrounded on all sides by low adobe houses. Many of these seemed to be used just for sleeping; they had wooden doors and a small opening for a window.

Amadou fascinated me from the start. He had a beautifully shaped head with fine features; it made me think of some of the heads depicted in ancient Egyptian tombs. He also had an innate air of nobility: his gestures were delicate and he walked with the lightness of a gazelle.

There was a lot of laughter when Amadou showed us the cooking pots where the women prepared their food. In no time, I was surrounded by numerous children with their huge velvety eyes and shy smiles. One small girl put her rough hand gently into mine; she reminded me of a little wild animal, timid and wary, yet curious and friendly.

By now the whole family had turned out to meet us and we were led towards Amadou's oldest uncle who seemed to be the head of the extended family. He was dressed in a magnificent pink *boubou* and was reclining in a wicker chair right in the centre of the group, radiating authority. He motioned to us to sit in front of him where two wooden stools had been placed, and after a few introductory questions, he started on the serious business of describing all the different ills he was suffering from. An extraordinary variety of aches and pains came to light. He particularly complained about pains in the abdomen; these seemed to me to be related to what he ate and drank and he admitted that, some time ago, he had been to see a doctor who had forbidden him to drink the water from the river. He had stopped for a while, but his mother had kept harassing him for not respecting tradition and finally, he had given in and was now drinking river water again. Unfortunately all the symptoms had come back. He ended by saying how much he appreciated our visit and told us that he was sure we would be able to give him medicine that would help him to get rid of all the pains he suffered from.

After we had given the uncle some medicine and advised him not to drink water from the river, I asked Amadou whether he would take us to his grandmother so that we could talk to her.

'I don't know whether she'll want to see you,' he replied. He hesitated for a while and then said, 'There is one thing I must tell you. She's a leper. Don't be shocked,' he added when he noticed Peter's instinctive withdrawal. 'She lives in that corner room over there, apart from the others. I take her food every day. She wants to die among us.'

A great sadness came over me when we left. How brave they were to keep looking after someone dear, afflicted by such a terrible illness. Yet there seemed to be no sadness in the house, only a feeling of happiness and lightness.

The vast majority of Africans are farmers or artisans, simple folk scratching out an unambitious existence for little reward. They lead an uncomplaining life, especially in those parts of Africa where modern ways of living have so far made little impact.

Projects, I thought, should concentrate on these people. I was therefore extremely pleased when I heard about such a project not far from Ségou: a non-governmental organisation was installing small windmills to pump water out of the ground to irrigate individual plots. The organisation drilled the hole and put in the pipes but each farmer had to pay for his own windmill. Windmills were made locally and didn't cost much by European standards but even so, they represented a considerable investment for an African farmer. The idea was that, having to pay for the windmill, the farmer would value it as a prized possession and take care of everything once it was installed. Here was a project to my liking! This was what we had come to Africa for: to learn about micro-projects and show people back in Europe what needed to be done.

We were put in touch with a farmer who had just installed one of those small windmills, and we accompanied the man to his plot. It was the first time we were going to film and we were very excited about it. At last, I thought, as I lifted the 16mm movie camera out of its metal box, fitted it onto the tripod, connected the battery, loaded a reel and measured the light while Claire got ready with the sound recorder.

The farmer was a dear old man, dressed for the occasion in his best blue robes, his white beard trimmed into a point. He was obviously not used to modern technology and things like a sound recorder and a movie camera must have looked like magic to him. Still, he was willing to be the spokesman for those of his people who had been brave enough to install a windmill, and he came prepared: he had his grandson of twelve with him. The young boy went to the mission school, spoke some French and was beaming with pride at the idea that he was going to be his grandfather's interpreter. The old man, too, was visibly proud of his bright grandson. He put his hand protectively on the boy's shoulder to give him courage for this most important task: an interview with what he was convinced was a film crew sent by the European organisation that sponsored the windmill project!

I explained the whole procedure to the grandson who next translated to his grandfather at length and with lots of gestures, whatever his limited French had allowed him to grasp. The boy obviously possessed more goodwill than French vocabulary and for the sake of the movie sequence, which could not run into many minutes, I repeated everything again before starting.

Finally all was ready. I had framed the old man nicely with the windmill in the background while Claire, who was crouching as low as possible at the man's feet, holding up the microphone, was just out of the picture. I stuck up my thumb and Claire asked the first question: how had the old man heard about the project and why had he decided to buy a windmill for pumping water into his patch of vegetables? The boy, who was standing next to me, translated this to his grandfather and as the old man began to talk, I started filming.

Within seconds I noticed that something was wrong. Through the viewfinder I saw the old man bending over to where Claire was crouching and he was talking to her! This was no good.

'Stop!' I yelled.

I instructed Claire to move away to a low bush on the right and hide in there. Then I told the boy that his grandfather was to look at the camera when he answered the questions and not at Claire. There was another long translation accompanied by gesturing and then we started all over again. I held my breath as the old man began to talk. He faced the camera as he had been told but then he hesitated, glanced over his shoulder at Claire – after all, she was the one who had asked the question – looked at the camera again and finally turned resolutely sideways, bent down towards the bush in which Claire was hiding and began a long story in which the word *yoyoyen* figured frequently.

At this point I gave up. Still, the old man was convinced that he had done well. He was beaming with pride and I thought it best not to make any comments. I did want to know, though, what *yoyoyen* meant and asked the boy. '*Eolienne,*' he said (windmill in French).

It was too late to drive out of town and we decided to go to a small hotel. We soon found out that it wasn't an ideal choice. Africans were talking late into the night and when they had finally quietened down and I had fallen asleep, I was woken up by an unwelcome visit. Something was crawling over my face! As I sat up, I heard a scratching sound as though many minute beings were scurrying around and when I stepped out of bed to switch on the light, I crunched something under my bare foot. I flipped the switch and as my eyes became adjusted to the light, I saw to my horror that the floor was covered with cockroaches. They scuttled away in panic; there was a great rush towards the shower and a real traffic jam as they all tried to disappear simultaneously into the hole in the middle of the cement shower tub.

Bamako

At last we reached Bamako, capital of Mali. A project leader further north had given us the address of a middle-aged French couple, and when we got to their house, they generously invited us to stay with them. They gave us a small, quiet bedroom in which to rest, a real luxury after life in the bush. We even had a separate bathroom without cockroaches! And we were served the kind of breakfasts whose existence we had forgotten: delicious, freshly baked bread, butter and jam, and fried eggs!

We began washing our clothes, cleaned out the Land Rover and then just rested for a day or two, enjoying the hospitality we were so generously offered. When we were ready to face the world again, our first call was to the anthropological museum, which Claire was very keen on visiting. To our regret, we were not allowed in. They told us that the museum was in the process of being renovated, though no traces of building or transformation were visible from the outside. When we asked whether it might be possible to see a small part of the collection anyway, they said, 'No, impossible.' It appeared that the collection had been stored away 'somewhere in the countryside' for the duration of the works.

When Claire told our French host of her disappointment later that evening, he shrugged. 'So it's in the countryside, they say? I wouldn't be so sure. A few weeks ago I was walking through a street not far from the museum when an African man came running towards me. "Please, please, buy," he implored, holding up an antique wooden statue he was carrying.'

'And did you buy it?' enquired Claire.

'Not me!' protested the man. 'I don't want to be mixed up with that kind of business. Life is good here, but you've got to keep within certain boundaries.'

'What exactly do you mean by "boundaries"?' I wanted to know. Our host was an engineer who had worked in Mali for many years and I was eager to learn from his experience.

'Well …' he began, 'you have to keep on good terms with the authorities. This means in particular that you should avoid getting mixed up with politics. And you must never criticise anything … not even if the lights fail,' he added half-jokingly.

'Does that often happen?'

'Well, at the moment, everything is fine because we've got a brand new power station, but while they were building it we had to live with the old one and that was a different matter. There were constant blackouts and everyone just hoped that the old station would last till the new one was completed. Then, one evening, there was a series of terrible bangs and all the lights went out: the generators of the old power station had exploded and some bits and pieces had literally shot through the roof. After that the town was in total darkness at night for a couple of months, until the new power station was up and running.'

'How could the generators have exploded?'

'You want to know?' Our host laughed derisively. 'It turned out that the African technicians responsible for the upkeep hadn't changed the engine oil for ages, as they were going to have a new station anyway. They'd sold all the fresh oil supplies on the black market hoping they wouldn't be found out!'

Theft was a fact of life here. This was the reason why expatriates employed guards to watch over their properties, especially at night. Our French hosts had a guard who spent the nights posted in front of the gate to their compound. I wondered how effective he was, though, because one night when we had been out dining, we found him fast asleep in front of the open gate when we returned home. We had to step over him to get in and he didn't even move!

When we had to park in town we were always preoccupied with the security of our Land Rover and its – for us – priceless contents, but finding guards was no problem: the moment we stopped anywhere, young boys would come running towards us offering their services. Sometimes there were several rival gangs and they would almost come to blows over the privilege of guarding the vehicle.

We always picked the fiercest-looking youth who, after being selected for the job, sat on the bonnet while his helpers positioned themselves along the sides and rear. When we returned an hour or two later, they expected compensation of course and we paid more to the boss and somewhat less to each of his helpers. It wasn't much and we were glad to contribute what we could to give them something to do and provide a little pocket money.

Now that we were in the capital of Mali, I hoped to be able to check the ideas, which I had so enthusiastically propounded before setting off from Europe, by talking to officials in responsible positions. However, it was disappointing to find out that the few I was able to meet seemed unwilling to answer straight questions. One such official didn't even attempt to reply when I asked him what he thought needed to be done. Straightaway he started a tirade against colonialism, staring accusingly at me as if I were the cause of all the wrongs that had befallen Africa.

It was clear that colonial occupation had left a lot of frustration and there were obvious reasons for it: in the late nineteenth and early twentieth centuries, Europeans went to Africa to plant the flag – they did not go to study local customs. In those days, Africans were considered 'inferior' races whose 'savage' practices had to be eradicated as soon as possible. And indeed, one of the main aims of colonisation – apart from exploiting Africa's wealth – had been the replacement of animistic beliefs and customs with the 'shining lights' of European civilization.

But not everything had been bad, I thought. The colonial era had also brought schools and health care, peace, law and order. And the Europeans had built infrastructure and begun modern economic development.

I diplomatically tried to tell the official that nothing had ever been perfect in history and anyway, colonialism and all its alleged misdeeds had ended more than twenty years ago, so why not turn the page and concentrate on solving today's problems?

'Which problems?' sneered the government official. 'You, Europeans, are always talking about *our problems* and telling us what to do. Why can't you leave us alone?' Then, after another virulent attack on European meddling, he began to criticise Europeans for their stinginess – their unwillingness to give enough aid and help Africans out!

As we drove away from the office of the government official and turned into a side street, we were stopped by a policeman. He'd been looking around vacuously but when he saw the Land Rover he shot into action. He rushed towards the middle of the street, raised his arm and blew his whistle sharply.

I got out. 'Anything the matter?' I asked nervously.

'Yes,' he replied with a wide grin. 'You didn't signal your intention to turn left.'

'But I did!' I protested. 'Look, the indicator is on.'

'Then it doesn't work,' he stated flatly.

I was unwilling to believe that. I told him it had been working perfectly up till now and went to check the left front indicator. The man was right!

'See,' said the policeman triumphantly. 'You have broken the law! This is going to cost you a lot of money.'

I stood there shaking my head in disbelief. Finally I muttered, 'How much?'

'Well,' replied the man, 'that depends. If you pay the fine directly to me it will be …' he reflected for a while, sizing me up, '… it will be 10,000 Malian francs.' (About £9.00 or the monthly income of a Malian in 1982).

'But that's outrageous!'

'As you wish,' said the policeman with a broad smile. 'If you don't want to settle directly I shall have to take you to headquarters where your vehicle will be impounded. And I can guarantee that you will end up paying much more.'

I reluctantly dug up a 10,000-franc banknote and handed it over. The policeman seemed very pleased, walked up to the front of the Land Rover and gave the left wing a good thump after which the indicator suddenly began to function. 'There,' he said as if he had performed an act of magic. 'I have fixed your problem. And you don't even have to pay me extra.' Whereupon he put the banknote in his pocket and went away cheerfully, looking like someone intending to give himself a day off.

> We spent an evening with our French hosts and some of their friends dining in an exotic restaurant full of brilliant, lush flowers. As we all squeezed in around small tables under a raffia awning, little lights above us were twinkling like stars. A fountain gave a feeling of freshness, the mood was cheerful and we chatted and laughed, listening to enchanting Malian music. But leaving our Land Rover out in the dark was risky. Returning to the vehicle we found that someone had broken off the handle at the back in an attempt to get inside. Yet it had been parked within sight, no more than 20 feet away from where we were dining!
>
> As we drove back from the restaurant, we noticed mats and covers in front of the houses and bumps underneath the covers. People were sleeping outside on the pavements to escape the furnace-like heat under the corrugated roofs inside!

As our hosts had to go away for a while, we went to stay with Richard, a French Canadian we had met, his wife and his two stepdaughters. Not far from where he lived, a vast area was stacked with the wrecks of discarded cars and young men were busy recycling these. Some were cutting up the carcasses and hammering them into flat sheets; others were welding the sheets together to produce strong travel trunks, which were then passed on to painters who decorated them in bright colours, making them look very attractive.

Although there were all sorts of activities going on in town, the sweltering heat of Bamako did not induce people to do more than necessary. They slept in the shade outside their shops when there were no customers, and work stopped altogether the moment it became too hot. And men didn't exert themselves if they could leave the work to their women. This could take unusual forms. One day, passing along the River Niger, we saw lots of women standing up to their ankles in the water while a few men were just hanging about, watching over them. The women were scooping up mud with their calabashes and then examining the contents carefully. It was a weird sight and we asked Richard what they were doing.

'Oh,' he replied, 'they're looking for gold nuggets.'

'For gold? In the water?'

'Well, you see, there were rumours that someone found gold in the Niger. So the men immediately sent the women to search in the mud.'

'But that's ludicrous!'

'Maybe ...' replied Richard with an even expression, 'but hope springs eternal. It's no good intervening. They will eventually find out.'

The 'gold-digging' went on for about a week. By then it was clear that there was no gold and the men gradually withdrew their women, putting them, I suppose, to more useful tasks.

I had been talking with the African woman who helped in Richard's house, we had become friends and she had begun confiding in me. One day she told me about a witchdoctor who was said to have the power to heal illnesses, even at a distance. He had arrived some days ago and people were very excited, visiting him in secret. The next morning, I quietly slipped out and went to the poorer part of the town near the river where he was said to reside. When I got there a woman pointed to a low house. 'Very good doctor,' she nodded. 'Give very good charm for protection.'

I felt exhilarated, yet afraid as I went through the door. Then, as my eyes got used to the dim light, I noticed the witchdoctor in a dark corner. His shrivelled and bony nakedness was covered in a grey blanket; long earrings hung from his earlobes and several ornaments and charms from his neck. He was sitting on a low stool, as impassive as a statue but his piercing eyes were staring at me with bloodshot fixedness.

'What you come for?' he asked abruptly.

'For a charm,' I managed to whisper. My throat was dry.

He made a brusque gesture towards a low African stool. As I sat down, I thought how mad I was to believe in occult powers, but I wanted to help one of my friends in Belgium who was seriously ill. So, gathering up courage, I said, 'Please make me a charm to cure a young woman of the illness that inhabits her.'

'She has child?' he asked.

'Yes, one daughter.'

He picked up some herbs from a bag that was lying next to him and sat there for a long time, muttering incantations. Then he pushed the herbs inside a small leather pendant and handed it to me. 'This drive away evil spirit.'

I was to put my hand on it every day, wish my friend to be better and after a while, the power of the charm would cure her.

I paid and was about to leave the gloomy room when I saw a tall Peul waiting for his turn outside. A broad friendly smile lit up his face as I greeted him and he allowed me to take a photograph before he disappeared into the dark room.

As I emerged into the brilliant sunshine, the world outside seemed so normal, so familiar that I was almost ashamed I could ever have dreamed of invoking the help of witchcraft. Could this be real? Yet when I walked away I was pervaded by the strange certainty that, surely, there must be many more things between heaven and earth than our eyes can see.

One morning, we heard shrieks near the house and were astounded to see two beautifully dressed young women shouting insults at each other from the opposite sides of the street. By the time people came running along to see what was going on, one of the women had crossed over and begun to hit the other. Soon a circle formed around them. The women were at each other's throats by now, pulling each other's hair out, scratching and biting, and finally rolling about in the dirt trying to tear their opponent's dress.

As no one intervened, Claire turned to Richard who was standing next to her.

'Can't someone do something?' she implored.

'No,' replied Richard. 'If you try to separate them they'll turn on you. Better to leave them.'

Later Claire asked the African woman who helped in the house why the women had been fighting.

'Oh! Jealousy,' she answered, as if this were the most natural thing in the world.

When Claire stared at her in disbelief, the African woman assured her that women would fight over the favours of a man.

'Let me explain,' intervened Richard. 'You see, if a man rises to an important position over here he takes a mistress. He will keep it quiet and tell his wife and his colleagues that he has to go to an office in town to justify his absence from home or from work. And the more powerful he becomes, the more "offices" he will visit: he will have a second and then a third "office". He will of course try to keep his "offices" separated, because you see what happens when they find out and meet in the street!'

It was Sunday and we were spending the day with Richard and his family when our host, who was a musician, said, 'I know of a village not too far away where they often play music. Shall we go and have a look?'

I was sitting happily talking to one of his stepdaughters, who was explaining about her work in a local orphanage, while Peter had just picked a ripe papaya from a tree in the garden and was devouring it with an expression of utter bliss on his face. It seemed a shame to interrupt such an idyllic scene. 'I'm not sure,' I said evasively.

'Oh, but you'll like it,' said Richard. 'It's authentic Bambara music.' And he kept insisting till we finally gave in.

To reach the village we had to cross the interminably long bridge that straddled the River Niger, and we had got only halfway across when the Land Rover's engine abruptly stalled. However much Peter tried, it refused to budge and he became extremely nervous. This was the only bridge over the Niger for hundreds of miles around and it was considered a strategic military target. Police usually patrolled it and would immediately arrest anyone who stopped on it or even tried to photograph it. Luckily for us, it was Sunday, there was little traffic and for once there wasn't a policeman in sight. Still, it was imperative to clear the bridge as rapidly as possible. Richard obligingly took the steering wheel while Peter put his shoulder behind the back of the Land Rover and I helped him as much as I could to push the three tons of metal and baggage. By the time we reached the end of the bridge, Peter was sweating profusely and was so out of breath that he couldn't speak for a while. Then, as he recovered, he stood there, looking at the vehicle with a face like thunder.

'Maybe it's another airlock,' I ventured hesitantly.

'Couldn't be!' he retorted. 'This must be a really big problem!'

'Why don't you give it a try, anyway?'

Peter shook his head but said, 'Well … just to please you.' He opened the bonnet and began bleeding the fuel circuit and, miracle, the capricious Land Rover started at once as if nothing had happened!

When we finally got to the village, we noticed a small crowd surrounding a few musicians sitting on low stools in the shade of a tree. I recognised some of the African instruments: one was a kora (a small, harp-like, stringed instrument) and another one a balaphone (a type of xylophone on which sound is produced by striking the tuned keys with two padded sticks).

We sat down in the sand amongst the Africans and listened, spellbound. We had never heard anything like it. This was totally different from the music produced for quick commercial consumption that we were used to in our 'civilised' world. The musicians seemed to be simply playing for their own enjoyment. One would lead with a few notes, another one would take up the melody and add some improvisations of his own and as the others joined in, the music would be flowing back and forth between them, blending together and growing in strength. Once the rhythm had taken on a life of its own, they would carry on, adding ever more variations to the melody they had created. Then, suddenly, one of the men would begin to sing, his voice melodious, light-hearted. This was music straight from the heart of Africa, as much part of it as the sun-drenched surroundings, the little villages, the dirt roads, the vast space and the endless repetition of work in the fields. It was in harmony with all that existed, the incarnation of life itself, an infinite variation of a melody according to the personality and momentary mood of the musicians. It was age-old, yet new, a creation every time a musician picked up his instrument. It was melodious, joyful and playful, like sparkling water bubbling from a spring, enveloping the soul with lightness and charm. It was the essence of Africa.

France, one of Richard's attractive stepdaughters, had a suitor, a young Libyan who worked for his country's embassy. The man appeared to be smitten by the young girl's dark, wavy hair, her grey-blue eyes, her mysterious smile and her shapely body, which moved voluptuously under the light dresses she wore. He was to be found around the house every time he managed to take time off, and that seemed quite often. Richard appeared rather pleased and received him with open arms: the young man was of a well-to-do family and had a first-class job. France, however, was not so keen. The Libyan was good-looking, but she confided to Claire that she thought his outlook on the world too different from hers. 'Marrying him,' she told Claire, 'would be like living in a prison.' She said she would never be able to adapt and accompany him to Libya.

The girl's reticence didn't discourage her suitor. He continued to woo her assiduously and to bring her presents, even though she had taken to withdrawing to her room whenever he appeared. France's mother didn't know what to do with him after having poured him several cups of tea and was all too happy to push him on to me. When he heard that I was interested in development, he immediately brightened up.

'Libya is a wonderful country,' he said. 'Its government is fully democratic and only concerned with improving the quality of life of its people. And its society is extremely progressive: there is total equality and everyone's rights are respected. What's more, the country has the best leader in the whole world! This is where you ought to go to study development.'

When I didn't seem to show the expected enthusiasm he insisted, 'Libya points the way forward to the future!'

Finally I told the young man diplomatically that I had an itinerary to keep to and couldn't possibly turn back north. He was disappointed but didn't give up. He had a solution! 'If I couldn't go to Libya,' he said, 'I must read Gaddafi's green book.' And the next day he brought me several copies, one for me, and others to distribute during my journey.

It was not the usual kind of book. Inside a green plastic cover, closed by a clasp, were two cassette tapes (green of course) on which the voice of Gaddafi could be heard in Arabic, two minuscule green booklets giving the French translation of the tapes and, to complete everything, a large photograph of the great leader himself (not green, but in bright colours). Each booklet gave the solution to the problems of, respectively, the economy and society. In a few thousand words, Gaddafi had solved two mind-boggling problems that had occupied the lives of hundreds of thinkers for centuries! I particularly liked the booklet on society. After telling us that democracy was the solution to all social problems, it ended, 'Nevertheless, in practice it is always the strongest one who rules.'

When I thanked the young Libyan for this most generous present, he just shrugged, 'Oh, I only want to help.' He stared hard at me, saying, 'It's all in here,' while tapping the green plastic cover with his forefinger. Then he began reciting the thoughts of the great leader.

As the days passed by, the young man became overbearing. It was no good trying to get away from him; he systematically cornered me and tried to draw me into discussions on politics and the Arab world. In the end it was France who saved me. She'd had enough of the man's attentions and told him that he was wasting his time because she would never marry him.

'That's for your father to decide!' countered the offended Libyan and he stormed off to find Richard and immediately asked him for the hand of his stepdaughter. When Richard called France down and told her that the man had proposed she refused point blank.

'I'm not asking you!' retorted the young man, turning away from France, 'I'm asking for your father's permission!' And he looked hopefully at Richard.

'Well …' said Richard, shrugging his shoulders, 'if France doesn't want to marry you, there's nothing I can do about it.'

'That's unheard of!' blurted out the young Libyan. And he turned and left the house in a huff; they never saw him again.

Through France, Claire met a young Belgian doctor. Claire had always been fascinated by the medical world and when she found out that the doctor worked in Bamako's central hospital, she immediately asked if we could visit him there. The young man had only recently arrived and wasn't sure whether his boss, the head surgeon, would be happy to have visitors, but she waved away his objections.

As we drove towards the hospital the next morning, Claire suddenly remarked, 'Did you see that?'

'Did I see what?'

'That man on a bicycle. His face looked African but he was white and his hair was yellow! Why does he look like that?'

'Oh! That must have been an albino.'

'What's an albino?'

'Well, some Africans are born without any pigmentation. It's a terrible condition because they can't really expose their skin to the sun. They also have very weak eyes.'

Suddenly she turned to me, 'Do you think we look like albinos to Africans? Pallid … with the unnatural whiteness of something that never sees the sun? Like … like maggots?'

'I hope not. But I did read once – I don't remember whether it was a Chinese or an African writing this – that white people smell like corpses.'

'Isn't that a bit far-fetched?'

'I don't know. I suppose that all races have their own smell.'

'Look over there!' exclaimed Claire, changing the subject abruptly. She was pointing at small groups of people sitting in the grass around a large, oblong, two-storey building. When we got closer we noticed that most of these consisted of women crouching around cooking pots stuck on top of improvised log fires; children were swarming around and there were also a few men sitting in the shadow of the sparse trees, gesticulating and talking animatedly. A scent of burning wood pervaded the air and the open space was littered with plastic bags and all sorts of food remains and human waste. We had arrived at the hospital!

Inside we found the young Belgian doctor with the French head surgeon and another young European doctor. It was coffee-break time and after we were introduced, the surgeon kindly offered us a cup of coffee. As we sat down on plastic chairs around a low table, Claire asked what the activities outside the hospital were all about.

'Oh,' replied the surgeon, 'those are the relatives of the patients. They cook food for them. You see, the hospital hasn't got a kitchen.' Then he corrected himself. 'Well, it did have one, but that's all a long time ago.'

'The grounds around didn't look very clean,' remarked Claire.

'They don't,' agreed the French surgeon. Then he sighed, 'To think that this used to be the best hospital in West Africa. And just look what's happened since it was taken over by the local authorities.'

'Are you running things here on your own?' I asked. So far I hadn't seen any African staff.

'Oh no. Quite a large number of Africans are working here.'

'Where are they all, then?'

'There's a meeting of the ruling – and only – party in Bamako today; that's where the director and most of the male nurses are.'

'But what about their duties?'

'I imagine that attending the meeting is more important for their careers than attending to their duties in the hospital,' commented the surgeon dryly.

'But that's awful!' I exclaimed.

'Well … that's the way things are.' The French surgeon sighed again deeply. 'Anyway, we do our best and everything still functions.' Then he added, 'But only just. It's not only absenteeism that's a major problem; the medical equipment we have is inadequate and there's also a shortage of medical supplies. Worse than that, whatever medicine there is has to be locked away or it's gone before you have time to use it.'

The surgeon now got up. 'Sorry to have to interrupt the conversation,' he said, 'but I have to attend to my patients.'

Claire turned to him. 'Could I possibly visit the hospital?' she asked enthusiastically.

'I don't know about that …' The surgeon hesitated for a few seconds but when he saw Claire looking eagerly at him he gave in. 'Why not?' he nodded. 'But I think that you'd better dress as a nurse. And if you expect European conditions you'll be in for a shock.'

And so Claire, dressed as a nurse, accompanied the French surgeon on his round through the wards and she was even allowed to take photographs.

> I followed the surgeon to his office, which he opened with his personal key. Inside there was a rusty chair and a metal table on which his files were piled up, a locked cupboard with his scalpels and other instruments, and shelves stacked with precious medicine, to be used for the worst cases only. He took a few instruments, some bandages, disinfectant and medicine, and after we had gone out again, he locked the door carefully.
>
> I had been looking forward to seeing an African hospital, but as we went through the different wards, I recoiled. The state of the rooms and equipment was appalling; conditions of hygiene were more horrible than anything I had expected and everywhere there was a moist smell of decay. Yet the French surgeon attended to his patients with great gentleness, all the while talking to them and encouraging them. What I thought unbelievable was that the patients, even the ones with terrible wounds or those who had recently been operated on, smiled happily at the surgeon with an expression of complete trust on their faces as he examined them and cleaned their wounds with competent movements of his slender hands.
>
> I felt a terrible sadness at the sight of so much effort to keep up a hospital that was going to waste. The French surgeon was here on a three-year contract and I dared not imagine what would happen after he left. And yet, there was something incredibly uplifting about the courage with which African patients accepted their suffering; they seemed to be able to cope with the most terrible pains. Then I sensed that life here was permeated by a vital force so strong that it would survive the greatest ordeals. And suddenly it came to me that Africa was indestructible.

In a town like Bamako, the expatriate community is a small world and any arrival is news. When we heard that Gerard, someone we knew from Brussels, was in town, we went straight round to see him. He told us that he had driven all the way from Abidjan in the Ivory Coast to bring supplies for a Belgian project in Mali. I was always on the lookout for projects I could film and without a moment's hesitation Gerard rang the project leader's home number. Unfortunately, the man was away and wouldn't be back for several days, but his wife promptly invited us all over for dinner. She lived in a large, walled compound on the outskirts of Bamako and we were wondering how to open the heavy, iron gate when an African guard appeared from the inside, opened it for us and told us to wait on the terrace.

'Madame is getting ready,' he said. 'She will come soon.' Then he disappeared.

Gerard and I walked over to the terrace and stood there chatting, when unexpectedly a fierce-looking cheetah emerged from the house. It eyed us for a second and then advanced towards us making a deep growling sound. We recoiled in fright till we had our backs against the wall and hardly dared breathe while the big cat stood in front of us, snarling.

Just at that moment our hostess came out of the house. 'Oh you've arrived,' she said. 'Welcome, welcome.' Then, as she spotted the cheetah, she beamed. 'I see you've already met my little pet.' When she noticed our terrified expressions, she began to giggle. 'You must excuse him. He's a male and doesn't like unknown men, but don't be afraid; everything will be OK as long as you don't upset him and stay quiet.'

We couldn't possibly have been any quieter than we were, glued to the wall with the cheetah growling menacingly at us no more than three feet away!

Claire had lingered in the garden to admire the lush vegetation and tropical flowers, and when I saw her appear I wanted to shout, 'Careful!' but not a sound came out of my dry mouth. I needn't have worried, though. She was a woman and blonde like our hostess, only more slender. She loved animals and the cheetah went towards her without any hesitation.

'Isn't he sweet?' remarked our hostess affectionately. 'And he's so useful. When I go into town I take him with me in the car and leave him inside while I do my shopping. And I don't have to pay anyone to guard my car because the young boys move over to the other side of the street when they see me arrive! My car and my cheetah are famous all over the town!'

Drinks were brought and as we all sat down, the animal lay at Claire's feet and let her stroke its head. Afterwards I asked her how it had felt.

'Rather rougher than I had imagined,' she said. 'More like a coarse brush than a soft cat's coat.'

There were two big dogs in the compound as well and as they came running through the garden, the cheetah shot forward like an arrow and with a few huge leaps overtook them.

'Isn't he impressive?' remarked his mistress with undisguised pride. 'He's got the freedom of the house and the garden. Isn't that wonderful for him?'

'Yeah,' I wanted to comment, 'maybe for him but not for visitors who come upon him unsuspectingly and nearly have a heart attack.' But I thought better of it.

The manservant now announced that dinner was served. Our hostess whistled and as the cheetah appeared from the garden with a few large bounds, she beckoned, 'Come, Pussy, bedtime,' and led the animal inside.

During dinner, Claire, who was sitting next to our hostess, noticed that her wrists and forearms were covered in scratches and asked her how she had got them.

'Oh these! I often tease Pussy and we play little games. Cheetahs are like cats you see, but unlike cats they cannot retract their claws. So that's how I got them.'

'Where did he come from?' I inquired.

'His mother was killed when he was only a small cub and they gave him to me. I brought him up and now he looks upon me as his mother.'

'I didn't know there were cheetahs in Mali.'

The woman sighed. 'Sadly enough, there are very few wild animals left in the country.'

'What are you planning to do with him when you leave?' Claire wanted to know. On the way to the house, Gerard had explained that his friends would be returning to Belgium in six months' time. 'Are you going to put him back in the bush?'

'That's out of the question!' replied the woman vehemently. 'He'd be killed in no time. Out in the bush they shoot at anything that moves.' She looked up defiantly. 'I'll take him with me to Antwerp. We've got a big apartment and he'll have space to run about there.'

'But how will you get him through customs?'

'Oh, I'll manage. I'll make my husband drill a few holes in the boot of our car and we'll put him in there with some food and drive him to the port of Abidjan in the Ivory Coast. You know the *Compagnie Maritime Belge*? They have a shipping service which runs between Zaire and Antwerp via Abidjan. We'll take the car on board with us, with the cheetah hidden inside.'

I shook my head in disbelief. What a scatterbrained plan, I thought, but I refrained from making any comment. I realised that nothing would make the woman change her mind.

After supper, as we were ready to say goodbye, our hostess disappeared for a moment and when she returned she motioned us to follow her to her bedroom. And there, on the end of a huge double bed, lay the cheetah on its back, its four legs stuck up in the air.

'Doesn't your husband mind him sleeping on the bed?' I asked, astounded.

'Oh no. When he's home, Pussy often sleeps in between us. I guess the poor little thing misses his cheetah family and feels safe with both of us around.'

Lord Almighty, I thought, imagine waking from your sleep wanting to kiss your wife to find you're holding a cheetah in your arms! There can't be much going on between husband and wife with a cheetah in the middle.

Map 2: Mali

Chapter 5: *Gao to Mopti, to Bandiagara and back to Mopti, to Ségou and to Bamako*
Chapter 6: *Bamako to Mopti and Goundam. To Timbuktu and back to Goundam. Return to Bamako via Ségou*

Above: Wherever you stop near towns…

Below: …they surround you…

117

Above: …and look inside the Land Rover

Below: The women delighted in plaiting my hair, which they said was 'the colour of the sun'

Above: On the way to fetch water. Note the goatskin gourds carried by the donkeys

Below: Talking about hairdos in sign language

Above: Meetings along the road

Below: Carrying goods to the market: a perfect balance

Above: Daily maintenance

Below: What! Not again! Rice and sardines…

Above: Claire getting ready for the night

Middle: Morning in Mali

Below: Making semolina pancakes for breakfast

Above: Arriving in Sanélou's village

Below: They follow our every movement

Above: A Dogon living room

Below: Sanélou's mother in her kitchen

Above: Pounding millet

Below: Young boys in Sanélou's village

Above: At Bandiagara mission: Sanélou

Below: Night in the bush

Above: Ségou: tea on the Niger

Below: Ségou: activities along the Niger

Above: Amadou and Peter

Below: Inside Amadou's compound

Above: Maybe there's gold in the river?

Below: Bamako, local activities: the hairdresser asleep, waiting for customers. His specialty: *défrisage* (straighten kinky hair). The text on the wall reads: "Here hairdresser. Master Abou, Doctor in hairstyles, open day and night." Note the drawings showing different hairdos, and also the assortment of electric wires coming out of the box on the wall above the motorbike

Above: A Peul visiting the witchdoctor

Below: Inside Bamako's hospital:
a patient in bed

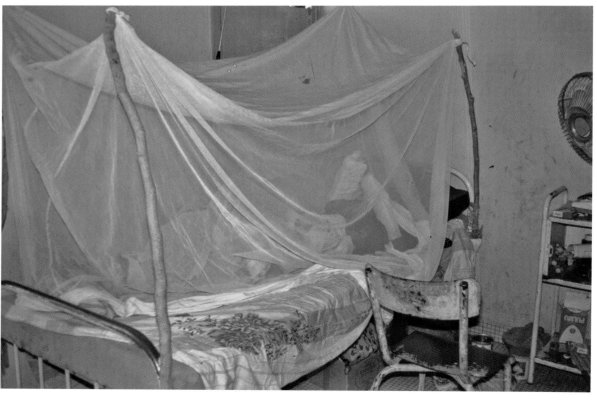

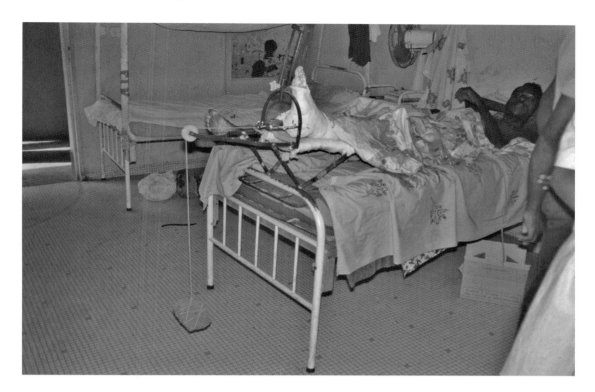

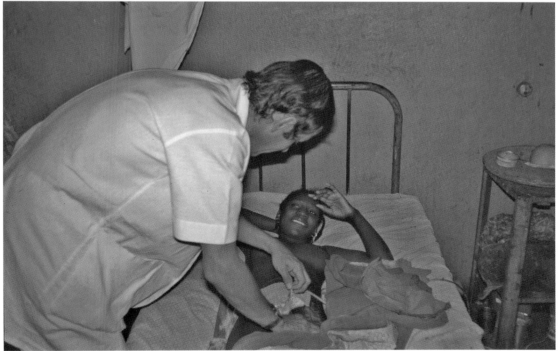

Above: The hospital in Bamako

Below: The French surgeon doing his rounds. Note the happy smile of the patient

Above and *Below:* Claire with the cheetah

CHAPTER 6
Back to Biblical Times

Life is an Eternal Surprise

In the modern world people are accustomed to planning everything, not just their holidays, but even their weekends. I had been no different. I had started this expedition with a strict time schedule: this week we were going to be here, the next week there. But we had stopped off at a number of places in Mali and also stayed much longer in Bamako than intended. We were well behind schedule and I wanted to hurry south to complete our itinerary, but first the Land Rover needed some urgent repairs. The bushes, which connected the leaf springs to the chassis, were worn out. They rattled constantly and it was imperative to replace them before anything broke down. Luckily there was a Land Rover garage in Bamako. When I drove there and began to explain the problem to an African mechanic, he put a finger to his lips.

'Don't come here,' he whispered. 'Much too expensive. Come back tomorrow morning. I wait for you at the corner of the street with my moped and guide you to my own repair garage. Much cheaper.'

I met the man the next day as arranged and followed him through a jumble of streets to where I supposed his garage was situated, but to my surprise he kept going on and led me out of town. Soon we were in open country without any sign of human habitation and still he continued. I was about to give up when, after some 6 or 7 miles, we reached a small hamlet and he drove through a gap in a wall. I followed him, expecting to see a garage, but to my bewilderment there was nothing but an empty compound flanked by a few low mud-and-wattle dwellings.

'Where is your garage?' I asked warily.

He made a sweeping gesture with his arm. 'Here. This is my garage.' He whistled and as a young man stuck his head out of one of the doors he said proudly, 'This is my assistant mechanic.' Next he shouted, 'Fetch the tools!' and after the 'assistant' reappeared with a toolbox, the two men set to their task with a great show of energy.

They had no jack but used mine to crank up the Land Rover. After half an hour it was sitting upon a few sturdy African stools; then they removed the four wheels and proceeded to take off the leaf springs. By the time they had got this far it was already past midday and they stopped when a pretty young woman came out of one of the dwellings carrying bowls filled with steaming rice, one for the mechanic who was her husband and the other for the assistant mechanic who appeared to be her brother. As the mechanic began tucking in, he asked if I wanted something to eat too but I said,

'No, thank you,' explaining that I had my own food in the Land Rover.

Lunch over, the two men hammered the old bushes out of the leaf springs and then the mechanic strode over to me, put his hand into his pocket and drew out eight new bushes as if he were pulling a rabbit out of a hat. I realised at once where he had got them from and why he had wanted me to come to his 'private' garage to do the repairs.

'With these, no problem,' declared the mechanic with a large smile. 'Repair finished in short time.' He went to the set of leaf springs lying nearest and held one of the new bushes against the hole into which it had to go, intending to hammer it in, but there was no need for that: it fell clean through the opening.

'Oh!' exclaimed the man, putting a hand in front of his mouth. 'Wrong size!'

'What a fool I've been to trust that man!' I began scolding myself. Here I was in a compound miles out of Bamako; my Land Rover was standing without wheels or leaf springs on four wooden stools; the old bushes had been damaged while being hammered out and couldn't be put back and the new ones were a size too small! I had no clue where I was, didn't have the slightest idea of a phone number where I could reach Claire and, anyway, the 'garage' had no phone.

'No problem,' said the man soothingly as he sat down, scratching his scalp. 'We find solution.'

He kept on scratching while I was getting more and more anxious. I found it impossible to sit still like the garage man and had to pace up and down to calm my nerves. I had told Claire I would be back within a couple of hours; she knew even less than me about where I was and she would by now be waiting for my return in front of the Hôtel de l'Amitié.

After having scratched his scalp for a long time, I suddenly heard the garage man exclaim, 'Ah! Got it!' He went inside a shed and returned with a number of empty sardine tins, which he began to cut up into strips. I couldn't imagine why he was doing this, but when I saw him wind a strip around one of the bushes and then, with great effort, hammer it into the hole at the end of one of the leaf springs, I couldn't help thinking, how clever! He had made up for the wrong size by adding the thickness of a sardine tin. Next the man and his assistant proceeded to hammer in the seven remaining bushes, each with added strips of sardine tins; then they fixed the four leaf springs onto the chassis, put back the wheels and cranked up each side of the Land Rover in turn to take away the supporting wooden stools. Darkness was setting in by the time the whole operation was finished. It didn't really cost all that much, but I would happily have paid more in a real garage to have avoided the nervous tension I had been through.

The man now guided me back to Bamako on his moped and finally, at around 7.00 p.m., I arrived in front of the Hôtel de l'Amitié where I found Claire in an advanced state of anxiety. She feared that I had been kidnapped and had been trying to drum up support for a rescue operation.

However, there is often a silver lining to a dark cloud, and the upshot was that she had met a French-Swiss couple, Joël and Marianne, who had come to Bamako to buy equipment. When she saw them driving past the front of the hotel, Claire, who was frantic by then, had stopped them and begged them to join in the search, and they were about to set off to look for me. I promptly invited them out for a meal and over dinner we talked about Africa.

They had been here for several years, working on an interesting micro-project: Joël was sinking wells for the Tuaregs in Goundam, a place not far from Timbuktu. When I told him that I had always wanted to visit Timbuktu but that we had been unable to get there and would never see it now, Joël became animated.

'It's never too late for anything,' he said firmly. 'You can see Timbuktu if you come north with us. We live only 60 miles away from it.'

Claire smiled when she heard this. 'I'd be surprised if Peter agrees to that,' she commented.

Indeed, I dismissed the whole idea out of hand. 'We're already way behind schedule,' I objected. 'We'll have to continue south as soon as we can.'

'But it's really worth it,' insisted Joël. 'There are several interesting projects to see and film, and …' he looked at Claire, 'you would also learn a lot about local customs.'

Claire turned towards me. 'Why don't we do it?' There was a shine in her eyes that I knew all too well.

I didn't fancy returning 600 miles to the fringes of the Sahara and tried one last stand. 'But … but our travel schedule. We really have no time.'

'You can easily be back in a week or so,' argued Joël. 'It'll be a great experience, I promise you.' He sounded very convincing.

When Claire in turn put on pressure, saying, 'I'd really like to go …' while looking at me with bright eyes, I gave up. Timbuktu had a mythical reputation and this was indeed an opportunity not to be missed. We had successfully crossed the Sahara and finished with it. And now, to my surprise, I found myself agreeing to return north. This was the first time in my life I had ever turned back on my tracks. It seemed madness, but Claire felt absolutely certain that it was the right thing to do. I didn't know then that we would spend nearly a month in Goundam, that this was to be a turning point in our journey and that it would change my whole outlook on life.

The Road to Goundam

Joël had told me that the trip to Goundam would take two days at most, but his Land Rover was light and speedy whilst ours wasn't; we were much too slow and delayed his progress considerably. After my engine had stalled due to another airlock on the morning of the second day, he decided to go ahead with a Frenchman who had come to Bamako with them to buy a few spare parts for his car, but he left us his wife to guide us and that was lucky. We would never have found our way without her, as there were many forks in the sandy track; much of the time it was even hard to tell the difference between the track and the surrounding landscape. The Tuaregs we met every now and then didn't have any such problems; they knew where to go, as did the Peuls who roam all over the

Sahel in search of pastures for their cattle.

Marianne immediately took command of our small group and when it was her turn to steer, she drove us expertly – if a little recklessly – through the sandy area. Goundam seemed far away though for our hopelessly overburdened Land Rover, and we had to spend the next night in the middle of nowhere.

As we were sitting in the sand eating a frugal supper, Marianne began to talk about her experiences in Africa. It was fascinating. She had accumulated a vast knowledge about the Sahel and its customs. Her alert eyes had taken in everything, but she had done more than just observe: she was a nurse and looked after the local people while trying to change their habits; cleanliness was paramount.

When bedtime came, she told us that she preferred to sleep on the roof rack, just to be sure. 'I don't want to be disturbed by wild animals in the middle of the night,' she explained.

We set off the next morning after a hearty breakfast and were immediately stopped by another airlock, but I managed to start the engine again. The Land Rover seemed to behave after this and I kept my fingers crossed as we progressed slowly through the hilly, difficult terrain, which obliged the driver to switch gears constantly. Then, when we had got to maybe 100 miles from Goundam, disaster struck. We were in a sandy area with dunes left and right, I was driving downhill and tried to switch from second to third gear when I found that I couldn't move the gear stick. The gears were stuck! I felt waves of panic going through my body. There's no way we'll ever make it to Goundam in second gear, I thought, but there was no other option. We had to carry on and I hung onto the steering wheel, my nerves extremely tense.

Every time we went downhill I tried to push the Land Rover as fast as it would go in second gear. The engine made a dreadful noise but I kept stepping on the accelerator all the same. Then, as we went up the slope of the next hill, we would gradually begin to slow down and I prayed that we would make it to the top.

I turned around to Claire, who was lying flat inside the back – Marianne was occupying the other front seat – and said anxiously, 'This is where we need all the protective powers you can muster.'

'Just be trustful,' came a tiny voice from behind. 'It'll be all right.'

I drove up and down the hilly terrain for what seemed interminable hours. Had we got stuck in the sand, or had the engine stalled on an uphill stretch, that would have been the end. We would have been unable to set off again in second gear.

Night fell and still there was no sign of Goundam. Then, by 8.00 p.m., the land levelled off, a few lights shone ahead of us and Marianne heaved a sigh of relief. 'We're there,' she said.

As we drove into the compound where she lived, Joël came running out of the house. He had expected us by early afternoon and as the hours passed by he had become ever more worried. Searching for us at night was impossible but he was going to set off at first light next morning.

Joël and Marianne lived in an adobe house which had a large living-dining room, an adjacent bedroom shut off by a curtain, a small kitchen and an outside shower. And – a great luxury for Africa – there was a spare room with separate outside entrance. During the first week of our stay we had to sleep in our Land Rover though, because the spare room was occupied by the Frenchman who had accompanied Joël and Marianne to Bamako. He had taken part in the Paris-Dakar Rally, his car had broken down and he had ended up here with Joël, who was helping him with the repairs.

The man told us that he and other participants had raced at 70 miles per hour over stony, irregular stretches where we had barely dared do 10 miles per hour.

'Chickens had been a bother,' he said because they scattered all over the place in a panic and many had been run over by the cars. In the outlying villages, children had been a problem, too. They were not accustomed to car races and often ran out into the road to welcome the approaching cars, only to have to dive away in the last split second to avoid being flattened.

The race had passed near the border with Burkina Faso. There happened to be a tense situation between that country and Mali at the time and when the inhabitants of one village heard the approaching noise of the Paris-Dakar Rally, they were convinced that it was the army of the neighbouring country invading them and fled in fright. But those in the race had no eye for such unimportant details and no idea of the emotions or havoc they were causing; keeping up their average speed was their sole aim. They imposed a mad strain on the mechanics of their cars because they had their set time schedule. They kept their eyes firmly fixed on the road, not to avoid squashing chickens but in order to spot the worst bits and speed around these. They had no time for greetings or welcomes; they might as well have been on Mars for all they cared.

After a week, the Frenchman's car was running again and he immediately set off for Bamako to try and sell it there. The moment he had gone we moved into the spare bedroom and Joël and I began to work on my Land Rover.

Settling Down in Goundam

The house had all the amenities one could expect from a place far away from the modern world. Next to it was a well that Joël had drilled, which supplied water. Before drinking it, the water was filtered and poured into bottles which were kept cool inside. Hot water was provided by 'solar energy': every morning an African was busy for an hour, manually pumping water into a metal tank on the flat roof where it was exposed to the full sun, and by mid-afternoon the water was hot enough to have a shower or do the washing up. And, supreme luxury, there was a toilet! It was situated inside a small adobe outhouse in a corner of the compound. The outhouse had a wooden door and inside, a pit had been dug out over which two wooden boards had been laid. The idea was to put a foot on each of these when crouching down. Every now and then Joël checked the boards for solidity since there appeared to have been a number of lively accidents with such toilets when boards, half eaten away from the inside by termites, had cracked under the weight of people using them. The whole setup seemed to be a bit hazardous to me, especially at night, and I was always very careful to take a torch.

Joël didn't have a generator, but after sunset he connected the battery of his Land Rover to a transformer to give us light till nine or so when everyone turned in for the night. It was primitive but ingenious. He also had a record player and a few records; among these were some of my favourite Beatles' songs: 'Strawberry Fields Forever' and 'Lucy in the Sky with Diamonds'. Otherwise, day after day, there was not a single sound of modern appliances such as radios or engines.

We soon settled down into the routine of living in an outpost. In the early morning we were woken up by a chorus of birds from the surrounding palm trees and then had breakfast on a table in the courtyard in the shade of a tree. An hour or so later – there was no hurry – Joël and I started on my Land Rover till it became too hot to work. During that time, Claire went out to explore the scattered mud houses on this side of the river. And sometimes she accompanied some of the young girls as they waded through the low water to go to school on the other side of the river where the main part of the town was situated.

I was extremely lucky; Joël turned out to be a first-class mechanic. He began working from inside the Land Rover, taking out seats and floor panels, while I started underneath, lying on my back in the sand and following Joël's instructions. After a few days there was a great gaping hole under the driver's feet. The floor had gone and the gearbox was lying on a raffia carpet spread out on the sand.

'Sand is the enemy of the car,' warned the Land Rover handbook, but here there was nothing but sand.

'It doesn't matter,' said Joël. 'We'll wash everything with fuel before putting it back.'

Joël took the gearbox apart and checked all the parts, but couldn't find anything wrong. Then he put his finger on the problem. 'It's the clutch,' he said. 'The diaphragm spring is broken.'

'Can you repair it?'

'No. We'll have to replace it.'

'And how on earth are we going to find a new one here, in the middle of nowhere?'

'A new one we shall not find,' replied Joël, 'but with luck we may find a second-hand one that fits. In cases like this we cannibalise a broken Land Rover; Africa is full of them. As a matter of fact,' he added, 'I know of one not far from here that's probably got the same clutch system. We'll go and have a look.'

'And why should the owners be willing to sell their diaphragm spring?'

'The owners probably wouldn't, but the users … maybe,' replied Joël mysteriously.

We got into his car and crossed the river over the only bridge there was – which meant a long detour – and entered the town. To my surprise, Joël drove straight to police headquarters. I didn't really fancy another visit to a police station and exclaimed, 'Hey! Why …?'

Joël put a finger against his lips. 'Shht …' he whispered. 'Leave this to me.' And he walked straight into the chief of police's office with the assurance of one who comes to do business.

And business it was. The local police had a Land Rover which had been ruined by the indifferent treatment meted out to it. It sat lifeless in the backyard and I kept staring at it while a lively discussion was going on around me.

'And what makes you think we'd be willing to sell our valuable clutch system to you?' I heard the chief of police ask in a scathing voice.

'Because your engine is broken,' argued Joël. 'It's finished …' He made a cutting gesture with his hand. 'And that's a big, big problem. So what difference does it make to add another much smaller problem?'

'But this is government property,' retorted the chief of police.

'Oh, but we'll pay the government! How much would you – I mean the government – want for it?'

The chief of police now showed interest. His eyes began to shine and after some deep thinking, he proposed a price.

'But that's more than the price of a new diaphragm spring!' protested Joël. 'And yours is a very, very second-hand one.'

After these opening shots, negotiations started in earnest and after ten minutes of haggling, they came to an agreement that seemed satisfactory to both parties: the price had more than halved, but we would have to take out the clutch system ourselves, replace it with our broken one and put everything back in place.

'I don't see the use of installing our broken clutch system,' I objected to Joël as we drove home. 'It's all work for nothing.'

'Well,' came his soothing reply, 'you must try to understand the chief of police. There may be an inspection. You never know.'

So we spent the next day at the police station, working away, and the chief of police had a wide grin on his face when I handed him the money for the government.

Claire had taken to Mali from the word go and was looking forward to finding out all about the ethnographic aspects of African life. We had spent about a week and a half in Goundam when she came to me, very excited. 'I can go on a camel trek with Mohammed!' she said. 'He is planning to visit his family in an oasis a day or so north from here, and he's just come to tell me that I can accompany him.'

'Who's Mohammed?'

'Well, he came here the other day to see Marianne and afterwards I was able to ask him about Tuareg customs. It was so interesting!'

I remembered now. One morning while I had been working on the Land Rover with Joël, Claire had been talking for a long time with a man. He was handsome, too.

'Just think! I'll be able to go on a camel!' Claire's eyes shone. 'And I would share everything in the camp where Mohammed lives. Wouldn't that be really wonderful? It's a unique opportunity to experience Tuareg life at first hand. Think of meeting the women and seeing how they live!'

When Claire noticed that I didn't seem very keen on letting her go up north with a Tuareg she hardly knew, she tried to reassure me.

'The trip would take a few days at most and you're busy with the Land Rover anyway. Don't worry. I'll be all right.'

I wasn't so sure that she would be all right. If she disappeared in the desert, how was I to find her? And I didn't really trust the intentions of that man. I vaguely recollected his shining eyes when he had looked at Claire during the conversation. She might find that she would be sharing more than she imagined, and not just by day. I remembered the nomad who had tried to carry her off on his camel in the Sahara; I didn't want to risk that again and told her so.

So Mohammed went off alone and Claire, after sulking for a day, resumed her previous activities: wading through the river with the girls on their way to school, trying to find out what they were learning. She often sat with them on the sand, communicating by drawing animals and people, which made them laugh. Or else she went about observing the details of daily life in and around Goundam: how the children caught tiny fish and boiled them with millet in huge earthenware cauldrons on open wood fires or how they made little toys for themselves. It was interesting, but I doubt whether it was as exciting as learning all the ins and outs of life in a Tuareg camp would have been.

One of my greatest joys was to wade across the river with the children on their way to school. They would laugh when my skirt trailed in the water and little hands would help me hold it up, or else slip into mine to reassure me that it was all right walking through the water.

After school I would sometimes fetch the girls. I would sit on the soft sand and they would surround me. We would usually just chat, but sometimes we would draw. I always brought paper and coloured pencils and as they looked on, a house would appear with a path leading to the front door and a dog running along it chasing a cat, and they would stare in wonder at the strange place where I lived. Then children would appear at the windows waving at them and they would wave back, all excited. Or there would be fields with all sorts of strange animals making them squeal with laughter: cows, horses, pigs, ducks …

Next I would begin drawing things from Africa. Suddenly an animal could be seen walking over golden sand with a man at its side. 'A donkey! A donkey!' they would call out. 'More please, more …' And then a camel would materialise on the page, stretching its long neck, staring haughtily at them. Oh, they knew the camel well – everyone respected camels here. Then a screech of horror: a crocodile coming out of the water. The girls jumped up ready to run. 'No, no please! Take him away!' They didn't want a crocodile – too dangerous – and I would rub it out. Afterwards we would go home holding hands, singing and laughing.

Sometimes, more rarely, the circle was made up of boys. I was happy when the young boys came, as it was more difficult to interest them and establish trust. I was a woman and a strange colourless being to boot, with eyes like the sky. With them I would draw different things: our land of rain, and snow covering mountains. They would all talk excitedly about this. 'Surely, such amazing things cannot exist!' And they would in turn show me things that were real: great sand dunes, caravans of camels, palm trees …

Somehow I wished these days would never end. The children were so beautiful, their huge, soft, brown eyes full of trust, shining with the simple joy of living. In this desert they seemed to have retained an innocence of heart, which broke through in their sunny smiles and laughter. Yet their toys were made of wood, wire and stone, and they drew with sticks in the sand. It seemed so far removed from the crazy world of Western toys.

'Look at this,' said Joël the next morning, digging into the bits and pieces that had come out of the Land Rover and holding up the gearshift lever. 'It's rusted at the base and is ready to break off. You're lucky that we took everything apart and I discovered the problem now. You would have changed gears one day in the middle of nowhere and been left with the lever in your hands!'

I sighed. This vehicle had become one long sequence of worries: its parts seemed to conk out faster than I could have them mended. 'What are we to do?' I asked, feeling discouraged.

'I've got a friend who can weld it, but I'll have to go to Diré for that.'

'Where's Diré?'

'Some 20 miles away on the banks of the River Niger. My friend is a technician who's working at the solar pumping station down there.' Suddenly Joël brightened up. 'Why don't you come, too? It's a project that may interest you.'

Of course I was interested. I had always thought that the future of Africa lay in solar energy and I was eager to see how a solar pumping station worked.

On the way to Diré, we noticed a bush taxi, which seemed to be stranded along the dirt road. Like most bush taxis in these parts of the world, it was a converted open Peugeot car, crammed full of people and laden with their goods amongst which I even noticed live chickens. As we passed, the driver waved at us to stop and asked if we had any spare petrol. His petrol gauge was no longer working, but he had set off all the same and had just run out of fuel! We were unable to give him any and had to abandon the unfortunate taxi driver and his dozen or so passengers, but we promised to send help the moment we got to Diré.

There was no maintenance crew and no director in the solar pumping station when we arrived – just the one technician we had come to see. He welded my gearshift lever in a short time and as he had nothing much on his hands, he was willing to show me around. While doing so, he told me the truly amazing story of the station.

In colonial times this had been a wooded area but as the soil was fertile, it had been decided to convert the land to agriculture and to irrigate the fields by building a thermal pumping station, which was to pump water from the river. Power was supplied by burning logs but year after year, as the nearby trees were cut and more land was turned over to agriculture, they had to go farther afield to supply the steam machine with wood. There had come a time when deforestation was almost complete and the thermal power station had been abandoned.

The colonial epoch had been replaced by the era of development projects and a few years ago someone in France had hit upon a grand idea: since agriculture needed irrigation, why not let the sun supply the energy required for pumping? After this, a delegation of specialists had come over from France to study everything in detail, a suitable spot had been chosen to build a solar pumping station and a French manufacturer had been selected to produce all the necessary equipment. A year later, the pumping station had been inaugurated; it was heralded as the beginning of a new era.

The solar pumping station looked impressive indeed. Outside there were about a hundred units, each consisting of a sizeable welded frame tilted towards the sun, in which a large glass pane just fitted. Underneath the glass ran copper pipes containing water to be heated and foam rubber insulated the pipes against heat loss from below.

The heated water coming out of the units was collected in a big pipe which entered the factory proper, a huge hangar with a red sun painted on the metal entrance doors. Inside the hangar the hot water went to a heat exchanger before it was pumped back outside and the heat was passed onto a separate freon circuit that drove the pumping engine. This engine then drew water from a branch of the Niger below and pumped it into an array of channels that led off in all directions into the fields. This was modern technology at its best and according to calculations done on a big computer in France, it should have worked perfectly. But it didn't; there were several factors that had been overlooked. Dust soon settled on the glass panes, reducing the heating efficiency of the solar rays. The solar-heated water was supposed to have been hot enough for the freon circuit to start operating before 9.00 a.m. In reality, pumping rarely started before midday and by that time it was so hot in the fields that the farmers were heading home.

So the glass panes were cleaned regularly but still, efficiency didn't improve much. Then it was discovered that the foam underneath had begun emitting gaseous compounds due to the great heat. These had settled as a thick, brown layer on the underside of the glass panes. It was whispered that the foam, which had been produced in Mali, was of low quality and so the French had it replaced. Then worse was discovered: the chemicals emitted by the foam had penetrated the glass panes and were impossible to scrape off. An order was therefore placed with a French firm to supply a hundred new glass panes. Getting them here had been a logistic nightmare – by boat from France to Dakar, Senegal; by rail to Bamako, Mali; and then another 600 miles by lorry to Diré – but they had all survived the trip intact. When the long-expected panes finally arrived and the first one was lowered into its metal frame, it fell clean through and smashed onto the copper tubes!

It turned out that there had been a misunderstanding. The people in the glass factory in France had believed that the measurements they had been given were those of the metal frames and they had taken off a few millimetres left, right, top and bottom in order for the panes to fit easily into their frames. The problem was that they had already done this in Diré when sending out the order and the result was that all the new glass panes were just a fraction too small!

Then another major problem came to light. The delegation of French specialists had visited Diré for the purpose of choosing the site in November. This was of course a cool and pleasant time of the year to visit Mali, but it was also the time just after the rainy season when water levels were at their highest and when the particular branch of the Niger close to which they had chosen to build the pumping station had been full, almost to overflowing. It had looked perfect and no one seemed to have bothered to talk to local people. However, a few years later, during a particularly long dry season when irrigation was absolutely necessary, that branch happened to have dried out.

So, finally, the whole project had been put on hold – for the time being, it was said – and the French project leaders kept just one technician on the spot to look after the station. When asked what they thought of the pumping station, local farmers just shrugged their shoulders and commented, 'That's nothing to do with us. It's the white people's business.'

Life out of Time

After supper, Peter and I often climbed up to the flat roof of Joël's house and sat there, sometimes for hours. There was no electricity anywhere and the milky-white moonlight created a fairy tale world. Far away lay the desert, an unreal landscape of dunes where shadows were deep and contours dimmed, and nearby, scattered amongst the palm trees, were the dwellings of the Tuaregs. In between glimmered the red glow of small fires and every night, around one or another of those, the women sang.

It was this entrancing sound of voices that had made us climb the stairs the first time. We vaguely discerned some women standing around a fire, their figures illuminated by the flickering flames while they clapped their hands, their song ebbing back and forth, and sometimes changing into a spontaneous ululation when they moved their tongues rapidly up and down in their mouths.

As we sat there under the vastness of a sky ablaze with stars and the magnificent sound of the women's voices wound its way around the palm trees and floated up towards us, I felt deeply moved. This was music of all ages, of people adapted to nature and living in concord with it without disturbing it – it was infinite beauty and harmony combined. After evenings like these we sensed we had almost touched eternity and when we finally retired to our room, we slept in perfect peace, knowing that life was as it should be.

In Europe, I had always been conscious of the passage of time. The day was cut up into sections of one or two hours and I would have to stop whatever I was doing and hurry to another place according to the time my watch indicated. Minutes had been so important. How often had I not exclaimed, 'Quick, only five minutes left!' There was no way around this. Modern working society would be unable to function without strict timetables. Then, barely a few weeks out of Europe, minutes had somehow become totally irrelevant and as if acting on cue, one day my watch disappeared; I must have lost it somewhere in the Sahara. I thought this a great misfortune, but I soon discovered that I no longer needed it, because I could use the sun as an indicator of the hour of the day. When it rose, it was 6.00 a.m., when it was at its zenith, it was noon and when it set it was 6.00 p.m. Yet I had continued to feel under pressure because we had got far behind my self-imposed travel schedule; I had to complete it and had felt obliged to hurry on. In Goundam, finally, I understood that my stress was caused by a profound maladjustment: I had been struggling with a code of conduct absorbed through years of living in a Western environment, which I had never questioned before. I realised that if I were to learn anything at all during this journey and feel Africa as it really was, I would have to throw many ingrained Western attitudes overboard – the sooner the better – and I would have to take things slowly.

As the days passed by, day following night following day, the importance of time began to recede. After a while I couldn't even remember the date, or which day of the week it was. Was it Monday or Friday? What difference did it make? I lost all sense of hurry and decided not to worry any longer about planning or dates and to go where the vagaries of chance encounters and fate led us. I had finally moved over to African time.

My mind had become contemplative, almost resistant to movement. We worked on the Land Rover, doing a bit every day; one day it would be finished and then I would start something else – or maybe not. In the meantime, there was companionship and sharing. I was content to stay here for a week, two weeks, a month … it didn't matter. Nothing mattered. I had fallen under the spell of Africa; it was an almost mystical pull, a soaring of the spirit.

Africa was offering me something that was hard to define, a quality of life I had only rarely glimpsed before. I often just sat there, losing myself in the limitless landscape where the sound of distant voices was as natural as the wind blowing through the palm trees, cleansing the land, cleansing the memory, cleansing everything. I felt truly alive, in harmony with all around; I had become content with my fate. I no longer needed more than I already possessed; in fact, much of what I had wanted before had lost its attraction. I had attained perfect peace of mind. This was total freedom indeed!

In the Sahara, I had become aware of the magnitude of space. If you climb a sand dune you perceive the hazy, mauve outline of mountains rising up from the plains fifty, maybe a hundred miles away. Nothing blocks your view – your mind can expand; not even the sky is the limit.

When you sit there very still, just gazing out into space, overawed by the vastness that surrounds you, you are almost unwilling to speak and when you do, you choose your words carefully, utter them softly. The loud chatter with which we fill the void of life in our cities feels irreverent here. There is no need to disturb the silence unnecessarily. This is something I had never learned before, and how could I?

It was in the Sahara that I had perceived the first glimpse of our true place in the cosmos. It is impossible to feel self-importance in the desert: its primeval strength, its seemingly unending space untouched by humans – its overpowering vastness – surpasses our nature by too much. Our urbanised ways of measuring, of cataloguing, of attributing value or the lack of it … they have no meaning there. Our successes, our failures … they are of little importance there. The struggle to become someone … it loses its sense. Only one characteristic of our nature stands out singularly: our vulnerability. Today we are here, tomorrow we'll be gone, but that's the way it is.

Now, in Goundam, I became even more aware of the futility of most human endeavour. In our modern world people are admired for attaining power, for making vast amounts of money, or for becoming famous. But is this what life is all about? I thought. Reducing the short span of time we spend on Earth to chasing the illusion of power and money? Or fame? Such 'great' people will have lived and will die without ever having known the timelessness of Goundam, the vastness of space or the wind of the desert which, when it comes, carries all before it.

But I learned more than that. There was the realisation of the miracle of being alive, this incredible feeling of being a thinking, breathing part of the moving, infinite universe. And when you open yourself to the throbbing pulse of the cosmos and feel one with it, your smallness, your finiteness no longer matters … Nothing matters, not even the numerous failures we all accumulate during the many difficult years of our existence.

From the roof of the house, Peter and I look out over the river, low now, so low one can wade through it. On the opposite bank women are washing their clothes. When they finish they spread them out, forming a patchwork of bright colours on the yellow sand. The wind carries the murmur of their voices towards us as they talk – a light-hearted sing-song sound. An old man in blue robes and black *chech* (a turban), sitting astride a small, grey donkey, passes along leisurely. His rhythm is slow, his lifestyle the same as that of his forebears; no need to hurry – time lasts an eternity.

This is how life must have been in biblical times and this is how life still is in remote oases where people live almost as they did 2,000 years ago. Here, far away from the hustle and bustle of the modern world, I felt as if we had been thrown back in time. Life was enchanting, in complete harmony with the deepest nature of being a human.

Goundam was a place out of time, a sheltered shell. As we woke up to the trill of birds singing in the palm trees and breathed the clear ethereal air of perfect dawn, everything exuded peace. A soft breeze would suddenly caress our faces, stirring the palm leaves and something deep inside ourselves. Truly, this was rejuvenation of our spirits and I wanted to stay.

Memories of that visit to Goundam have never left me: the tranquil expanse of lazy water; dugouts drifting by very slowly in the morning light, the water so still, so quiet; the voices of the people from the oasis below floating through the palm fronds and amongst the dunes; the setting sun reddening the smoke of small fires; the millions of bright stars in a velvety sky.

Sitting on the roof at night, I recorded the sounds and singing. I very much wanted to have that music to keep it forever as a memory. When we got home it was the only tape we were unable to find. Like all exceptional moments in life, this one was to live on only in our hearts.

Return from a Dream

We all tend to get stuck in places we like, but never in my life had I felt more unwilling to leave than here, where I had discovered our insignificance and accepted it. And we had found people we loved. Of all the many who gave us shelter on our way through Africa, Joël and Marianne were without doubt those who made the greatest effort without ever so much as showing the slightest displeasure at the bother we must have caused them. But there was no longer any excuse. The Land Rover was repaired, so we said goodbye to our hosts and headed towards our reason for coming here: Timbuktu, 60 miles east through difficult, sandy terrain.

We had barely left Goundam behind and started to tackle the first dunes when we got stuck. I put the gears in four-wheel-drive mode, high gear ratio, but only the back wheels turned; the front ones didn't seem to be connected!

In Brussels, Bernard had equipped the front wheels with a special system, which allowed them to turn freely. If we wanted the front wheels to be connected to the drive shaft, as they should be in four-wheel-drive mode, we first had to turn a knob in the centre of the wheels. I had failed to see why we really needed this system but Bernard had insisted that it was an essential improvement.

'What if it breaks down?' I had asked, but Bernard had been adamant.

'This will never break down.'

It now appeared that, when turning the knobs into the on-position, the new system no longer connected the front wheels to the drive shaft. Whatever Bernard had said, it had probably worn out under the strain the Sahara had imposed upon it. But we were lucky; I remembered that he had put the old system, which he had removed, up on the roof rack.

'Look here,' he had said, 'you no longer need this, but as you seem to be worried I'll put the old system in the spare parts box. There's still room up there.'

Putting the old system back in place meant returning to Joël and bothering him once again and this we hesitated to do. The end of his project was approaching and he had to leave Goundam within three weeks. He had been kind enough to help me out with my repairs so far, but he needed all the remaining time to check his own Land Rover and pack.

Yet deep down we were pleased, almost relieved, to have an excuse to go back, but we didn't dare to return within a few hours of leaving. So, after we had managed to get out of the sand with the help of the sand ladders, we decided to spend the rest of the day there, camping behind some low bushes away from the track. It was a unique spot between the dunes and we sat in stunned silence, looking at the succession of clear-cut crests rising up from a sea of sand while the setting sun painted the purity of their curves golden-red.

The next morning, we drove into Joël's compound saying we were very distressed about our new misfortune and telling him how it had taken us hours to dig the Land Rover out of the sand. Poor Joël! He put on a brave face and started the repair job straight away. He also found room for us in a jeep that was driving to Timbuktu early the following day and would be back late at night. So we made it to one of the most mythical towns of Africa after all.

The Sahara had fascinated Europeans for centuries and Timbuktu particularly so. Its lure had been so great that a substantial prize had been offered in the early nineteenth century to the first European who could reach the fabled city and come back alive to report on it. It had been a disappointment to René Caillié when he finally got there in 1825; it was even more of a disappointment when we got there. We had been forewarned not to expect too much and indeed, there was nothing special to see. Famous Timbuktu had no more to offer than dusty streets and mud houses. To us it lacked everything we had found in Goundam.

Before we left him, Joël had given us directions to a project, one day's drive west, run by Fabricio, an Italian. The man, who lived alone, didn't often have the chance to meet European visitors and was delighted when he saw us. He had wavy, dark hair and fiery eyes, and overflowed with attention for me.

'Are you hungry?' he asked. 'You know what? I'm going to cook my favourite recipe.' He stared at me with a romantic look in his eyes. 'This is going to be a special treat for a very special occasion.' Then he added, 'I like cooking,' before disappearing into his kitchen.

I could well believe that. He was plump and already beginning to develop a paunch although he couldn't have been older than thirty-five.

While Fabricio was getting busy with pots and pans, I looked at Peter. He seemed extremely pleased.

'A special meal,' he said. 'What a wonderful surprise. I can't wait.'

I had never had the opportunity to observe an Italian cook in action and was curious to see what was going on, so I went into the kitchen where I found Fabricio with a happy expression on his face. He was stirring a red sauce while keeping an eye on a steaming pot that smelled strongly of spaghetti. 'What are we going to have?' I asked warily.

'You like good cooking?' He beamed.

'Yes, but what –?'

'Hah, normally I wouldn't reveal. You taste it and it will be *delicioso*. But as I see you're interested in Italian cooking, I will reveal.' He stared at me with two big dark eyes, as if getting ready to let the cat out of the bag. 'It's going to be spaghetti with sauce of tomato, unfortunately from a tin, and corned beef. But it will be nice! Extremely tasty! Shall I show you how I prepare it?' He put an arm around my waist and pulled me nearer.

I suddenly felt panicky. Peter would have a fit if Fabricio put this dish on the table. I managed to free myself, stuttering, 'Just a moment.'

I slipped out of the kitchen and found Peter sitting quietly on a chair at the dining table. He had an expectant look on his face and my heart sank.

'Is there a problem?' he asked when he saw how distraught I looked.

'Darling, don't be disappointed but … guess what the special dish is going to be?'

'It doesn't matter. Whatever it is, it'll be a nice change from our monotonous diet.'

I winced but I plucked up my courage, leaned forward and whispered in his ear, 'It's going to be spaghetti with tomato sauce and corned beef.'

Peter uttered a stifled groan. 'I don't believe this …'

'Please,' I implored, 'pretend to be delighted when he brings it in. He's so proud of his cooking.'

Peter looked disgusted as I left the room and I had a feeling of impending doom. Back in the kitchen I kept well away from our host and tried to engage in small talk about the great qualities of Italian cuisine, hoping that Peter would have recovered by the time supper was served.

Finally all was ready and Fabricio brought in a steaming pot heaped up with spaghetti covered in a thick, brown-red sauce. He carried it as if he were holding a prized treasure.

'Here,' he said, putting it on the table and dumping a big ladleful onto our plates. 'Eat up! You're going to enjoy this.'

I shot a worried, sideways glance at Peter as he put the first forkful into his mouth. Then, to my relief, I heard him say, 'How delicious! This is quite unexpected. How do you manage to cook this out here in the bush?'

Fabricio beamed. 'Well …' he replied, 'it's not easy. Cooking is an art, you see; many try but few master it.' And I saw his chest swell with pride.

When we had worked our way through the heaped-up plates Fabricio had served us, he immediately wanted to give us second helpings but we declined politely, saying that our life in the bush had accustomed us to a lean diet and that our stomachs had probably shrunk.

'What a pity!' exclaimed Fabricio. 'Maybe I serve the rest for breakfast tomorrow, yes?'

Later that night, as we lay in our Land Rover, Peter commented, 'And you know what? It wasn't even as tasty as yours!'

The following morning, we visited Fabricio's project. He was trying to introduce improved crops and took us proudly around the tilled fields with row upon row of healthy-looking vegetables. I was, however, more interested in the activities that were going on next to his project: a young boy was making bricks in an age-old fashion. He filled a wooden mould with clay, smoothed it with his hand and then turned the mould over to smooth the other side. Then he emptied the mould on the ground where the mud brick was left to bake in the sun with hundreds of similar ones. When they were ready, the bricks would be piled onto a bullock- or donkey-drawn cart and carried to their destination.

Many houses here were made from rough clay mixed with straw, but some of the best had walls made of sun-baked clay bricks. The ceilings consisted of beams of more or less regular, round branches, over which reeds were spread on which mud was piled and smoothed. Mud played the role of cement in local construction. The walls, too, were finished off with a layer of mud. Towns in the Sahel all looked clay-coloured, the houses hardly distinguishable from the earth on which they stood.

Clay is very cheap, locally made and has excellent insulation properties; in the cold season it keeps the warmth inside and in the hot summer it keeps the interior relatively cool. The flat roofs in particular are very practical. One can sit on them or sleep on them during nights when it is too hot inside. The only problem is when it rains which, fortunately for the buildings but unfortunately for the land, doesn't happen very often: the outside of the walls and the exterior roof surfaces turn into soft mud and have to be patched up and repaired, rainy season after rainy season. But then, people over here have time.

It's a shame that imported corrugated iron is beginning to be used as roofing material. Although it keeps the rains out, it is totally inappropriate for insulation purposes. In the summer, people suffocate underneath the scalding metal and in the winter they shiver. But it has all the attributes linked to progress: it is imported, easy to put into place, timesaving, and totally ill-adapted to Africa. And so, it is more and more replacing traditional materials.

Joël had advised us to return to Bamako via the western route around the inner Niger delta, which was longer but less sandy. All went well until we lost the track and while searching for it, drove into soggy soil near the Niger delta. I put the sand ladders under the wheels, but they were useless in wet soil and in spite of all my efforts, we got well and truly stuck. I couldn't think how we were ever going to get out of this when I saw a few men come towards us. Oh no, I thought, more problems. Then I noticed the men's large smiles and relaxed. They shook hands and when I asked if they had any idea what to do, one of them immediately ran back to his nearby village. Within less than half an hour, twenty men turned up to help us and they all began to push while I got behind the steering wheel and revved up. For a while nothing happened, but they didn't give up and after some heroic pushing, the Land Rover began to move and finally shot out of the boggy area. Then they all came to congratulate me and instead of asking to be paid for their efforts, they showed us how to get back to the track and wished us a safe journey!

The next day, we were advancing slowly towards the south when in the early afternoon the engine stalled. 'Another one of those blasted airlocks!' I exclaimed irritably. I opened the bonnet and set about bleeding the fuel circuit, but the engine simply wouldn't start. 'One of the tubes must be defective and is letting in air,' I explained to Claire. 'It won't take a minute.'

I began to check the diesel supply tubes but there didn't seem to be anything wrong with any of them. All the same, there had to be a leak somewhere and I began by replacing the tube that seemed to be in the least good condition. Since that didn't help, I replaced the next tube and then the following one. It was no good; however much I bled the circuit after changing a tube, air always remained in the diesel fuel.

Hours later, I was still working under the full sun, sweat was dripping in my eyes and trickling down my body while Claire, who had installed herself on a low folding chair on the shady side of the Land Rover, supplied me every now and then with water from a gourd. She tried to keep up my morale, saying all would be well, but gradually despair took hold of me. We were in the middle of an empty landscape on a track that was rarely used. All I had seen for the last few hours were a few wild asses moving along very far away near the horizon. We had enough water to stick it out for a couple of days maybe, but who was to find us here once we had run out of water?

I climbed up on the roof rack and began fumbling through the spare parts box, wondering what else I might be able to do, when I noticed a small cardboard box containing a new fuel pump. Bernard must have bought it and put it there, just in case. The old one seemed OK but, I thought, I've replaced all the rest. I might as well replace the old pump. You never know.

When I showed it to Claire she put a hand on the new pump, closed her eyes in deep concentration and then said, 'I feel this is going to work.'

It had better, I thought. This is our very last chance.

Changing the pump took another half hour of toil. After bleeding the circuit again to remove air bubbles, I crawled behind the steering wheel, utterly exhausted and convinced that this was all useless anyway. I pressed the starter and suddenly the engine began to turn. Waves of relief swept through my body. You cannot imagine the emotions one goes through in such a situation. I was nearly in tears, muttering, 'Thank you, Bernard.'

It was getting dark by now and I wanted to call it a day, when I heard Claire say, 'Let's drive away from here. Now the engine's running again it's better to carry on. I feel that we shouldn't stay any longer in this unlucky spot.'

So we drove half a mile further and stopped behind the next range of dunes, set up camp, had a perfunctory wash and a frugal meal and were soon asleep under the starry sky. We reached Bamako the next day.

The trip to and from Goundam had been extremely difficult; it had been a long, hard slog, a battle against breakdowns and fatigue, but it had been well worth the effort: I was no longer the same person I had been when I set out on our journey through Africa.

Before entering the Sahara, we had faced the unknown. Now we knew: we had been overwhelmed by the magnificent expanse of the desert; we had seen the starry skies at night, had felt the overpowering vastness of the cosmos and become aware of the true dimension of our existence. But we had also realised that we were part of it all – an insignificant part, yes, but one that was intimately linked to the whole; we belonged. And now we had been allowed to spend the most wonderful month of our lives in Goundam, a place where a part of us would remain forever.

We knew that the first section of our journey was behind us and that we would never experience anything like this again. The discovery of the solitude of the desert – the feeling of awe when, for the first time ever, you abandon yourself to its endless space and absolute silence – and the magic peace of Goundam could never be repeated.

Nothing is ever as deeply touching as when it happens for the first time: there is no longer that same breathless expectation the second time or that incredible, overwhelming feeling afterwards. But the amazing thing was that there had been a first time at all. We were well aware that fate had smiled upon us, that life had opened its treasure chest and had let us have a look at what was hidden inside. And what we found in there was something so precious, so unique, that we would carry it with us deep down in our hearts for the rest of our lives.

Above: On the road to Goundam, Tuaregs

Below: On the road to Goundam, Peul cattle

153

Above: On the road to Goundam: Marianne and Peter at breakfast

Below: Claire with schoolgirls wading through the river

Above: Joël and Peter repairing the Land-Rover

Left: Peter's head through the hole under the driver's seat

Above: Handsome Mohammed posing for a photo

Below: Preparing fish soup

Above: Claire with schoolgirls

Below: Claire drawing stories for boys

Right: Peace in Goundam: Peter writing next to the entrance to Joël's house

Below: Brick making

Above: Transport of bricks

Below: Claire and children in front of mud houses

Above: All pushing together

Below: The tree of Africa is the baobab with its gigantesque bulk and primitive appearance

CHAPTER 7
Into the Primeval Forest

Out of Mali

Throughout our travels in Africa, we were to discover that departures were often heart rending. It was always sad to have to say goodbye to people who had offered us generous hospitality and opened their hearts to us, and this was especially so when we had to leave Joël and Marianne. We would have loved to stay in Goundam where our spirits had soared. For days afterwards our eyes missed its palm trees and the tranquil river, the vast expanse of the golden dunes and the starry nights. What could possibly surpass the infinite beauty of the desert and the peacefulness of Goundam?

But life goes on and after a short sojourn with our friends in Bamako, we were again heading for unknown destinations. As we drove away, somehow the open road seemed less appealing. Then, gradually, as the landscape unfolded, we fell under the spell of the bush. It felt good to be nomads again, to be free to go where we liked, and once more the thrill of discovery caught hold of us as we headed south towards the equatorial forest.

First, however, there was an obstacle to clear: the border. The guards on the Malian side gave us exit stamps without any bother but we still had to cross into the Ivory Coast, and entering a country is often a serious affair in Africa. I was well aware of the fact that it was forbidden to carry weapons or even to posses a radio transmitter, which might indicate that you were a spy, but as we had no weapons or radio equipment with us, I felt completely unconcerned. Then, as we drove slowly toward the barrier of the Ivory Coast border post, I suddenly thought of the ornamental Tuareg sword we had purchased in Gao as a present for our friend Bernard. We did have a weapon with us!

I was racking my brain to find a way out of the predicament. As I stopped and saw the customs officer come toward us, a purposeful expression on his face, I felt panicky. He was sure to discover the sword, confiscate it and make a lot of trouble. Then, in a flash, I knew what to do. It might not work, but it was worth a try.

The handle at the back of the Land Rover had been wrenched off one night in Bamako and ever since, it had been impossible to open the back flap from the outside. Whenever we needed to get into the sleeping area I would have to pass head first through the narrow opening in the plywood panel that separated the steering cabin from the back compartment. This forced me to perform a set of acrobatic movements but as I had lost a stone by now I managed easily enough to wriggle through. Then, lying stretched out on our mattress, I would reach for the inside part of the handle, which was still intact, and open the back flap to let Claire in. However, the customs officer didn't know that and when he told me that he wanted to inspect the contents of the vehicle I pointed at the missing handle, saying apologetically, 'I'm afraid it's not possible to open the back.'

'But I have to check what's inside!' retorted the officer, staring at me with marked disapproval.

'Oh, but you are very welcome to do that,' I hastened to reply. I opened the driver's door and showed him the narrow opening in the plywood partition. 'You can climb in through there,' I said making an inviting gesture.

I saw the officer recoil. He was quite tall and slightly corpulent, like many Africans who can afford to eat plenty. He didn't seem at all keen on attempting to crawl through the narrow opening; as likely as not, he would have got stuck.

'You want me to go through there?' The officer rolled his eyes in disbelief. 'That's not possible!'

'Well, I'm afraid it's the only way.'

'You can't expect to cross borders like that!' barked the man. 'You must repair this immediately!'

'I've tried to,' I replied, looking despondent, 'but they didn't have the spare part in Mali. You see, it all happened very recently. A few nights ago burglars attempted to get inside and broke off the handle.' I managed to sound very upset. 'I'm really sorry that those Malians should have put you in such a position. I've been keen to get to the Ivory Coast because I'm sure they'll be able to do the repair in your country.'

I glanced at the customs officer, holding my breath. He stood there, a picture of indecision, staring at the Land Rover, his face set in a deep frown. Then, suddenly, I saw his expression change. Victory, I thought. He has found a face-saving exit! And indeed, he had. Wagging a disapproving finger, he declared, 'Malians are very bad people. They're not to be trusted.' Then he beamed at us like a benign father and added, 'Fortunately you are now in the Ivory Coast and such things do not happen here. *We* are honest people! And rest assured. Just go to any garage here and they will repair this immediately.' He then rubber-stamped our passports and vehicle carnet with a great show of energy, welcomed us into his beautiful country and waved us on with a broad smile.

Now that we had successfully crossed the border, we wanted to celebrate and instead of bothering with searching for a safe spot in the bush, we decided to stop at a hotel in Odienné, a large town further south. It was a luxury stop. The hotel had a swimming pool and we were soon splashing about in the refreshing water. A couple of Europeans were sitting in deck chairs and when I heard them talk I couldn't believe my ears: they spoke Flemish and judging from their accent, they came from a place not too far from where I was born. Imagine their surprise when I addressed them in their local tongue! It was a lucky encounter. It turned out that they were running a micro-project some 20 miles further in the bush.

'Why don't you come with us?' they said after I had explained what we were doing in Africa. 'You'll find the project very interesting and you can film everything.'

We didn't have to think twice and so, the following day, they guided us to Kaniasso, a small town lost in the countryside, which we would never have found on our own. The project's main aim was empowering women and this was vital. Women are the ones who toil in the fields all day long; then, when they get home, just before sunset after a long slog through the countryside, carrying firewood or water on their heads and babies on their backs, they still have to cook supper. And as they receive no pay for their work, they have no say in anything. The Belgian development project in Kaniasso not only attempted to make the women partly independent, but also taught them to diversify their food base. Food tends to be monotonous in rural Africa and lacking in vitamins and minerals, and the aid workers showed young women how to cultivate a variety of vegetables. The women took part of their produce home and transported the rest to local markets where they sold it and kept the income. After only two years, changes had started to appear. Having their own income, the women had become visibly less dependent on their husbands. They were now able to buy nice clothes for themselves, and the necessary uniforms, books and pencils for their children so that they could go to school.

The next day, we visited the green vegetable gardens. There were rows upon neat rows of cabbages, lettuces, onions, leeks, potatoes, turnips and many other varieties – all looking healthy and luscious – and even flowers, grown for their beauty. The women watered the plants morning and evening, and in the daytime they kept the weeds and pests at bay. It was an arduous task, all done by hand and with very few funds, but they still found time to follow educational courses and health seminars. The project had brought about a mini-revolution: the women certainly didn't want to go back to their previous state of ignorance and dependence and the men, strangely enough, seemed rather proud of the bright clothes and good health of their women and children.

The project had sunk a well to provide clean water that could be hand-pumped, thereby doing away with the back-breaking task allotted to women of hauling up full buckets from open wells 20- or 30-feet deep, a baby slung on their backs. The women, dressed in their colourful clothes, took me to the new concrete well to show me how easy it was now to fetch water.

African women can carry anything on their heads with grace and great ease. I had often admired them and had wanted to try it out, too, so I told the women I was eager to carry a bucket just like they did. They thought it great fun, stuck a cloth crown on my head, filled a large bucket with water, lifted it up and placed it on my head. I shrank under the heavy weight and quickly clutched the sides of the wobbling bucket to steady it before it toppled over. As I began to trundle off slowly, water kept splashing out and I had staggered no more than a few paces when my neck began to hurt. How can these women do it? I thought, as I begged them to take the bucket off quickly.

The women were laughing away while they freed me and my face reddened with shame when I heard them joke that they should have given me only a small bucket and just have filled it half – the quantity old grandmothers carried!

When I turned to Peter who, strangely enough, was looking at me with admiration in his eyes, I couldn't help saying, 'You think me young and strong, but have no illusions. What you see here standing before you is in reality no more than a very weak old grandmother.'

While we were in Kaniasso, there was a funeral. The deceased had been an important chief and the whole village had come out to pay homage. Groups of wailing women surrounded the house where the chief's body lay in a small room and people entered in shifts to pay their last respects to the mortal remains of the great man. As some left, others immediately took their place; the wails continued for hours.

A few days later, they celebrated a wedding. A procession carried the bride, dressed up in bright finery, to the house of her husband-to-be. The atmosphere was frenzied; crowds of people were singing and clapping their hands amidst great outbursts of shouting and laughter; colourfully dressed horsemen were galloping around on their horses; drums were pounding and shots were fired into the air out of old muskets. We felt as if we had stepped back in time.

Most striking was the whirling mixture of dazzling colours. Africans tend to dress in the brightest materials they can find. A multitude of people in Africa looks like a patchwork of strong and highly contrasting tones, vivid, joyful and very much alive. This was quite different from Europe where people tend to move about like dull shadows, especially in the winter, their clothes a drab grey or very often black. In Europe, crowds appear gloomy, so much so that it has led to the French expression, *C'est noir de monde* (it's black with people).

Maybe it's all due to the climate, I reflected. Sunlight most definitely influences character and behaviour. The dim light of the northern climes makes us cautious and anxious, and sometimes leads to depression, whilst the brilliant African sunshine creates an enjoy-the-moment outlook, openness, laughter, light-heartedness and optimism. But such carefree attitudes can lead to reckless behaviour. When Africans burn the bush, which happens every now and then, they do so for a variety of reasons. One of these is hunting; they set fire to the grass and wait downwind to catch any game that flees.

'The last time they burned the bush around Kaniasso,' the Belgian project leader told me, 'one of the local men caught sight of an agouti – a big rat – running away from the blaze. Agoutis are considered a delicacy here and when the man saw it, he just went for it. The agouti turned round in panic and rushed back toward the flames with the man in hot pursuit. Having reached the wall of fire it stopped, undecided, but noticing the man close behind, it made up its mind and sped on, whereupon the African, who had eyes only for the agouti, dived straight into the flames to catch the animal before it disappeared! The agouti cleverly moved sideways and shot out of the fire, escaping with a few light burns, but the man fell flat into the flames, got horribly burnt and had to be rushed to the hospital in Odienné!'

The people in Kaniasso had given us directions to a Belgian mission in Zélé, a small place a day's drive south. I was in two minds about stopping there, remembering the reaction of the Belgian missionary in Bandiagara, but I needn't have worried: Sister Mathilde welcomed us with open arms. She bubbled with enthusiasm and soon took us around to show us the different activities. The mission supplied education, did health counselling and also tried to interest parents in social programmes. I had expected the conversion of people to Christianity to be one of the main activities of the mission, yet here in Zélé there was no coercion and the atmosphere felt light.

This was a happy place indeed. When school finished, hundreds of children came running out through the trees, their voices like twittering birds. Soon they were crowding around us, a mass of moving arms, heads and big smiles. We had already given away most of the notebooks and Biro pens we had brought from Belgium, but the few children who received the last of our small gifts seemed very pleased with them.

In the Ivory Coast, children start learning French at a very young age and this was lucky because it allowed us to communicate. Like most African countries, the Ivory Coast is made up of dozens of tribes and languages; when I asked an Ivorian if any of those languages were used for official communication, he replied, almost offended, '*Mais Monsieur, nous sommes des Francophones!*' But, sir, we are French speakers! At least, the problem of communication here seems to have been solved by the French colonial occupation.

At night it was so dark that the world around was reduced to the small circle illuminated by the petrol lamp on the outside table where we had supper with Sister Mathilde. Even our torch, when we walked around, didn't illuminate much, but one of the amazing phenomena which struck me was how the teeth of Africans lit up in the torchlight. It was uncanny! You didn't see the Africans – just their shiny teeth, which seemed to move about on their own some 5 feet above the ground. The teeth were not just white; they sparkled. For a while it was a mystery to me how they kept them in such a good condition that any of the Africans here could have been an advertisement for toothpaste. Of course, their diet contained little or no sugar and they only ate natural foods, so they didn't ruin their teeth as our sweet-addicted children begin doing from a young age, but still, they had no toothbrushes in the bush – or so I thought – until Sister Mathilde put me right.

'Of course they have toothbrushes,' she affirmed.

'But where would they get them from?' I looked at her, convinced she was pulling my leg. 'The nearest shops are in the small town fifteen miles from here and anyway, toothbrushes would be too expensive.'

'They get them from the toothbrush tree,' she replied, dead seriously. And indeed, there is a tree over here which has twigs people break off, split open and use to rub their teeth clean.

We loved our dinners, shared with Sister Mathilde on the outside terrace of the mission while listening to the chirping of cicadas. Night would fall, a few stars would begin to appear here and there, and soon the bull-frogs and toads, quiet all day, would stir to life and start to croak in the marshy area behind the mission.

By the time supper was over and we walked back to our Land Rover, the sky was blazing with stars, the darkness had come to life with a myriad of sounds, and fireflies were dancing at chest height like miniature magic lanterns. As we crawled inside the back compartment and got ready to sleep, crickets were rubbing their legs, producing a shrill sound and I could hear the loud croaking of frogs and toads nearby … an interminable concert of animal noises that would continue through the night and only stop when dawn crept in. We felt invigorated by those nights out in nature and by this simple but truly rejuvenating way of life.

It had been getting hotter as the months advanced. We were in March now and as we drove south towards the rainforest, the heat was becoming hard to bear. Our old Land Rover had no modern luxuries such as air-conditioning, and the additional warmth produced by the engine was sheer torture. The exhaust pipe passed underneath the driver's seat and I felt the heat mounting through the floorboards; the soles of our sandals might as well have been made of paper for all the protection they gave us. Claire lifted her legs from the floor and put her feet on the dashboard, but her face was glistening and sweat trickled down her blouse, leaving ever-broadening patches of dampness.

I had to keep my foot on the scorching accelerator and although Claire had wrapped towels around my feet and legs, the excruciating heat seeped in through the thick wadding and made me want to cry out.

Our tyres were another worry. Though they were solid and made of six layers of rubber, thorns, pointed stones and the bad state of the tracks and roads in Mali had taken their toll, and we had already had one flat tyre. Now, although the dirt roads of the northern Ivory Coast were excellent, there was a new, even worse enemy: the heat of the roads attacked the rubber, which then lost its resistance.

We were moving along steadily when we heard a loud 'bang'. We slowed down and as I pressed hard on the brake pedal, we skidded to a standstill.

'Not a flat tyre again!' exclaimed Claire.

I clambered out to inspect the damage. It was a blow-out; the tyre was ruined. There was nothing for it but to get out the jack. Changing wheels was an unpleasant job. It was extremely hot in the full sun, I was sweating profusely and the wheel nuts refused to yield; I had to pull myself up onto the roof rack, arms bent, and then let myself drop down onto the wrench to loosen the wheel nuts.

The Rainforest

At last we entered the rainforest. Giant trees bordered the dirt road, rising like pillars from the undergrowth. I gazed in amazement at their huge fin-like roots and then up and up along their smooth, interminable trunks to the canopy of great leafed branches seeking their share of the light above; the force of nature's unrestrained vitality was overwhelming.

Lianas hung like curtains from gigantic trees. Straining my neck, I saw them cascading down from far above, so far I almost couldn't see where they started and I felt reduced to ant-like proportions. Holding a liana for the first time I could feel its supple strength. I had a vision of swinging on a liana from tree to tree, of flying between branches, but when I tried I only managed to move a few very inadequate feet.

There was a path that led into the darkness of the primeval forest and as we followed it, a sense of excitement pervaded me: this was virgin, untamed nature! We found a liana bridge suspended over a stream. I crossed it slowly; it swayed with every step.

We came to a glen from which several trails split off. Only dim light filtered through the dense green foliage, the air seemed to stagnate and I felt as if we had stepped into a magic world peopled by witches. I was irresistibly drawn by its mystery but Peter held me back.

'Don't,' he said. 'If we go off into the forest along one of these trails we might easily lose our way and never return. Africa would simply swallow us up.'

We kept driving along unmade roads, penetrating ever deeper into the equatorial forest. The sparkling play of light and shade upon the leaves was enchanting. Trees enclosed us on both sides and the shelter of the forest created a feeling of belonging; it felt almost like being in the safety of nature's womb.

When we drew up close to the edge of the forest for the night, the dense mass of jungle shut off most light. The sun set swiftly and great was the contrast between the brightness of the day and the shadowy world of the night. Even when the moonlight flooded down it illuminated no more than a few trees in the deep darkness that surrounded us. I will never forget the wonder of our first night in the forest. It was different from anything we had ever known in Europe where you could sometimes hear the gentle call of owls or the sharp bark of a fox. Here the whole forest seemed to come alive with unknown cries, snorts and screeches as we lay inside our Land Rover.

The next morning, we came to a large, open clearing and saw a man sitting in front of his mud hut. He was sharpening his machete but as we stopped and got out, he came over to greet us. This would be ideal material for my documentary movie, I thought, seeing that he had cut down a part of the forest to make a plantation, but when I asked whether I could film him he seemed to hesitate. Maybe this was the moment to bring out the Polaroid camera?

I asked the planter whether he would allow me to take a picture, which I could give him immediately. He protested that such a thing wasn't possible but all the same, he stood up and let me take his picture. As the photograph slid out of the Polaroid camera and I handed it to him, he stared at it uncomprehendingly: it was completely white. Then, slowly, as the development fluids did their work, his face began to appear and as the picture got ever clearer, he became very excited; it must have seemed pure magic to him.

'But this is Amadou!' he exclaimed, pointing at the photograph. By the time the fixation process had ended he was dancing around with his picture repeating, 'This is Amadou! This is Amadou!'

In the West, we have dozens of photographs of ourselves, but we easily forget that many Africans do not even possess a single one and Amadou was obviously one of them. Filming was no problem after this. I just followed Amadou with my heavy cine camera and tripod on the shoulder while he walked proudly ahead to show me his plantation.

As I started filming I thought that he had done a really good job. He had cut his plantation out of the forest all by himself and planted a cash crop – cocoa trees. But he also cultivated bananas, sweet potatoes and yams for himself and his family. That was more difficult than it looked, though, because the jungle fought back. Every week he had to go around cutting down weeds and clearing the ground between the cocoa trees.

'And there's an even bigger problem,' he said. 'There are intruders who come to steal my crops!'

'But who would come to steal here?' I asked, surprised.

Amadou didn't know the name in French, but he was a resourceful man and made a sign that he would show us. He disappeared into the forest and we were just wondering where he had gone when we heard a hooting sound; the leaves at the forest's edge began to rustle and then Amadou's face appeared between the greenery. He tiptoed out slowly, his shoulders bent, rolling his eyes, looking to left and right like a born actor and then moved stealthily toward the nearest cocoa trees. We couldn't think what on earth he was doing and stared at him in bewilderment, when suddenly he began to hop about while scratching his armpits and making loud grunting noises, and we got the message: monkeys!

I had of course read about baboons and monkeys and their noisy, thieving and destructive activities. Their troops sometimes invade farmlands, sacking and pillaging whatever they find – maize, bananas and manioc plants – and pulling up potatoes and other vegetables in kitchen gardens and fields near villages, but however much I looked at the forest, there wasn't a single monkey to be seen.

'No,' said Amadou. 'In the daytime they keep quiet, but when I'm gone at night …'

I pointed at his hut. 'But don't you live here?'

'No!' he exclaimed, looking shocked. 'Stay alone in the forest at night? I wouldn't dream of it! I return to my village before nightfall.'

While we sat talking in front of his hut, Amadou offered to share his lunch with us. He took a few yams out of a pot, which had been cooking all the while, and started to peel them and slice them into small pieces with his long machete! He had two of these and used them for everything: to chop down big trees, to clear the grass that grew between his cacao trees and to cut up his vegetables, too. We were astounded at his ability to use his machete, but were even more amazed that he still had his ten fingers!

Ivorians seem to be born with a machete in their hands. I've seen toddlers, just about able to walk, already wielding a machete. Boys no older than six or seven walk along the roads through the forest as they go to school in their uniforms, holding a satchel in one hand while in the other they carry a machete; there's always something to cut on the way back home. There are variations: satchel slung over the shoulders and machete flat on their heads; satchel on their heads with the machete inside, the ends sticking out; or any conceivable combination.

As we drove on we found the villages very different from those we had passed in the north of the country. Building materials were still the same: the walls were daubed with clay, which eventually dried in the sun, and the mud-and-wattle huts had grass roofs, or were sometimes thatched with banana leaves. What differed, though, was the layout. The further south we went, the more the huts were clustered together; some villages were even surrounded by a palisade of strong wooden posts. It was as if those living there wanted to shield themselves from the forest. In the daytime, children ran about between the huts and we met people along the roads; they would walk to their plantations or go foraging in the forest. But not at night. Then they all huddled together in their villages, seeming to seek safety in numbers.

I loved the sight of those rounded huts with their pointed, sometimes lopsided, straw roofs. They seemed to grow out of the earth like mushrooms, their hues changing with the light of the sun from pale mother of pearl and straw gold to the colour of the soil itself. Deeper in the forest, though, we found that people lived in large communal huts. We came to a clearing along the track and noticed a great hut with a domed roof. It seemed to defy the towering trees and climbing plants that rose up around it. As we stopped to look, a few young women in bright flowery skirts and blouses waved to us and made gestures inviting us in.

Inside the light was dim. This was a shadowy world, even at noon. Tall bamboo pillars supported the framework of the high dome; smoke rose from wood fires that burned constantly underneath big earthen pots, and cereals hung in rusty-coloured bunches from the rafters. Though this was a one-room hut, there was a feeling of space.

The scent of the drying bunches, mingling with the smoke and the aroma of cooking, delighted me as I sat with a baby on my lap, listening to the babble of the young mothers – it felt very comforting. They turned towards me with broad sunny smiles, the light filtering inside throwing a soft golden glow on their faces as they told me how happy their life was with so many lovely plump babies around, and how they never felt alone. They were part of a supportive community. Their sisters helped with the youngest babies while their mothers and grandmothers cooked for the whole extended family.

The space was thronging with women and children, as if clustering close together gave them greater protection against the threatening powers of darkness.

'At night,' they told me, 'malevolent spirits come out and roam in the gloomy shadows of the forest, ready to harm people.'

Obviously, to them, nights were very frightening, but we didn't fear the forest. Towards nightfall we would start looking for a space amongst the trees wide enough to park. The moment we stopped the engine and stepped out, we entered an enchanted world. The light would begin to fade rapidly, darkness would close in around us and we would hear strange noises deep in the jungle, some high-pitched and loud, others muted. Insects in all shapes and colours were attracted by the Land Rover's lights – dragonflies with long, transparent wings and giant beetles with shiny carapaces. And the setting darkness was punctuated by coughs, hisses, sighs and a hundred unidentifiable sounds.

As we crept into the sleeping compartment after a frugal supper and switched off our lights, the forest would come alive and the noise became indescribable; there must have been great numbers of animals out there judging from the calls, cries and growls, and some animals must have been very large: every now and then we heard the loud snap of a branch breaking.

Being in the forest in the darkness of the night gave us a primeval thrill. We lulled ourselves to sleep with intervals of listening to the weird sounds, snorts, grunts, screeches and chatters. Once, shortly after midnight, there was a great cracking so close that it woke me up. I lay perfectly still, straining my ears, my heart beating fast, but whatever animal had made the noise must have gone past; nothing happened.

I felt overawed, but never threatened. I didn't believe in malevolent spirits and wasn't nervous about wild animals. They don't usually harm you unless you threaten them or get in their way. I felt safe at night, protected within the shelter of our home on wheels.

We slept in our Land Rover on a soft foam mattress set upon a wooden board on top of the luggage. Don't imagine that we had the whole width of the back compartment to ourselves; there was a narrow cupboard running along one side, containing all the kitchen utensils and the small fridge in which Peter stored his exposed films. That left about two thirds of the width for sleeping and it wasn't much.

The length of the sleeping area wasn't quite sufficient either. It was about 4 inches shorter than Peter. He could never sleep on his back and stretch his legs unless we left the flap at the back open so that he could stick his feet out. It had been safe to do that in the Sahara where Peter didn't risk having his toes nibbled by wild animals. Even in the Sahel we had left the back open, although there were jackals about, but once we were in more densely populated areas, and especially after the head-cutter episode, we preferred to lock the Land Rover at night. This forced us to sleep on our sides and we had been trying out different ways of fitting together, but nothing was ideal. Peter always slept with his head towards the front and after a while, I found that if I slept with my head towards the back we fitted much better inside the restricted area; it gave Peter just a little bit of extra space for his broad shoulders. Even so, when one of us got tired of sleeping on one side and turned over, the other one had to turn too. When I woke up at night I would try to remain immobile as long as I could stick it out, even though I often found myself wedged into a space no more than fifteen inches wide, with the top of my head squashed against the inside of the metal back-flap.

It all seemed very difficult at the beginning but after a few weeks we got quite used to our way of sleeping and only turned over once or twice a night. And sometimes I even had the joy of lying on my back, squashed against Peter, my bent knees stuck up. In the end I felt like a bird in a nest and, strangely enough, when the journey was over, I would sometimes miss the closeness and cosy feeling of our moving home.

The forest was eerily quiet at dawn. Everything was extremely humid; dampness hung almost tangibly among the trees in great misty blankets. As the light grew in intensity, the mist slowly dissipated, leaving behind great sparkling droplets of dew hanging from every leaf and bough around the small clearing in which we had parked, dripping on us as we sat down for breakfast.

'Would you believe it?' said Claire one morning. 'We've still got that mouse!'

'Which mouse?'

'The one that's hidden inside the Land Rover.'

'Oh, *that* mouse! I haven't heard it for a long time. Are you sure it's still there?'

'Of course I'm sure!' Claire sounded upset. 'I heard it just now. And you know what it's doing? It's eating our rice.'

'Well, it's got to eat something I guess.'

'Yes, but not our rice!'

The mouse had been with us for a long time. We first heard it just after arriving in Goundam. It must have worked its way amongst the reserves shoved underneath our mattress and decided that it had found a perfect home: food was plentiful, but I couldn't think what it drank. Still, being a desert mouse, it probably got enough moisture from the food it ate.

We had tried to track it down but without success. We had emptied the whole back compartment onto the sand in Joël's compound and when we hadn't found the mouse we had reloaded everything, certain it had gone. Unfortunately, the next night we again heard it scurry amongst our belongings underneath our bed. After that we had given up, hoping that it would leave one day of its own accord. But now, more than 1,000 miles further south, it was still with us! However, a few days later when we reached the Atlantic, it was no longer there and I felt concerned about our adventurous stowaway. Would a mouse, used to a dry desert climate, be able to survive in the humid forest? But then, nature is strong and maybe the mouse would learn to cope with this radically new environment. Even better,

I hoped that one day it would meet a forest mouse of the opposite sex and, I fantasised, maybe this would give rise to a brand new mouse lineage?

The following day, to our surprise, we ran into two young Europeans who were eating sandwiches sitting next to their Land Rover. Christian and Brigitte told us they had left the South of France less than a month before and intended to drive all the way to South Africa. Since we were going southwards, too, we decided to carry on together until our ways parted. The only problem was that Christian wanted to drive much faster than we liked or could manage.

'That doesn't matter,' he said. 'I'll carry on and wait for you every now and then.' He seemed quite pleased with this arrangement, as the pauses would allow him to eat a sandwich and make a cup of coffee, of which he was a great consumer.

We had been following a straight, well-kept forest road for maybe two hours without seeing a single vehicle when we noticed a stop sign. Christian was standing next to his vehicle some 10 yards further on, surrounded by several uniformed men. When he saw us approach he began to jump up and down, making wild signs to attract my attention. His antics so distracted me that I kept looking at him instead of the road surface, until suddenly my front wheels bumped over something. I stopped at once and opened the door: under the middle of our Land Rover, from one side of the road to the other, ran a rusty tyre deflation device. It consisted of a foldable steel frame from which 5-inch-long, thick iron spikes stuck out. And I had driven over them!

When Claire saw the long, pointed spikes she flared up. 'They've ruined our tyres!'

I was furious and when the uniformed men came towards us I shouted at them, 'Are you out of your mind? To put a thing like this across the road!'

I saw the armed men stiffen. 'This is to stop smugglers,' said one of them with a stern face.

'Smugglers? Here? In the middle of nowhere?'

'Missié,' replied the man, 'we're only twenty kilometres from the Liberian border.'

'But this road doesn't go into Liberia. It runs parallel to the border!'

The chief of the uniformed men now came forward. 'Missié,' he said pointing an accusing finger at me, 'you are not to criticise the government. And you've acted against the law. There's a sign here to warn oncoming traffic to stop, and you didn't stop!'

'But I did!'

'Not in time!' retorted the officer. 'You should have stopped well before the sign, not at it.'

I was livid by now. How stupid officialdom could get when it tried hard. 'Yeah, not in time to stop my front tyres from being punctured,' I hissed. As I spoke I looked at the tyres and my mouth fell open: they seemed intact! I went to have a closer look. There wasn't a mark on them, but the spikes of the tyre deflation device were completely flattened down where my wheels had run over them! This bucked me up no end and I calmed down at once, but it was too late.

The officer drew himself up in front of me with a face like thunder, held out his hand and barked,

'Missié, your passports.'

I had been warned that in contacts with officialdom in Africa, success depended on your patience and your ability to keep calm. And I had failed abominably on both accounts! I resigned myself to the inevitable, dived inside the Land Rover to fetch our passports and handed them to the officer who put them inside his pocket. Then the uniformed men all went towards a small wooden shelter that had been erected further along the road and turned their backs on us, clearly showing their intention to ignore us.

So that was that! Here we were, stranded between the green walls of the forest; our front wheels had passed the rusty, shoddy tyre deflation device that ran from one side of the red earthen road to the other, but the back wheels hadn't; it was stiflingly hot and armed men had confiscated our passports.

Christian, who had stood by silently during the whole exchange, now turned to me. 'You should have been more careful,' he said disapprovingly. 'Why didn't you stop? I tried to warn you not to run over the obstruction.'

I lifted my eyes to heaven but refrained from making any comment.

'We've already wasted twenty minutes waiting for you,' he carried on, 'and look what you've got into now. We can't just hang about here forever. If you can't get your passports back we'll have to leave you behind.'

I wished I could get our passports back and leave, but how was I to do that? First of all, I thought, I must get past this stupid obstruction. Seeing that the armed men weren't looking, I decided to act swiftly and began to pull the tyre deflation device from underneath the Land Rover. When they heard the scraping sound the soldiers turned and came running along at once, but before they had time to intervene I had already hopped behind the steering wheel and quickly drove a few feet further. As I began to pull the device back into place, the officer nearly blew up and roared, 'You're not allowed to touch anything!'

It certainly wasn't the moment to ask for our passports, but I tried all the same.

'You have broken the law on several accounts,' the officer barked, barely able to hide his anger, 'and I shall have to report your conduct to higher authorities. In the meantime, your documents are confiscated and you will have to wait here.' He gave me a cold stare and turned, ready to go back to the shelter.

The whole affair was taking on the ridiculous proportions of a diplomatic incident and it was important to defuse it before it escalated further. One of us had to back down and the officer certainly wasn't going to do it: he had his pride and would rather be seen dead than lose face, and he held all the trump cards and knew it. So there was nothing for it but humiliate myself. After all, I had got us into this predicament and it was up to me to get us out of it.

'I'm sorry,' I said, trying to sound as if I admitted guilt. 'Can't we settle this? I shouldn't have been in such a hurry.'

The officer looked at me blankly.

'The problem is,' I carried on, smiling as amiably as possible while quickly making up a story, 'I have an appointment with the Belgian ambassador in Abidjan tomorrow afternoon.'

That didn't seem to make any impression on the officer. He snorted derisively, 'And why would this concern us?'

'It does concern your country,' I replied politely, making up an even wilder story, 'because I have been sent by the Belgian Government to visit development projects. I cannot miss the appointment because the ambassador and I are expected to meet a minister of your government afterwards to discuss Belgian aid to the Ivory Coast.' And I repeated, 'I'm really sorry all this has happened.'

A worried frown had begun to appear on the officer's face while I was talking. He now withdrew and I saw him confer with the others in a low voice. After a while he returned with his men. 'We can drop most of the charges,' he said sounding more amenable, 'but there's one thing we cannot overlook. You have destroyed government material and you will have to pay so that we can have it repaired.'

'Which government material?'

The soldiers pointed all together at the bent spikes of the tyre deflation device.

'Oh that!' I looked at them eagerly. '*I* will repair that for you if you like.'

The officer seemed disappointed but after a few seconds he made a sign that I could go ahead. I climbed up on the roof rack of the Land Rover, got a heavy hammer out of the toolbox, knelt down in front of the tyre deflation device and started banging the bent spikes to straighten them. Within no time the army people had all gathered around me and I heard them snigger; as I turned my head upwards I saw the smirks on their faces. They hadn't been able to extract money but I'm sure that humiliating this 'important European official' made up for it. The sight of me on my knees in the dust, sweating away while they were looking down upon me, must have been very gratifying!

I did get our passports back after that, but as I drove away I never wanted to see another one of those frustrating roadblocks again. Little did I know then that check points were the staple of daily life in some African countries and that, by the time I was halfway through Zaire, I had got so used to them that I was almost looking forward to the challenge.

The Atlantic

It was late afternoon by the time we reached the coast and we decided to call it a day. We found a sleepy lagoon and were ready to drive on to the beach when we noticed five or six huts at the far end. Good manners demanded that we ask for permission to stay on the beach and so we went to find the chief of the little hamlet.

'You're welcome,' he replied, 'but under one condition …'

What now? I thought, but then I heard him continue with a twinkle in his eyes, 'You must join us for a drink tonight.'

The drinks were to start after the moon had risen and in the meantime, Claire and Brigitte started preparations for supper while Christian began to clean out his Land Rover. I sat there, wondering what I could do, when my thoughts went to the spare wheels. The two we carried had been used and if we had another flat tyre or a blow-out we would be left stranded on the road. After the scare with the tyre-deflating device, I felt it was high time to prepare at least one wheel for a possible emergency. It now seemed providential that Bernard had bought us four new tyres, which were stacked up on the roof rack.

In Belgium I had been to garages where they changed tyres in no time. They had specialised equipment for this, of course, but all the same, it seemed a job I could do. I took a used wheel and new tyre down from the roof rack, got out my tools and started with a great show of energy. However, I soon found that the job wasn't as easy as I'd imagined. The old tyre refused to budge and it took me ten minutes of jumping up and down on it before the rubber became unstuck from the rim. Removing the tyre was even worse. Half an hour later, I still hadn't managed to yank it off the wheel.

I finally decided to ask for help and went to the huts where a few Africans, who had been out in a fishing boat, had just arrived.

'No problem,' said a tall fellow who looked like a heavyweight boxer. And indeed, it wasn't a problem for him. He just wrenched off the old tyre and ten minutes later a new one was in place. Then, as I stood there gaping, he asked with a large smile, 'Shall I pump it up for you?'

That evening we were sitting on a log near the huts. Our hosts had made a small wood fire, which created a circle of light in the darkness of the tropical night; two of the men began beating tom-toms with the palms of their hands and slowly a few of the Africans stepped forward and started shaking their bodies in rhythmical movement. One of them was a little girl; she couldn't have been much older than three but she was already stamping her feet and twisting her small body as if dancing were as natural to her as drinking her mother's milk.

The chief now filled a couple of plastic cups from a large vessel, came over and handed them to us, saying proudly, 'Our palm wine.' Then he returned to his stool near the fire.

'What's palm wine?' whispered Claire into my ear.

'It's made from the hearts of palms.'

'I thought wine came from grapes. How do they make wine from palms?'

'The women do it. I've read that they chop up the hearts of young palms into small pieces, put these into their mouths, chew them for a while and then spit them out into a big vessel where they leave the lot to ferment.'

I saw Claire abruptly straighten up. 'What!'

'You see …' I explained, 'the women's saliva helps to start the fermentation process.'

Claire looked at her cup with undisguised disgust. 'And we're expected to drink *that*?'

'I'm afraid we'll have to. They'll be very upset if we don't.'

'Well, I'm not going to,' said Claire with a determined expression on her face and when nobody was looking she poured the contents of her cup onto the sand behind her back; then she pretended to be drinking from her empty cup. But I put my lips to the cup and drank. The palm wine wasn't bad at all; it was sparkling and slightly alcoholic. And I tried hard not to think of all that saliva as I downed my cup.

The following day we drove along a sandy track to reach a village close to the ocean. I was always on the lookout for pure water, which we tried to collect wherever we found clean wells. When I discovered that there was a covered concrete well, we stopped to top up our six bright-red, plastic water containers.

The track petered out in the village but the people told us that further along there were beaches firm enough to drive on. We thought that we might just as well have a look and carried on in four-wheel-drive mode. When we reached the ocean, the view was breathtaking. Magnificent deserted beaches stretched into the far distance, narrow strips of curving yellow sand bordered by the white foam of the rollers of the Atlantic on one side and fringed on the other by a dense, dark-green wall of coconut palms. The sand was firm and we drove along until we found a really lovely spot where coconut trees were leaning over at quite an angle. We parked right under a huge tree which spread its leaves wide, providing shade for our Land Rover, and installed our mattress on the roof rack. Christian carried on another 50 yards, preferring to park nearer the water's edge where he could feel the spray.

The ocean seemed inviting, but I soon learned that the undertow of the Atlantic was so strong that swimming was extremely dangerous. Walking innocently into the waves, my feet were swept clean from under me before I realised what was happening and I felt a strong current pull me out towards the open ocean; then, just as suddenly, I was turned upside down and my head hit the bottom; next I surged upwards and a great roller threw me onto the beach like a piece of flotsam.

Christian, who had come over to see if I needed help, laughed at my misadventure. 'You have to dive into the breakers,' he lectured, whereupon he left to go for a swim.

I hadn't yet fully recovered from my encounter with the Atlantic when I heard Brigitte scream. As we ran over we saw her, half hidden by the foam, trying to hold on to one of Christian's arms. The current was pulling at his seemingly lifeless body and we arrived just in time to drag him out of the thundering waves and stretch him out on the beach, where he lay gasping and regurgitating water. Apparently he had been about to dive into a breaker when it hit him fully in the stomach and knocked the breath out of him. Had Brigitte not been just behind him, and had we not arrived within seconds to help her, his body would have been carried out to the ocean where nothing could have stopped him from drowning.

An hour later, a man from the village arrived on a bicycle to sell us a huge fish, which had been freshly caught that day. Brigitte skinned it and filleted it expertly and then fried it on a small fire of dead branches we had collected. We had supper on the beach with our hair waving in the breeze, and as the western sky began to turn orange, I felt like Robinson Crusoe!

We climbed up to the top of our Land Rover and attached our mosquito net to the overhanging leaves of the coconut palm so that it made a protective curtain above us. We lay there for a while, looking out at the star-speckled dome of the African sky and listening to the waves racing up the African shelf and roaring against the coast. To sleep like this was to enjoy a feeling of peace and freedom such as one could never experience in a city. I closed my eyes in perfect contentment and knew no more until I was awakened the next morning by the sound of the surf on the beach.

We felt like castaways, alone in a world of unspoilt beauty. There was no sign of human presence, just endless space, rocks jutting out into the waves and yellow beaches curving away as far as the eye could see between the green wall of vegetation and the blueness of the mighty ocean. The strong rollers of the Atlantic were breaking with thunderous noise and far away over the ocean, just above the hazy line of the horizon, hung a bank of white fair-weather cumulus clouds.

If this wasn't paradise, then what was? We stayed there for two days and would have liked to stay for much longer, but Christian wanted to move on and there was no stopping him. Soon we were back on the roads and a day later, as we entered Abidjan – a modern city by any account with wide avenues, high-rise buildings, traffic jams and whistle-blowing policemen – we knew we had returned to civilization.

Christian and Brigitte went their own way from here on, while we drove to an address friends in Belgium had given us. We were slightly apprehensive since we didn't know the people, but yes, our mutual friends had written about us and of course, they were happy to welcome us. And they gave us their daughter's bedroom as if this were the most natural thing in the world. Once again we were amazed at the extraordinary hospitality people showered upon us.

The following morning we went to the Belgian Embassy. When the secretary who received us found out who we were he immediately went upstairs and a few minutes later we were ushered into the ambassador's office.

'So there you are!' exclaimed the ambassador. 'Thank God you're alive.'

When we stared at him in total surprise he explained, 'It's your parents. We understand that they are without any news from you. They are very worried and …' he turned to Claire, 'your father contacted the Belgian Ministry of Foreign Affairs some time ago. According to your travel schedule you were supposed to have arrived here by mid-January and we are now in March! We feared that you had got lost – or worse – and were about to launch a search party, but we didn't know where to start. Thank God you're here.'

The ambassador was right, of course. It had taken us a long time to reach Abidjan: a mere three and a half months into the journey we were already two months behind schedule. We had been oblivious of time, living each day so intensely that we had forgotten all about Europe and our families back home. We had not written since that letter I had sent from Reggane just before Christmas!

'Here,' said the ambassador, handing Claire the phone. 'You'd better call your father.'

Claire did as she was told and when she heard her father's voice and sensed the immense relief he felt that we were alive and safe, she was full of remorse.

'Don't you want to phone your parents, too?' the ambassador asked me when Claire had finished her call.

'That's very considerate of you,' replied Claire, 'but my father is going to phone Peter's parents immediately.'

'Good, good,' commented the ambassador. 'Now, let me see … there was also a letter from the Ministry of Foreign Affairs. Now, where did I put it?' He thought for a while and then decided, 'I'm going to ask my secretary,' and left.

'How is Papé getting on in his studio?' I asked when we were alone.

Claire looked embarrassed. 'Well … actually he's not living in his studio.'

'What do you mean? We specially transformed the garage into a studio for him. You don't mean to say that he's still in the house, do you?'

'Well … yes … and so is Philippe.'

Suddenly the problems we had left behind in Brussels caught up with a bang and hit me fully. 'But then … but then … that means they haven't let the house!'

Claire shook her head. 'No,' she said slowly. 'They haven't been able to let it.'

'But why? They should have let it by now. Everything was ready when we left Brussels. And your father promised he would take care of everything. He assured us he would let the house!'

Claire lifted her head defiantly. 'I'm sure he did his best!'

'But don't you understand what a disaster this is for us? We'll never be able to travel to India and back on the money we've got!'

'Well … we'll have to, won't we?' said Claire.

'What about those articles you were going to write for that women's magazine? I'm sure the Embassy will forward them. Then at least we could make some extra money.'

'I've decided not to send any articles,' replied Claire, turning her head away.

I found it hard to believe this. 'Why?'

She seemed embarrassed. Then she blurted out, 'How can I make money on the backs of poor women such as Fatima who confided in me? I must have been mad. How could I ever have thought of revealing their intimate secrets to the public, betraying the trust they showed in me? It's unethical.'

'But I've seen you fill up pages and pages with notes, even recently.'

'That's for myself because I like remembering.'

'But we haven't got enough money to complete our journey!'

We both fell silent for a while. Then Claire looked at me encouragingly. 'I'm sure we can do it.'

I emitted a hollow laugh. 'And how do you propose to do that?'

'That's easy. We just cut out all hotels and superfluous expenses from now onwards.'

I stared at her, flabbergasted. 'Superfluous expenses? When we've been living off tinned food for months and done nothing but sleep in our Land –'

Just at that moment the ambassador returned to his office and we both managed to force a smile.

'I can see that speaking to your father has really cheered you up,' he said to Claire. 'It's always so nice to have news from home.' He looked at her, beaming, and then turned to me. 'My secretary has just retrieved the letter from Foreign Affairs. Apparently you want to film development projects in the Ivory Coast. Now, there are several interesting projects up north …'

'Well, ahem …' I managed to reply. 'We've already been in the north and filmed a few projects there.'

The ambassador was taken aback. 'But you should have come to me first! The Foreign Office is asking me to lend you my assistance … within the limits of the acceptable of course,' he hastened to add.

'Thank you very much for such a generous offer,' I replied diplomatically, 'but as you rightly observed, we are well behind schedule. We should be leaving the country soon.'

'Quite, quite …' The ambassador seemed to mellow. He stood there for a while, nodding his head and then asked, 'So you plan to study the problems of development on the ground? At least,' he clarified, tapping the letter he was holding, 'that's what they say here. Now, that's an intelligent idea. Tell me, what have you learned so far?'

I didn't know what to reply. What had I learned so far about development? I had tried to make the best of chance meetings and had talked to as many people as possible, hoping to learn from them. I had heard a lot of criticism of the colonial epoch. Government officials in particular had recited a litany of all the ills colonisation had brought Africa: that it had created artificial borders; that the colonisers had exploited the Africans; that all of today's problems had their roots in the colonial epoch; and so on.

I had also found out that African countries were a muddle of tribes, which often didn't get on and that neighbouring nations didn't seem to get on well either. People from poorer countries who went in search of work over the borders were frequently treated as unwanted immigrants and those from more advanced countries looked down upon the others, considering themselves a cut above the rest. I realised this when I heard a Ghanaian in Bamako say with disdain in his voice, 'They're completely underdeveloped down here in Mali.'

Then there was that Nigerian student who told me, 'You Europeans can never leave anything alone. You're always thinking of improving things, of how to make us work more. You keep telling us what we need to do and how we ought to live when you don't understand us Africans at all.'

But apart from a few general observations, I hadn't found out much. Nothing was as I had expected back in Brussels where I had conferred with people from the EEC, suggested a blueprint for Third World development and drawn up a programme of what we were going to do during our trip.

And what had we done so far? Nothing one could call useful! I had visited a few projects here and there, but had come away with more questions than answers. In fact, the deeper we penetrated into Africa, the more perplexed I had become. How was I ever to understand Africa, let alone suggest solutions to its mind-boggling problems?

Basically, our attention had been taken up with solving practical problems as they arose, avoiding obstacles of all sorts and surviving on poor food rations. We had no idea what the next day was going to bring and most days we didn't even know whether we would find a safe place to sleep. I didn't realise it at the time, but this was in fact a fair summary of the life and outlook of many Africans.

'Well,' said the ambassador, shaking his head after my muddled exposé, 'and where do you plan to go from here?'

The ambassador's words brought me back to reality. I didn't know where to go. The rainy season was about to start north of the equator and this would make it impossible to drive through Nigeria and Cameroon to reach Zaire and Uganda as we had planned. If we attempted it we would be stuck in the mud for the next three or four months! It was clear that I would have to radically revise our schedule. I was at a total loss as to how to proceed when the secretary suggested a possible solution. A boat from the *Compagnie Maritime Belge* – the *S.S. Fabiolaville* which had left Antwerp more than a week before – was due to arrive in Abidjan harbour within a few days. It would sail on to Matadi, which was Zaire's port at the mouth of the Congo River well south of the equator where the rainy season was about to end. If they had room for us and the Land Rover, we would avoid the rainy season altogether!

We kept our fingers crossed as we drove to the company's office the following morning. If they didn't have a free cabin I intended to plead with them to let us sleep in our Land Rover inside the hold or wherever they might be able to put it. But luck was with us: they told us that a couple of passengers were going to disembark in Abidjan and this would free one upper-deck cabin. To our relief, they charged no more than 28,000 Belgian francs (about £400 at the time) for the cabin plus full board for two.

'And the Land Rover?' I asked hesitantly.

'Oh,' they replied, 'that'll cost nothing. We'll just put it on the deck. We'll count it as hand luggage.'

We still needed to have our visas for Zaire renewed. The time limit for using them had run out and we went to the Zairean Embassy full of dire forebodings, but we were lucky again. We had an introduction from the Belgian ambassador, the Zairean ambassador received us personally and when he heard that we planned to sail on the *Fabiolaville* he was well-disposed toward us because it turned out that his wife was returning home on the same ship! He renewed our visas there and then, and allowed us to enter via Matadi but he told us that, as the old visas were for one week only, he couldn't give us more than that. We would have to apply to the Ministry of Home Affairs in Kinshasa for an extension.

And so, at last, we were ready to leave the country. Two days later we said goodbye to our kind hosts, drove to the port, went through emigration, carried on along the docks and stopped some 20 yards from where the *Fabiolaville* lay moored. Then I went up the gangplank to show our tickets, leaving Claire alone in the Land Rover.

I sat there, thinking of my father and the phone call I had made a few days ago. For months he had been waiting for news while I hadn't even thought about him! How could I have forgotten my home and my family so completely? How could our worlds have diverged so much? And then I realised what had happened: Africa had captured my heart. Discovering its warmth, roaming freely through parts of the world unknown to us, had been so unique that it had totally entranced us. The civilised world had receded, time had lost its meaning and days stretched endlessly. It was such a heavenly feeling, so alien to anything I had known before.

While I was lost in reveries, a young African came strolling over to where I was sitting and, leaning on the open window, he started chatting to me. The man was telling me such a complicated story that I couldn't make head or tail of it, but I didn't want to seem impolite and tried to listen while he kept grinning and gesticulating. Then, from the corner of my eye, I saw an arm shoot through the other window and grab the bag that was lying on the driver's seat; a split second later the thief sprinted away, followed by the man who had been chatting to me.

We had been so careful all through the journey. Our papers had always been stowed away securely, but Peter had just shown them to the border police who had given us exit stamps and for once all our documents had been lying in a bag on the driver's seat and both windows were open! I should have kept an eye on our passports and car documents, but I was feeling relaxed and completely safe so near the boat.

As the disaster sunk in, I sat there stunned: our passports and car documents had been stolen. We would be unable to go back to the Ivory Coast, or go forward to the boat and on to Zaire. We were stranded in no-man's land!

Suddenly all hell broke loose. A sailor began to yell and several men rushed forward in hot pursuit of the thieves.

I was on the upper deck when I heard loud screams and as I leant over the railing to see what was happening I noticed a great commotion below. Some men were hitting an African while others were running along the docks. Why are they beating up that poor man? I wondered as I went down the gangplank. I was about to go to the Land Rover when one of the sailors came running towards me waving a pile of papers which somehow looked familiar. Then I recognised our big orange vehicle carnet.

'Hey! What's this?' I cried out. 'These are my papers.'

'You … huh … don't know … huh … how lucky you are …' the man gasped, still out of breath. When he had recovered somewhat he told me that he was the one who had spotted what was happening and had sounded the alarm. When the dockworkers had begun to pursue the thief, the accomplice had turned round to stop them and enable his partner to get away; he was overpowered and immediately beaten up, while some of the men continued to chase the other African. The thief then began to throw papers out of the bag, one by one, to slow down his pursuers; the strategy had worked and he had managed to escape!

The sailor handed me the pile of documents he had picked up. I scanned through them with beating heart and to my relief, I found the vehicle carnet, our passports, our car documents – everything was there. We were saved!

'Isn't there anything left in the bag then?' asked the sailor, intrigued.

'Yes, a wallet.'

'Hell!' he exclaimed. 'Your wallet! No wonder the thief didn't mind throwing out all the rest.'

'Oh but I don't really care about the wallet. It was a present. I never liked it.'

'But you've lost all your money!' The man looked very worried. 'How much did you have in the wallet?'

'Oh! It was empty. I never keep my money in a wallet.'

A smile of satisfaction now appeared on the sailor's face. 'I have a feeling that our thief is going to be very disappointed when he opens that wallet,' he grinned. 'Serves him right!'

A quarter of an hour later, we watched our Land Rover being hoisted aboard. At the gangplank we shook hands with the people from the Belgian Embassy who had come to see us off, and went up to our cabin. It was not very large, but after sleeping for so long within the narrow confines of our 'home on wheels' it seemed spacious to us. It had comfortable bunk beds, which felt like a real treat. We would be able to lie down at night and stretch out without pressing against the sides of the Land Rover. It also had a small porthole through which we could look out over the ocean, but what pleased us more than anything else was that we had our own bathroom. We could shower as much as we liked and there was hot water gushing out of the tap any time we turned it on! This was sheer luxury after more than three months in desert and bush.

The ship was only due to sail on the morning of the following day and the night spent in the port of Abidjan was not as safe as we had imagined. Around 2.00 a.m. we heard banging and angry shouting. It appeared that some Africans, sneaking up in a small launch, had tried to climb on board, but the sailor on watch had pushed them back into the sea with a long pole.

'It's getting worse every year,' one of the sailors told us the next morning, as the ship began to move out of the port. 'And we're lucky we don't have to anchor off Nigeria. There the pirates have guns.'

As the African Coast disappeared, a brisk breeze arose, lifting our spirits. After several weeks spent in the humid atmosphere of the southern Ivory Coast, the fresh air of the ocean invigorated our senses. Within hours, the discomforts and problems of the past months receded into the corners of our memories. I had lost a lot of weight, but was much fitter than when I started the journey. We were far behind schedule but we didn't care; we didn't even want to think about the future. It was glorious not to have to worry about finding a safe place to camp, to have no anxiety about the morrow, no particular spot we absolutely had to reach, no rendezvous to keep. We just lived in the moment.

Above: A stop in the bush

Below: Beware of obstacles! As no one is going to move them, you'll have to drive around them

Above: Women returning from work in the fields at nightfall

Below: Hauling up water the traditional way

Above: Claire in Kaniasso: let me try it!

Below: Peter and schoolchildren at the mission of Zélé

Above: Changing a wheel

Below: Into the forest

Above: The suspended liana bridge

Left: Claire holding a liana

Below: Morning in the forest

Above: Amadou showing his cocoa trees

Below: Amadou and his machete: an all-purpose tool

Above: There is safety in numbers

Below: The great domed hut

Above: Holding babies

Below: Inside the great domed hut

Above: Claire and the waves of the Atlantic

Below: North of Abidjan: a giant communal 'launderette'

Above: Port of Abidjan: ready to go.

Below: The Land-Rover is hoisted on board the *Fabiolaville*

Interlude: Crossing the Equator on a Boat

When I awoke the next morning I found the gates of bondage wide open. Suddenly there came the full realisation that I was free! For years I had been leading a life of captivity, doing what others wanted me to do and being what others expected me to be. For years, deep down, so deep that I had hardly been aware of it, I had dreamed of escaping the strict rules of conventional society that keep you on a leash and the demands people make on you. I thought I would never be able to break away from servitude, from everything that held me back. And now I was free!

Looking out over the ocean, I knew that life was eternal and beautiful, and that I was deeply and irrevocably a part of it. I was living the life I had always desired, a life of travelling without time restrictions, of exploring everything we wanted to or dared to. Freedom!

Awaking to a new dawn was precious; each day brought fresh excitement, the thrill of wandering into the unknown, of discovering amazing landscapes, sights, people, animals – pure adventure! It was like gazing into a kaleidoscope that revealed all the different facets of life, each instant full to the brim, each moment perfect because there was 'time' to dwell upon it.

This journey through Africa was Peter's gift of love to me – our first great journey together. It contained everything we had both dreamed of since our earliest youth and I knew that nothing could ever surpass this first time.

I revelled in the life on board the *SS Fabiolaville* as I never thought I would. We felt within a sheltered shell, part of one big family. All the passengers were on easy terms and everyone seemed good natured and happy. And we were pampered: the upper deck passengers ate at the officers' table and the food was out of this world. A heavenly aroma came out of the kitchen, dishes were exquisitely prepared and there was such a variety and abundance of everything that it was dazzling. After months of monotonous, solitary meals in the bush, it seemed wonderful just to sit down, put your feet under the table and be served divine meals. Breakfast, lunch and supper were copious and you could eat as much as you liked. And to make sure passengers wouldn't go hungry they also served mid-morning and afternoon coffee and tea with a wide choice of scones, cakes and pies!

I had justifications for feeling ravenous, having lost more than a stone since leaving Brussels, but the truth was that the food was too tempting to resist. The first day we sat down to all the meals and teas, and had second and even a few third helpings. The freshly baked bread was heavenly, as was the steaming coffee, the cream, the pies and cakes, the sauces, the succulent dishes, everything! The second day we began to skip third and even second helpings; the third day we no longer went down for tea and by the fourth day we were eating no more than minimal quantities.

But not everyone managed to withstand the temptations of the kitchen. One of the passengers, a woman in her late thirties, had been on board since the boat sailed from Antwerp. She was going to join her husband, a major in the Belgian Army who had left for Zaire several months earlier to train young African officers. Was it a need to compensate for being alone or the excitement of going to join her husband? Whichever it was, she had been unable to resist the rich food and by the time we reached Zaire, she had put on twenty-five pounds and was bulging out of her clothes! It was only then that she began to panic.

'My husband won't recognise me,' she kept repeating. 'I was a slim woman when he left. He'll have the shock of his life when he sees me come off the boat. I'm sure he won't want me anymore. What am I to do?'

One morning, after a lavish breakfast, the upper deck passengers were told to get ready for a very special event. The ship was going to cross the Equator, festivities were being organised to celebrate the crossing in style and it was whispered that an extremely important visitor was expected on board for the occasion.

When I came out onto the deck in my bikini as requested, there he was, sitting on a bench, holding his trident: Neptune had appeared from the depths of the ocean to honour us with his presence and preside over the festivities! He was accompanied by his wife, a mature lady, and both had crowns on their heads. Strangely enough, they were bone dry although they had supposedly just emerged from the waves.

The King of the Seas and his Queen were assisted by a female judge who cut an impressive figure in her red cloak and white sheet, which was bulging like a sail caught by the wind. I recognised her immediately as the plump young woman who had put on such a lot of weight since boarding the *Fabiolaville*. She was to pronounce judgment over the few unfortunate passengers who had never crossed the equator before, and she was playing her part with great enthusiasm.

Four victims were awaiting judgement: a French couple – they had decided to risk everything and had sold all their belongings in France to start a small business in Kinshasa; then there was a young woman who was about to join a mission as a sister; and myself. In the days of sailing boats, sailors who were crossing the equator for the first time were lowered on ropes and plunged into the foaming waves. Fortunately we were merely to be thrown into the small swimming pool on the upper deck and our heads to be pushed under seven times – once for each of the seven seas – while the audience counted aloud; and the ship's doctor was standing at the ready to rescue us from drowning.

When I heard the judge announce the punishment I felt quite frightened. I don't like being pushed under water. Luckily, Peter was the one who would have to push our heads down each time we rose to the surface. He had been selected for the role of executioner and was dressed as a pirate, one eye covered by a black patch.

The fun began with the young woman who was going to join a mission. After she had gone under several times she began to splutter and gulp and I couldn't help calling out to Peter, 'Wait, wait! Leave her time to breathe,' but she had to go down the full seven times and ended up so out of breath that Peter had to help her out of the pool. Now it was my turn. When I came up the first time I whispered to Peter, 'Please, don't push my head. Let me go down by myself.' He gave me a wink and handled me gently, so I managed, only swallowing a mouthful or two at the end. Then the Frenchman had to go in and all the passengers were cheering and egging Peter on to push him firmly under each time he popped up; the man stood it out bravely. Finally it was the turn of his young wife. She got cross at being ducked, struggled for a while and ended up gasping and coughing; she came out all wobbly, her beautiful hairdo completely ruined and she was so upset that I had to comfort her.

After loud applause from the public, the judge decreed that next, the victims were to be painted one side red, the other green. Peter, who had been given a long brush, set about with great gusto smearing the gluey liquid all over us. It was quite horrible, but the onlookers fully enjoyed the show. Then we were allowed to shower, terribly pleased it was over and were awarded our certificates for crossing the equator.

In the evening, the captain and his crew offered us a sumptuous banquet and the night was full of fun and laughter. Later, lying on my bunk bed, I had a nightmare. I dreamed that I was a sailor who was thrown again and again into a gigantic wave by a merciless pirate, and I woke up with a start, gasping for breath. Then I realised that I was safely in our cabin; Peter was breathing quietly on the bunk bed above mine, deeply asleep; the ship was moving gently through the waves and all was bliss.

For four glorious days the boat glided over a dark-blue, glassy sea while we played childish games or just lay in our deck chairs, lulled into beatitude by the ship's gentle motion. Life was there to be lived in the here and now; we didn't have to think; there were no chores to be done, nothing to worry about. Everything felt just right. Time seemed to have been suspended. We were immersed in a misty, dreamlike ambience, as if a silken glove had wiped out the past and pushed the future to a remote distance …

Map 3:
Boat from Abidjan to Matadi

Above: Neptune on board

Below left: Punishment has been meted out

Below right: Painting Claire

PART 3

South of the Equator: From the Atlantic to the Indian Ocean

Africa is a string of surprises

Map 4:

From Zaire (Congo) to Zambia, Zimbabwe and Tanzania

CHAPTER 8
The Congo: Life is There to be Lived

How the Congo Became Zaire

On the morning of the fifth day on the *S.S. Fabiolaville*, we sighted the African coast. As the ship began to enter the mouth of the Congo River, moving slowly through the muddy-brown waters against a strong current, we hung over the railing, looking at the low hills and beautiful landscapes gliding by. This was the Congo at last!

So much had changed since I'd dreamed of the Congo at the time of the World Fair in Brussels in 1958. I was sixteen at the time and rebelling against the stupid rules and regulations imposed by my school. Unfortunately, one day I was caught scaling the wall with three of my classmates, and the director – a narrow-minded man – used this minor infraction to ban me from school for a week.

I was rather apprehensive about the punishment my father was going to mete out when he came home that evening, but to my immense relief, he said, 'How lucky! As I've got a day off work this week we can go to Brussels together and see the World Fair.' I will always remember his reaction with deep gratitude.

The World Fair had just opened and that day we visited the pavilions that my father chose, but I returned a number of times over the next few months, undertaking the two-hour train journey alone. I repeatedly went to see the Brazilian pavilion, where I immersed myself in a profusion of tropical flowers through which wafted an aroma of coffee, but I spent most of my time in the Congolese pavilion. Whole trees had been brought over to create a tropical forest; there were stuffed animals lurking amongst the tree trunks and imitations of animal sounds; and a village had been built complete with tom-toms, masks, spears and musical instruments. To me, this was the real Africa. I spent many hours there, and time and again I had to tear myself away from it at night to rush to the station to catch the last train home.

In those days, the Congo was still a Belgian colony and not a single Belgian politician considered setting it free in the foreseeable future. Jef Van Bilsen, then lecturer at the Higher Institute for Overseas Territories in Antwerp, was virtually ostracised by the establishment after he dared to suggest that it would be advisable to begin preparing Congolese personnel for future independence (he presented a thirty-year plan in an article published at the end of 1955). But the wind of change was blowing over Africa in the late 1950s. Armed revolts had broken out in several colonies and some had recently become independent. Encouraged by what was happening elsewhere, Congolese intellectuals were making ever more strident demands. Then, when riots broke out in 1959, the Belgian government unexpectedly caved in. Elections were held in a hurry and the colony became independent on 30 June 1960 without adequate preparation. The Congolese people had had access to lower-level jobs but no African had been admitted to any post of command or responsibility. Now, literally overnight, postal clerks became ministers of state in the new Congolese Government. It was a recipe for chaos.

The Belgian establishment believed that business would continue as usual in spite of independence and that they would be able to carry on running everything, but within days the Congolese troops mutinied against their Belgian officers, a number of colonials were killed, women were raped and the Belgians fled in a panic, leaving the Congo without a functioning administration. To make matters worse, inter-tribal wars broke out. In the Congo, as in other parts of Africa, there had always been friction between neighbouring tribes, often culminating in bloody conflict. Colonial occupation had put a lid on this, but the moment decolonisation removed that lid, the old tensions flared up again. On top of that, some provinces seceded (the most prominent was Katanga, the copper-mining province), and a communist-inspired rebellion erupted in the northeast. The Congo seemed to have irrecoverably fallen apart.

At this point, Mobutu decided to act. He was a secondary school dropout who had been a sergeant in the army before independence, but through networking with the right politicians and with a knack for manipulation, he had managed to become Chief of Staff of the Congolese Army. In 1965, finally, his moment came. With tacit American support, he grabbed power in a coup d'état, sacked all the politicians – whose main activity had been squabbling amongst themselves – and created a one-party state. His army marched into the breakaway provinces, putting down one rebellion after another, and eventually Mobutu managed to unite the Congo once again.

His military rank continued to rise quickly after he had declared himself president. By 1967, he was already a general and in the end he considered his position so exalted – well above that of those ordinary generals and admirals elsewhere in the world – that he created a unique title for himself.

At first, Belgian politicians and industry had supported him, relieved that he was 'cleaning up the chaos'. They believed that he would protect Belgian interests and allow them to continue as before, but Mobutu had other plans. He didn't wish to remain beholden to Belgium; he wanted a clean break with the colonial past.

Already in 1966 he had Africanised the names of towns in an attempt to return to African authenticity, outlawed neckties and proclaimed that all Christian first names be stamped out. To show the way forward, he changed his own name: Joseph-Désiré Mobutu became Mobutu Sese Seko. Not satisfied with that, he gradually added a string of other African words behind his name. According to some slanderous people, these translated into: 'The rooster who reigns over the henhouse and cannot leave a single hen alone.' There was probably some truth in this. A friend of ours whose husband was a trader in the Congo happened to be staying with a doctor in a region reconquered by Mobutu's advancing army. She told me later that her friend the doctor was woken up by soldiers in the middle of the night and taken to a house where he found Mobutu in great distress. Apparently the man had been overexerting himself with young women for hours on end and had suffered an apoplexy some time after midnight. My friend also told me that Mobutu preferred lighter-skinned African women, and that his troops picked these up and brought them to their commander as they 'liberated' towns.

Mobutu now began to nationalise industries, including the most profitable of all, the mining industry in Shaba (ex-Katanga), and introduced a new monetary unit, the zaire, to replace the old Congolese franc. In 1971, he went further and re-baptised the country and the Congo River, calling both Zaire (although Congo was an African name, whilst Zaire was a sixteenth-century Portuguese mispronunciation of Nzere, the name by which the Congo River had been known to one of the local tribes). The names were changed back to Democratic Republic of Congo and Congo River respectively after Mobutu's demise.

In 1973, oil prices quadrupled while the price of copper, Zaire's main export product, fell dramatically. Blaming foreign speculators for the dire situation in which his country found itself, Mobutu began a move towards what he called self-reliance – his Zairianisation – which basically consisted of driving out all foreigners active in production and commerce, and handing their enterprises to his entourage and members of his party.

Reality caught up quickly: production fell rapidly and this showed in the exchange rate of the zaire, which had been fixed arbitrarily at $0.5 US (then 25 Belgian francs) in 1967. By 1982 the official exchange rate had already fallen to 9 Belgian francs, but only those who could not avoid it changed at official rates; you could get 1 zaire for only 3 Belgian francs on the black market.

However, Mobutu was seen as an ally of the West in the fight against the spread of communist influence in Africa and he milked this for all it was worth. The IMF intervened and bank loans and aid flowed in to stabilise the currency. This could not, however, compensate for Mobutu's economic mismanagement, and in spite of receiving no less than $20 billion US in foreign aid during the period he was in power, Zaire's economy deteriorated rapidly and the national currency began to collapse. Over the next ten years average annual inflation was 400%. The banknotes bearing Mobutu's image, which had been introduced with so much pride in 1967 to herald a new era, had become virtually worthless. By 1991, Zaire, one of the richest countries in the whole of Africa, had become a failed state.

This was not the end of the story. Since communism was no longer a threat, Mobutu was now put under international pressure to restore democracy and allow political opposition. He systematically reneged on his promises while the economic situation went from bad to worse: between 1992 and 1997 average annual inflation was 1,600% and Zaire was in ruins.

In 1997, Mobutu was finally chased out of the country and fled to Morocco, which gave him asylum, but he had provided for his old age. He had stacked away no less than $6 billion in private

Swiss bank accounts! Alas, the poor man wasn't to profit from his nest egg. He died of prostate cancer in December 1997, aged 67.

Arrival

It was dusk by the time we arrived at the port of Matadi, 85 miles up the estuary of the Congo River. No sooner had the ropes been fastened when gang planks were put from the quay to the ship, and men ran on board as if they were pirates taking the *Fabiolaville* by storm. Within minutes, the deck swarmed with Africans, some wearing no more than ripped trousers. The few Zairean passengers who had been on board and whom we'd hardly seen until now, suddenly appeared and started shouting orders at the men who immediately began to offload their luggage and the bales that were stowed on deck.

I thought we would have to disembark too, but the customs offices were already closed and European passengers were requested to stay on the ship until the next morning when immigration officers would come on board. It was a relief. I had not been looking forward to setting off again towards the unknown in the pitch dark and sweltering heat of the African night. All the same, I was worried about the Land Rover's safety with all those Africans milling about on deck for what seemed endless hours.

Thankfully, although meals were included in our tickets only until arrival, the ships officers invited us for dinner and we sat down once more to a delicious supper. However, I didn't enjoy it as I had in the past few days. Maybe it was because my carefreeness was gone. I was thinking about the future once more and I was apprehensive about what it might have in store. Corruption and bribery seemed to be rife in Zaire and problems often began at customs. I remembered that the Zairean Embassy in Brussels had not been welcoming and this seemed to be part of a general pattern. I had heard some tall tales about government officials doing their very darnedest to annoy Belgian citizens in one way or another and generally making their lives difficult.

The next morning, immigration officers came on board, stamped our passports and made us fill out a form on which we had to declare all foreign currency we carried on us. This form had to accompany our passports. When we left the country, customs officers would check our remaining cash and verify whether bank receipts accounted for the difference. These formalities over, the Land Rover was finally lifted onto the quay and we were told to drive along the back of some warehouses to reach the customs building. When we went in, to our surprise, the customs officer turned out to be a Belgian! He was very courteous, if a trifle rigid. He accepted my international vehicle carnet, checked whether it was valid for Zaire, went out to see if the vehicle plates and car particulars corresponded, stamped the carnet and then wished us a pleasant journey. It was all over in less than ten minutes without any hassle or bribes.

This doesn't feel like independent Africa, I couldn't help thinking. It's like colonial times. What's a Belgian doing here? Later I heard that corruption had been so rampant over recent years that customs duty had all but dried up as a source of government revenue. The African customs officers had got into the habit of pocketing the money themselves instead of sending it on to Kinshasa (where Mobutu took a fair cut of it to pay for his personal expenses). Mobutu had finally had enough. He had decided to stop this and asked the Belgian Government to send some trustworthy officers to supervise operations!

Just past Kinshasa, the capital, the mighty Congo River begins its descent from the high plateaus of Central Africa through a series of treacherous rapids and gorges to Matadi some 200 miles further, where the river widens and becomes navigable again all the way to the Atlantic. Nearly a hundred years before, a railway had been built under Stanley's supervision to bypass the rapids and provide an ocean link for the otherwise landlocked Congo Free State. The railway was to be Congo's lifeline, of vital importance to its economy. It was to be built whatever the cost, and the cost had been very high indeed: an African life for every sleeper. It remains important today, although less so than in the past now that an asphalted road has been built alongside it and road transport has become easier.

We started the slow climb out of the estuary of the Congo River, left Matadi and the last human habitations behind, and gradually emerged onto the plateau of Bas-Zaire, a country of ever-changing rolling hills. As we stopped and got out, the peace of undisturbed nature enveloped us. Nothing seemed to have been touched here; there was only beauty as far as the eye could see. A warm breeze caressed our faces and the rustling of the tall golden grass, gently blowing in the soft wind, accentuated the silence. This is what the Earth must have looked like before humans started moving in, I thought. We felt as if we had returned to the beginning of creation. We were completely alone in a bright-coloured land where unspoilt views stretched to the far horizon. We were back in the Garden of Eden! Looking upon these luminous landscapes of infinite beauty, where nothing had been sullied or disfigured, brought home to me how magnificent our planet could be if only humans left it alone.

Kinshasa

Back in Brussels, a young friend of ours had given us the address of her parents who worked in Kinshasa, saying that if we ever passed their way they would be delighted to put us up. When we finally reached the Cottrils' house, we found them somewhat peeved. It appeared that the Belgian Ambassador in Abidjan had informed his colleague in Kinshasa that we were on board the *Fabiolaville* and they had heard the news. They knew that the ship had docked in Matadi and had organised a surprise party the evening they reckoned we were going to arrive at their house. We had apparently become mini-celebrities. Many Belgians in Kinshasa had read about our expedition, we were considered intrepid travellers, and our hosts had invited a number of friends and colleagues to welcome us.

Unfortunately we had been so overwhelmed by the enchanting beauty of Bas-Zaire that we had spent an extra night in its golden hills, and our hosts had held the party the day before we arrived in Kinshasa! The Cottrils' welcome was less cordial than it would have been had they been able to show us off but still, they put us up and kindly offered to help with any problems we might encounter.

For a day or two, I felt dazed. Was it the miles of glorious, ever-changing landscapes and the enthralling visions we had seen, which kept unrolling before my eyes? I just wanted to indulge in a bath and then lie on my bed so that I could dream about our adventures and the many fascinating encounters our nomadic way of living had brought us, but it was not to be; the Cottrils were going to dine out. All the people they had invited two evenings earlier would be there, and there was no escaping them this time. Even worse, they told us that we *had* to dress up because the Belgian Ambassador would be present.

I tried to shake off the torpor and, wondering what I could possibly wear, rose slowly looking at the bundle of clothes dumped on the floor. Everything was rumpled; there was nothing I could put on. Then I noticed the long, white cotton kimono with dazzling pink fuchsia flowers printed all down the front – a present from Richard's stepdaughter France in Bamako. I had used it as a nightdress, but it was clean. It might just pass off as a dress though it was slightly transparent, but there was nothing to be done about that, as no petticoat was available. I slipped it on and put the heavy Dogon sun pendant around my neck. It would be different from the silks and jewels other ladies would no doubt be wearing, but I thought I looked presentable for what they considered 'an adventuress', until I saw my hair in the mirror: it was a tangle of tight, unruly curls!

Minutes later, I was still desperately pulling at my hair, trying to smooth out the tangles, when Peter came in. He had been checking oil levels and looked like a tramp.

'Put on some decent clothes,' I urged. 'Be quick! The Cottrils are waiting.'

Peter washed, picked up a clean shirt and trousers, and began to dress without any fuss. I sat spellbound as he changed from the dusty tramp he had been a short time ago into a tall, handsome man. I handed him the comb, wiped a smudge from his face and forgot all about my own appearance. Then, when he was ready, he smiled at me, held out his arm and said, 'You look lovely – like an exotic flower. Come, let's go.'

We thought the Cottrils would take us in their car, but to our surprise they told us to follow them in our own vehicle.

Eight other people had been invited for dinner and they all shook hands and seemed keen to meet us. I was seated next to the ambassador who immediately plied me with questions. He wanted to know all about our adventures and in the end he got me talking enthusiastically. All went smoothly until we reached the end of the main course and the ambassador suddenly wanted to have a look at our Land Rover.

I flushed pink. In my mind's eye I saw the horrendous jumble inside and I mumbled evasively, 'Oh, well … maybe tomorrow if you like.'

He leaned towards me. 'But you have brought your vehicle, haven't you? I specially asked for it.'

'Yes, it's here, but … but I'm afraid everything is in rather a mess.'

'Oh … I don't mind that. Come on,' he motioned, 'let's go before they serve the dessert. I'm really curious to see how real adventurers travel.' And before I could do anything to hold him back, he got up, took a torch and went outside looking for the Land Rover. I followed, dragging my feet and found him, his nose glued to the windscreen.

'Can you open the door?' he asked eagerly.

Oh no, I thought, but it was too late. He already had his hand on the handle and when he found the driver's door unlocked, he opened it and straightaway got into the driver's seat.

'Well, well …' he said, holding on to the steering wheel, 'imagine driving all the way from Belgium like this.' Then he turned around, looked at the opening in the plywood partition and shone his torch inside.

My eyes were wide with horror as he peered into the back compartment. We'd had no time to clean anything; the inside was a huge muddle and everything was covered in red dust.

The ambassador seemed in a state of shock. 'Is this where you've been sleeping for all these months?' He stared at me with incredulity. 'I can't believe it! And how do you get in there?'

All right, I thought, I'll show him. After all, it can't get worse than it is already. So I crawled onto the seat next to the ambassador and before his mesmerised eyes, I disappeared through the plywood opening, felt for the handle of the back flap, opened it and called out, 'Come round!'

As I lay on my belly looking out, the ambassador's head appeared at the back; he heaved up his heavy body, trying to crawl inside next to me, but he slid down and nearly fell. Then, as he steadied himself, we looked at each other and burst out laughing. Suddenly all was fun. After the ambassador had stared at our sleeping quarters with bulging eyes, he helped me to lock up everything and then lent me his arm, saying, 'It's an honour to walk with such an adventuress.'

We went back to the house under the bright starry expanse of the sky and the ambassador was in high spirits for the rest of the evening, explaining to a spellbound audience what he had seen in the Land Rover and egging me on to talk about our journey and tell a few tall stories.

Over the next few days, I was busy attempting to solve administrative problems and trying to work out how to proceed from Kinshasa. What bothered me most was the extension of our visas. I drove to the Ministry of Home Affairs hoping they would be amenable and allow us enough time to drive out of the country, but when I entered the building I was in for a shock. A dense crowd of Africans was milling around, all gesticulating and shouting. This was not just confusion; it was total chaos. After a quarter of an hour of patient pushing, I had worked my way through the throng and at last reached one of the counters. I had prepared a little speech to present my case, thinking of arguments to counter any objections, but it was all useless. The employee I was facing didn't even look at me but kept talking to another civil servant behind him, and when I finally managed to attract his attention and explain my reason for coming, he stared at me, totally uninterested, and said, 'I don't know.' Then he held out an indifferent hand and added, 'Just leave the passports here.'

I glanced at the pile of papers and scattered documents around him and recoiled. Suddenly I saw red. I'll be damned if I'm going to leave our passports here, I thought. I might as well throw them straight into a dustbin. And I turned on my heels, fuming, and worked my way out through the mass of people.

Back at the Cottrils, I was pondering our predicament while staring at our passports. This whole administration – nay, this whole government – is a joke, I reflected. Who wants to depend on the whims and benevolence of incompetent employees? Not me! No way. And I decided there and then to take my fate in my own hands. I put our passports on the table, opened them on the page where the visas for Zaire indicated: duration 1 week, took a pen and changed the 1 into 6 and added an s to the word week. And to hell with officialdom, I thought.

Many annoying things can happen on a journey such as ours, but one thing I had not foreseen was toothache. This is no problem in Europe; you just go to a dentist. But in Africa there are no dentists outside big cities. All you may be able to find in the bush is a witchdoctor with a rusty pair of pincers, eager to pull out your tooth without any form of anaesthesia. And you just pray that he pulls the right tooth. So you'd better have your teeth checked and all old fillings replaced before you set off. I had, of course, not thought of that but, fortunately for me, the toothache began in Kinshasa and before it became worse, I managed to find a French dentist who put in a filling. And that wasn't all. When I asked him how much I owed him, he replied with a large smile, 'Nothing. Consider this my contribution to your expedition.'

My toothache had been no more than a small inconvenience but it made me realise how well organised modern society has become and how we take that organisation for granted. Developed societies want security; everything is insured and the value of everything is measured in money: your car, your house, your health and even your life. This web of security protects us from everything, even from our own stupidity. You can drive aggressively or too fast and cause an accident: no bother, your car is insured; you can live irresponsibly and eat unhealthily: no worry, your medical insurance will take care of your medical bills. Responsibility is shifted onto insurance companies and if their managers behave irresponsibly and the companies run into difficulty, the government is sure to step in. But here in Africa, this supporting web of security doesn't exist. You are responsible for your own actions. There's no insurance company to come to the rescue, no one else to hold responsible for your misfortune. You've only got yourself to blame. And if you make a mistake, you pay for it yourself in effort, sweat and money; and you have to pay immediately.

I needed to exchange some money and asked Mr Cottril for the address of the nearest bank.

'You'd be mad to change money in a bank,' he replied. 'Nobody does it. Everybody changes on the black market and for a good reason: they give you three times the official rate.'

'But I've got to report any foreign currency I spend,' I protested.

'No one's asking you to spend any foreign currency,' he retorted. 'How many zaires do you need?'

I hesitated for a few seconds, but I had to admit that he was right. If tyrants apply ridiculous financial policies and make laws to impose these, I thought, they just incite people to do what they can to circumvent those laws. I made a quick estimation of the cash we were likely to need over the next five weeks and told Mr Cottril. He went to his study and returned a minute later with a thick wad of banknotes. Counting them in front of me, he said, 'Just write me a cheque in Belgian francs. I'll cash it when I return home.'

'Would it be possible to have some notes of a higher denomination?' I asked, hoping to reduce the bulk of the stack of banknotes.

'Sorry,' he replied, 'but this is the best I can do. Until recently the highest denomination was ten Zaire (about forty pence at black market exchange rates); fortunately they've now brought out fifty Zaire notes, but they're still difficult to come by.'

We sometimes watched TV. One of the regular appearances on the small screen was President Mobutu. He always spoke as a father would to his small children, or else would whip up his people to perform great patriotic deeds. His speeches invariably ended with the slogan, 'One Country! One Party! One Guide (the guide being, of course, Mobutu himself)! Then he would make way for groups of musicians and dancers, the women with large portraits of the president printed on their colourful dresses. Mobutu was a great showman and a clever manipulator, and the broadcasting skilfully combined his bombastic rhetoric with popular themes, music and dances. The message was: all is perfect in Zaire, which is the most beautiful country in the world.

'Wouldn't you like to phone home?' Mr Cottril suggested to us one evening.

'I've already phoned my father from Abidjan,' replied Claire evasively.

He turned towards me. 'And what about you?'

'Well … that's very kind of you but phoning Belgium would be far too expensive.'

'Not at all. It's very cheap. I ring my children in Belgium every week and I talk as long as I like.'

When we stared at Mr Cottril in disbelief, he explained, 'I know a man at the telephone company; he's always on duty on Sunday evenings; let me speak to him.' He got up and I was about to follow him when he raised a hand to stop me. 'Leave this to me. Just give me your parents' number.' And he went off and I heard him talk into the phone in the hall.

A quarter of an hour later, the phone rang and this time Mr Cottril beckoned me over. 'Here's your call,' he said, handing me the receiver.

My father was on the line and he couldn't believe his ears when I told him I was phoning from the very city where he had spent a couple of months in 1960, supervising the repair of the telephone connections that had been destroyed during the riots just after independence. He was one of the rare Belgians who had volunteered to fly to the Congo at a time when all Europeans were fleeing the country. My parents were extremely pleased that we'd got this far and relieved that we were well and still in good spirits.

'How much do I owe you?' I asked Mr Cottril when I put the receiver down after a long and enjoyable conversation.

'You don't have to pay me. You pay the man from the phone company. He'll come to collect the money tomorrow morning.'

The next morning the doorbell rang. 'It's the man from the telephone company,' whispered Mr Cottril. 'Don't come. Just give me fifty zaires.'

When our host came back I stared at him with suspicion. 'I bet you that man is going to put the money in his own pocket,' I couldn't help saying.

'Of course he does.' Mr Cottril shook his head contemptuously.

'But … doesn't someone have to pay the bill?'

'You really want to know?'

'Yes.'

'You see, I'm not the only one phoning Belgium. Lots of people do it and not only Belgians. The Zaireans phone their relatives in Brussels all the time, or else they ring up their embassy over there. So the Zairean phone company – in other words, the government – runs up a huge bill with the Belgian phone company, which of course is also a government service. And Zaire will refuse to settle, just as Mobutu refuses to pay taxes on his properties in Belgium. In any other circumstances Belgium would have cut all phone communications with Zaire a long time ago, but the Belgian Government is not going to do that. They want to stay on good terms with Mobutu.'

'So, what will happen?'

'Well, eventually the Belgian Government will cancel all Zairean debts as they have done before and then everything will start again from zero.'

For months, tropical storms had broken over Kinshasa, usually in the early afternoon, but the thick steamy cloud cover was now following the sun towards the northern hemisphere.

The rainy season wasn't yet over, though. We were sitting inside the Cottrils' house when black whirling clouds suddenly began to move overhead amid gusts of wind. Within minutes the sky, which had been bright blue in the morning, turned a deep black while the branches of the trees along the street began to shake furiously. The light faded rapidly, a suffocating heat weighed down upon us like a heavy blanket and the atmosphere became unbearably charged with electricity, making us all tense. Then the skies exploded in deafening thunderclaps that seemed to shake the whole world and lightning enveloped the house. The wind steadily increased in intensity until suddenly the rain came, approaching like a dark moving curtain with a deep rumbling sound. Torrents of water thumped so violently against the windows that no one could hear what anyone was saying.

The other side of the street vanished from sight behind a wall of rain and nothing could be seen except leaves and broken branches whirling by. One branch cracked against the building and when at the height of the storm a door flew open, the sudden rush of wind swept the table clear of dishes and cloth.

This cloudburst bore no resemblance to any kind of rain we were used to in Europe. Water came down in bathtubfulls, an almost solid downpour, so much so that if you stepped out for a second you would be as soaked as if you had fallen into a river. Towards the end of the storm the street had become a torrent in which thick raindrops splattered, making bubbles that kept bursting.

After an hour, it was all over. The mass of black clouds thinned out, patches of the sky turned blue again and then a brilliant sun appeared and shone on the water in the streets, heating it to steam, which drifted upwards like a hot, quivering mist – a real Turkish bath. The air felt humid for hours afterwards.

Mr and Mrs Cottril's daughter was due to arrive for Easter and as we were occupying her room, they asked us to look for somewhere else to stay. Fortunately we had met so many Belgians by now that this was no problem. Jo and Henri, a couple of teachers at the French Lyceum, whom we liked very much, had a large apartment with an extra bedroom, and they were willing to put us up. They seemed happy to be working in Zaire, and no wonder. As Henri explained, there were many advantages.

'Do you realise that the Belgian Government pays us double salaries?' he said. 'They pay us over here and again into a bank account in Belgium where the money just accumulates. We'll be able to buy a beautiful country property by the time we retire; and we can retire early!' Henri smiled contentedly. 'None of this would have happened had we stayed in Belgium. Think of the lives of teachers over there: low pay, lots of administrative chores and unruly classes, whilst over here everything is perfect. African students are extremely well behaved; we have no chores outside our teaching, long holidays and free plane tickets home. And this apartment is free, too! We're really leading a life of luxury.' He sighed. 'It's almost too good to be true.'

But even they could not escape the downside of living in Zaire. Their apartment was situated in an attractive area of the town. A row of tall trees lined their driveway and behind these trees there was a thick hedge of flowering bushes, separating their apartment complex from a modern villa. Unfortunately a branch had broken off one of the trees during the recent storm and fallen onto the roof of the neighbour's villa where it had damaged a few tiles. The man, an African, was enraged and swore that he would have his revenge.

Some days later, when I entered the driveway, I found it blocked by branches scattered about everywhere. A few Africans were high up in the tall trees, chopping off branches with machetes while clinging on in a precarious position. I backed up, parked in the street and ran inside.

'They're cutting the branches off your trees!' I shouted when I saw Jo and Henri. 'Can't you stop them?'

They shook their heads in sadness. 'It's not just the branches. The man on the other side has given order to cut down all the trees.'

'But most of the trees are a long way from his villa! And they're not even on his property! He has no right to do this!'

Henri shook his head in resignation. 'We've protested but it's useless. The man's a big shot in Mobutu's government and his word is law around here.'

But the man didn't escape retribution altogether. Some branches fell onto his roof, making gaping holes and then, to our intense satisfaction, as they chopped down the trunks, one of the tall trees fell towards his villa and crashed straight into it, almost cutting it in two. We couldn't help thinking that there was some justice after all and felt much better after that.

It was Jo's day off from school and we were standing in her kitchen, talking animatedly, when through the window she saw a boy dragging a skinny little monkey along by a string tied around its neck.

'Oh those heartless boys!' she exclaimed. 'How they treat animals!'

She quickly ran down the flight of steps and called out, 'Hey! What are you doing to that poor monkey? Leave it alone!' She barred the boy's way and stood glaring at him.

The boy just shrugged his shoulders. 'Madame,' he muttered, 'if you want him to live you must buy him. You pay me and you take him.'

Jo hesitated. What would Henri say if he found a monkey in his apartment when he returned from school?

Suddenly the little monkey, who had been looking down with dispirited eyes, sprang up and clasped his thin arms around Jo's neck making soft cooing noises in her ear. Jo melted at once.

'Right,' she said, handing over a ten-zaire banknote, 'but don't you ever dare catch another monkey!' She wagged a warning finger.

Maybe he'll behave after this, I thought, but the boy didn't seem to show any remorse. He just pocketed the money and scampered away gleefully.

A few hours later, Henri came home, hot and tired after a day of teaching, and sank down on the sofa. 'Ah, a nice cool drink,' he said as Jo brought him a glass. He smiled, 'Peace at last,' when suddenly a flying mass of fur landed on his head and pulled his hair, trying to hang onto it while uttering small piercing shrieks.

Henri dropped his glass in fright and jumped up, yelling, 'What the hell is this?' He pulled the struggling monkey from his head and held it up by the scruff of the neck. The little animal was dangling at arm's length and when Henri shook it furiously, it started emitting strange cries sounding like sobs. Jo immediately rushed forward, grabbed it and wrapped her arms protectively around it.

Henri was livid. 'What's this little monster doing in our apartment? Are you mad?'

'Listen,' Jo pleaded, 'just listen …' And she told him the story of how she had seen the little monkey outside, ending, 'So you see, I had to buy him.'

By the time she had finished her story the tense atmosphere had lifted. Jo now turned towards her husband beseechingly. 'I'm sure you would have done just the same to save an innocent life.'

Henri tried one last objection. 'But we already have a dog.'

'The two seem to be getting on very well.' Jo sounded firm. 'And I love this little monkey,' she added, stroking the head of the monkey who by now had buried his face in her neck and held on to her as if he were a little baby seeking protection.

'He's an ugly thing, but if you really want him …'

'Oh yes!' Jo beamed. 'So we keep him?'

'Well …' Henri bowed before the inevitable. 'All right.'

'What shall we call him?'

Henri stood there for a while, undecided, trying to adjust to the fact that he was now the proud owner of a monkey. 'It'll have to be something like Scruffy or … Scraggly,' he said after a while. 'No … wait … something really ugly would suit him much better. Let's call him … Gargoyle?' He looked at Jo with undisguised mischief.

She cut him short at once. 'He's much nicer than that! I think we'll call him Grippy, no … Gribouille … that's it: Gribouille.'

The little monkey had not moved while they were discussing his fate, but when Jo called out, 'Gribouille!' he began to make funny faces and clapped his hands as if he understood that all was settled now. 'See how happy he is,' remarked Jo. 'He'll be our mascot and bring us luck.'

But soon they got more than they had bargained for. Gribouille started swinging from the curtains and the chandelier, opening cupboards and hiding in the most impossible places, sometimes making them burst out laughing but more often making them mad. He became a little tyrant and would not eat from his bowl unless he could sit with them at the table. He ruled the roost. The final touch was sleeping in their bed with his arms around Jo's neck!

As we had to stay for a while in Kinshasa, we gradually began to know it better. Its centre had been planned in the colonial era when the capital was called Léopoldville, and it had imposing buildings and hotels and wide avenues intersecting the city, in particular the one now called Boulevard du 30 Juin (June 30, Congo's Independence day). Its infrastructure had been ample in 1960 when there were just half a million inhabitants, but the African population had been growing rapidly since then and internal migration had been intense. When we arrived in 1982, 2.5 million people had already come to live in Kinshasa. The inner city was showing signs of fatigue and the outskirts had become a muddle of shantytowns, which were growing by the day.

What do all the people here live off? I wondered. There were some government jobs, lots of small shops and bars, and some open-air markets where they sold anything imaginable, but few industrial activities, even if you counted as industry the banging and clanging made by low-skilled craftsmen. What I saw in Kinshasa didn't look to me like a real economy but more like survival from one day to the next.

And yet the younger generations continue to flood in from the countryside. In the villages, young people are controlled by the elders; life out there is boring and without a future, whilst in Kinshasa, life is free and promises the wildest illusions. The bright city lights are irresistible – who doesn't want to come to Kinshasa?

I was told the story of a diamond digger who finds a big diamond in Tshikapa in the Kasai and sells it. And what does he do with the money? He hops on the first lorry to Kinshasa, installs himself in a luxury suite in a grand hotel, buys expensive clothes, eats loads of rich food so that he becomes plump and attractive, hires a car with a chauffeur – because he cannot drive and anyway, rich Africans are driven around by chauffeurs – entertains in his hotel suite and, of course, surrounds himself with lots of pretty young women. He lives like a king and has the time of his life. Unfortunately, after six months, his money runs out and when the hotel management discovers that he can no longer pay his bills, he is thrown out. So he returns to Tshikapa as poor as before, lying on top of a load of sacks on a lorry and once again becomes a diamond digger. He's back in a deep hole on the banks of the Kasai River with other men in rags, up to his knees in the muddy red earth, but boy, oh boy, what memories! What a life he's had! And you never know. Maybe luck will smile on him a second time. Maybe he'll find another large diamond. And what will he do then? He'll go straight back to Kinshasa and start all over again.

In Zaire, as in most African countries, there are quicker roads to riches than finding a diamond or working hard, and the quickest road of all runs via cultivating ties with the ruling party, and especially with the president … if you can. High political rank confers great power. Unfortunately, that road is open only to a small elite but once you're part of it, your life is set apart from that of the common man. There is a clear distinction between those who have power and the opportunities to use or misuse it, and the rest – the vast majority of the population.

Africans know they can do little to change their fate. You'd better be happy-go-lucky and accept life as it is if you want to survive in Africa. Luckily most people here seem to be endowed with a huge capacity to enjoy each moment. And they can always hope for better times. Today they're poor but tomorrow … who knows? Maybe they will be lucky … or even very lucky. Maybe … they'll get rich?

The people in Kinshasa were as nice as the authorities were abusive. I felt strangely attracted to the town with its easy-going men, its smiling women and its carefreeness. There was an innocence of life different from anything we were used to in the West.

Africans are often known by their nicknames. They habitually use these next to their names when they advertise for their businesses, and this sometimes leads to very funny ads. A startling one I saw, proudly painted in big, bright letters above a shop entrance, was the owner's name: *Muzungu Nzaya*, followed by: *known as The Idiot*.

People are endearing. You often see young women plaiting each other's kinky hair and creating all sorts of attractive hairdos. The most striking, maybe, is the one known as 'the antennas of Zaire'. The plaits stick out impressively like the quills of a porcupine.

No matter how rapacious the government and how awful people's living conditions, life beats strongly. Africans seem to have an inexhaustible capacity to survive; music is in the air and nothing can resist the sheer force of sensuality. Here in the city, every moment, with every breath, Africa exudes sensuality, unadulterated, raw. You find it in the bright colours and strong body scents; in the swinging movements of the women; in the sensuous dances and vibrant music. Here black women wear elegant dresses and have no inhibitions; they look you straight in the eyes, staring at you with insolence as they pass by, swaying their hips. Sexual desire is in the hot humid air, everywhere, daily. Who could resist the attractions of the city?

I liked Kinshasa. I even got used to its policemen. The street on which Jo and Henri's apartment was situated crossed a wide avenue a few hundred yards further on. This crossing was a strategic point because cars had to come to a halt there. And this, of course, was where the police were lurking.

As I was driving a vehicle with a foreign licence plate, I was considered a potential milk cow, and whenever I stopped at that crossing on my way into town, looking left and right to see if there was any traffic on the wide thoroughfare, a policeman would invariably jump out from behind a tree and start blowing his whistle. The first time this happened it caught me by surprise. I was sure I hadn't done anything wrong, but that wasn't the problem. I was told that my licence plates were not the correct colour and the policeman asked for my passport. I argued that I had Belgian licence plates, whose colour was obviously very different from Zairean plates, which were bright blue, but it was no good. The policeman insisted that he was right and demanded I pay a heavy fine!

However, after my experiences with policemen in Mali and soldiers in the Ivory Coast, I was not keen on paying fines of any sort or handing over my passport and so, perceiving a lull in the traffic on the thoroughfare, I revved up and crossed, leaving a flabbergasted policeman behind.

After that, encounters with the police became like a childish game. The scenario at that crossing repeated itself, even though there seemed to be a different policeman whenever I arrived. The third or fourth time a policeman tried to stop me I got so annoyed that I leaned out of the open window, made a rude gesture and drove on. I was low on diesel fuel, though, and as there was a petrol station just on the other side of the avenue I pulled in without thinking. Unfortunately the policeman had seen me do this and I had just begun to fill my tank when I saw him crossing the wide thoroughfare, running, gesticulating and blowing his whistle.

When he got to where I was, he grabbed the diesel pistol from my hand and continued to fill up the tank! Then, after I'd paid the pump attendant, the policeman held out his hand and demanded my passport. That was of course the last thing I wanted to do and I quickly jumped behind the wheel and started up the Land Rover, but before I had time to drive off, the man ran round and hopped in on the other side!

'Your passport,' he kept demanding as we drove along, but I just ignored him and carried on. We had covered maybe half a mile when the policeman began to get worried.

'Where are you going?' he wanted to know.

'I'm going to the Belgian Embassy,' I replied – and for once this was true. 'And there, in front of the ambassador, I will hand you my passport.'

'Why didn't you tell me?' said the man in a plaintive voice. 'You should have told me you were going to the embassy!' As I carried on, he began to panic: 'Stop! Let me out!'

I continued for another quarter of a mile and then, feeling the fun had lasted long enough, I stopped. The policeman jumped out without so much as a goodbye and as I continued on my way, I saw him in my rear-view mirror, running back at top speed, his image getting smaller until he disappeared from view.

However much fun Kinshasa was, we had to move on; sooner or later we would have to leave Zaire. The north, where it was raining, was impassable, while the south, Angola, was off limits. Its communist government, aided by Cubans, was fighting rebel forces supported by the West and South Africa. Anyway, my aim was to reach Dar es Salaam on the other side of Africa and to set sail to India from there. But how were we going to cross Africa from west to east? Directly east of Kinshasa lay impenetrable rainforest and somehow we would have to bypass it.

Maybe we could catch a boat up the Congo River to Kisangani in the northeast of the country and then join our original itinerary through eastern Zaire into East Africa? I was told, though, that riverboats were always overcrowded, noisy, unhygienic and unsafe; total chaos reigned on board. And even if we made it to Kisangani, a boat journey of maybe two weeks, we would still have to cross the forests of eastern Zaire. The rainy season had not yet ended up there and I was warned that the dirt road out of Kisangani was in such bad condition at this time of year that lorries sank almost entirely into the huge muddy potholes. Anyway, no riverboat was sailing just now, so we finally gave up the idea.

If only we could get to Lubumbashi in the southeast of the country we would be out of trouble! I tried to have the Land Rover airlifted on a C130 plane, but all in vain. There was one and only one way to reach Lubumbashi and the Zambian border, no less than 1,800 miles away: drive there! Most of the road was unmade, but since it was marked as a thick red line on the map, I hoped that it would at least be in reasonably good condition.

I asked Mr Cottril but he said he had no idea and sent me to one of his acquaintances who had been in the Congo before independence and was reputed to know everything about the country. The man didn't seem very enthusiastic about the road through southern Zaire.

'It's a bad stretch of mud,' he commented.

I was foolish enough to ask, 'Don't they flatten out dirt roads at the end of the rainy season?' when my interlocutor cut me short.

'This was common practice in colonial days when roads were kept in good condition. And did you know that the colonial authorities were planning a complete network of roads, to be built and surfaced in the early 1960s? But unfortunately independence intervened and the Belgians passed control overnight to incompetent subalterns. Very little has been added to the infrastructure since then.' He snorted. 'Unless of course you want to count as infrastructure the airport in Gbadolite – the village up north where Mobutu comes from – and the asphalted road from that airport to the president's marble palace. We're no longer in the Belgian Congo, remember,' he said sneeringly. 'We're now in Zaire.'

'But look at the Ivory Coast,' I objected. 'It became independent at about the same time as the Congo and there the dirt roads are well kept. In fact, the whole country seems in excellent condition. And they've even got a stretch of motorway.'

'The Ivory Coast is not a typical African country! Are you not aware that there are forty thousand French in the Ivory Coast, including some armed forces? And that many companies over there have remained in French hands? And let me remind you that the stretch of motorway you mention runs from Abidjan to Yamoussoukro, President Houphouët-Boigny's native town.'

'But isn't the Congo – I mean Zaire – a rich country?'

'Well, it was ...' He sighed and shook his head. 'But the colonial era finished in 1960 and now the country has Mobutu, his clique and his Zairianisation. Whenever any money is made, the government is there to take a large cut. And no prizes for guessing into whose pocket most of the money ends up.'

The man was getting irate and I diplomatically changed the subject. 'So you don't think I should drive through the Kasai?'

He strongly advised me not to go that way. Apart from the awful condition of the road, we would be passing through areas that weren't very secure. Tribal warfare had flared up in the Kasai after independence but I had heard that the situation was stable now and told the man.

'Don't you believe what the authorities say,' he countered. 'The unexpected is never far away in this country.'

Other Belgians in Kinshasa agreed. Comments ranged from general statements such as, 'You'll never get through all that mud,' to more specific ones like, 'It's too dangerous; you're sure to bump into army patrols or worse, and you're not going to enjoy that.'

It was obviously foolhardy to attempt getting to the other side of Zaire over a dirt road when the rainy season had not quite ended. And I was not at all keen on driving through unsafe areas. Somehow, though, we had to get out of the country and by now it was clear that it was either taking the road through the Kasai and southern Zaire, or ending our expedition here in Kinshasa.

I had been told that we needed special authorisation to drive through the Kasai because of the diamond mines in the area. So I went to a government office, gave all the information and a passport photo to one of the employees, spent days waiting and then, when the document was finally ready, it cost me no less than 270 Zaire! Even at black market rates this came to £13.00. And all I got was a typed page with my passport photo stapled onto it and a stamp from a ministerial department. The employee had probably typed it himself and pocketed the money!

If we were to drive all the way through southern Zaire it was imperative to have the gearbox repaired; changing gears had become difficult. When I consulted Mr Cottril, he advised me not to go to the official Land Rover garage. 'That would be much too expensive,' he stated. 'I know a competent African mechanic who is much cheaper.'

The mechanic, an Angolan refugee called *Vieux Papa* (Old Daddy), immediately set to work. Within a day he had taken out the gearbox and had opened it up.

'This is culprit,' he said holding up a part. 'Is completely worn. You give me money, I get new part.'

Two days later he was ready and the repair was indeed cheap as Mr Cottril had predicted.

We packed and left Kinshasa the next day, heading off alone for the unknown, but we had done no more than 20 miles when, trying to change gears from first to second, I heard a loud cracking noise. It was impossible to change to second! We had to turn around, and limped back into town in first gear.

'Sorry,' said the African receptionist at the Land Rover garage when we got there, 'we're fully booked until the end of next week. Come back later.'

As we drove away, Claire flared up. 'I'm not having any of this! I'm going to see the Belgian ambassador. He'll find a solution.' And she was right! The ambassador knew the director of the Land Rover garage personally and immediately phoned him, asking him to give the repair of our vehicle the highest priority. We were taken on straightaway and the director put two mechanics on the job.

The breakdown turned out to be not as bad as I'd feared. *Vieux Papa* had put in the spare part the wrong way around. When two days later I returned to the garage to pick up the Land Rover, to my utter surprise, I found Christian and Brigitte waiting there; they seemed immensely relieved to see me. After they had left us in Abidjan they had tried to drive towards Cameroon just as we had originally planned to do, only to get stuck in the mud. They had turned back, gone to the Belgian Embassy in Abidjan to find out what had happened to us and had decided to do the same and sail to Matadi. They caught the next boat and reached Kinshasa almost three weeks after us, convinced that we must have left by now. They had nevertheless driven to the Belgian Embassy where they heard that, with luck, our Land Rover was still in repair. Seeing them again was a relief for us, too. We felt much better having them with us for the long trip through southern Zaire.

As Christian would be driving through the Kasai with us, he too needed authorisation, but he was adamant: he wasn't going to sit here another week waiting for the document and he flatly refused to pay all that money. I drove over to Mr Cottril, asking him what he advised and of course he had a solution. He knew someone who would arrange everything the same day for 50 zaires; and so Christian and I set off for the man's house.

Mr Cottril's friend didn't seem very pleased at being interrupted, but he showed us his photocopier, told us what to do and then disappeared into another part of his house. I took the letter authorising me to cross the Kasai, unstapled my passport photograph and handed it to Christian who photo-copied it. Then he glued a strip of paper over my name and photocopied the page again, stuck the new copy into a typewriter, typed his name into the blank space and stapled a passport photograph of himself onto the copy.

When I looked around for our host to say goodbye, I had a shock. There he sat, sweating profusely, his arms around two scantily-clad young Congolese women, one on each knee; his fat belly was bulging out of his open shirt and he had an expression of contempt on his lips. His attitude was like that of a lordly colonial of the old times who, on coming to Africa, lets go of all his inhibitions and preys on any pretty-looking black women. I felt ashamed of the man as I left.

Needless to say, when we crossed the Kasai, no one ever asked for any document authorising us to do so.

To the Kasai

Don't grumble when reality turns out to be very different from what you expected.
Just be thankful for the good things you receive.

I had tried a few times to inquire how long it would take to get to Lubumbashi, but no one was willing or able to tell me. 'It depends,' they had said evasively.

'It depends on what?'

'Well, on all sorts of circumstances …'

In the end I realised that it was no use asking and so we set off along the trunk road through southern Zaire, clinging to the hope that it wouldn't be all that bad. And indeed, just after leaving Kinshasa, we were on an asphalted road. We'd been speeding along happily for a couple of hours when we came upon a village where a great deal of shouting was going on. As we stopped we saw that the bush behind the village was on fire. The area around villages doubles as the local loo, and the blaze had been started to clean up the bush and at the same time kill snakes and all sorts of vermin. The burning of the grass is a centuries-old custom all over Africa, but it is a dangerous one. As the flames spread, sparks fly everywhere and sometimes the fire gets out of control.

We were watching the progress of the flames from a safe distance when the wind suddenly turned and sparks fell on some of the nearby thatched roofs. To our horror, they caught fire; within seconds the dry straw began to burn like a torch and the huts were devoured in a roaring blaze. We stood there feeling distressed and thinking: poor, poor people … how awful, when to our utter surprise we heard the villagers standing nearby burst out in loud guffaws. Soon they were all doubled up with laughter and we heard them repeat, as if it were a good joke, 'We put fire to the grass, ha ha … then the wind turns, ha ha … and now our own huts are burning, ha ha …'

Of course, those huts hadn't taken long to build but still, they were these people's dwellings and contained everything they possessed. And yet they were laughing at their own misfortune! It showed a sense of humour totally alien to the European mind. Their reaction brought home to me that the African attitude to life was entirely different from ours.

When we had entered Zaire several weeks before, we had declared all the foreign currency we had brought into the country. The border police had written down the total amount on an official document, which they then stapled to my passport, and they had told me that when we left the country, customs officers would check the remaining foreign currency. I would have to account for the difference by showing bank receipts. Mr Cottril had provided me with a huge pile of local banknotes but I realised that I would have to change at least some money officially because the border authorities would never believe that we had crossed Zaire without spending any foreign currency.

As we reached Kikwit and drove through the town we passed a branch of the National Bank of Zaire. Why not change here? I thought and I stopped, dug out my passport and some travellers cheques and went into the bank. I had expected to have to queue up or push my way through throngs of Africans as I'd had to do in the ministerial departments in Kinshasa, but no, I was the only customer. This was a pleasant surprise and I thought that the business of changing money would be over in a short time, especially since there were five or six employees sitting behind tables with nothing much to do, but I was sorely mistaken. It took three quarters of an hour to change a £20.00 travellers cheque!

All my particulars were taken down and typed on an old typewriter by a female secretary who used only one finger, reading each letter of my name slowly and then carefully looking for the same letter on the typewriter's keyboard. And she repeated the operation twice, as there was no photocopier or even carbon paper! When she had finished, she took the pages to the other employees who studied them attentively, checked them against my passport and filed them away in different cupboards at the back of the room. Next my travellers cheque was taken to the director who took a very long time to check its authenticity. And after all that, I left the bank with just a handful of dirty local banknotes – a third of what I would have got on the black market!

I decided there and then not to repeat the frustrating experience of changing money officially. In the evening I picked up the bank document stating that I had changed 20 pounds, and just added a zero to the number twenty and to the amount of zaires I had received. We'll see what happens at the border, I thought. I'll find a way.

To our regret, the surfaced road on which we had been so far ended in Kikwit. We were back to African reality: a track through the forest just wide enough for one lorry. Although the thick cloud cover had moved north by now, a late shower would sometimes strike us, turning the track into a muddy stream of running water. This forced us to move slowly over a red slithering ribbon stretching between two green walls of jungle, so thick that we felt our senses begin to choke with confinement. But every now and then we would come to a clearing in the forest where a village had been built.

We passed a small settlement in the rain. There was no one in view. All the people were probably sheltering inside their huts. Only a few ducks were out and even they seemed to be looking for a shelter. The scene was an artist's dream of beautiful misty hues.

When the sun was out the world was very different. We enjoyed stopping at the villages, where the people we met seemed to be happier than any we had come across so far. There was a feeling of lightness, of carefreeness as though they led an easy life, yet they lived in mud and wattle huts without any kind of comfort.

Very few villages had clean water, which obliged the women to walk long distances to fetch water from the nearest streams in the dry season, but in one of the villages the schoolmaster had had the idea of collecting the rainwater running off the tin roof of his school. He had rigged up a system to divert it into a well, and kindly allowed Peter to fill up his water containers. And the schoolchildren helped to carry them back to our Land Rover in a joyful procession.

The sun goes down swiftly in the tropics. At dusk you will see everyone returning to his or her shelter to escape the perils of the night. Around the fires inside the huts everything is warm and secure, but the countryside is believed to be peopled by malevolent ghosts, which come out at this time to do their evil deeds. The local inhabitants will urge you to sleep in their village, and the chief will be keen to give his permission for you to do so. People here cannot understand why anyone would want to sleep out in the bush. Only witches and sorcerers would purposefully stay out at that time, and those who are outside at night are therefore, by inference, not to be trusted.

Spending the nights in villages has its drawbacks, though. People never leave you alone and children follow you everywhere, trying to practice the few words of French they know. However lonely the world may seem when the last light fades and you find yourself alone in the infinity of the bush, after sleeping in villages a couple of times you long for some privacy.

We had, therefore, decided to spend the next night out. I badly wanted to shower and Christian was eager to cook a proper meal. Around five in the afternoon we all started to look for a suitable place to camp and we seemed in luck: a track split off from the main dirt road, leading into the countryside. Imagine our annoyance, therefore, when after a bend in the track we came upon a settlement. We tried to slip by unnoticed but men ran out of their huts, gesticulating to us to stop. However, we were determined to ignore them and drove on. About a mile further on the track ended in a flat expanse that looked like a landing strip for small airplanes. It seemed ideal for camping. The grass was soft and green, and there was plenty of space to set up a table and chairs for supper. Christian grandiloquently declared that he would cook us a meal we would remember, brought out his stove and started preparations with Brigitte, while Claire began to wash some clothes and I set about improvising a bush shower. Water from a jerry can, tipped at an angle on the roof rack, ran into a tube which was connected to a showerhead; all I had to do was undress, stand next to the Land Rover underneath the showerhead and open the tap above.

But solitude is never guaranteed in Africa. I had just set up the shower and was climbing down from the roof rack when two men appeared from the direction of the settlement, accompanied by a young boy; the latter spoke some French and acted as interpreter. Christian and Brigitte were sitting behind their vehicle further away and as I was nearest, they turned to me.

'You come to village,' they urged. 'No good out here. You come and sleep with us.' They kept harassing me for a full twenty minutes, insisting that we must accompany them, until finally the sun began to set and they left in a hurry. At last, I thought, I can shower.

I quickly took off my clothes in the setting darkness and was standing naked under the improvised shower, soaping myself while water was running over me, when suddenly my whole body began to itch and I screamed out. Only then did I notice that I was surrounded by clouds of mosquitoes; my bare body was black with them and they were injecting their poison into my wet skin.

Claire and I dashed inside our Land Rover where the mosquito net was rigged and ready, but at least a hundred mosquitoes had managed to come in before we had time to pull it down. As they settled upon us we began to slap ourselves and each other to kill the little horrors before they had time to bite. Meanwhile hordes of mosquitoes clustered about the outside of the net, stinging through the mesh whenever any part of our bodies – an elbow, a hand or a toe – touched it.

I was lying on our mattress, dripping wet, but there was nothing I could do about this since the towel was lying outside, guarded by thousands of malevolent mosquitoes.

'I don't believe this!' I exclaimed, scratching myself like mad. 'Where the hell do they all come from?' We seemed to have struck the home of the largest and most ferocious mosquitoes in the world. The moment the sun went down they had come out in force and the air had become a humming mass of insect life.

Suddenly a shadow appeared behind our Land Rover: it was Christian, covered in a long sheet, his head wrapped in a dark-blue towel. 'Quick,' he said, shoving a pot of food under our mosquito net. 'Here's your supper.' And he immediately rushed off. A few mosquitoes had entered with the food but I pursued them relentlessly until there were none left inside. Then we chewed the half-cooked meal, sitting cramped under the net. Our dream supper had turned into a mosquito nightmare.

The high-pitched sound made by thousands of mosquitoes went on all through the night. They seemed possessed by a malignant obsession to get in, while we were lying huddled together in the stifling heat, trying not to touch the net.

The sun rose the next morning to find us all tired out and in a bad mood. After breakfast we turned our vehicles round and began to drive back. As we approached the settlement, people came out of their huts and made us stop; amongst them were the two men who had walked over to us yesterday. I stared at them with antipathy. Had they not come, holding me up for twenty minutes, I would have finished my shower before the mosquitoes arrived. When they saw my face swollen with red bites, one of the men shouted something at me, pointing an accusing finger while a young boy translated.

'You wrong not to come to village. That there place very bad. Many mosquitoes there. That place is swamp.'

I nearly screamed, 'Why the hell didn't you say so yesterday?' but looking at the sullen unfriendly crowd around us, I controlled myself, thanked the man for his information and drove away waving goodbye.

Before setting off on our trip, my backer at the European Commission in Brussels had given me a thick stack of documents describing a number of EEC projects in Africa. Unfortunately we had, so far, not had the opportunity to visit any of these, but now I found that there was an EEC project in the Kasai not very far from the road we were following.

The EEC document seemed to be very enthusiastic about the project. Apparently, European agronomists were showing the local farmers how to grow maize, and this intrigued me. It seemed surprising that Europeans should be teaching Africans how to grow maize when the latter had been doing it for centuries. Furthermore, this was a region of forests, which didn't seem very suitable for agriculture. You never knew, though, I thought. A modern scientific approach might well be able to change soil conditions and if they could grow abundant food for the poor in this kind of area, it might radically change the development perspective. This was surely a new approach to agricultural development. If the EEC thought it useful to pour a lot of money into that kind of project, I reckoned

PETER PEETERS AND CLAIRE VAN VELSEN

that it must be of special interest and worth filming.

Christian and Brigitte were not very enthusiastic about the detour but we managed to convince them that they wouldn't regret it. Europeans often live isolated lives in the African countryside and the people who ran the project were sure to receive us with open arms and offer us all a meal. And Christian and Brigitte would be able to do their washing and clean their Land Rover the next day while the project people showed us the scientific work they were doing.

We had been driving for hours between tall trees, enjoying the coolness of their shade when, by early afternoon, we came to a fork in the road where the track to the project split off and dipped down into a shallow valley from which the trees had been cleared. In the centre of this clearing stood a brick and wood house, and just as we were heading for it along a narrow lane, a powerful four-wheel drive appeared and sped towards us until it faced us head-on. Two Europeans jumped out and asked us in a tone verging on rudeness what we were doing here blocking their driveway.

'Isn't this an EEC project?' asked Peter, taken aback.

'Yes … so what?'

Peter seemed surprised by their discourtesy but he explained politely that we were filming projects for the European Commission, and that this one had been recommended to us. This didn't seem to have the effect Peter had hoped for; there were no smiles on the men's faces.

'Can we see your letter of recommendation?' asked one of them abruptly.

'I'm afraid I haven't got a letter,' replied Peter.

'Then I'm afraid we can't receive you,' retorted the man, a tall portly fellow.

'But it won't take up much of your time.'

'We've no time for that sort of thing. Anyway, it's Friday afternoon.'

'What difference does that make?'

'It means that we're off to Kinshasa,' said the other man. 'We spend our weekends there.' He had a smug smirk on his red face.

'But … it'll take you days to drive to Kinshasa,' argued Peter. 'We've come from there.'

'Don't be daft,' cut in the portly man. 'We're flying there. We always hire a small plane and the pilot is waiting on an airstrip not far from here. Move over. We're in a hurry.'

'Maybe your wives could receive us instead?' I intervened, trying to save Peter from further unpleasantness.

'No they can't.'

'Why?'

'We have no wives.'

I sat there, not knowing what to answer, when I heard Peter say in a rather sharp voice,

'Can't you at least have the decency to let us spend the night here? Your project has been specially recommended to me in Brussels and we've driven all this way to see it.'

The eldest of the two men looked slightly uneasy. 'All right,' he finally decided. 'But don't go near the house. Leave the people in there alone. There's a shed further down, which has a concrete floor and a water tap.' The man spoke as if he were doing us a great favour. 'You can stay there till we're back ... that'll be on Monday around midday. In the meantime, you're not to film anything. You wait for us.' The man now looked at his watch, exclaiming, 'Sorry. We must be off!'

After they had rushed off we looked at each other, our spirits rather dampened. We had maybe visited a dozen projects in Africa so far, but this was the first time we had ever come across such uncooperative people.

As we passed the house a young African woman came out, carrying a lighter-coloured baby in her arms; when she saw us she didn't wave at us but turned away.

We drove along several fields, delineated by low fences, in which maize of different height was growing. Nothing seemed very special and we carried on till we found the shed, put our cooking equipment out on the concrete floor and started a meal. Christian and Brigitte were not impressed.

'So this is the promised hospitality!' they grumbled. 'We're certainly not going to hang around here till Monday.'

The following morning we went to the house and knocked on the door; four young African women were sitting inside and a few lighter-coloured toddlers were crawling over the floor. When we asked the women if they would be kind enough to tell us about the project and show us the maize fields, we were met with an embarrassed silence. Then one of them replied in broken French that they couldn't help us; we would have to wait for the return of the bwanas.

'Christian's right,' Peter said after this. 'We're not going to wait here till Monday.' And we went back to the shed, packed and set off.

The next day, we approached the Kasai River, a wide expanse of water. In Zaire, rivers are usually crossed on pontoons, which are for the most part precarious structures consisting of a wooden platform fastened over a number of canoes. Furthermore, to get your vehicle aboard you have to drive over two unsteady planks and these tend to bend dangerously.

When we got to the Kasai, we found a queue of lorries blocking the muddy descent towards the river and I feared the worst. Maybe a lorry had crashed through the flimsy planks or even through the pontoon itself? When I asked one of the drivers what was happening, he just replied, 'Ferry not running,' and carried on eating from a large bowl a woman had brought him, but I insisted, 'How long has it been "not running"?'

The man went on munching for a while and then mumbled, his mouth half full, 'Oh! A number of days …'

I shouldn't of course have asked for any precise measure of time. So I walked down to the riverside to see for myself, counting the lorries as I passed by. There were thirty-eight of them, and at five or six lorries a day that meant that the ferry must have been out of order for a week!

When I got to the river's edge, I discovered that the ferry was not a traditional wooden pontoon but a modern, almost brand-new, steel structure. How could it be 'not running'? The crew was just hanging about and I asked the nearest man what was going on.

'We've had to suspend service,' he explained.

'Why?'

'Because the engine suddenly stopped.'

'Can't you repair it?'

'Well, no … it's burned out.'

'How come a new engine has burned out?'

'Oh, it just happened … there was no more oil.'

'And what are you going to do about it?'

'Hah, we've sent word to the public riverboat service and asked for a new engine.'

'And where's that going to come from?'

The man looked at me as if I were asking him to reveal a government secret but he finally made up his mind. 'The ferry is a gift from the German government and so,' he said as if this were the most natural thing in the world, 'it's their responsibility. They will have to send a new engine.'

'And how is that going to get here?'

'Oh, via South Africa, how else?'

'Good Lord!' I exclaimed. 'And how long is that going to take?'

The man looked at me as if I were a nitwit. How could I ask such a stupid question? He shrugged his shoulders and turned away.

I guessed that if we waited for the engine to arrive, it would be weeks before we would be able to cross. The drivers of the lorries that had been piling up on both sides of the river didn't seem to mind. Some were sleeping in the shade underneath their lorries, while others were eating and chatting. In fact, a whole new village had sprung up around them. People had come from all around and a lively trade was going on in food and the 'services' women provided to the drivers. By now many of them had formed amorous attachments with local beauties and they viewed the broken ferry not as an obstacle, but as a unique opportunity. We were probably the only ones who weren't rejoicing at the prospect of being stuck here.

There must be a way out, I thought, and we turned around and drove to a nearby village to inquire if there were no other ways of crossing the river.

'Yes,' they told me, 'there is a ferry some twenty kilometres further but it belongs to a foreign company and doesn't take any private cars or passengers.'

However small our chances of success, we set off on the long detour and after struggling for half an hour over a muddy track, we came to what I supposed was the platform where the ferry docked. The place was enchanting. The mighty river flowed at our feet, the air was sweet with the scent of flowers and there were huge numbers of coloured butterflies – some as large as my hand, and a nimbus of smaller, white ones with black markings on the edges of their wings – but there was no ferry or human presence. Our situation seemed pretty hopeless.

I shouldn't have worried about the lack of human presence, though. This was Africa and we had been alone for no more than a few minutes when, as I turned around, I found two men standing just behind my shoulder. It was scary! They hadn't been there a moment ago and now, suddenly there they were. But I was glad all the same, for like Africans anywhere, they were smiling and eager to help.

I plied them with questions and, yes, they confirmed, this was where the ferry docked but it was not here. It was on the other side of the river just now. No, they didn't know if it was going to come to this side, or whether it would be willing to take us, but they knew it belonged to white people.

'Is it possible to meet those people?'

'It is possible but they live on the other side.'

I stared out over the wide waters of the Kasai River but all I saw was a solid green wall of trees. 'Where?'

'Oh, not very far. Just behind those trees.'

'And how can I possibly get there?'

'No problem,' said one of the men. 'This dugout here is mine. I can paddle you over the river if you pay.'

'And I'll guide you through the forest,' offered the other man, looking at me with an engaging smile.

And so we set off. I clung on to the edges of the small dugout, wary of falling into the water and ending up as the meal of a crocodile. I scanned the surface of the river but however much I looked, there was not a crocodile or hippopotamus in the water and no bands of chattering monkeys in the trees: the riverside of the Kasai was silent. The total absence of animal life came as a complete surprise. Where had all the animals gone? Nothing moved except the paddle, which the man dipped into the brown muddy water to the timing of sharp rhythmical grunts. Slowly we began to move towards the other side while the strong current carried us downstream.

> When Peter came to say that he was going to cross the river, my heart missed a beat. I looked at the few canoes lined up at the edge and couldn't help fearing that such unstable contraptions might capsize in the middle of the river, or else be carried away by the strong current. I wanted to accompany him but no, he wouldn't let me. I had to look after the Land Rover, he told me, and anyway, he would be back in less than an hour. But I did manage to make him put on a white turban to shade himself against the sun.

My heart sank as the distance between us grew and the canoe and its occupants dwindled into a small speck. I was filled with apprehension and a feeling of intense loneliness overwhelmed me when I saw him disappear among the trees on the other side; I felt vulnerable, abandoned in the middle of Africa.

I mustn't be silly, I encouraged myself, and went to sit in the shade, trying not to worry about Peter. Clouds of butterflies swirled in front of my eyes, nearly touching my hands and face as they moved in noiseless flight. Their wings were the colours of the rainbow, a vision of unearthly beauty, mesmerizing.

As they fluttered lightly in front of his eyes, Christian became very excited. He tried to catch some to take home to his father who was a lepidopterist, but without a net he was unsuccessful, which I thought very fortunate; these delicate wonders of nature just flitted away, completely eluding him.

When an hour had elapsed, I began searching the horizon for signs of Peter, for something that would look like a canoe, but nothing moved. My stomach was a tight knot and with every passing quarter of an hour, I became more anxious. Peter seemed to have been swallowed up by the forest. If the headquarters of that company were just on the other side, why hadn't he reappeared ages ago?

There was a good reason for this: I was still plodding through the forest. As we walked on and on amongst the tree trunks, seemingly forever, I kept asking my guide if we still had far to go and he invariably answered, 'No. It's just a bit further.'

'Just a bit further' appeared to me incredibly far and after half an hour or so, I began to realise that the man had no idea of distance. Africans never seem to tire of walking, but I was sweating profusely in the sweltering heat. Believing we only had a few hundred yards to walk, I had not taken any water but now, after several miles, I felt extremely thirsty.

At long last we emerged from the forest into an open space flanked by buildings and warehouses, and my guide led me to what appeared to be an office with the inscription 'Nepa Company' above the door. As I stepped inside and faced a European, my throat was so dry I was unable to utter a word. I stood there, panting, and was just about able to gesture that I needed a drink.

The man immediately fetched me a glass of water and when I was somewhat restored, I explained what I was doing in Africa and why I had come to him. To my relief, the man, who was Portuguese, replied with extreme courtesy, 'I'll be delighted to help you out. Consider my home to be yours.' He shut his office, brought out a light lorry, drove me to the ferry and told his men there to go and fetch our Land Rovers on the other side of the river.

The Nepa Company

That night, he arranged rooms for all of us in his house and then invited us to supper.

'We Portuguese are born traders,' our host, Mr Pereira, explained during supper. 'My father started this business and I have carried on. We buy agricultural staples and goods, stock them in our warehouses and deliver them to shops all over the Kasai Province and even further according to demand. Without our distribution network the local economy would return to subsistence level.'

As I looked slightly sceptical, he insisted, 'Believe me. It did so a few years ago.'

'Why was that?'

'Because we were thrown out!'

'You were thrown out?'

'Yes. One day the boss of the local party cell walked into my office accompanied by a few armed men and just told me to get out. "We're taking over," he said and he ordered me to leave everything behind: our stock of goods and food, our six lorries, the money in the till, my car, the furniture in our house, everything. And we were sent out of the country. That's how the Zairianisation began.'

We had heard rumours about it in Kinshasa. Foreigners seemed to have lost a lot in the Zaireanisation. 'It was just a pretext,' they told us, 'to take over all foreign assets.' Apparently Mobutu had first choice amongst the richest possessions and most profitable businesses. The rest of the spoils were divided amongst family, friends, ministers and members of his party. In most cases they immediately emptied the tills and over the following months sold the contents of the business, furniture, machinery, etc. After little more than a year there wasn't much left to sell and commerce collapsed. There was, for instance, a flourishing ranch in the Bas Zaire, which had 30,000 head of cattle when it was taken over by a Zairean bishop. Two years later the number had dwindled to 500.

'Within a few years the country was in ruins,' Mr Pereira continued, 'and Mobutu decided that foreign owners could come back. Most of them declined but trading had been my whole life and I was willing to return. There was no question of compensation, of course, but we were handed back the remains of our business. We found a few lorries lying around, mere wrecks, and from these we managed to put together one that functioned, and started again. And we're still here,' our host said proudly, 'but for how long only God knows …'

Later, as I was lying in bed, I suddenly thought of the two young French people who had been with us on the *Fabiolaville*, and wondered how they were doing. They had sold up in France and were going to invest all they had in Kinshasa, trying to set up a small business. What was going to become of them?

The following day we visited the installations of the Nepa Company with Mr Pereira as guide. There were several warehouses, a workshop for the vehicles and a small health clinic. Mr Pereira explained that Nepa employees and their family were treated free of charge, but outsiders had to pay for health care.

I wanted to find out more about the unusual story of the Nepa Company but there was no need to ask questions. Mr Pereira's was an eager talker and now that he had an interested audience, it was almost impossible to stop him.

'I've expanded my business,' he said. 'Today we've even got a riverboat to transport merchandise from Ilebo to Kinshasa. Now, having a boat is not the panacea you might think. Do you want to hear the story?' He looked at me expectantly.

Before I had time to nod, Mr Pereira had already started.

'When I let it be known that I needed a captain, no less than eighty candidates turned up. Imagine! I took on someone who had sailed riverboats since 1953 and had excellent references. His job was strictly limited to ferrying goods for the company and there were two things I absolutely forbade him to do: he was not allowed to take passengers on board or to push other riverboats along. I bought a small plane after we started again and the first time he set off in the boat I told him that I would fly along the river to check on what he was doing. Unfortunately I was held up and unable to fly that Monday, but on Tuesday I took off and what did I see when I finally caught up with the boat on the river? That it was pushing a big barge along! Monday had passed, it was now Tuesday and so, the captain must have thought, the coast was clear. And this was the very first time he was steering the boat! But what could I do about it? Sack him and hire someone else who was possibly even less competent and might do worse things? The sad truth is that you really can't do anything about this sort of abuse. Africans will exploit any occasion to earn money on the side.'

I tried to put in a question but Mr Pereira was not to be interrupted.

'Take our lorry drivers, for instance,' he continued. 'Lorries are loaded to the limit with the bags they are transporting for the company, and they're not allowed to take passengers, but of course they do it all the time. There's no public transport between towns here and so lorries perform that function. We close our eyes to this as long as the drivers don't overdo it and limit themselves to taking a few passengers, but you won't believe the cases you come across here. It's not unusual to see a few dozen people clinging on for dear life, piled on top of the load of bags with their luggage, food and live chickens, and this when the words *Passagers interdits* (Passengers not allowed) are clearly inscribed on the sides of the lorry! Such heavily overloaded lorries will inevitably get stuck in the mud or may even break an axle, and then it's the company that loses. And it doesn't bear thinking about what might happen if someone falls off the top and is killed!

'Our lorry drivers earn money on the side in many other ways. My lorries often have to cross rivers, and I make them carry sturdy planks. That's essential: it often happens that traffic is blocked at a river crossing because one of the planks over which vehicles drive onto the ferries is broken. If I accompany a lorry, which I sometimes do, and we are blocked in front of a river because one of the ferry's planks is broken, I lend our own until all the vehicles in front of mine have crossed the river. Then, when it's my turn and I've got on to the ferry, I pick up our plank and take it with me. Those who crossed before me are the lucky ones, and too bad for those behind. There's no reason why they shouldn't take precautions like I do!

'Of course, when I'm not there, I suspect our drivers of exploiting the situation. I'm sure they don't drive on once they've crossed; instead they rent out our planks for the rest of the day to all those behind. When I'm accompanying a driver, the lorry will cover the distance in one day, but when I'm not, drivers regularly arrive a day late and then they tell me all sorts of wild stories about heavy traffic on the roads and busy river crossings. From their point of view, everything is all right. They have delivered the load and on top of that have been able to make some extra money for themselves! They fail to understand why their boss is so strict on rules and regulations. Why make such a fuss over taking passengers or about a day's delay when time is irrelevant in Africa? But since the boss cannot accept this, they are forced to invent a story. Isn't it better to tell him something he can accept than to blurt out things that might upset him and could have nasty consequences? That's Africa for you!'

Mr Pereira shook his head. 'I check my lorry drivers constantly but what I cannot control are the authorities! Corruption is part and parcel of daily life in this country, and when you are trading that's a real problem. Zairean government officials love bureaucracy, permits and documents. Everything that needs to be exported requires signed documents and you need to pay for every signature; a small amount of money to lowly placed officials and a lot of money to those at the top. And officials will check your documents whenever an occasion presents itself. Even if all the signatures are complete, they will claim that something is not correct. Then you pay twenty zaires or so and the officials immediately drop the charges. They stamp your documents, pocket the money and everybody is happy. And to be honest, it's not entirely their fault that they have to act like this. Salaries are so low that, even if they are paid, the officials are unable to live off them.'

Mr Pereira sighed deeply. 'And it's not just exports. The government taxes most imports heavily. Only salt can be imported tax-free, would you believe this? Importing anything was a big problem until the era of containerships. When they came, this created a unique opportunity for Zairean importers. Containers stuffed full with textiles, machines or whatever were imported as salt. Who could tell what was inside since the containers were padlocked? But soon the war between customs officers and importers began to escalate. The former armed themselves with metal saws and pincers, while importers added ever-stronger padlocks. Finally they hit upon the idea of welding their containers shut and this completely defeated the customs officers.

'"Why work for three days to undo this," an importer would say as he accompanied the customs officer to see the container. "It's only salt. Look, here's a hundred zaire. Just sign the import licence and you won't have to do all this useless work."

'And who gains? The customs officers and the importers. Who loses? The state. And who is the state? Mobutu and his clique who are rich enough already. But still, Mobutu was not pleased that import taxes had dwindled and so he asked for incorruptible Belgian custom officers to put an end to such practices.'

I chuckled. We had come upon one of these when we arrived in Matadi and it had made a difference.

However much I enjoyed talking to Mr Pereira – or rather listening to him talking – we had our own problems to solve: we had been unable to buy any diesel fuel so far; another 300 miles or so and we would be stuck somewhere in southern Zaire. I didn't know how to solve this when Mr Pereira came to the rescue.

'We've just received a large consignment of fuel for our lorries,' he said. 'It's come all the way from South Africa. How much do you need?' He allowed us to fill up all our jerry cans and tanks at the price he had paid for the fuel, and he did Christian the same favour!

We were now ready to set off again. Before arriving at the Nepa Company, Christian and Brigitte had been held up by us. They didn't like our snail's pace and, what's more, we were always stopping at villages. Now they decided to abandon us altogether and to continue forward at their own fast pace. They had only one thing on their minds: to arrive in South Africa as soon as possible.

Landscape in Bas-Zaire

Above: Kinshasa: chopping down trees

Below: Peter with Gribouille

Above: Antique African art (Museum of African Art, Kinshasa)

Below: Modern African art made out of the body of a discarded car (along a street in Kinshasa)

Above: Rain, rain…

Below: Local traffic has priority: sacks of charcoal are pushed along on bicycles

Above: Filling up at the village well

Below: Carrying the water containers

Above: Driving off the ferry after crossing a river

Below: The ferry over the Kasai River: waiting for a new engine

Above: At the Kasai River: Peter in the dugout

Below: Crossing the Kasai River in the dugout

The 'antennas of Zaire' at the Nepa Company

CHAPTER 9
A Thousand Miles of Mud and Dust

The Villages of the Forest

As we were on our own now, at last we had time and were rewarded by seeing tropical Africa as it truly was. Day after day, we passed through villages strung along the road and it always caused a stir. Chickens would invariably run in front of our wheels cackling in panic, desperately trying to keep ahead of us instead of swerving off the road; how we never once ran over one of them was a miracle. And people would come out to see us; for weeks nothing unusual had happened here and then, suddenly, strangers had arrived from a faraway world.

Whenever we stopped in a village, children would rush towards us with great demonstrations of joy crying, 'Mundélé! Mundélé!' (White man)! They would crowd the windows and little hands would reach into the Land Rover trying to touch me. The uninhibited curiosity and cheerfulness of these forest children went straight to my heart, moving me deeply.

When we got out, men and women would interrupt whatever they were doing and come to shake hands, their faces alight with great sunny smiles. Their welcome somehow conveyed all the warmth and friendliness of Africa. Peter would answer their many questions as well as he could and I would be given a baby to hold while the women told me the names of their children. Older women would come along, shyly pushing their grandchildren forward, wanting me to admire them as all grandmothers in the world would.

The villagers never asked us for anything. Instead, they gave us some of their own precious possessions. They made me accept many small gifts – things women value – like the bracelet a girl in one of the villages took off her wrist and slipped over my hand. One woman gave me something I treasured for a long time: a lovely woven pendant with cowries and blue stones – for luck, she said – which she attached around my neck. I wore it all through our travels and even for years afterwards until one day, to my extreme sadness, I lost it somewhere.

I was also offered a beautifully woven basket, which a young woman had been carrying on her head when she returned from the forest. And in one village I received an ankle band made of seedpods, which unmarried girls wore during dances. I tried it on and as I jumped up and down it made a wonderful swishing sound, but the girls shook their heads. They didn't seem impressed and made me understand that I was no good.

'You will never be able to seduce a man,' they said, putting their hands in front of their mouths to hide their giggles.

But most surprising of all were the babies I was offered. As we were travelling on our own, the people thought we were childless, and in nearly every village mothers wanted to give me a baby! If we had accepted them all, we would have returned with our Land Rover crammed full of babies!

We were touched by the kindness and generosity of these people and at a loss as to what we could give them in return. Living in extended families they felt secure and didn't seem to need much. Fortunately we discovered that they were crazy about photos, so it was lucky we had a Polaroid camera. We made numerous group photos and they jumped with joy at recognising each other on the photograph. Each time we left one of those little villages that had welcomed us so warmly, a fan of small hands would wave us on our way and we would set off with their cheerful farewell wishes in our ears.

At noon it was so hot that we wondered how people here were willing to do any work at all. We would see the men reclining in the shade, chatting, but women weren't idle. Grandmothers would be sitting with their legs stretched out, leaning against a hut, busy making some close-woven fibre-bags; most of the other women had, of course, gone off to the fields.

From sunrise to sunset, women dig and plant, hoe, water the crops and reap, while carrying a child on their backs. Aid agencies often appoint a local man at the head of agricultural projects. This is a recipe for failure. In Africa sowing, cultivation and harvesting are women's occupations; they are the ones who grow the crops. It is also their task to fetch water at the stream or from the water hole and to return with the huge vessels full of water on their heads; or else they carry back heavy loads of firewood to cook the meals. They bear numerous children and raise them; and always, however urgent the task at hand, they are at the beck and call of their man. If African society survives it is largely thanks to the women who toil continuously. They are the true sustainers of the African world.

On the other hand, we seldom saw a man at work. Chiefs, of course, wouldn't be seen dead doing manual tasks. They were often thickset men. In the now long-ago past, tribal kings were usually extremely overweight and corpulence is still a sign of wealth. But most other men didn't seem to do much manual work either. Instead, while the women were slogging away in the sun, the men occupied themselves with the really important tasks: discussing the affairs of the village and settling disputes, which seemed to take an interminable time. We would often see some of them sitting in the shade around a big tree in the centre of their village, drinking beer and palavering. Other men were squatting in the shade playing draughts, or a complicated game with beans dropped into shallow holes made in a flat piece of wood. Africa really is a man's paradise.

The villagers were always curious to see how we lived in the Land Rover and how we cooked. Everything about us interested them, especially our food, which was very different to theirs. We found that they ate the most extraordinary things. I saw a boy pop a huge live caterpillar into his mouth and devour it with relish. Large, white worms from the palm trees were considered delicacies, and they also appreciated beetles, grubs extracted from rotten logs and termites which were made into cakes and roasted. People seemed to get their protein wherever they could find it.

We met a sweet girl with her hair fashioned into tiny plaits sticking out around her head. She had just been foraging in the forest and as she came along and looked into our Land Rover, she discovered an orange. Her eyes clearly showed that she wanted it and when I gave it to her she immediately offered me her harvest of worms in return! She must have spent hours collecting them and they were still alive and writhing. I took a handful not to disappoint her and then she ran off happily. Sadly, I hadn't been brought up in Africa and wasn't keen on eating worms, so I returned the wriggling things to the forest.

Africans differ from us in many other respects. These days, most people in the West have little time for non-essentials or for any form of nicety not directly useful. Work rules our lives – our feelings, our personalities, have to be brushed aside for the sake of efficiency. Not so in Africa. Here they haven't yet got to the quick 'Hello and let's get on with business' stage. It was maybe not so surprising that expatriates opened their arms to us, but we had not expected to find such hospitality amongst Africans. Poor as they were, they would share the little they had and if we were in trouble, they would immediately gather around to help us out without sparing their time or efforts. Would this happen in rich Europe?

I just loved the African villages. The walls of some huts were covered in raffia mats woven in geometrical patterns, and all the weaving and dying was done locally. The people showed us how they used all kinds of natural materials to produce their own fabrics.

We were also lucky enough to observe some local ceremonies. In one village, as we arrived in the wide, sun-drenched clearing between the huts, an initiation ceremony was under way. A crowd was gathered in the shade of the surrounding trees, several warriors were standing about in full attire and other men were dancing, dressed in home-made loincloths. There was no singing, but a great banging of drums accompanied the dancers as they went into an eccentric sort of movement, throwing their legs and arms about. They seemed to be running but always remained on the same spot. Even a young boy, no more than a few years old, executed the rhythmic movements perfectly.

It was there that I met an old witchdoctor. I sat quietly near him for a long while, listening to him as he spoke slowly. He gave me a shallow woven bowl, black with grime with a pungent scent used, he said, to mix potions to cure the sick and wounded.

Not so long ago, Africans spent their days in a constant state of dread. They were afraid of the witchdoctor and lived in terror of the evil spirits. To my surprise, I found that, despite great efforts to stamp it out, the spirit world was still alive in the countryside. Many continued to believe that the spirits of the deceased shared this world with the living and needed constant appeasement by sacrifices if they were to be kept in a benign frame of mind.

Much worse were the evil spirits. They were no one's relatives and were just out to harm people. As in the Ivory Coast, we were warned never to go into the forest at night because that was the time evil spirits came out to do their foul deeds. Stories about malevolent things that roam through the darkness abounded and were told to children around the fires at night, scaring the wits out of them.

Sorcery was still there, as Claire never ceased to tell me. An image of a witchdoctor we saw in a museum was so charged with magic, we were told, that if you touched it you would instantly drop dead. In one village we ran into men armed with spears and bows, who were brandishing magic objects. I wouldn't have fancied seeing them appear next to us at night when we were camping out.

I have often wondered whether the all-prevailing insecurity has not fashioned some of the African character. Here nature is too overpowering and life too unpredictable. Man is powerless in these surroundings; living conditions are precarious and death often violent. This breeds fatalism, but cruelty lies dormant just below the surface. Fear for one's life and for the unknown can lead to outbursts of ferocity, as if people have suddenly blown a fuse – you have to be careful what you do, for retribution is swift and can be deadly. We were soon to find out that not all villages were as welcoming as the ones we had visited so far and that there is only a narrow line separating life from death in Africa.

A day in Africa

You will never know the many pitfalls you have avoided in life …
But you know very well the ones you did not avoid and fell into.

We were progressing slowly through the Kasai Province deep in the centre of Africa, when Claire suddenly burst out, 'For heaven's sake, can't you keep level?'

We were on the main road – if that was the appropriate word for the kind of track on which we found ourselves – that linked Kinshasa via Ilebo to Lubumbashi, a distance of no less than 1,800 miles. To put this into perspective, envision driving all the way from London to Moscow over a narrow, muddy track; add that you'll be lucky to find diesel fuel or any sort of services along the way; then imagine that there are bandits and untrustworthy, unpaid troops scattered throughout the area.

So far we had covered half the distance and driving had been a struggle. The rainy season had nearly ended apart from an occasional shower, but when it rains in the tropics it pours. However much I dreaded another week of this, there was no turning back now. All we could do was try to carry on, keep our fingers crossed and hope that we would emerge one day on the other side – whatever awaited us there.

The last village had been left behind ages ago and the world seemed to be reduced to a rutted track between two impenetrable walls of tree trunks. I had to keep all my attention on the portion of track just ahead of the wheels but Claire, who was sitting in the passenger's seat, had decided that this was the moment to keep her notebooks up to date. Staring at the narrow dirt road spattered with sunshine or into the dense forest had clearly lost its attraction.

Alas, as this was the only 'road' through southern Zaire, it was used by lorries. There were never more than a few a day passing through this part of the world, but they were always vastly over-loaded and ended up cutting deep ruts on both sides of a central ridge. Sometimes the left rut was deeper, sometimes the right one, depending on which side of the track was harder. Unfortunately for us, drivers of humble Land Rovers, the wheels of a lorry are spaced further apart than those of four-wheel drive vehicles. So, if I put our left wheels inside the left rut, the right wheels were on the elevated middle part – or the other way around.

The Land Rover was therefore either tilting dangerously to the left, with Claire towering above me in the passenger's seat or else, as I changed over without any warning, Claire would suddenly sink away on my right shoulder. This made writing extremely difficult for her, and every now and then I tried to put one set of wheels on the elevated part between the ruts and the other two wheels on the narrow space near the forest's edge, so that the Land Rover was almost level, but I was to find out that the ground near the forest's edge was not always as stable as it seemed.

We had been driving for some distance on the left side of the track when suddenly the ground gave way. The left wheels sunk into the earth and with a bump the left wing bored itself into the embank-ment, and the engine stalled. Claire screamed, her notepad flew out of her hands just missing my head and hitting the windscreen instead, and I swore as Claire landed on top of me, arms wrapped around my neck. After sorting out our arms and legs and disentangling all body parts, we managed to crawl up to the passenger door and clamber out, letting ourselves drop onto the track.

From the outside things looked less bad than from the muddled inside. The Land Rover was lying at an angle with the two wheels on the passenger's side up in the air, but the embankment had prevented it from falling on its side and nothing essential seemed to have been damaged. Then I saw the winch and felt on top of the situation. That winch was my pride. It stuck out in front of the vehicle and such a prominent example of Western technology did not pass unnoticed in Africa. A number of times I had been asked by inquisitive, admiring Africans to explain its use and I had never failed to boast about its near-miraculous qualities. It was powered by the battery and had a strong steel cable wound around the rotor; unwound, the cable was 60 yards long and could take a strain of no less than four tons. I had had no use for it until now, but this was the time to show how well equipped we were. It was just a pity that there was no one around to admire the performance.

I climbed up to the roof rack, unlocked the toolkit and got out the 10-foot-long, electric command cable that came with the winch. On one end of the electric cable there was a cylindrical plug that fitted into the box above the winch. I plugged it in then picked up the other end.

'Look here,' I explained to Claire, 'there's a button and a switch on this side. In one position of the switch the winch unwinds and if you flip the switch it rewinds. Now press the button and see what happens.'

As Claire did so, the winch's rotor began to turn with a plaintive, rusty sound, and the heavy hook at the end of the steel cable started coming out of its rest position.

'Good!' I nodded approvingly. 'This is the unwind position. We're in business. Carry on.' I grabbed the hook and pulled the steel cable along as it unwound, shouting over my shoulder, 'I'm going to pick out a solid tree further ahead on the other side of the track, hook the cable around it and I'll get us out of this in no time. Don't worry!'

I shouldn't have been concerned about a lack of spectators. I was no more than 10 yards away from the Land Rover, pulling the cable along, when I suddenly noticed that a couple of Africans were watching me; they seemed to have materialised out of thin air. By the time I had chosen a huge tree some 30 yards further, wrapped the steel cable round its trunk and fixed the hook around the cable, another three or four men had popped up.

You imagine yourself to be completely alone in the forest, but this is obviously an illusion. If you stop – better even, if something dramatic befalls you – you're surrounded by people within the hour. Africans seem to have a sixth sense for knowing that something interesting is happening somewhere. As there are extremely few foreigners travelling through the Kasai, a foreign vehicle in trouble is of course a special treat for them. I have never been able to make out, though, why they should be hanging around in dense forests miles away from their villages, but there you are: this is one of the many unresolved mysteries of Africa.

As I walked back, I was accosted by one African after another. They all came to shake hands, their teeth shining white in their faces, which were all smiles.

'*Bonjour Missié*! Can we help, *Missié*?'

Then, without waiting for an answer, they rushed towards the steel cable and took up position along it. They seemed to have taken stock of the situation with one look. A cable was obviously meant for pulling and here they were, ready to lend a helping hand, happy to pull the unfortunate vehicle out. And without further ado they set to it with all their strength.

Claire seemed a bit worried about the bustle going on in front of the Land Rover but I shrugged it off with a, 'Leave them. Their pulling the cable won't do any good. They cannot possibly move a vehicle that's stuck and weighs three tons. But it won't do any harm either and they're happy to help out. Don't bother about them.'

I now strode forward with measured steps like a conjurer who walks onto the stage full of self-importance, ready to perform an amazing magic trick in front of an admiring audience. I gave Claire her final instructions. 'Flip the switch to the rewind position, then move away from the front end of the Land Rover as far as you can and once I'm inside, look out for this sign: when I stick my thumb up, you press the action button.'

I climbed inside the cabin via the passenger door, started the engine, switched to four-wheel-drive, high-gear mode, stuck up my thumb to signal to Claire to press the button and slipped the stick into first gear. And yes, yes! It happened! The Land Rover jerked into action, scraping the embankment while crawling forward inch by inch, slowly but surely. Another 5 yards and we would be out of this hole and safely back on the road. The wonders of Western technology! The Africans were sure to be greatly impressed by this!

The Land Rover had shifted a couple of feet when suddenly the forward movement stopped. I revved like mad but nothing happened. Claire must have stopped pressing the button.

'Hey!' I shouted. 'What are you waiting for? Carry on! We're nearly out of here.'

As an answer she held up the electric cable. At the end there was no longer the cylindrical plug that had gone into the winch box. Instead, three thin ends of broken wire stuck out of the black protective lining. I was out of the cabin in no time, staring at Claire in disbelief.

'How could you do such a thing?' I shouted.

'It's not me!' she retorted vehemently. 'It's one of the Africans!'

Then I realised what had happened. One fellow had come out of the forest well after the others and, finding the places along the big cable occupied, he must have caught hold of what he considered to be a small cable, thinking, aha, this is a special cable for me. He must have given it a good jerk and pulled out all the connections.

I suddenly lost my temper and yelled, 'Who is the idiot who's done this?' When he heard this, one of the men turned on his heels and disappeared into the forest like a hare.

A great tumult now ensued and as I tried to fix the problem, the Africans began to press in, looking over my shoulders to see what I was doing.

The problem was not as simple as I had thought. There were three wires, a red one, a black one and a blue one, but there were four holes in the cylindrical plug! I made a quick calculation: this amounted to no less than twenty-four possible combinations, but there was nothing else I could do and I set to work while a cacophony of voices was going on around me. I pushed each wire at random into a hole and pressed the contact button. Nothing happened. I tried a second combination, then a third one. By the time I got to the fifth combination so many people were looking over my shoulder and pushing me that I had forgotten which combinations I had already tried out.

I started again, but the situation was completely hopeless. I was incapable of concentrating and after a while I gave up, pushed through the crowd and sank down by the side of the track. The Africans had become ever more numerous – there were also women and children among them by now – and the ones who had seen it all were explaining everything that had happened to the newcomers. A great deal of talking was going on in shrill excited voices, accompanied by telling gestures and interrupted by great whoops of merriment and the slapping of thighs as some of the men exploded in loud laughter. What unexpected fun this was! What news to relate in all the villages deep in the forest. This really made their day!

As I was sitting there amongst the trees at the side of the track, staring at the scene with empty eyes, I was overcome by the deep realisation that I had fallen into a sort of parallel world. I had been told that Africans had an uncanny propensity for going straight to the weakest point and were capable of undoing the most carefully conceived plans. I had not believed it at the time, but now I had been outmanoeuvred in the blink of an eye by an innocent African hand.

More than anything, there was a sense of total defeat. When we had set out four months before to study the problems of development, I had been sure that Western technology was part of the solution. I looked at the winch I had been showing to everyone with such pride. There's our Western technology, I thought bitterly: a winch with a steel cable that has the potential of pulling four tons! And there it was, this steel cable, hanging taut. And our Land Rover – that other technological wonder – was not only stuck in a hole but also tied to a giant of the forest, and it could be moved neither forward nor backward. Western technology in Africa!

Claire was sitting next to me, still holding onto the command cable with its three broken wires sticking out of the plastic lining, while I kept shaking my head. Here we were, somewhere in the middle of Africa, with trees towering above and a crowd of merry Africans milling around us. What are we doing here? I couldn't help wondering. Why the hell had I ever wanted to come to Africa?

When you're stuck in Africa it's no good moaning; neither should you despair. Sooner, but more often later, help will arrive. All you need is patience.

About two hours later, we were shaken out of our stupor by a deep rumbling sound further down the track. '*Camion, Missié!*' Lorry, Mister! shouted the Africans, all excited. More fun was coming their way. What a day! And indeed, a few minutes later, a blundering lorry appeared, lumbering over the potholes of that dreadful track, piled high with heavy bags and lying on top of them, clinging on for dear life, were a number of Africans. As it came to where the crowd blocked the track, the lorry shuddered to a halt and the driver got out, visibly annoyed. A lorry driver is an important man in this part of the world and everyone pressed close to him. They all began talking at once, while a few fingers pointed accusingly at us. The man nodded, pushed the people nearest to him out of the way and turned to me.

'Missié,' he said in a voice that tolerated no contradiction, 'your cable is blocking the road! You have no right to do that! Take it away immediately!'

This was so preposterous that I burst out in a hollow laugh. Then, as I saw the man's eyes darken, I replied in a soothing voice, 'I am very willing to oblige but, as you can see, I am unable to do anything about it.'

The man now strode towards the cable, clearly intending to judge for himself. He tried to pull it, but it was so taut that he was unable to move it. 'Hmm …' he said with the air of an inspector who is not satisfied, and began to follow the cable all the way to where it was slung around the tree, with me trailing at a respectful 3 feet and the rest of the company even further behind.

When he reached the forest giant, the lorry driver began to scratch his head. The cable had cut into the bark and even into the wood as it had tightened when the Land Rover moved.

'We have problem here,' the man finally said. 'Big problem.'

'I'm sorry to hold up your lorry,' I apologised. 'Any suggestions as to how we get out of here?'

The man stood there scratching his head for a long while. Then, suddenly, his eyes lit up. 'We cut tree!' he exclaimed.

I stared in disbelief at the mighty forest giant, which had a diameter of two to three feet, but as the lorry driver shot into action and ordered the passengers to bring their machetes I had to admit the soundness of his reasoning. We couldn't possibly detach the steel cable from the winch – there was still some 30 yards rolled up around the axis of the rotor – but clearly, if they cut down the tree we would be able to pull the end of the cable over the stump and free it that way.

The strongest men now set to work chopping at the tree and soon wood splinters were flying in all directions. I wanted to take part in the action and motioned to one of the men to give me his machete, but I made little headway and after a few minutes my arms started aching. This was really heavy work and I handed back the machete.

The tree resisted for maybe half an hour. Then, suddenly, the forest giant began to lean over with a great cracking sound, making the men scatter in panic. It tilted ever more rapidly while the branches of nearby trees snapped as if they had been matchsticks, and then the giant came down with a great crash while the earth shook beneath our feet. The tree might have fallen in any direction but, of course, it had fallen towards the road and ended up lying directly across it, completely blocking the passage!

I saw the lorry driver stare at it in disbelief while scratching his head and I heard him say, 'We have problem here … big problem.' He was visibly pondering how he could solve this new problem. He had been scratching his head for quite a time when all of a sudden he turned around and commanded, 'We push tree!'

This is ridiculous, I thought. It's quite impossible to move a tree like that. But there were many men now and they all rushed forward to obey his orders. I pulled the steel cable off the stump and then, not wanting to stay behind, I too went over to the huge trunk.

It was hard to believe but as we set our shoulders under the tree and started heaving all together, little by little, it began to move!

I was just thinking how easy everything really had been when suddenly my whole body began to itch: I was being stung almost frantic by tree ants. In Africa it's not just big animals or snakes you have to look out for; smaller creatures can be much nastier. You can be walking peacefully in the jungle, sublimely unconscious that you are treading upon a caravan of warrior ants concealed by the thick underbrush. And then there are black ants. They make their mud nests in the branches high above the ground and as it happened, the tree was home to a large ants' nest. Unfortunately, I found myself in the exact spot where the nest was located. In my eagerness to help, I hadn't noticed that the ants were swarming over the giant tree and that I was pushing against the nest. The ants clearly didn't like it and within seconds they began a counter-attack and were crawling inside my clothes and all over me. They did this so stealthily that I hadn't the slightest notion of it until suddenly they all began to bite as if they had been synchronised. As I felt the burning pain of hundreds of little pinchers simultaneously closing in on my flesh, I yelled and began to pull off my clothes as rapidly as possible. Within seconds I was stripped almost naked and began to pick the little biting devils off my skin, all the while jumping madly about.

The Africans stopped, surprised to see me hop about wildly. One pointed his thumb at me and I heard him say, 'Maybe magic tree dance of white man? We dance, too?' but the lorry driver didn't want to hear of it and after I had plucked the ants off my body and put on my clothes again, we all continued pushing. A quarter of an hour later, the tree had been moved sufficiently for the lorry to pass and the driver told his passengers to get back onto the sacks. 'We off now,' he said to me.

'Hey, you couldn't just hook the cable behind the lorry and pull us out?' I asked quickly.

'Why not?' replied the driver. 'This we can do.'

I hooked the cable behind the lorry, ran towards our vehicle, got in and started the engine while the lorry began to move. As the cable tightened, the Land Rover was pulled forward with a jerk, and within seconds it was out of the hole and back on the track. I thanked the driver profusely and then the lorry set off with a thundering noise in a cloud of fumes.

So that was one problem solved, but there remained another one. We still had 30 yards of steel cable hanging in front of the winch and we were unable to rewind it.

'We have problem here,' the lorry driver would no doubt have said.

I turned to Claire who had remained remarkably calm throughout all the events and even seemed to have enjoyed them. 'What do we do now?'

'Well,' she chuckled, 'why don't we wind the cable around the roof rack till we come to the end and then make a big knot.'

'Like a parcel in the post?'

She nodded. 'Like a parcel in the post.'

We set to work with gusto, wound the cable around the roof rack as best we could, made a big knot and ten minutes later, after having shaken many hands, we climbed into our Land Rover and set off, ready to continue our journey along the main highway of southern Zaire.

We had driven for some time when I heard Claire say, 'How about stopping soon?'

I didn't need any encouragement. There was still an hour to go before sunset but I'd had enough adventures for one day and just longed for a good rest and something to eat.

'Look!' exclaimed Claire, pointing at a large open area on our left. 'Why don't we camp there?' The place seemed indeed ideal. There was about 100 yards of flat space and towards the end grew some trees behind which we would be able to hide.

I veered off the track, but we hadn't covered more than 20 yards when the vehicle began to slow down as if it were struggling against thick mud. I immediately tried to turn back but it was too late. The Land Rover began to sink and then the engine stalled. We had driven straight into a swamp! I swore a couple of times, grabbed the spade and started digging at the mud around the wheels, but to no avail. The foul stuff ran back as soon as I shovelled it out. We were well and truly stuck.

'We might as well go to sleep like this,' suggested Claire. 'Tomorrow is another day,' she added, trying to keep up the morale. 'People are sure to pass by and get us out of this.'

That was all very well, but I didn't see how we could possibly sleep with the Land Rover tilted at that angle. The left front wheel was at least a foot lower than the right and two feet below the back wheels. And I was filled with dread when I thought about the mosquitoes, which would soon begin to come out in droves. I wasn't going to wait. I wanted to get out now!

When you're in a desperate situation like this one, you find your power of concentration magnified. The winch, I suddenly thought. There were some medium-sized trees not too far away. If I could make the winch work again, it would pull us out! I shot into action, got out the electric command cable and began to stick the wires into the holes in the cylindrical plug while Claire began to unwind the steel cable from the roof rack. This time there were no Africans looking over my shoulder, I could concentrate and, yes! When I tried the seventh combination the winch began to rewind with a plaintive sound. We were saved! I pulled the steel cable towards the clump of trees some 20 yards away, slung it around them, ran back and pressed the rewind button of the command cable. Slowly the slack cable started to rewind and became taut. This is it! I thought, and carried on pressing the command button. The rotor kept turning, the steel cable kept rewinding, and yet … the Land Rover didn't move! What was going on? Then I turned around and couldn't believe what I saw: the trees were coming slowly towards us! It was hallucinatory. Instead of the trees pulling us out, the Land Rover was pulling out the trees! Obviously, trees in a swamp have shallow roots but still, this was just too much.

Claire shook her head, unhooked the cable from the trees, took the command cable out of my hands and rewound the steel cable completely, while I sank down on the bumper wondering if things could get any worse than this.

I looked up at the heavens in misery and only then did I notice that the sky, which had been blue just moments before, was darkening rapidly. Walls of black clouds were piling up in the sky, there was an eerie silence and the air had become very oppressive. A mighty storm was rapidly building up, driving whirling masses of dark, rain-swollen clouds towards us. If they burst overhead, the Land Rover would sink into the swampy ground. This was surely the end!

Then I saw them: a dozen men carrying machetes appeared silently along the road, turned towards us, moving purposefully, and stopped 10 yards away. They took up position in a semicircle and began to stare at us with undisguised hostility.

The men looked fierce and menacing and terror suddenly struck me. They're going to kill us, I thought, and I desperately tried to think of something to say to make them change their minds. There wasn't a friendly face amongst them, only bloodshot eyes and cruel grimaces. Then a young man detached himself from the group and approached us, whispering, 'Speak, for heaven's sake. Say something.'

My mind seemed to have gone numb but I heard myself say in a strange choked voice, 'What a relief you have come to help us.'

My words met with blank stares. Finally an older man, probably the chief, barked out as if he were accusing us, 'What you doing here?'

'Oh,' I replied, trying to steady my voice, 'we tried to find a place to sleep before nightfall.'

'Why you not come to village?' The chief sounded outright hostile.

'We didn't know there was a village, otherwise we would have come.'

'Why you not on road?'

What could I reply to that? I thought feverishly and blurted out the first idea that came to my mind. 'If we camped on the road we would have blocked the traffic.'

I waited anxiously for the reaction. No one moved for a while; there was a tense silence. Then, at last, the chief replied, 'Hah, yes …' He sounded a bit less hostile. 'But this no good,' he objected. 'This is swamp.'

'We didn't know that.' I looked at the chief imploringly and saw him relax.

Contact had been established and I felt the atmosphere become less tense. This seemed the moment to appeal to the men's better selves. 'Why don't you help us out?' I pleaded. 'Then we can go to your village. You are all strong men and I'm sure you can do it.'

The chief hesitated, but finally said, 'Good.' He made a sign to his men and to my great relief they put down their machetes and placed themselves around the Land Rover, ready to lift it out of the marsh by sheer muscular force.

I breathed a sigh of relief and quickly climbed up on the roof rack to throw down jerry cans, spare wheels, tyres and our plastic water containers to lighten the load. Then I got behind the wheel, switched on the engine and put the gears into backward position, four-wheel drive and high-gear ratio. The men were heaving with all their might while I revved up, but nothing happened; the wheels were just spinning in the mud. But the men kept hauling and suddenly I felt the Land Rover budge; it began to move very slowly and then, all at once, it shot backwards. I kept pushing the accelerator until I was out of the quagmire and back onto the track!

At that very moment, the heart of the storm came with a roar. Black thunderheads were boiling and tearing across the sky, driven into a frenzy of motion by a violent wind. Suddenly a great jagged flash of lightning split the sky, closely followed by a crash of thunder, and the storm broke.

Claire and I immediately rushed towards where our equipment was lying in the swamp, fetched a heavy jerry can each, returned to the track and kept running back and forth while the rain was lashing us, soaking us to the bone, until there was nothing left in the marsh. In a hurry, I dumped everything onto the roof rack while counting the number of jerry cans, wheels, tyres and water containers to check if everything was there. It was then that I noticed I was barefooted; my shoes must have remained stuck somewhere in the mud, but I couldn't possibly go back to look for them. It was pitch dark by now and the Africans were getting very impatient. They had picked up their machetes and stood there in the rain, looking more displeased with every passing minute until suddenly the chief could stand it no longer and ordered, 'You take us to village now!'

How the hell does he expect me to take all his men to the village? I wondered, but I soon found out. Several Africans climbed up on the roof rack where they settled down between the jumble of containers, jerry cans and wheels, whilst two, who had been in the process of joining the others up there and found there was no space left, just stood on the back bumper, clinging on to the end of the rack. I shook my head but there was nothing I could do to stop them.

I clambered behind the wheel and Claire had only just got in on the passengers' side when the chief came in after her. He was a big man but he moved up and managed to make room for another stout fellow by pushing Claire literally onto my lap. Four men were still standing about looking for a place and I was just asking myself where they could possibly go when, to my utter horror, I saw them crawl up on the bonnet straight in front of my eyes!

We'll never make it, I thought as I started. The track had become a running stream by now; the rain kept coming down in sheets; it was pitch black outside and visibility was reduced to nothing. The Land Rover is sure to collapse under all this weight, I kept worrying, or else we'll get sucked into the mud or slide off the track and end up in a ditch.

Fortunately, lightning flashed every few seconds, illuminating a surreal world. Each time there was a vivid flash the muddy track leapt to life amidst torrents of water, but I couldn't see very clearly with four men huddled on the bonnet right in front of me. The rain kept drumming noisily on the Land Rover; the windscreen wipers were working at full tilt; everything was damp inside and water vapour condensed on the windows. I felt like a sardine in a tin: I had Claire on my knees and was squashed against the door by the fat chief and his companion who took up all the space. I was just about able to steer.

Please, please, I kept praying while we skidded along, let us reach that village. Most of the time I could only guess where the middle of the track was; we banged into several potholes and once the wheels slipped uncontrollably towards the side and into the muddy bank, but we slid on.

An hour or so later, we saw the light of fires loom up in the darkness and limped into an open space surrounded by huts. The rain stopped as abruptly as it had started and the thunder and lightning gradually passed into the distance. As the Africans leapt onto the ground, the Land Rover seemed to heave a sigh of relief and rose several inches; and then the entire population of the village came running forward, surrounding us with shouts of excitement while we stumbled out.

We stood there, not knowing very well what to do when we saw the chief stride towards us. I had seen him confer with some of his men and was wondering what surprise he had in store. He placed himself squarely in front of me and said with a face like stone, 'We have done big towing job. Now you pay.'

I sighed, slipped a hand into my pocket, brought out all the local money I had left – some 300 zaires (about £15.00 in those days) – and handed it over. The chief just took one look at the banknotes, spat on them and threw them on the ground. Then he stared at me with furious, bloodshot eyes, which made me recoil.

'We want big money!' he shouted in my face. There was an intake of breath all around, the men began to surround us and I dearly wished we were somewhere else.

'And … how … how much do you want?' I asked, almost stuttering.

Shadows were flickering while the chief stood there, pondering the question. We were his prisoners, he clearly wanted to get the most out of the situation, and abruptly blurted out, 'Thirty-thousand zaires!'

This was outrageous! It was a sum of money those men had never seen together in their whole lives! I didn't have 30,000 zaires anyway and I was racking my brain trying to think how we could get out of here. I took a step back towards the Land Rover in the vain hope that I would be able to jump in and drive away, but there was no possible escape. The men closed in upon us with threatening looks in their eyes, holding their machetes at the ready … There was a tense silence; the hostility of the men was almost tangible.

I shut my eyes, waiting for the inevitable end, when I heard Claire say, 'We haven't got money but we have medicine. Would you accept that instead as payment?'

I held my breath, waiting for the chief's reaction, but his face remained closed. Then, to my relief, I saw him become interested. 'You have vitamins?' he asked.

I was thinking, no we haven't got any, when I heard Claire reply, 'Of course we have vitamins. Lots. As many as you like.'

Suddenly the chief looked pleased and I sensed a change of mood. Some of the men began to smile and the atmosphere relaxed almost visibly.

'Can we have them now?' The chief held out a hand.

'Could we give them tomorrow morning?' suggested Claire. 'We are very tired and want to sleep.'

'No problem,' replied the chief while making a sign to one of his men to pick up the 300 zaires he had thrown on the ground and hand them back to me. 'You are guests of this village. You under my protection.'

We summarily washed our grimy, mud-caked hands, feet and faces and disappeared inside the Land Rover to change into dry clothes. While I was rubbing my hair with a towel I whispered to Claire, 'How could you promise to give them vitamins? You know very well that we haven't got any. All we've got left are those …'

'Shht …' Claire put a finger on my lips. 'That's exactly what I plan to give them.'

'You wouldn't!'

'And why not? Can you think of any other way to get us out of here?'

'All right,' I sighed. 'We'll see about that tomorrow.'

We opened a tin of sardines, dug up a piece of stale bread, ate the lot and felt so exhausted afterwards that we lay down and immediately went to sleep.

The eastern horizon was only just brightening when we were woken up by the sound of women pounding manioc in their mortars; roosters began to crow with a great show of energy, almost as if they were trying to burst their lungs, and we heard a pig foraging and grunting nearby. Morning in the tropics! Soon children were scampering around the Land Rover, pushing each other, trying to peep in; little fingers began to scratch our windows, but fortunately our curtains were drawn.

We would have liked to sleep on but this was impossible with all those little voices around, hens cackling and women beginning to bang pots and pans for breakfast. We got up, made a cup of tea and had breakfast sitting on low African stools surrounded by children. Our clothes were a messy damp pile waiting to be washed but the sun shone and there was that unmistakably joyful feeling mornings give you in Africa.

We hadn't even finished our breakfast when men began to surround us, looking at us with eager eyes. It brought me back to reality. I knew we couldn't postpone the hour of reckoning any longer, and I just hoped we would get away with it.

All that remained of the medicine we had brought from Belgium was that big box of suppositories; no one had been keen on them, although they were supposed to be good for headaches. As Claire dug the box out from underneath our luggage, I turned to her and said, 'Shall I tell them how they work?'

'You'll do nothing of the sort.' Claire was firm. 'We've had enough problems already. Just tell them they are vitamins and distribute them.'

This was it then. However little I was looking forward to distributing suppositories, I didn't see how I could possibly escape from it. Claire passed me the box and I called out, 'Let all those who want vitamins come forward!' trying to look authoritative, which wasn't easy with so many tall, strong men around. They immediately pressed forward, holding out their hands, and a great confusion ensued; a few women came hesitantly out of their huts, too, but the men immediately sent them away.

'Please!' I called out to the chief who was standing in front of me, his face split by a wide smile. 'I can't distribute the vitamins like this! You must form a line!'

After some energetic pushing and pulling, the chief managed to line up his men and then moved to the head of the long column which trailed away between the huts. I solemnly deposited ten suppositories into the chief's cupped hands and then moved onto the men immediately behind him, who were the ones who had helped to lift the vehicle out of the swamp the previous night; they got six or seven each; after that I gradually reduced the dose until I got to the end of the line where the last men had to be pleased with only one or two suppositories because by that time the box was nearly empty.

We were about to hop into our Land Rover when the chief's son came towards us. He wanted to go to a town 20 miles further and asked if we could take him.

'All right,' I said, 'jump in,' and we drove off without any further delay. It was a relief to be out of that village.

The chief's son was a bright young man who spoke perfect French. He was the one who had urged us to speak the previous night and I was interested to find out what had really happened.

When I had driven into the swamp I thought we hadn't been seen but, of course, there's always someone around in Africa and two women who were returning to their village had noticed us and immediately alerted the chief. Unfortunately for us there had been bandits around in the area a week before and they had attacked a neighbouring village and killed several people. Everyone was out for revenge and when the women who had seen us told the men we were camping out, they wanted to go and kill us since, obviously, only witches and badly intentioned people would willingly stay out at night!

'But I intervened,' said the young man proudly. 'You see, I have been to the mission school and have learned many things. So when the women who had seen you said you were white I told my father, the Chief, that this made a great difference. You don't kill white people straightaway; you first talk to them to find out about their intentions and then, if necessary, you can kill them. That's why I urged you to speak last night.'

I sat there, stunned. Only now did I fully realise that, from the start, they had intended to kill us. The scenes in the marsh the previous night unfolded again before my eyes. We had escaped death by a hair's breadth … It might so easily have turned the other way.

'Tell me,' I asked after a while, 'why did the men in your village want vitamins?' It was something that had intrigued me the whole morning.

The chief's son stared at me as if I were asking him to talk openly about a taboo subject and he kept an embarrassed silence.

'You can tell me,' I insisted.

He sighed and hesitantly began to speak, 'It's got to do with …' he hesitated again, 'It's got to do with why white people rule the world.'

This was totally unexpected and it aroused my interest. Here was an occasion to have an African's view on what was a very complex subject. 'And why do you think they rule the world?' I asked him.

'Because they are clever.'

'And why do you think they're clever?'

'I have been to school and know it's because they have learned so much but ...' he seemed ashamed to admit it, 'the elders don't think so ...'

'What, then, do they think?'

'That white people are clever because they eat vitamins all the time!'

'They can't really believe that?'

'Yes, they do. And they say that this is why white people don't want to give us any vitamins, because they want to keep us backward!'

I sat there, gaping. Then, in my mind's eye, I saw the chief and his men swallowing the suppositories I had given them in quick succession, expecting cleverness to follow instantly. I was glad that we were out of that village and would never have to pass that way again.

Out of the Kasai

I had been told that we would run into army roadblocks in southern Zaire. Soldiers were badly paid and what with the insecurity caused by rebels and armed bandits, their lives were dangerous. They were sure to try to confiscate our passports and extort money, but anything might happen. Their reactions would be unpredictable.

I was therefore extremely wary the first time we bumped into an army roadblock. Fortunately I had learned a great deal from my encounter with soldiers in the Ivory Coast. I stopped at a respectful 10 feet from the roadblock and waited for the boss – in this case a sergeant – to come over. He did so with a determined expression on his face, held out his hand and shouted, 'Passports!' This was the last thing I wanted to give him, but I couldn't just blankly refuse. I knew by now that if you try to be difficult with African officials, or start impressing your importance upon them, they will hassle you if they are in any position to do so. And it wasn't a good idea to talk to the sergeant while I remained seated either. This would have shown disrespect for him and so I opened the door and jumped down.

Now, the world over, men like to be considered. They tend to react according to how you treat them; they are particularly pleased if, when addressing them, you use a title well above the status they occupy in life and they are even more delighted if you do this in front of their subordinates. It makes them swell with importance. So I walked over to the sergeant with outstretched arms, got hold of his hand and shook it vigorously while saying, to his utter astonishment, 'How are you, Captain?'

The sergeant at once raised himself a couple of inches to the size that befitted a captain, turned around towards his men with pride written all over his face as if he were thinking, see, this feller knows my true value, and then smiled benignly at me.

Before he had time to recover, I began asking after his health and family, as Africans would do when they meet. Were his father and mother still alive and in good health? Yes. Did he have children? Seven! What a man! I had only managed one. And how were his brothers and sisters? And so on, and so forth … It was like playing a part in a drama on stage.

About five minutes later, well into the exchange of family information, I enquired about the conditions of the road and, Lord, I had never seen a worse track in the whole of Africa: mud, ruts, deep holes, you name it. But the sergeant obviously wasn't going to disappoint me now that we were on such friendly terms.

'Oh, the road,' he said, 'not bad; regular.'

When an African affirms that the place you want to reach is not far, or that you will get your papers back the same day, or that the road is good, you are not to take this literally, of course. It is just an expression of politeness, of a desire to please and not upset you.

Next I asked innocently, 'Do you think then that we can get to Mbuji-Mayi before nightfall?'

'Mbuji-Mayi!' the sergeant exclaimed, breathing out hard a couple of times. 'That's going to be difficult. If you want to get there you'll have to leave immediately!' and he shot into action and ordered his men to open the barrier at once, shouting, 'Hurry up! Let these people pass.'

I thanked the 'captain' profusely, shook his hand again, jumped into the Land Rover, started up and moved off slowly, waving goodbye. We might not reach Mbuji-Mayi that night but one thing was certain: we had passed the roadblock and the passports were still safely in my pocket.

The road through southern Zaire seemed to go on endlessly, and it didn't improve. Heavy lorries, grinding their way through the mud after rainstorms, had gashed long ruts in the track, at times a foot deep. It was difficult to manoeuvre over the still soggy ground and sometimes we had to switch to four-wheel-drive mode. It required alertness of mind and great control of the vehicle. Every now and then a wheel, becoming caught in a gully, would suddenly spin the vehicle sideways, almost rolling us over. Driving like that for a whole day was tiring and I always hoped to find a place where we could sleep safely. Every now and then, if there wasn't a village in view towards sunset, we would leave the dirt road and move into the bush in search of a camp site. In places the grass was two-feet high and could easily have concealed a lion, but all the same, Claire would get out and courageously walk in front of the Land Rover to make sure we weren't driving into a swamp again, and to guide me around deep holes, and I would advance slowly behind her. We were lucky. She never ran into a wild animal, not even a snake, and we didn't get bogged down again.

The forest had begun to thin out. It was the first time in days that the solid green wall was behind us and we could look out over the open savannah. The grass rippled under the sun, birds flew across the blue sky and, far away, white fair-weather clouds drifted along slowly in the clear air.

As we drove on, vast landscapes unfolded before our astounded eyes, expanses more brilliant than anything we had ever seen in faraway Europe, the pure gold of the rolling hills meeting the bright azure of the sky at the far horizon. How lucky Africans are, I thought, to live in such a paradise.

Some evenings we would set up camp in the bush and, away from all human intrusion, watch the glorious sunset, pervaded by a sense of belonging to this earth, a feeling of total peace enveloping us in the dusk.

We arrived at a Catholic mission and asked the Belgian missionary if he would allow us to spend the night there.

'Make yourself at home,' he replied, as if this were the most natural thing in the world.

The next day was a Sunday and the missionary invited us to mass. People from the nearby small town had gathered in the church and as we entered it to join what we believed was going to be an ordinary Sunday's celebration, we found the church resounding with the sound of drums, flutes and guitars; and people were singing their hearts out.

This was a spontaneous happening, rather than the usual kind of mass. When the African priest appeared, the assembled congregation rose and they all began to sway their bodies in time with the music. And the priest! He was not saying mass in a monotonous voice. He was singing it in front of the altar, rocking his hips, both arms raised. At one point he turned around, stamping his feet and swaying his arms, causing an outburst of joy. We looked at the people gathered together, a medley of colours, an explosion of emotion. That Sunday we lived a moment out of time as we sat in the packed church while all around us pure, melodious voices rose up in fervour, lifting the divine within the souls. This was far removed from the way mass was said in the cold churches of Europe! Here faith was fully alive, vibrant, an overflow of tropical warmth. When the celebration was over and we came out of the church, we felt like embracing all those smiling, happy people.

In the afternoon, the missionary took us round on a tour; he made us visit a small school and dispensary, but his greatest pride was his biogas installation. Most of the bits and pieces were homemade and welded locally, the missionary had personally assembled everything, and now he produced gas for cooking from all sorts of organic leftovers. He was truly a man of great resources as well as of kindness.

Later in the day, we washed our clothes and cleaned the Land Rover thoroughly. Unfortunately, the next morning, we discovered that Claire's canvas shoes, which she had washed and left standing against one of the wheels to dry during the night, had vanished. Her sandals had already disappeared in the swamp a few days earlier and now she had nothing left to put on her feet.

'It doesn't matter,' she said. 'I'll buy sandals in a local market.'

'But you can't go barefooted!'

'Why not?' she protested. 'African women do it all the time.' And she started preparing breakfast.

We left in high spirits after a hearty breakfast. The rainy season had ended apart from an occasional shower, and by now most of the mud had dried into dusty dirt. We were looking forward to a pleasant drive; all problems seemed behind us. But you can never take anything for granted in Africa. Occasionally there were mud holes concealed under a thin crust and it was better to swerve around them because some could be quite deep. It wasn't always easy to spot them, though, and they made driving hazardous. I should have kept on the alert, but that morning I was mighty pleased with myself. We had slept well and had been able to shower. I had freshly washed clothes on and the Land Rover gleamed in the morning sun. I felt relaxed and was enjoying the day and the landscape.

We were advancing slowly over the rutted dirt road through the wide plains when suddenly we heard a squelching sound and the Land Rover tilted to the right. Peter had driven straight into a mud hole several feet deep! He revved up in a vain attempt to get through, the wheels churned through the mud and the engine stalled. Peter swore and then there was silence.

When I tried to open my door, red mud oozed in and I quickly slammed it shut. Peter had already jumped out on his side and as I crawled out after him, I slipped and fell straight into the slimy mud puddle. By the time I got up, Peter was already running around the Land Rover to take stock of the situation.

'We're stuck!' he said, stating the obvious.

Our strong electric winch was useless as there were no trees around, but Peter was determined to get out of the hole and thought that he might be able to do so if he could put the sand ladders under the wheels – although this was mud, not sand. He immediately undid the spade and shot into action, digging away. I saw the mud ooze back into the hole as quickly as he shovelled it out, but he kept on digging all the same.

Soon several Africans appeared. The men were willing to push and Peter desperately tried to organise them; he even unloaded the roof rack to lighten the Land Rover, but it was no good. When you get to this point the only sensible attitude is not to bother. What does it matter? I thought. The sun is shining and a lorry is sure to pass by sooner or later. And I just sat down on the roadside with all the friendly children and women who had appeared by now and had gathered around me.

Meanwhile everybody was enjoying the fun. The Africans were all laughing at the state we were in. Peter's freshly washed shirt was lying on the left wing of the Land Rover, crumpled and dirty; his second pair of sandals had vanished in the mud hole and he was barefooted just like me; and his trousers were caked with red mud, which the hot sun was drying; after an hour they were so stiff he could hardly walk!

Three hours later, a jeep passed along and the driver was willing to help us. We hooked the cable of the winch behind his vehicle and were pulled out within seconds. Everyone now helped to put our jerry cans and all the rest back on the roof rack and after shaking many hands, we were cheered on our way by all those smiling people. We stopped a mile or so further to clean up as best as we could (see photo front cover) and then continued our joyful journey along the 'great' highway through southern Zaire.

The next days were relatively uneventful apart from a few minor incidents. At one point the road was blocked by a huge tree lying directly across our path. We had an African with us, whom we had met along the road pushing his broken bicycle; we were taking him to the next small town where he hoped they would be able to repair his bike.

'Let me help you!' exclaimed the young man when we stopped in front of the tree, and he jumped out and clambered onto the branches. He looked at our Land Rover and next at the tree, and then, after carefully weighing up our chances, he shook his head, shouting, 'I don't think you'll be able to pass underneath!'

We had to back up until we found a place where we managed to climb up the bank into the bush, kept moving slowly through the grass in four-wheel-drive mode till we were certain we had passed the tree, and eventually slid down onto the 'road' again at a point where the bank wasn't too steep.

Here and there, along the interminable road through southern Zaire, we came upon relics of colonial times: abandoned missions or crumbling buildings overgrown by weeds; the bush was reclaiming its own. Less than a quarter of a century after decolonisation, the traces of colonial times were disappearing fast.

And the infrastructure was decaying everywhere. Sometimes we still found an old Bailey bridge with half-rotten planks strewn over its metal structure, allowing us to pass slowly while praying the planks would hold; but how long would it be before everything rotted and rusted away? At most river crossings we had to put our faith in wooden platforms supported by a set of dugouts. Maybe as a consequence, there was extremely little traffic on the road – just a few lorries a day. How, I wondered, do they manage to transport everything? But then there were of course the women.

The road was beautiful, a red ribbon stretching in front of us, running up and down the low hills under a dazzling sun, and all along we met women carrying heavy loads. A slim, young woman came walking gracefully towards us, a huge bundle balanced precariously on her head; she stepped in between the yellow daisies growing wild along the roadside to make way for us. Further along, two young women had just emerged from the bush. One was carrying a basket piled high with cassava; the other was balancing a thick 15-foot-long branch on her head. I noticed their slim arms and ankles and thought how tough these girls had to be and how brave they were.

A man was strutting in front of three women staggering under head packs; they were following like a train of donkeys, as if linked to him by an invisible chain. Peter shook his head. 'Women really are the lorries of Zaire,' he remarked.

'And the men?' I asked. 'What are they? Look at that one. He isn't carrying anything!'

'Well …' replied Peter with a twinkle in his eye, 'I suppose they are the drivers. Driving is a man's job, you see! That's why they don't carry anything. They like to keep their hands free to steer their lorries.'

We had left the rainy season behind, the track had dried by now and mud was less of a problem. Instead, dust was becoming a constant annoyance. As we drove along, the wheels churned up clouds of red dust, filling the Land Rover and covering its contents in a fine red film. Every evening we had to clean out our mattress before we were able to settle down to sleep. Everything was red – red is the colour of Africa.

Gradually the landscape changed. The bush became less dense, big boulders and wind-bent acacias were scattered through the spiky grass and here and there anthills, some of them 10-feet high, stuck out of the savannah like gnarled fingers. The views and colours were extraordinary, but if I relaxed and became distracted by the scenery, suddenly there would be a deep crevasse cutting the track from side to side and the wheels would hit it with a loud 'clang'!

All day long the Land Rover was rattling and everything that could come loose came loose. Towards sunset, as we were looking for a place to camp, there was a sound of shearing metal. I stopped immediately and discovered that three of the studs and nuts holding the right front wheel had broken off and that the remaining two were bent and ready to snap. Fortunately Bernard had had the foresight to stow a set of spare studs and nuts in the toolbox, but removing the broken and bent studs was far from easy. Repairing the damage took a long time but in the end I managed to fix the wheel again.

The next day, the road began to climb up towards the mountains of Shaba (Katanga), the copper province. It was a truly frightening experience. On our left rose high cliffs from which boulders might come crashing down at any moment and on the other side was a sheer drop of hundreds of feet. In places the track had so degenerated that it was merely a sequence of deep potholes and gaping cracks. There was nothing between the precipice and us, and the idea that we might go over the edge was truly scary. At times I held my breath as I felt the road surface crumbling, or the movement of the wheels started a runnel of rubble down the abyss. Far below I could see clumps of trees clinging on among jutting rocks, but I didn't dare look much at the astonishing mountain panoramas.

For what seemed ages, we ground our way over the narrow track, edging carefully around the hairpin bends of this appalling road, our eyes wide with fright at the spectacle of the abyss so close to our wheels, and finally we began a hair-raising descent towards the high plateaux of Shaba. Then, suddenly, the mountains were behind us and we hit tarmac. We had returned to civilization!

Night was falling. We always avoided driving in the dark but friends had given us the address of a

Belgian doctor in Likasi, only 50 miles away, and we decided that we might as well try to get there now that we were on tarmac. I was utterly exhausted and glad to leave the steering to Claire who put her foot down on the accelerator. The Land Rover immediately shot forward; with luck we would get to our destination in an hour.

Then, with a bang, we hit a deep pothole which we had failed to spot in the pitch dark. The Land Rover was making a loud rattling noise and we should have stopped, but the thought of sleeping in a real bed made us persevere and Claire carried on in first gear. Hours later, we limped into Likasi and found the doctor's house. He was out but his wife welcomed us, invited us to supper and generously gave us her children's bedroom. We collapsed onto the beds and were asleep within minutes.

'I was surprised when I came home last night,' said Dr Van der Veken next morning. 'I went up to kiss my children good night and found a bearded man in my daughter's bed!'

He was a good-humoured man and when Claire told him of our misfortune, he immediately took us to the workshop of the mining company he worked for. They were extremely kind, welded the broken part and refused any payment!

Afterwards I asked Dr Van der Veken if I might see where he worked. He nodded and guided me down a dusty road till we came to a small hospital. Everything was spotlessly clean and well organised, patients were waiting for him and their faces brightened as he approached. The doctor dedicated his time and knowledge to bettering the local people's health, giving his energy without restraint to alleviating their illnesses and pains; and he also taught the women how to take care of themselves and their children. It showed how the efforts of just one dedicated man could alter the lives of many and change their condition from miserable suffering to a healthy existence.

We were now able to continue. From here on, driving was easy. An asphalted road led to the Zambian border and even all the way to South Africa if we wanted to. We had re-entered the modern world and were speeding along at 50 miles an hour, instead of doing 50 miles in a day as had sometimes been the case previously.

For a while we enjoyed it. There were towns where we could buy consumer goods imported from South Africa; there were modern, relatively efficient services and we could again plan ahead. But after a day the satisfaction with easy modern life began to wane. We were loath to admit it, but deep down we regretted leaving behind an authentic world of simple human contact, of smiles and, yes, of fun.

Our priorities had changed. The consumer goods we had thought absolutely essential in Europe now seemed superfluous. Over the months we had whittled down our necessities until nothing remained but what was strictly necessary for survival – and we had come to realise that we didn't need much to live. We had also become fully aware of the vulnerability of our bodies, but had learned to protect ourselves and keep within our limits. We had ended by taking things as they came, didn't ask more from a day than it could deliver and felt immensely happy just to be alive.

A problem loomed ahead as we were nearing the end of our Zairean adventure. I had to get out of the country with visas and a money declaration I had tinkered with. Expatriates had suggested that I should slip a banknote into the customs officer's hands, or else put money into the passports when I handed them over, but I wasn't convinced. I feared that, on the contrary, this would make the officer suspicious. Then, a few days before we had to cross the border, I knew what to do.

As we approached the customs building, I stopped and walked over to one of the officers who was sitting behind a large desk, trying to look important.

'The documents,' he ordered.

I handed him my vehicle carnet, our passports and the declaration of the bank in Kikwit where I had changed money, and waited anxiously for him to find the pages on which the Zairean visas were displayed. He was just staring at them when I coughed politely.

'Yes?' he said, looking up.

'Officer …' I tried to appear confused. 'I have a problem.'

'You got a problem?' he asked, surprised.

'Well, yes … somebody told me that it is forbidden to export Zairean currency. Is that true?'

He eyed me sternly. 'Of course that's true! It's strictly forbidden.'

'But …' I held up a 50-zaire banknote, which I had especially kept for the occasion. 'But I've still got 50 zaires. What am I to do with this?'

The customs officer stared at the banknote as a snake would at a rat. 'You must leave that here,' he hissed and his hand shot forward, snatching the banknote from my fingers. He quickly stuffed it away in his drawer, glanced furtively around to make sure that none of his colleagues had seen anything and hurriedly slammed exit stamps on our passports and vehicle carnet. Then he urged, 'Go!'

'What about checking the vehicle?' I asked, tongue in cheek.

'That's not necessary,' blurted out the man. 'Just go!'

Above: Stopping in a village: children rush towards you

Below: A village along the road

Above: Offering us organic protein fresh from the forest

Below: A boy and his uncle playing on a hand-made draughtsboard with beer bottle caps

Above: Claire talking to the chief in one of the villages

Below: Weaving raffia is a man's job

Above: Doing what comes naturally.

Below: A local warrior.

Above: Brandishing magic objects.

Below: An image of a witch-doctor. Don't touch this object! It is charged with evil power.

The road through the Kasai

Above: Checking how bad the situation is

Below: Shovelling out mud

Above: Three hours later a jeep arrived.
Notice my shirt lying on the left wing; it was clean before starting

Below: Victory! We're out of it again!

Above: A mile further: all pleased, posing for a photograph.
Note: no more sandals

Below: An unexpected obstacle on the road

Above: Local transport along the highway of southern Zaire

Below: Look what we're bringing home!

Above: Camping out

Below: Repairs along the road

Above: An old Bailey bridge of WWII vintage: watch out for rotten planks!

Below: So young and already carrying a baby

CHAPTER 10
From the Congo to the Indian Ocean

Zambia

Great was the change as we crossed the border. Zambians dressed in cheap, Western-style clothes as people do anywhere in the modern world; they even wore sunglasses. And the towns, with their cottage-like houses in neat rows and well-kept front gardens, were somehow reminiscent of England. Had British colonial occupation fashioned people's character, too? There wasn't a hint of a smile from police officers or anyone in uniform. In colonial times, the French had treated the Africans in a free and easy manner. The British, on the contrary, had believed that in their dealings with Africans – as with Indians – they must retain their distance; the result had been the colour bar. Authority was there to be respected; life was a serious affair.

Even the children didn't behave like those from other parts of Africa. Many straightened up when we took photographs and stiffened for the pose. We met a schoolboy who had fashioned a pair of imitation sunglasses from cheap local material, copper wire. It was funny, but he didn't smile when I photographed him.

Leaving Zaire … losing Zaire …
In Zaire, there had been wonder in my heart, awoken constantly by the beauty and strangeness of all we had seen, touched, lived through and felt deeply. That wonder had gone, vanished, lost to this civilised world. That uplifting feeling of freedom of the Kasai where young girls wandered into the forest to collect worms, roaming unscathed for hours, fearless … it seemed so far away here. How tidy Zambia looked after the carefree muddle of Zaire! Of course people here were well-fed, well-housed and their children went to school in uniforms, but somehow they no longer radiated the warmth and joy of Zaire. They seemed mere shadows tamed by discipline and order, by the strict rules that dominated society. Where had all the fun gone?

The Zambian copper belt – a prolongation of the copper region of Shaba in Zaire – was a relatively rich area and the road system that linked the Zambian copper belt to South Africa was very good by African standards. Main roads were asphalted and there was little traffic. Where's the challenge?

279

I thought, used as I had become to the struggles of Zaire, but there was a challenge: people warned me never to drive at night and in particular, to keep off the roads on Saturdays. I knew that it wasn't safe to drive at night because there might be unforeseen obstacles, 'But why,' I asked, 'keep off the roads on Saturdays?'

'Because Saturday is payday.'

I was puzzled. 'And why should that make driving dangerous?'

'Well … some lorry drivers immediately convert part of their wages into beer.'

And indeed, we saw the wrecks and debris of some spectacular accidents. At one point a lorry, loaded with beer crates, had gone off a straight stretch of road and ended up against a tree. There was no one to be seen, just the abandoned wreck and scattered crates. The road hadn't been cleared and broken beer bottles were strewn all over the tarmac.

Some miles further on, we came across the wreck of what had been a new lorry with a trailer. The lorry was resting on its side while the trailer was lying back to front, its wheels up in the air, yet nobody seemed to care. Children were clambering around among the big tyres and young men were playing football in the middle of the road.

We arrived at a large town and decided to visit the local museum, which had an exhibition of masks and carved objects but also an unusual collection of toys made by African children from any materials they had been able to lay their hands on: wire, tins, discarded tyres, pieces of wood – leftovers people in Europe or America would have thrown away.

We were the only visitors. The director gave us a private guided tour and we ended up in his living room chatting over a cup of tea. I was surprised to find how pleased he was to have been posted here, far away from his parents, uncles, brothers and sisters. From what I had seen so far, I had come to the conclusion that Africans didn't like living alone; instead, they preferred being embedded in a web of extended family relationships. 'So why,' I asked him, 'do you like being here in the north of the country with your wife and two children when all the rest of your family are in the south?'

'That's simple. If I lived near my family they would come to live in my house and eat up all my money.'

'If that's what happens, how can people ever get rich by working hard?'

'They can't!' exclaimed the director. 'So no one works hard. What's the point?'

We were still in the north of the country when Claire asked, 'Is Lusaka far away?'

'Some two hundred miles. Why?'

'Because if I remember rightly, that's where my Uncle Ralph's gardens are.'

'We're not going south,' I said firmly, determined not to give in. 'We're going east to Tanzania. We need to reach Dar es Salaam to catch a boat to India.'

'But I've always dreamed of seeing Uncle Ralph's gardens!' Claire sounded disappointed. 'And now that we're so close it would be a shame to miss them. It'll only take a few days. You don't mind that, do you?' She looked at me entreatingly.

And so we headed south towards Lusaka … What else could I have done?

As a young girl in England, stories about Uncle Ralph had captured my imagination. He loved gardens, but Grandpa had already put his two eldest sons in charge of the orchid firms in St Albans, England, and Bruges, Belgium, so there was no room for Ralph in the firm. Instead, Grandpa sent him off to join the Navy where he was enrolled as a cadet. It was not to his liking and he lasted only few months, lack of discipline causing his downfall. After this he went from one job application to another, going from refusal to refusal – those were the years of the Great Depression. Grandpa had to intercede once again and managed to secure a place for him with a big London store. They had been told that he had an artist's eye and so, on his first day at work, Ralph was given the job of piling up jars of marmalade into a tall pyramid in the store window. He was doing his very best to build an artistic display, up and up went the pyramid, and Ralph was just stretching an arm to add the last jars to the top when suddenly the wooden ladder on which he was standing toppled over. He came crashing down and lay, dazed, amidst the sticky remains of hundreds of broken marmalade jars, to the dismay of the people in the street who had been gazing interestedly into the store window.

He was immediately thrown out but this time, when he found himself outside on the wet pavement, jobless once again, he'd had enough and decided to follow his inner dream whatever the cost. He had always wanted to create botanical gardens where people could wander for hours admiring all the different species of flowers, shrubs and trees. There was no way he could ever fulfil his dream in England and so he decided to escape. He was only just twenty but managed to sail to South Africa, paying for his passage by slogging away at the filthiest jobs on board. He landed penniless, yet he was filled with the courage of someone following his dream and eventually made his way to Zambia – then Northern Rhodesia. Many years later, my mother received a letter from him saying that he had created beautiful botanical gardens amongst the vast landscapes south of Lusaka! Was it surprising then that I longed to go and see his life's work?

Every now and then, on our way south, we met school children returning to their villages. They were all wearing uniforms, the girls in dresses, the boys in shorts and matching shirts. Most had no shoes, but that didn't stop them from moving at a fast pace. They weren't exactly running; their movement was a sort of quick step on rather stiff legs, almost as if they were trotting. They seemed to advance without any waste of energy and they could keep it up for miles without getting tired. I knew by now that Africans never hurry if they can help it – it's part of their attitude towards time. They walk, even when they have to cover long distances. But not these children! They seemed keen to get home as quickly as possible. Yet once home, the girls generally couldn't relax or concentrate on doing their homework; they were expected to do their share of the household tasks. We often saw them standing outside, pounding maize in wooden mortars.

Maize was the main food ingredient here, even in prisons, as we were to find out. Driving along a track in a dry, dusty area, we came upon a prison camp. It wasn't a traditional sort of prison surrounded by high walls or even barbed wire. We found the prisoners out in the open with just a single armed guard watching over them! And they were roasting maize!

The guard didn't mind us stopping and the prisoners clearly enjoyed the opportunity to talk to someone from the outside world. These men were not hardened criminals, though; they had been caught rustling cattle. They invited us to share their meal and Claire, who loves maize, immediately sat down with them and was handed a cob, but biting into the burnt maize she nearly broke a tooth.

The guard told us that theft was a big problem in Zambia – as was the case in most African countries. And as ever, the worst thieves always seemed to be those living on the other side of the border. Several Zambians had already warned us, 'Those Zaireans are real bandits; don't ever trust them.' Yet the people on both sides of the border were Bembas. Their ancient tribal area had been split in two by the vagaries of colonial occupation, but we found that the Zambian Bembas looked down upon those of their tribe who happened to live on the other side of the border. Zaire was considered a backward country.

The Zambian police were in the habit of rounding up any Zairean they found and dumping them back over the border. But then we learned that in Zaire a man (if he had a job) had to work for two months to buy a bag of maize flour which his family would consume in two weeks, while in Zambia the price was less than a week's wage. Small wonder then that Zaireans migrated into Zambia in search of work and that they tried to help themselves to part of the 'bounty' they found in what, for them, was a rich country.

A hundred miles from Lusaka, we met a white man in front of an Indian goods store; he was just getting into his battered pickup truck as we drew alongside him. It turned out that he was a farmer. Des Hunt had come out here when the country was still Northern Rhodesia and had decided to stay on after independence. When I told him I was interested in agricultural development, he suggested, 'Why don't you come to my farm?'

We had expected to sleep in our Land Rover but Heather, Des's wife, wouldn't hear of it and gave us their son's bedroom. It was a pleasure to be able to shower; we put on fresh clothes and when we came down, we found to our surprise and joy that we were invited to sit down to supper. We felt accepted into the Hunt's household, welcomed with simple but generous hospitality.

The next morning, we had breakfast on a veranda covered in bougainvillea. Afterwards I sunk down in a tempting wicker chair, my mind at peace, my body relaxed. The house and adjoining veranda stood on the shoulder of a hill from which you looked out over green fields sloping down towards a small lake, which Des had dammed to retain water for irrigation in the dry season. Here was agricultural development, respect for the environment and natural beauty perfectly combined. I would have liked to stay there for a long time but Des had many things to do and, somewhat reluctantly, we followed him on his tour of the farm.

First we went to visit the storage rooms where a dozen young African women were sorting out maize cobs by hand amid constant chatter and laughter. It appeared that the farm provided a large part of the seed maize the Zambian Government distributed to African smallholders, and Des wanted to make sure they were selecting the best and thickest cobs.

'Come along,' said Des afterwards. 'I've got to fix one of the tractors. It broke down some weeks ago and the spare part arrived yesterday – that's why I went into town.'

Des had trained three men as mechanics and after having checked that they were putting in the new part correctly, we drove along to an irrigation pump that was giving trouble. We spent half an hour there and then set off again in Des's pickup truck towards fields of waving golden wheat and maize where several Zambians were at work, one on a tractor, the others sorting out the harvest and heaping it into trailers. Not far from there, we came upon an African village of small houses surrounded by minute plantations of maize and bananas.

'This is where my workers live,' said Des with pride mingled with affection. Not only did he pay them a decent salary, but he saw to it that they were all housed and that their children were educated and their health cared for; and above all, he knew everybody personally.

Next he took us to see what looked to me like a field of rust-coloured tall grasses, but Des explained that these were in fact cereals whose seeds were reported to have a high protein content. He had read about their potential in an agricultural magazine and was now trying to develop these promising cereals.

'If this works,' he said enthusiastically, 'it might solve the lack of protein Africans suffer from.'

And on we went in Des's pickup truck. Dressed in shorts, an old shirt and a pair of worn boots, he was out amongst his workers in the fields all day long, repairing machinery and supervising the innumerable tasks that had to be done, his skin tanned and wrinkled by the incessant radiation of the sun.

'It's hard work,' he admitted, 'but that's how it is and I don't wish for any other life. But I hope my children will have it easier. We've managed to send our son and daughter to boarding schools in South Africa.'

When I asked why he hadn't sent them to school here, he hesitated. 'Well … you see …' he said finally, 'the quality of education is not so good here. It's much more expensive to send the children abroad but they're intelligent, hardworking kids; they deserve it.'

We left Des and Heather, our hearts filled with admiration. They had toiled unsparingly for years to develop their farm and had succeeded in creating an agricultural property of great beauty as well as value, but what impressed me most was Des's sense of justice and how much he cared for his workers. It was rare to see this in Africa.

The next day we reached the capital, Lusaka. It wasn't a pleasant town to be in. There had been many camps in the area which had housed those fighting for the liberation of Southern Rhodesia – now Zimbabwe – and though the camps were now empty, a large number of handguns and small weapons had been left behind in the south of the country. Insecurity was in the air and we were fortunate to be able to stay with the First Secretary of the Belgian Embassy. Every night he unchained two huge mastiffs, which watched over the house after the lights were switched off, patrolling the garden behind the tall walls that surrounded it.

'I never go out at night,' said our host. 'And even in the daytime I never stop at red traffic lights. I just drive through them, because when you stop, that's when they attack you.' And he told us that only a few days earlier a young white woman had parked in front of a school, waiting for her son to come out, when an African opened the door of her car and told her to get out and leave all her belongings inside. When she refused he pulled out a gun, shot her and ran away.

'But that's horrible!' exclaimed Claire.

'Yes, and I can't get used to it,' said the First Secretary, 'although I have seen some pretty awful things in Africa. Four years ago, I lived in Kolwezi in Zaire and that wasn't a very good time to be there. The Katangese gendarmes, as they were called, had been chased out of Katanga, now Shaba, by Mobutu's army in the 1960s, but they bided their time. Supported by Angola, they launched a surprise attack in May 1978 and Mobutu's troops fled in panic.

'It left me and other expatriates in an extremely dangerous situation. Had the gendarmes found me, they would have shot me on sight. As I heard the gunfire get closer, I rushed into my bathroom, filled the bathtub with water and fled to the end of the garden where I hid under some thick bushes. For the next few days I lay flat on the ground behind those bushes without moving, coming out of hiding only towards the middle of the night to drink from the bathtub after having checked there wasn't anybody around.

'Then the French came to the rescue. Paratroopers of the French Foreign Legion were dropped over Kolwezi and *they* were no softies like Mobutu's soldiers. They went systematically through the streets walking in single file, one every ten yards, shooting at anything that moved; they took no risks! The town was cleared out in a short time, the Katangese gendarmes vanished as mysteriously as they had come, and then Mobutu's army took control, the victors once again.'

I hated living behind high walls with fierce, yellow-eyed dogs guarding the entrance. This was an Africa we had not met with before and it saddened me.

The next day, we had to go to a bank in town and as we parked and Peter went inside, I found myself alone on the pavement. Two men passed by, sizing me up, a cold glare in their eyes. For the first time in Africa, fear invaded me and I was glued to the pavement, holding my satchel tightly pressed against me. As the men carried on and reached the corner of the street, someone came up to me whispering, 'Don't stay here. I've heard them talk. They're going to attack you and take your car.'

I didn't know what to do. It was like a nightmare. Wherever I looked – left and right – unsmiling faces stared at me. Then I saw the two men reappear around the corner: two others had joined them! Just at that moment, Peter emerged from the bank. I clutched his hand and we hurried into the Land Rover and drove quickly away. We continued, never stopping for red lights as the First Secretary had told us, until we reached his high-walled house and were safely inside.

Why is man incapable of stopping himself from turning life into hell?

By now we had found out about the Munda Wanga Gardens created by Claire's uncle: they were south of Lusaka and were open to the public. We decided to drive there, but first we had an appointment to visit the Agricultural College.

When I told the British garage supervisor in the Agricultural College that I had come to study development and was filming projects, he snorted, 'I'll show you some development you can film. Come and see,' and he led us to a part of the garage where a few students were learning about the upkeep of tractors. They had taken off one of the big wheels, but the tractor had slipped off its support and the axle had hit the concrete floor and was damaged.

'This sort of "accident" happens all the time,' the supervisor hissed between clenched teeth. 'I don't know how much longer I'll be able to stand this.'

The man seemed to be on the verge of a nervous breakdown as he took us around the workshop, urging me to film the disastrous state of the equipment. I could well understand his exasperation. There were some very unusual examples of the abuse of equipment, such as a hole in a lorry's engine where one of the cylinders had exploded. But one of the most macabre sights we saw was a ruined coach. It had been full of students when the driver had taken a 90-degree turn into a street without slowing down. The coach had turned over and had continued to slide forward on its side till it hit the opposite wall. Seats had come loose and a number of students had been killed; bloodstains were still visible everywhere.

'And these are just the results of working with practical things,' the supervisor grunted. 'When it comes to abstract concepts such as productivity or planning, things are a great deal worse! Take planning, for example. It should be high on the list of requirements of those running government services because many things, which in any normal country are left to private initiative, are centralised in Zambia. Believe it or not, the importation of basic goods, such as cooking oil or soap, is the responsibility of the government! So you would expect a certain amount of planning to take place, and imagine that those in charge of imports would keep an eye on stock levels and realise that there's just enough for, say, five more months of consumption. You would, furthermore, expect the bureaucrats to take into account that the time lapse between placing an order in South Africa and delivery is about four months, and you would hope that they would come to the conclusion that it's high time to place an order. Not so! In this country those in the government responsible for placing the order begin to get active – if that's the right word – the day stocks run out. The consequence is that recently we've had to spend months without cooking oil or soap!

'If you want to see a well-functioning African country,' he said, 'you should go to Zimbabwe. There's an example of what Africa could be. That's the Africa of the future.'

If the British garage supervisor was so full of praise for Zimbabwe, I wanted to see it, and so I decided to carry on southwards after visiting the Munda Wanga Gardens instead of turning back to the man-made terror of Lusaka.

I was glad to escape from Lusaka. Stark fear seemed to be lurking around the town as we drove southwards the next morning. At each corner we held our breaths, awaiting some unknown menace, and it was only when the dread of Lusaka receded that my spirits gradually lifted and I began to think of the Munda Wanga Gardens. There was an air of expectancy, of excitement at going to discover what a young man, setting out to follow his inner dream, had been able to achieve in this harsh African land.

When I told the warden of the gardens that Ralph Sander was my uncle, he was overjoyed and, 'Although Bwana Ralph unfortunately died a few years ago, his gardens are still here,' he said, 'and it will be an honour to take his niece around.'

There had obviously been love between these people and Uncle Ralph; he had lived among them and looked upon them as his own family.

The gardens will always stand out in my mind as homage to a man's dream. It was a vision of extraordinary beauty and harmony, a perfect balance of nature's treasures and man's gentle touch. We were surprised as we wandered, enchanted, between flowering shrubs and roses: a piece of England had been transplanted onto the African soil. Herbaceous borders lined the well-kept lawns, sloping down to a pond covered with water lilies, in which fish swam. We walked over an arched stone bridge that spanned a narrow stream and stepped into a walled garden enclosing a cottage. This was where my uncle had lived. The walls were hidden by a screen of bougainvillea flowers climbing high towards the blue sky, all entwined, in a glory of colours – pink, white, yellow, mauve, gold, red, fuchsia – an earthly rainbow retaining Uncle Ralph's vision of life. It was a world set apart where time had stood still.

But now the unkempt bush around threatened to invade; the wind blew wild seeds into the gardens. A man who was clearing the weeds told us they were trying to keep everything as it had been, but it was a hard struggle. Tears welled in my eyes as the old gardener said, 'We do not know what will become of the bwana's gardens now that he has gone, but we will go on working as he taught us.'

I left with joy and sadness lingering in my heart.

Zimbabwe

After crossing the Zambezi at the Kariba Dam, we were greeted by a smiling Zimbabwean customs officer.

'Why don't you stay in my country?' he suggested when he learned that I was a scientist. 'It's people like you we need – scientists and professors.'

I had no intention of staying in Zimbabwe more than a week or so but all the same, it was a great welcome and a hopeful sign for the country's future. Ian Smith's minority government had been overthrown only a few years earlier and I had expected to experience resentment against white people, but this certainly didn't sound like it.

As we followed the Zambezi, we came upon a farm run by white Zimbabweans who employed a large number of Africans. It turned out to be a crocodile farm where they produced the raw hides from which handbags were made. We were intrigued. In Europe or America they farm cows, sheep or pigs, but how do you set about farming crocodiles? They're not exactly animals you can breed, tame and trust.

Indeed, crocodile farming was a rather complicated affair. The eggs had to be dug up from the banks of the river and brought to the farm where they hatched. The baby crocodiles were then put into ponds where they were fed and as they grew in size, they were rounded up and moved to ever-larger ponds. The crocodiles had to be handled with great care. Barely a foot long, they were already very vicious. Their teeth were like fine needles and if they caught your finger they would inflict painful wounds.

Going into the river was a particularly dangerous job. Crocodiles sneak up under water, snatch their victims by the legs, drown them and carry them off to their larder – a sort of scooped-out airlock under an overhanging part of the riverbank – until such time as they consider the flesh ready for eating. One huge crocodile, which they called Satan, had been the terror of the nearby village. He had killed several women while they were washing their clothes in the Zambezi, but he had finally been caught and put inside a stone enclosure on the farm.

As I climbed onto the wall of loose, piled-up stones to film, Satan stared at me with malevolent eyes and produced a sinister deep grumbling sound while striking the wall with his tail, making it shake under the impact. I felt extremely nervous: he never stopped lashing out, trying to unbalance me; I wouldn't have stood a chance if I'd lost my footing and found myself inside the enclosure with that monstrous crocodile! I was relieved when the filming was over.

As we drove into Harare, the capital, we were surprised to see some large houses looking vaguely like fancily decorated cream tarts. They weren't to our taste but those mini-palaces behind high walls were certainly impressive. They belonged to Indians.

Indians could be found all over East and South Africa. The British brought them over as cheap labour in the early twentieth century. They were poor then but they had stayed on and worked hard; some were very well-off today. They ran shops or were involved in trade and often dominated commercial activities: import and export, retail sales, building, engineering, great public works, etc. Indians were the ones who kept much of East Africa running.

We stayed for a couple of days with a family of Belgians who had settled down here many years before. They had been ready to flee when Mugabe took over because their son had been a fighter pilot in the armed forces of Southern Rhodesia, but then Mugabe made his reconciliatory speech on television.

'It was such a relief,' they told us, 'so unexpected.'

Reconciliation and building a new future together were also the words used by Mr Hendricks after we met him in his textile workshop. 'There is no longer any future for textiles in Europe,' he said, 'but here there is. Coming to Zimbabwe was a gamble, but I'm sure I did the right thing.' He had arrived just after independence and invested all his money and knowledge into creating a big textile workshop in Harare. 'We work long hours,' he explained, 'but my workers are willing and well-educated.'

As long as he abided by the government's demands that 80 percent be sold locally at cost price, he was allowed to sell the remaining 20 percent abroad and keep the profit.

Mr Hendricks was full of enthusiasm. 'This is a wonderful country!' he exclaimed. 'I want to stay here. I've just bought a farm up-country, one of my sons is running it and my wife and I go there for the weekends. That's where I want to retire.'

Aware of what Zimbabwe has become today, I wonder what has happened to him?

Now that we had got this far, we decided to head further south and visit the ruins of Great Zimbabwe, the oldest stone buildings south of the equator in Africa. We drove along well-kept tarmac roads, neat houses and shops stocked with merchandise; we even passed an imposing inn near Bulawayo called the Churchill Arms, which looked like a replica of some grand English hotel. Had it not been for the weather and the landscape, we could have imagined ourselves in England. By any measure, and especially by African standards, Zimbabwe was a developed country.

We spent a pleasant afternoon in Great Zimbabwe; there were no guards, no visitors and we simply drove into the enclosure. Then, after staying for the night in a well-organised campsite set in beautiful lawns along a lakeside, where we met a number of white South Africans, we decided to turn back. This kind of Africa was too much like our own modern world!

Somehow this way of life, the prosperity and riches so suited to European countries, felt alien to the buoyant, carefree spirit of the Africa we loved. After a few days of ease and spoiling, surrounded by all the luxuries that money makes available, I awoke knowing there was a void. Something precious to us, difficult to define, had gone out of our lives … We longed to return to the bush, to the thrills of adventure and discovery, and to meeting people whose ways of life were totally different from ours. And so we turned our Land Rover around and drove back north.

Our guidebook showed that there was a cave with Bushmen paintings not far from the road we were following, and we decided to head for it. We found it, parked the Land Rover and climbed up an uneven, rocky path between boulders and cliff walls till we reached the cave where the Bushmen had left this wonderful testimony of their existence. It felt like a very special, almost sacred place.

These extraordinary rock paintings depicted the daily lives of the Bushmen: men walking along with spears and bows, and women carrying loads on their heads. Most striking was the profusion of animals. There were hundreds of them, all delicately executed, some small, others large: giraffes, antelopes, drawn true to life as if they were moving gracefully. They were often painted one on top of the other, probably in the course of centuries, some standing out in vivid colours, others almost faded. It was a wonder to behold, a testimony to the Africa of long ago at its most beautiful. In Western countries, this would have been a cultural heritage site, a national monument, fenced off and guarded, but we were completely alone here. Anyone could have come along to spoil these paintings, or even cut them out to sell them to rich private collectors. Why wasn't the government doing anything to protect this unique site?

The Bushmen had been driven off lands that had been theirs for millennia when the Bantus invaded this area centuries ago. Were these paintings looked down on as no more than the work of primitive people, not worth bothering about?

We left the cave, pausing to steady ourselves against the cliff wall while our eyes gradually adapted to the bright light outside. Then, as we slowly began to climb down, I could have sworn that something had moved between the boulders further down. What could it be? Suddenly I froze in my tracks.

'What is it?' asked Claire, very tense. I held a finger against my lips, pointing down below, and then she saw it, too: a leopard crossing the path and vanishing between the shadows of the boulders.

The leopard is one of the least trustworthy animals on earth. It is one of the rare creatures besides man known to kill just for the sake of killing and is extremely dangerous when cornered. When it attacks a man, it strikes fast, jumping up and clinging to its victim's shoulders with its forefeet, digging its razor-sharp claws as far in as they will go while biting at the man's throat and at the same time disembowelling him with its hind legs.

I stood there, my heart pounding, but nothing seemed to move below. After an anxious wait, we went down, step by step, staring in fright at the boulders as we slipped by, hoping the leopard wasn't lying in ambush. It was an immense relief to reach the safety of our Land Rover!

I had been looking forward to photographing animals in their natural habitat in Africa and studying the map, I noticed that we would be passing close to Wankie National Park (now called Hwange National Park) on our way north. We decided to visit it, but it was dusk by the time we reached the park and we had to spend the night in the campsite at the entrance. A convoy of four-wheel drive vehicles full of tourists accompanied by park wardens was leaving next morning and they invited us to follow them, but somehow we weren't keen. We were sure that the noise the tourists made would scare away the animals, and so we set off on our own.

> My heart lifted when we entered the open parkland where animals roamed freely, obeying their own laws. I soon forgot that somewhere beyond these undisturbed landscapes lay a man-made world where animals had become mere food or else were kept as pets. Time had stopped.
>
> We followed dusty tracks with tall grass and scattered trees growing on either side. We had no idea where we were going, but it didn't really matter; we were immersed in a world where the savannah grasses shone golden under the sun. I felt surrounded by beauty and the sounds of wild nature, and there was a feeling of freedom and intense happiness. Everything was just perfect.

It was early morning, the best time for observing animals. The park must have been full of them but, surprisingly enough, they seemed to be invisible. Maybe we passed within yards of dozens of animals; maybe the whole area was teeming with wildlife, but however much I peered into the bush, I never saw more than the astonished eyes of a few antelopes gazing at the Land Rover from the safety of a grassland thicket; the red flash of a rump retreating amongst the scattered trees and tall grass as we arrived; or the silent vanishing of soft shapes into bush and forest the moment we stopped. It was disappointing. By the time we sat down for our picnic, I hadn't been able to take a single picture in which you could clearly distinguish an animal.

We were chewing on a few stale sandwiches, sitting on the side of a track in the shade of what is commonly called a 'sausage tree' because of the thick, iron-hard, foot-long, sausage-like fruits it bears. Some had fallen down and were lying on the ground around us and I was looking warily at the many sausages hanging precariously from the branches above us.

'What if one of these falls on our heads?' I pointed out to Claire, but she just shrugged her shoulders and carried on chewing.

Suddenly I noticed a herd of zebras some twenty yards away, half hidden by the tall grass; they were watching us with suspicion. Then a frightening thought struck me and I turned to Claire. 'It's known that where there are zebras, there are lions. We shouldn't be sitting out here in the open.'

'I can't see any lions.' Claire looked around carefully. 'But if one does come along,' she continued, picking up one of the long sausages that was lying on the ground, 'I'll give him a whack on the head with this. I'm not afraid of lions!'

'Well …' I got up, speaking quietly. 'I'd better fetch my camera and take a picture of those zebras before they run away.'

'You're not going to take another picture of animals, are you?'

'Don't you think these zebras look nice?'

'All animals do,' commented Claire dryly, 'until the moment you get your camera out and then, whoops … they vanish.'

Maybe she was right. Animal photography didn't seem to be my strongest point. So far I had taken a number of pictures in which you vaguely saw the tail ends of antelopes, zebras, gnus and other fleeing animals …

'What you need,' suggested Claire, 'is someone who chases the animals towards you.' She looked eagerly at me. 'I can do that for you if you like. I'll crawl through the grass and when I get behind those zebras, I'll suddenly jump up and startle them. Then they'll all run towards you and at last you'll be able to take a picture where you can see their heads.' She laughed at her own wit.

I was about to tell her not to do such a stupid thing, but she had already set off on a wide detour, crawling on all fours through the tall grass, attempting to circle around the zebras. They seemed intrigued. I saw them turn their heads, following Claire's movements through the grass with great interest. She had finally got behind them when suddenly, from the other side of the track, I heard a mighty, 'Aarrooh!' There *was* a lion hidden somewhere in the tall grass! The zebras turned and thundered away, crashing through the bushes, while Claire shot out of the grass like a Jack-in-the-box. She dashed straight for the Land Rover, jumped in panting and slammed the door. I think she must have broken the 100-metre record.

After this, Claire agreed to stay inside the cabin while I climbed onto the roof rack and took up position in a deckchair I had installed there. I was sure to spot many more animals from this vantage point, but Claire drove around for several hours without me being able to film anything extraordinary. The few scattered grazers we saw seemed as distrustful as ever and immediately darted off when we approached.

We had been driving for a while on a narrow track between bushes and low trees when, rounding a corner, we found the way blocked by a large herd of female elephants with their babies. As she saw us, the leading matriarch raised her trunk and trumpeted loudly.

Wonderful! I thought, pointing my movie camera at the elephants, but before I could film anything Claire had thrown the gears into reverse and the Land Rover whizzed back around the bend.

I will never forget that wonderful vision of the matriarch, her big ears moving like sails.

She stood there just in front, towering high above me. One push forward of her mighty body, one movement of her strong trunk and she could have destroyed us. I was overawed by her majestic presence, yet I wasn't afraid; I trusted her. She held back, just waving her ears, and I knew what she wanted to tell me. It was a signal for me to make way and without hesitating a second, I switched into reverse gear and freed the track for her and her herd.

'What did you do that for?' I heard Peter grumble from above after I had stopped some 30 yards back where the track was wider, pulling into the bush as much as I could.

'Don't worry,' I said to appease him, leaning out of the window, 'they'll come along and then you'll be able to film them.'

But the elephants must have been camera shy. Minutes later, we heard small trees to our right snap as if they had been matchsticks and saw the herd, mothers and babies, a grey mass of elephants, moving slowly through the dense wood. It was a scene of incredible beauty, the mothers pushing thin trees out of the way for their little babies and encouraging them to go on. It brought tears to my eyes.

Then I heard Peter exclaim from the roof rack, 'It's useless trying to film the elephants! There are too many trees in the way.'

It was getting towards sunset – time to leave the park. I had spent many uncomfortable hours on the roof rack and hadn't been able to film a single animal or take even one decent photograph; it was really disappointing. I was about to shout to Claire to stop to let me come down, when suddenly we ground to a halt in a cloud of dust and I was flung out of my deckchair and thrown amongst the spare tyres. Then the engine stalled. As I crawled up from between the tyres rubbing my elbow, which had hit the tool chest, and peered over the row of jerry cans, I saw a huge rhinoceros accompanied by a baby standing right in the middle of the track. Claire had just avoided a head-on collision! The rhino was eyeing us malevolently, then it began to paw the ground with one front foot, snorted and lowered its head with its massive horn: it was about to charge!

Claire desperately tried to restart the engine, but it just went bzzz … bzzz … I bent down from the roof rack, whispering, 'Quick!' but however much Claire pressed the starter, the engine stubbornly refused to start.

Rhinos are always searching for something on which to vent their wrath. They are the most bad-tempered animals of the bush, in a constant state of irritation because of the large number of parasites that feed upon them. They charge in sheer outraged fury and have been known to hurl themselves against cars, running their horns though the metal bodies and even overturning them.

These incidents flitted through my mind as I sat paralysed, afraid to make the slightest movement that might provoke action. Then, after some tense moments, the rhino snorted again, turned and trotted off into the bush behind its baby without giving us a second glance. And so, at last, I was able to take a good photograph and a very rare one, too: that of a baby rhino walking in front of its mother – only white rhinos do that!

The moment the rhino had disappeared I jumped down from the roof rack ready to find out what was wrong with the engine, but before I had time to do anything Claire pressed the starter once more and now that the danger was over the capricious engine started immediately! We drove off into the fading light of the setting sun, wiping the sweat from our faces.

Rhinos are such mighty beasts. For millions of years their heavy armour has shielded them from danger, yet it no longer protects them. They are now up against a species infinitely more ruthless and ferocious than themselves, armed with guns, shooting them relentlessly for their horns. I couldn't help thinking that they are fighting their last and hopeless battle.

Before leaving Zimbabwe we made a detour to the Victoria Falls on the Zambezi. The falls were a miracle of beauty and as they thundered into a chasm, the mighty sound was overpowering. A column of spray rose up high into the air, creating the famous cloud of rising rain that can be seen from many miles away. Long before Livingstone discovered the falls and named them after Queen Victoria, the local inhabitants called them 'The Smoke that Thunders'. To me it was a much more appropriate name.

Tanzania

I had been looking forward to reaching Tanzania, not just because we were going to sail to India from there, but because this was a country that had devised an authentic path towards development, different from anything we had seen so far. Julius Nyerere, who had led the country since independence, had promulgated African socialism as the solution. He was known in particular for having created Ujamaa villages where people from different parts of the country were grouped around schools and hospitals in an effort to overcome ethnic divisions and facilitate development.

After the end of colonialism, the West wanted someone to believe in and in Nyerere they had found their man. Here at last was someone who hadn't monopolised power solely for the sake of lining his own pockets. He was that rare African – a sincere, simple man living by rigorous principles – who put the interests of his country first. He was a man of great charisma, the West liked what he said and did, and aid flowed in. So far, during the first twenty years of its independence, Tanzania had received more aid per head of population than any other country in the world. I was eager to learn about the Tanzanian development model and to find out how all that aid money had been put to good use.

After leaving the Victoria Falls behind, we re-crossed Zambia without delay and reached the border. I felt relieved when the Zambian customs officers let us leave their country without any problem. At last we're in Tanzania, I thought, but as I stepped into a frame building on the Tanzanian side to have our passports examined by the official in charge of immigration, he stopped me saying, 'No, it's too late.' I couldn't think what he was talking about but then he pointed at his watch which indicated 6.00 p.m. and added, 'We're closing.' The immigration officials were indeed locking up everything, including the border, and there was no persuading them to be flexible, leave the border open a few minutes longer, stamp our passports and let us in. They had finished for the day and nothing I suggested could alter the rules and regulations of bureaucracy. 'We're opening again at 8.00 a.m. tomorrow,' one of the officials informed us. 'Come back then.'

What a joke, I thought. How could we go anywhere else and come back? It was impossible to return to Zambia, as they had given us exit stamps in our passports. So we remained stuck on the narrow strip of no-man's-land between the two border posts, and that's where we cooked a frugal supper sitting on the tarmac and where we spent the night.

The customs people showed up again at the official opening time the next morning, unlocked the border and after some extensive checking of our passports to make sure we hadn't been to 'apartheid' South Africa, they finally let us in.

In the first large town we came to we started looking for a bank. When an Indian shopkeeper whom we asked for directions realised we wanted to change money, he made a sign to come inside his shop and to our surprise locked the door behind us.

'Don't go to a bank,' he whispered. '*I* can change your money.'

I stared at him, surprised. This was not what I had expected, but he insisted.

'I give you much better rate,' and he offered five times the official rate. It was too good to refuse! I nodded my agreement and passed him some pound notes, which he stuffed into the bottom of his socks; he then put on his shoes again, gave us a wad of Tanzanian banknotes, pressed a small packet of rice into my hands to make people believe we had gone into the shop to buy something, unlocked the door and quickly let us out.

It somehow reminded me of Algeria. One of the side effects of 'socialism' there had also been an unrealistic official exchange rate and a flourishing black market. I'd been hoping Tanzanian 'socialism' would be different!

We were driving along the main highway towards Dar es Salaam, night had just fallen and we still hadn't found a place where we could camp. Then, suddenly, the headlights of the Land Rover shone on a dark obstacle blocking the entire width of the road. Slamming my foot on the brake pedal, I just managed to stop a few feet away: it was a long trailer attached to a lorry, which had gone off the road and seemed to be stuck in a clump of trees. The trailer was barring the way for any oncoming vehicle and as I hooted furiously, a head popped up over the side. I had woken the driver who, not having anything better to do, had decided he might as well go to sleep inside the empty trailer!

We reached Dar es Salaam two days later, found the Indian Embassy and asked for the letter from New Delhi authorising us to film in India. The employees were happy to help but seemed somewhat disorganised.

'A letter?' they repeated. 'From New Delhi?' They checked our passports, noted that we had visas for India, took all our particulars and promised to start looking through their official documents. 'But,' they warned, 'it could take some time.'

As we had to hang around for a few days, we decided to go to the EEC office. We had more luck there. They had received news of our coming and had been waiting eagerly for our arrival; it seemed there was an interesting EEC-funded project in Morogoro that was nearing completion and they absolutely wanted me to film it because it was an example of the new approach to development. Although this meant returning 120 miles, there was no escaping the EEC people's insistence and so, off we went.

For more than half a century, Tanzania (or Tanganyika as it was then called) had been growing sisal, a type of agave, and had exported the long, resistant fibres extracted from its leaves. Then the government came up with a grand idea. Why not turn the fibres into canvas here instead of exporting the raw material? It would keep all the added value inside the country and would simultaneously contribute to jump-start industrialisation.

The government had wanted a modern factory, asked for the best, and had received the best as part of an aid package: a top-of-the-range factory – a gift from the EEC. As to their side of the deal, the Tanzanian government had promised to install a new power station with enough capacity to run everything.

As we approached Morogoro, we passed vast plantations of sisal and met two girls balancing heavy sisal roots precariously on their heads, carrying them home for firewood. I made Peter stop to have a chat, but we didn't have much time. A mixed EEC-Tanzanian delegation was already waiting for us at the factory in town and they soon ushered us into what looked like a vast hangar. Inside we noticed row upon row of hyper-modern machinery, all painted olive-green, but there was none of the noise and frenetic activity we had expected, no workers busy at their tasks, no sisal leaves going in at one end and rolls of canvas coming out at the other.

'You couldn't switch on the machines so that I can film turning wheels and flashing lights?' asked Peter.

His request met with an embarrassed silence. Then a Tanzanian official replied lamely, 'We're waiting for the electricity.'

'And when is that going to come?'

The official looked away, but finally replied, 'When it is ready.'

There was no point in filming equipment that was sitting silent and as another

Tanzanian official was pressing us to continue with the rest of the visit, Peter decided to leave his heavy movie camera behind.

'Wait,' said the official, and he called for a soldier, an *askari*, to stand guard over the camera. 'Otherwise,' he explained, 'it might no longer be there when we return.' As the government had decreed sexual equality, young women too were enrolled in the army and so it came about that a female *askari* in full uniform stood to attention next to Peter's camera. She provided the only human touch in what otherwise turned out to be a very disappointing visit.

As I was pressing him to tell me why there was no electricity, one of the Europeans finally revealed that, unfortunately, the power station, which should have been finished a long time before, wasn't there. By cutting off other customers, the town of Morogoro had been able to supply just enough power to allow each unit of equipment to be tested separately to make sure it worked properly, and thus it could be claimed that the factory functioned. The European specialists were ready to fly home and Tanzanian officials were going to take over everything, and particularly the cars of the Europeans.

As we stepped out into the dazzling sunshine, I couldn't help shaking my head. The Tanzanian Government had failed to keep its promise. There wouldn't be any electricity to run the factory and so £1.5 million worth of brand new, highly specialised equipment, delivered with the best of intentions and installed within the promised deadline, was destined to rust away.

We got back late into Dar es Salaam and thought we might as well escape the sweltering heat of the town by opting for a hotel on the beach. The setting looked all right but as we sat down for supper, we were in for a nasty disappointment. There were lots of items on the menu, but nothing we ordered seemed to be there; not even fish.

'Never mind,' I tried to console Claire who had been looking forward to having fresh fish. 'Tomorrow we're going to the Indian Embassy. They're sure to have found the letter by now; soon we'll be on a boat to India and there'll be lots of fish on the menu.'

Early next morning we stepped into the embassy full of hope, only to hear that there was no letter from New Delhi. We had got this far against all odds just to find out they wouldn't let us film in India. As I left, feeling totally dispirited, I felt Claire's hand on my arm.

'It doesn't matter,' she said soothingly.

'But it does! To think that I planned everything so carefully and made such an effort to get here,' I grumbled, 'and all for nothing!'

'I'm sure something good will come out of this.' Claire smiled encouragingly at me. 'Why don't we go to Kenya instead?'

She was right of course. We often think we have missed something important and then the important thing turns out to be of no value, whilst something else we hadn't even thought about turns out to be of surprising significance. Had we been allowed to sail to India we would never have gone to Turkanaland in northwest Kenya where we would spend some of the happiest weeks of our lives; meeting the Turkana was to have an enormous influence upon us.

A few hours later, we went to the EEC office to see what could be done.

'It's difficult to cross the border between Tanzania and Kenya,' said the man who received us, 'but it can be done if it's for "diplomatic" reasons. I'm sure we'll be able to arrange it.' They had to communicate with the EEC delegation in Nairobi, Kenya, and also needed to obtain the necessary authorisations from the Tanzanian authorities, and that would take a few days.

I decided that we might as well make good use of our time and started to look for a shop where they developed photos. So far I had taken maybe a thousand colour slides, which I had sent to Europe via diplomatic bags, but I had no idea of the quality of the slides. There might be problems since we had dropped the camera (a Canon) a couple of times; it had even fallen on a hard rock. After searching around we found a small photography shop where I bought a roll of black and white film and then went out in the street to take twelve photographs with different settings. The owner of the shop immediately developed the film and printed the photographs; to my relief everything seemed to be all right.

While we were in the darkroom, I asked the owner, an Indian, about life here. At first he seemed reluctant to talk, but as trust was established he became more outspoken and gradually began to complain.

'Sometimes,' he said, 'it's impossible to buy certain supplies for months on end.' He was most upset about the fact that his little son hadn't had any milk for six months. 'It's showing in his bones and teeth,' wailed the father, looking very worried.

I returned to the Land Rover without delay, fished out a quart of milk powder, which was all we had left, and gave it to the man who thanked me profusely. Then, as I was about to leave, he held me back.

'Be careful,' he warned, 'this is a dangerous place.' And then he told me about an Indian shop-keeper who had been robbed in his shop only a week ago, and when he resisted, he had been killed. 'And what do you think the police did?' the photographer asked, almost shouting in my face. 'Nothing! The government doesn't do anything to protect us, Indians. On the contrary, they pester us all the time. They want to ruin us! They want to push us out of the country and I can tell you that many of us would be pleased to get out of this place, but how can we? If we go we would have to leave all our possessions behind, everything our grandparents, our parents, and we have toiled for. We would be destitute!'

That night we moved to an African guesthouse in town, which was much cheaper than the hotel on the beach. That was about all that could be said in its favour. It was stiflingly hot inside our room and there was no mosquito netting in front of the windows, so we had to keep them shut because of the abundance of the buzzing little horrors. We stayed for two nights until we could no longer endure the mosquitoes, flies and other insects, winged and crawling, which infested the place, and decided to drive back to the mission at Lugoba where we had spent a night on our way towards Dar es Salaam. It was 70 miles away, but well worth the drive; it was much cooler than the coastal area and was a haven of peace and cleanliness.

The sisters received us again without hesitating for a second and as this time round we stayed for several days, we were able to learn more about their lives. They always got up at the crack of dawn, prayed, had breakfast and then set about their daily tasks. One of the sisters, Marie-Esmeralda, had trained as a nurse and after finishing breakfast, she would open the door of her dispensary and tell the first of a long line of patients waiting outside to come in – medical care was one of the few activities the government allowed the mission to perform. And she would continue her care with just a few short breaks until nightfall.

I was fascinated to see Sister Marie-Esmeralda clean festering wounds, bandage burns and treat infections with the sparse medicine she had, and to hear her explain patiently to mothers when they came with their sick babies that they must avoid contaminated water. She gave her time and energy to these forsaken people unsparingly.

Sometimes patients came from the government dispensary carrying notes asking if she would take care of them because they simply didn't know what to do or had no medication.

'But we haven't got enough medicine either,' the sister told me. 'An organization in Holland sends us a parcel of medical supplies every month, but it rarely gets here. We know that on several occasions the packet addressed to us was diverted to a camp where they train guerrillas; corrupt officials have also been in the habit of intercepting it in order to sell it for their own benefit. But we do our best.'

After spending the morning in the dispensary, I was curious to find out why patients were coming to the mission for treatment instead of going to the official dispensary, and so I walked to the nearby Ujamaa village. It was an indifferent cluster of low houses. The walls of the little houses were made of any material at hand – mud, pieces of wood or tin sheets – and the roofs were in corrugated iron. It all looked miserable. I had been told that the idea behind creating Ujamaa villages was to group people around schools, shops and hospitals so that they could get free health care and education, and be able to buy goods. Yet the school was just an earth building where pupils sat on the ground and wrote in the dust. There was no hospital, only a miserable dispensary; it lacked medical supplies and patients were treated with indifference. And in the shop there was nothing much for sale. Everything seemed to be lacking here, even clean water. To me the whole village looked like a disaster. People seemed bereft and disorganised, without hope or initiative.

We did, however, meet some happy people. To our surprise, there were a number of Maasai women amongst those coming to the mission's dispensary; they must have walked many miles to get here. They looked fabulous and I was keen to photograph them, but they simply turned their backs to me when I came closer. Despite their contact with 'civilization' the Maasai seemed to be wary of anything they weren't used to. I was wondering how to handle this when I had a brainwave. I showed one of the older women how to look through the viewfinder and she thought it great fun to see her companions reduced to tiny beings. Others now wanted to have a look too, and finally they were all laughing happily. After a while they got used to my camera and no one bothered any longer when I walked between them and took pictures.

> The Maasai women had a proud bearing, their magnificent bodies draped with a length of blue or dark cloth, leaving one shoulder bare. They walked with majestic grace, their backs straight, their heads held high, bracelets tinkling on their wrists as they moved; the dignity of queens was naturally ingrained in them.
>
> The young Maasai women in particular were enchanting. They were breathtakingly beautiful with their silky skins, large eyes and smiling lips. The stiff, wide collars of tightly woven red, white and blue beads standing out around their necks like corollas and their headbands and earrings created an appearance of delightful, luminous flowers – a fascinating picture of beauty I could have looked at for hours. Barely seventeen or eighteen, they were already carrying a baby on their backs, but the smiles of these young mothers spoke of happiness and freedom. They were among the most eye-catching people we had ever met.

Although Africa must have been full of snakes, we had so far not seen a single one. But one morning we had a near-fatal encounter.

> We had settled down for the night under a huge tree somewhat away from the mission building, the branches overhanging our Land Rover like an umbrella, and we felt safe and protected. We slept peacefully through the night, but we were awoken at dawn by shouts, a great thump startled us and then the thud of a heavy weight landing on the roof rack shook the vehicle. Surprised we peered out from the back flap we had left open to let the cool night air come in and saw a man standing a few feet away with a long snake hanging from a sturdy stick; it was dead.
>
> 'This very bad poison snake,' said the man, a broad smile across his face. 'I see him hang down from branch ready to bite you when you come out, so I kill snake.'
>
> We were shaken and kept thanking him for his courage. Later the sisters told us this was

one of the most dangerous snakes. It had a habit of sliding along branches and dropping soundlessly upon innocent prey. Within seconds the victim would be paralysed and soon all would be over as the poison was fatal.

After this, we shut the back flap of our Land Rover at night, even if it felt stifling inside.

Before coming to Africa, I was not very partial to missions because I imagined that their main line of activity was trying to convert people, but little by little I had to revise my opinion. I particularly had to take off my hat to the work these sisters were doing. They were carrying out their tasks from the crack of dawn till nightfall with only short breaks, sustained by their unwavering faith and driven by their devotion to others.

Sister Mathilde, plump and homely, was a wonderful cook who turned out tasty meals. How she managed to feed us all seemed a miracle, till she took us to the fields and gardens beyond the mission. Here they grew all the maize, vegetables and fruit they needed. A man from the village was busy all day long, weeding and watering under the supervision of the Mother Superior. And then there was Margaret who, besides doing the cleaning, also helped in the gardens. It turned out that she had twelve children to feed, hers and those of a sister!

One day Margaret had told the sisters about an old man in the village who was facing certain death, as there was no one left to support him; his son had just died in the village dispensary from an illness they had been unable to treat. Horrified, the sisters had taken him into the mission and entrusted him with the task of roasting maize cobs in an iron stove in the outhouse where he now lived. He seemed happy with what he considered to be his new family and was totally devoted to the sisters. As he had no clothes, they had given him one of their nightdresses and a coat. The man had a wonderful, gentle face and great dignity; we got fond of him and always praised his delicious roasted maize.

As we sat down for supper in the peaceful dining room in the evening, the Mother Superior would tell us strange stories. I still remember an intriguing one about a cancer tree.

'In the heart of the forest,' the sister began, 'there grows a tree which, if you touch it, causes cancer.' The witchdoctor sometimes ordered those he had judged guilty to be attached to that tree as punishment, and one day a young woman had been found tied to the trunk. She must have been there for several days and was suffering from terrible lesions all over her skin. But the really amazing thing was that around that cancer tree grew a plant whose leaves could cure the wounds it caused and they managed to save the young woman.

'Many years ago, a young doctor who passed by had discovered this plant's incredible properties,' explained the sister. When he left he hoped to return to collect and study this plant, but the sisters had never heard of him again. The story made a deep impression on me and I wanted to go into the forest to find that plant, but to my great regret Peter wouldn't hear of it.

The Mother Superior was not only a source of strange stories, but she also organised everything, from the people working in the vegetable gardens to the upkeep of the mission. The sisters were kindness itself and really heroic. In my heart I shall always retain the image of those three brave sisters, so welcoming in their fresh white robes, surviving against many odds and never abandoning those who came asking for help.

A few days later, we returned to the EEC office in Dar es Salaam and they had a wonderful surprise for us: they had all the necessary authorisations ready. We would be allowed to cross the border and drive into Kenya! Claire decided to celebrate by splashing out on an extravagance. Having had an English mother and having been brought up in England, she loved butter and would spread nothing else on her bread if she could. We had a mini fridge in the Land Rover, but it was filled with exposed rolls of film. It was supposed to keep them cool, although the fridge didn't function very well in the great heat. But, of course, Claire's priorities were entirely different. To my annoyance, a number of times my films had to share the limited space with half-melting butter, and if there wasn't enough space for both, it was the film rolls that went out!

Every time we reached a town of any importance I had to do the round of the shops and hunt for butter. Fortunately the smaller shops never had any, but supermarkets, those epitomes of Western civilization, had penetrated deep into Africa. Very large towns usually boasted at least one of them; they were better stocked and generally had a supply of butter, which pleased Claire no end.

When we found out that Dar es Salaam had no less than three supermarkets, Claire's hopes soared, only to fall rapidly after we had done the round of the first two and discovered that there was precious little food to buy. We managed to find some rice, sugar and two packets of rather stale biscuits well past their sell-by date, but no butter.

There was, however, one thing they had in abundance: what they called educative books and magazines. One, which seemed interesting, was called the Africa-Asia Magazine. I picked it up from the shelves, opened it at random and came upon an article on Afghanistan. To my astonishment, I read how the people of Afghanistan had received their Soviet brothers with open arms; how they had been waiting for the benefits of socialism to be bestowed upon them and how happy they were now that they were liberated from oppression. Then I looked at the author's name. I can't quite remember it now, but it ended in -ov, like Popov or Andropov.

When we got to the third and last supermarket, asking for butter, and a sales assistant pulled an apologetic face, my hopes began to soar. Our small fridge was choc-a-bloc with films and I needed all the space I could get.

'Sorry,' I said to Claire who had become very quiet by now. 'No butter. You'll have to eat margarine.'

'But I've been eating margarine for weeks now!' Claire could be very stubborn when she set her mind to it. 'I want butter! This is more than I can stand. I'm going to see the manager and give him a piece of my mind!' And she resolutely knocked on a door marked 'Manager' and went in without further ado. A minute or two later the manager came out, looking rather shaken. He went in search of an assistant and followed by Claire, they disappeared through a back door into what appeared to be the reserves. They began to search through different freezers and finally, at the bottom of one of these, they found a pound of butter, which Claire carried away triumphantly!

That night we drove back to the mission of Lugoba, which was on the north-south trunk road, and when Claire told the sisters how she had obtained a pound of butter, craving was written all over their faces. They hadn't had butter for two years! To do honour to Claire, I must say that she didn't hesitate a second. She went to our Land Rover, retrieved her pound of butter from the small fridge and gave it to the sisters, who were overjoyed.

The main north-south trunk road, which stretches north of Lugoba all the way to Moshi near the Kenyan border, is marked on the map as a thick, red line, suggesting a road in good condition. It had indeed been asphalted with foreign aid only a few years before, but there had been no maintenance since, and tropical rains and overloaded lorries had caused enormous damage. The tarmac was broken in many places, there were deep potholes and it was often safer to drive next to the road.

As we stopped at one of the Ujamaa villages further north, we were told by the official in charge that there was an agricultural project close by, run by a German woman. When we found her she asked us what we were doing here.

'Just passing by on our way to Kenya,' I replied.

She immediately set out to convince me not to go. 'Vhy you not stay in Tanzania?' She pointed a finger at me, moving it forwards and backwards. 'Zis is a gut country! Zis is gut regime. Vhy you vant to go to Kenya? Anyvhan in Tanzania can tell you zat ze zituashion is bad in Kenya. Zey are dying of hunger zere. Zey all vant to come to Tanzania.'

I was about to ask, 'How do they know all this when the border is closed?' but I held back. It's no good arguing with true believers and this woman was clearly a true believer.

'Zey have evryzing in Tanzania,' the woman carried on. 'Zey produce evryzing in abundance here. Zey are pluffing all the time. You can go anyvheir and you zee people pluff.'

After we left, I turned to Claire. 'I don't understand. What do you think she means when she says people are pluffing all the time?'

'Well … you know … the English *ough*-ending can be very confusing to foreigners. When she says pluff she pronounces it as in *rough*, but what I think she means is plough … that they are ploughing all the time.'

'My God!' I exclaimed. 'That woman must be East German!'

302

Driving further north, our impression that Tanzania was on the east side of the iron curtain was only reinforced. It was not only in Dar es Salaam that we found an abundance of socialist literature. Elsewhere in Tanzania, bookshops were stacked with it, too. Prominently exhibited of course were the speeches and complete writings of President Nyerere; there were also the works of Marx and Lenin, and more in the same vein; but there wasn't a single book by any Western author, not even a book on tourism.

As we strolled through Arusha, a big town in the north of the country, I noticed that half the front window of a bookshop was taken up with one title written by a Jamaican author: *How Europe underdeveloped Africa*. I went inside and bought the book out of pure curiosity, only to find out that it was an inflammatory diatribe about how colonisation had brought nothing but ills to Africa; that it had created artificial borders; that the colonisers had exploited the Africans; that all of today's problems had their roots in the colonial epoch; and so on and so forth.

Tanzania accepted Western aid, even counted on it, yet criticising the West seemed to be an officially sanctioned attitude. But I hadn't heard a single word of criticism levelled against government policy. In the name of African 'socialism', millions of people who had lived in scattered dwellings near their plots of land had been rounded up and resettled by force in Ujamaa villages. The results, as far as I had been able to make out, were food shortages, abuses by government officials who controlled everything and apathy amongst the population in general. There seemed to be few positive results to show for all the planning, nationalisation and forced collectivisation and for all the aid the country had received.

I had obtained permission to film one more project before leaving Tanzania – a coffee plantation on the slopes of Mount Kilimanjaro. It was supposed to be a showcase and two employees were going to demonstrate the spraying equipment the project had received through foreign aid. They were handed new overalls for the occasion, which they took out of their plastic wrapping and proudly put on, but unfortunately there were no pesticides. The official in charge couldn't explain why. Perhaps state planning had overlooked these, or maybe they had gone somewhere else? So I filmed the employees as they gave a demonstration, spraying coffee beans with water!

To make up for our disillusion, we were hoping to behold the sight of snow on Mount Kilimanjaro, the highest mountain in Africa – its name means 'the shining mountain'. To our regret, the peak of the Mount Kilimanjaro was wrapped in a dense cloud. However much we waited to get a glimpse of the promised beauty, it never materialised. As we were about to leave Tanzania, somehow this seemed symbolic.

Zambia

Above: Returning from school with exercise book, a fish and sugar cane

Right: Sunglasses come in all styles

Above: A spectacular accident

Below: School is out

Above: Girls' tasks never end

Below: A prison camp

Relaxing at Des Hunt's farm

Zimbabwe

The crocodile farm

Above: Mr Hendricks and his workshop

Below: Claire and local worker in Mr Hendricks' workshop

Bushmen cave paintings

Above: Peter filming from the roof rack

Below: White rhino following its baby

Victoria Falls

Tanzania

Above: Sisal plantations

Below: A female askari guarding Peter's camera at the Morogoro factory

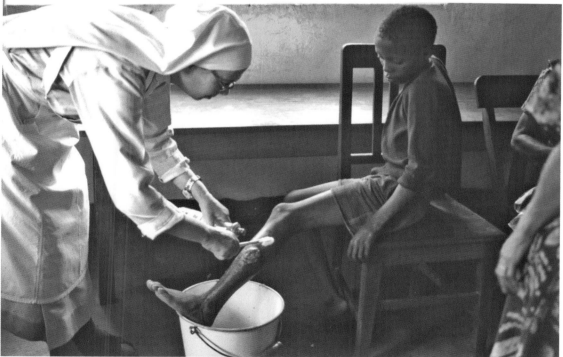

Above: The mission at Lugoba

Below: In the mission's dispensary

Above: Lugoba mission: the old man roasting his corn

Below: African splendour: Maasai girls

PART 4

Kenya
The New and the Old

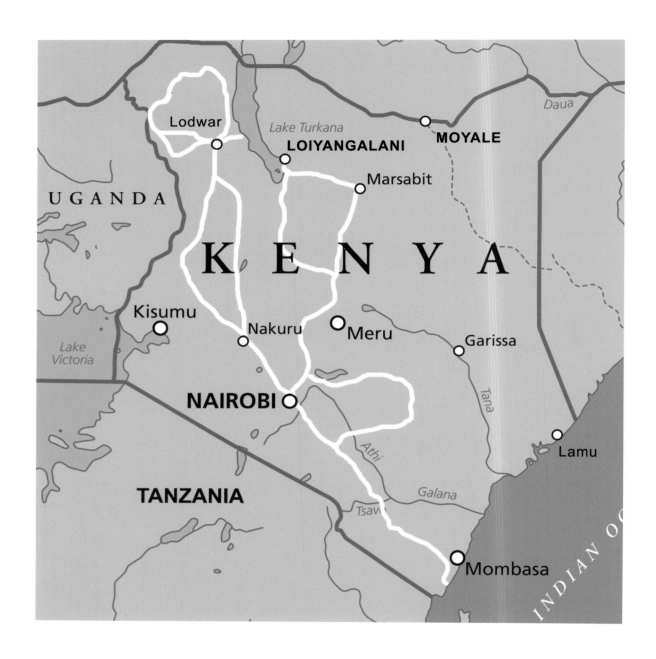

Map 5: Kenya

CHAPTER 11
The Many Colours of Kenya

Projects and Safaris

We were expecting to see malnourishment and poverty in Kenya, as the German woman in Tanzania had led us to believe, but we were struck by how healthy and contented everyone looked. By African standards Kenya was a rich country. As Jean-Paul Jesse, the head of the EEC delegation in Nairobi, observed, 'I can't think of any better assignment in the whole of Africa.'

Jesse was a dynamic Frenchman and as he was a friend of the man I knew in the European Commission in Brussels, he immediately set about organising our stay.

'Now that we have a cameraman,' he said, pointing at me, 'we're going to make the most of it. There are a number of projects I need to visit and you're coming with me to film everything.'

'What about my wife?' I asked hesitantly. 'She does the sound recording.'

Jesse turned to Claire. 'Don't worry. We're not going to leave you behind.' He laughed. 'We'll manage to find a small place for you somewhere in a corner of the car.'

Barely two days later, we were heading eastwards in a comfortable Range Rover, seated behind Jesse, who never stopped talking. 'As you will soon see,' he explained, 'we have a new approach to development aid. In the past, many projects failed because local people didn't have to pay for them and therefore didn't value them. Think: if something is given away for free, how can it have any value?'

I nodded while Jesse continued as we passed alongside a shrivelled plantation of banana trees.

'At last, we have understood this and our projects are taking it into account. We now ask the local population to cover part of the cost. Of course they have no money, but they have to put in some work representing maybe a third of the price before receiving the equipment that represents our contribution.'

This principle was fully illustrated by the project we visited in Tawa where men and women were digging a trench designed to drain away surplus water in the rainy season; it would stop the erosion caused by water running freely down exposed hillsides. Some of the people were standing next to the trench, singing and playing drums and flutes to cheer on those who were working. To me almost all the energy the men and women digging the trench were expending seemed to go into swinging their bodies to the rhythm of the music, and maybe only 10 percent into shovelling out earth, but at least the work was getting done and the villagers were enjoying it.

Jesse's safari was well organised. Whenever we arrived at the site of a project, we found dozens –

sometimes even hundreds – of people waiting for us, and the moment all the important men were seated, someone would get behind a microphone and start talking. The number of speeches we were treated to was impressive. Jesse was expected to reply and he dived into it with great gusto. Being a Frenchman, I suppose it came naturally to him, even if he had to do it in English and wait every two or three sentences for an interpreter to translate what he had said into the local language.

As I was the cameraman, I wasn't expected to make speeches, but they did make me come forward in the Meru area and placed a mask of ostrich feathers over my head, saying they had done me the honour of making me a warrior of their tribe! Since women couldn't be warriors, Claire only received a colourful, locally woven shoulder bag, but she was extremely pleased with her present.

We spent most of our time in the Machakos district, a region of dried-out riverbeds shaded by doum palms. The rains, which came twice a year, turned the deep, sandy courses into wildly running streams, which swept down the gullies with furious strength, but soon everything dried out again. The last rainy season had ended two months before and there appeared to be nothing left except dry sand. But if you dug a few feet down you would reach water!

The heat pressed upon us as we descended into one of those sand rivers through a tangled mass of bush. Here and there we came upon holes in the riverbed; a small girl was scooping water out of one of these as we passed by, filling up a canister with the help of her little brother. Finally we reached what was called a 'subsurface dam', the object of our visit. From below it looked like any normal dam but behind there was nothing but sand. It seemed most unpromising but in fact the sand acted like a big sponge. It was full of water and it shielded the precious liquid inside from the sun's heat, thereby preventing the water from evaporating and making it available all year round. At the bottom of the dam there was a tap, which I opened. The water tasted slightly brackish, but it was all right to drink.

In the course of our trip we came to a spot where a number of European aid specialists had arrived in a small plane that morning. A group of nomads were looking on from afar at these strange people who were sitting in camp chairs while being served lunch on folding tables; I noticed several bottles of champagne in ice buckets.

A nearby area had been fenced off and month after month, local aid workers had tied strings of different colours to the extremities of all the little shoots and branches of bushes and trees within that area to show how fast they grew. In a neighbouring control area, a number of camels had been left free to wander and browse, and several aid workers were busy measuring the differences with the fenced-off area. We went to say hello and found the specialists discussing how to process the data in Europe in order to obtain an estimate of the number of camels the area could support.

Strangely enough, the Europeans didn't even bother to speak to the nomads. These were kept at arms' length by askaris who had come over by Land Rover, and the nomads in turn stared at the European specialists as if they had been extraterrestrials who had landed for a short visit and would soon be off again without so much as leaving a ripple on the surface of their lives.

As we left, I felt a volcano rising inside me!

After we got back to Nairobi, Jesse told us to prepare for a prolonged safari (the Swahili word for trip). So far we had lived very sparingly to make our funds last. Upon entering Kenya, six months after leaving Brussels, we had spent no more than half the cash and travellers cheques we had with us. But travelling with the people from the EEC delegation, we now had to sleep in lodges and hotels and as we were expected to pay our own costs, our funds were melting rapidly.

We were on our way to a bank and I'd just stopped at a red light when an African came up to the Land Rover, hissing, 'Psst … Change?' I hadn't expected a black market in a country like Kenya, but then you can never tell, and when the African offered me three times the official rate, I nodded agreement; it was almost too good to be true.

'How much do you want to change?' asked the man.

I made a quick estimate. 'A hundred and fifty pounds sterling.'

'No problem,' he replied, passing me an airmail envelope. 'Just put the cash in here, park the car and when you're ready, follow me to the boss's office.'

After I had parked I followed the man into a side street, until he stopped in front of a door and turned to me, 'Have you got the money?'

I took the envelope out of my pocket and was just about to open it when, with a quick movement, the man snatched it from my hand and put it into his own pocket!

'Hey!' I shouted, stepping forward. 'What's this?'

'You don't trust me?' The man looked surprised. 'OK.' And he handed me the envelope back.

At that very moment, several Africans appeared, shouting, 'Police!' In a flash the man turned on his heels and ran away. I didn't want to be arrested either and rushed back up the side street, jumped into the Land Rover and immediately drove off.

'Phew!' I exclaimed, explaining to Claire what had happened. 'That was a narrow escape. But at least,' I said, digging the airmail envelope out of my pocket and holding it up triumphantly, 'I haven't lost our money.' Claire opened the envelope; it contained nothing but a few tightly folded newspaper cuttings!

Two hundred yards further on, as we stopped in front of a red light, another African came towards us, hissing, 'Psst … Change?'

I flew into a rage. 'Thief!' I shouted in his face. 'Swindler! I'm going to call the police!'

The man stared at me in shock and moved rapidly off.

Claire put a hand on my arm. 'Don't get so upset,' she said. 'After all, it's only money we've lost, not our lives. Let's go to a bank.'

We soon set off on a safari around a number of projects. It was to be a blitz-type of trip, much like that of the European aid specialists we had seen before; we had chauffeurs and were going to sleep in luxurious – and expensive – lodges.

The EEC had invested heavily in education and Jesse wanted to see for himself how things were faring. We started in the Samburu area around Maralal, stopping in a number of secondary schools where we were entertained by the students who executed a few typical dances. For the occasion, the dancers, young men and girls in their late teens, had swapped their school uniforms for traditional attire. They delivered their performance with great enthusiasm and shouts of merriment, yet it all seemed artificial, a pale imitation of what the real thing must have been. However, the mothers of these school children were still wearing shiny copper wire wound tightly around their upper arms and rows of brilliant beads around their necks. One of them was even encumbered with such impressive coils of wire, hanging heavily on her shoulders, that I wondered how she was able to sleep with all the paraphernalia she was carrying around her neck.

In one of the schools there was a choir of Samburu mothers – a particularly splendid sight. They were dressed in brightly coloured cottons, were decked out with the wide collars of tightly woven beads we had already seen amongst the Maasai and wore matching ear ornaments and headbands, which they had decorated with mauve bougainvillea blossoms, making them look like flowers themselves.

Unfortunately we couldn't stay very long. It wasn't that Jesse didn't appreciate the welcome shows put on for him, but his agenda was full to the brim with engagements and soon we were speeding north again. At this point, an open Land Rover full of askaris joined us. They were going to protect us from shifta, armed bandits from the area near the Somalian border. I had seen askaris in action before. They often strutted about with an arrogant air, but the moment they saw an officer they brought their feet together with a loud smack and, standing rigid as pokers, would give their superior a quivering salute. Was this part of the colonial legacy?

We were the last of a line of five four-wheel-drive vehicles. The askaris drove ahead in an open Land Rover, scanning the surroundings for any sign of danger; then came two other Land Rovers with American and British aid specialists who wanted to visit some of their projects on the way; a Range Rover with Jesse and a delegate from the EEC office, and finally Claire and me in another Range Rover with Joseph, our driver. We were very pleased not to have to steer and being driven around in a comfortable vehicle seemed sheer luxury to us.

After visiting another project, we carried on towards Lake Turkana. It was a stifling afternoon. Every now and then we saw a dust devil whipped up by the wind, rising like a spinning top as it whirled upwards. Never had we seen a countryside more parched; even the trees appeared lifeless, their dust-powdered branches hanging limply down. As we approached Lake Turkana the hot, sticky air seemed to be shimmering above jagged streaks of coagulated lava. Here and there beside the track was a tuft of yellow grass, but otherwise there was nothing, no cicadas, not a single bird, just black, volcanic earth.

Emerging from the volcanic plains stretching away for miles into nowhere, we descended towards the blue lake and then we entered a dream setting, Loiyangalani, an oasis surrounded by palm trees and lush vegetation. Jesse headed towards Oasis Lodge with its large swimming pool and after the men had dived into the clear spring water and we had been served cool drinks, I went out to explore the surroundings. Next to the oasis there was a village of bedraggled straw huts with nothing to shield these from the heat in this parched, sun-scorched land. Here lived the poorest of poor amongst total nothingness, so close to this unbelievable luxury! As I walked between the huts a small hand slipped shyly into mine and when I saw the naked child's bony frame just covered with dusty skin, sorrow choked me. How can we come here, I thought, with nothing to offer but words? Yet, they were smiling, the undemanding women and children of this village.

The next day, we veered eastwards through a semi-desert. Around us, as far as we could see, stretched a dusty landscape of low bush and thorn trees; this was where the Rendille lived. Their young women were strikingly beautiful and whenever Claire noticed some she would ask Joseph, our chauffeur, to drive towards them through the open landscape and to stop so that she could get out and take photographs. Each time he politely complied with Claire's wishes and then rushed on to catch up with the others, but the last time this happened we found the other four vehicles waiting for us along the track. As our chauffeur pulled up, Jesse came forward waving a warning finger at Claire.

'Don't think I haven't noticed what you've been doing,' he said, 'but this time you have really gone too far; we've been waiting a full twenty minutes for you!'

'I'm so sorry,' replied Claire. 'I didn't realise. I was just taking a few photographs.'

'This won't do,' Jesse continued. 'It just won't. I planned this whole safari very carefully, but how do you expect me to stick to my programme if you constantly disrupt my schedule? I'm going to put a stop to this right now.' And to make sure he would be able to control Claire, he placed our Range Rover in second position, between the Land Rover of the askaris and his own Range Rover, and told our chauffeur not to stop unless he specifically authorised him to do so.

At last we reached our northern destination, Marsabit – the centre of the area where the Boran, a cattle-herding tribe, lived. We visited another secondary school where a choir made up of schoolgirls in their uniforms was waiting for us, and we were treated to songs specially composed for the occasion of Jesse's visit. It wasn't very interesting, but then came the schoolgirls' mothers and the contrast couldn't have been greater. They were dressed in strikingly beautiful bright cottons and wore bead necklaces, and bracelets and earrings in silver. Their almond eyes, thin, classical noses and high cheekbones, typical of east African populations, gave them an air of great dignity. As they advanced, pride radiated from their faces and everything in their behaviour conferred the impression that they were doing us a favour and that we, non-Borans, should feel honoured to be allowed to attend.

The Boran women had no instruments other than a cowhide, which they pulled tight over a stone on the ground, and then they began to sing the bull's song with some of the women acting the part of the bull, their arms lifted in a graceful curve symbolising the horns. They drummed on the hide with their bare feet, producing a resounding rhythm and as they started clapping their hands and their voices rang out deep and melodious, the gibbering schoolgirls suddenly became silent, gazing in awe at their mothers. As I looked at the girls, all identically dressed in light-blue school uniforms, I thought, how wonderful that they are being educated, but what an irreplaceable cultural loss.

Nobody made a sound while the women were singing. The music held us all spellbound; we were transported to another, timeless Africa.

The following morning we headed south towards Nairobi via Isiolo. The route was not without danger: north of Isiolo there was a stretch of 30 miles where shifta were known to attack; over the years they had robbed and killed several travellers here. Jesse told us that, only weeks earlier, they had shot at a passing MP. They had immobilised his vehicle but the MP had managed to escape. Two days later, he reached a small town quite a distance away, extremely thirsty and hungry, without shoes and in his underpants! How he had lost all his clothes was a mystery to me, but I thought it best not to ask.

As we approached the dangerous stretch, Jesse became increasingly nervous and gave strict orders to all the drivers to go as fast as possible. Claire, who doesn't like high speeds, kept leaning over to our chauffeur pleading in Swahili, '*Pole, pole*, Joseph.' Slow, slow! But Joseph took no notice and continued to race over the uneven dirt road at a reckless 70 miles per hour. Then, as we came to the most exposed part of the road, there was suddenly a loud bang and the Range Rover veered off towards the side; fortunately Joseph managed to control the vehicle, which shuddered to a halt in the ditch below without overturning. We threw ourselves down on the back seat expecting the worst but no other shots followed. Then we realised what had happened. It was only a tyre that had exploded!

We thought the askaris in the Land Rover ahead of us would stop and immediately come to our rescue, but they just carried on driving at high speed. Seconds later the other vehicles caught up with us and when Jesse found us immobilised at the side of the road, he nearly blew his top. 'Always the same ones making trouble!' he shouted at Claire who tried to make herself very small. Then he realised what had happened and our chauffeur was treated to a collection of loud French swear words. Joseph had already got out the jack and wrench but the wheel nuts didn't yield easily. Jesse, who by now was hopping about with impatience, couldn't stand it any longer. He pushed Joseph away and began banging the wrench with a hammer. The sun was hot and Jesse was sweating profusely, but he did manage to change the wheel in record time. Then everybody helped to push the Range Rover out of the ditch and we all jumped back into our vehicles, which set off again at top speed. And we eventually caught up with the askaris who were responsible for our safety. We found them in the next town sitting on the terrace of a café behind pints of cool beer, chatting animatedly.

In Nairobi, we found a room in an affordable guesthouse run by an American missionary society. The people staying here were a mixed group of Americans, Africans and the two of us; there was a pleasant family atmosphere and we liked it very much.

Meals were served at fixed hours. We all sat down together at long tables and after saying prayers, steaming dishes were put on the table. We helped ourselves to reasonable portions but we soon found that not everyone acted that way. The African women sitting at the table were always the first to finish their plates and then quickly served themselves again, heaping up their plates without caring if this left a second helping for others.

Most Africans we had seen so far were skinny. This wasn't because slimness was fashionable, but because they didn't have enough to eat. Was it surprising then that Africans, when they had enough food, would eat almost till bursting point? In the past maybe, they had to go hungry and who knew what the morrow would bring?

In fact, being fat was a sign of wealth in Africa, just as it had been in Europe in the days of Rubens, and this could take extreme forms. All the Maasai we had seen were very slim people, but I learned that the Maasai MP Oloitipitip was so obese that he had to be driven around in a Range Rover, occupying most of the back seat all by himself.

We had been lolling about for a few days, pleased to have nothing to think about, when we heard from the EEC office that we were expected to visit some development projects in central Kenya and that we had to leave immediately; and could we please go in our own vehicle? Claire didn't hesitate for a second – she would be able to stop whenever she liked to take photographs – and I was happy, too: our funds were dwindling rapidly and we would be able to sleep in our own Land Rover instead of in expensive lodges.

As we came to the central highlands, we passed young boys herding shiny-coated cattle and women plodding along under heavy loads. As was the custom here, these were suspended by leather straps that bit into the women's foreheads. Stretching up the hills on both sides of the dirt road was a patchwork of fields in which crops grew all mixed together – maize, beans, sweet-potatoes, groundnuts and millet. The maize and millet crops stood waist-high and many women were out weeding, their babies bobbing about on their backs.

People lived close to their *shambas* (agricultural plots) in mud and wattle huts with open apertures for windows, each hut surrounded by minute plantations of bananas. The lush, deep green of drooping banana fronds, the sight of ripe vines clambering up on the huts, the gourds of all shapes and sizes and of many shades of orange, brown and yellow … it was Africa in all its abundance.

For generations, Africans had produced at subsistence level and that had been ample. Food grew the whole year round here, and anyway, what was the point in producing more than they needed and then having to store it? Rats, pests or fire were sure to destroy the stored food before it could be eaten. But now that food could be sold to towns, things had begun to change. We saw many granaries, which looked like huts in miniature standing on poles several feet high. One of the suggestions made by aid workers was to fix disks of tin, like collars, round these poles to prevent rats from running up them and to smear the poles with insecticide. And it worked! It was encouraging to see so many huts flanked by granaries.

> A girl stood outside her hut, pounding maize in a wooden mortar. She looked about seventeen or eighteen, the age at which young women attain the perfection of their beauty in Africa, but a baby's head was already hanging out from the sling on her back. By the time they are thirty, childbearing and hard work have often ruined women's beauty here.
>
> Women have to do all the daily tasks. You see them bent over while searching for firewood, or walking down the steep hillsides to the river and then climbing up the hills again, burdened with a heavy gourd or container full of water. I even saw an old woman clamber out of a riverbed struggling under the weight of a calabash filled to the brim. In the dry season they might have to walk 4 or 5 miles to fetch water, or else dig for it in the sand of dry riverbeds.
>
> Women were the patient beasts of burden, toiling all day long. Many bore furrows on their foreheads where the strap, which had supported thousands of burdens, had left its mark. I felt sorry for the women.

As we reached our destination, the village people welcomed us warmly. They had expected us the day before but they didn't show the slightest displeasure at our being late and expressed the hope that having to come out here hadn't inconvenienced us. Then they all looked at me; they were waiting for me to make a speech! As I started speaking I heard myself utter the most commonplace things. I just couldn't imagine how Jesse took such a delight in delivering speeches and especially how he managed to convey anything sensible with a translator interrupting you after every other sentence, but I did my best and rambled on. I doubted if any of the public understood much of my incoherent babble but several nodded wisely, gazing at me reverently. I was glad when the ordeal was over. It all ended with loud applause. Then a few women snatched me by the wrists, pulled me along and executed some lively dance movements as if for my personal enjoyment!

Afterwards a delegation from the village directed us up a long sloping hill and took great pride in showing the work they had done. The whole village had contributed towards digging trenches in which water pipes, to be donated by the EEC, were to be laid to provide irrigation water in the dry season. They had done their part, they conveyed to me while I was filming; would it be possible to deliver the pipes soon?

When our official duties were over, to our delight, the local chief told us there were dances that evening not far from there and asked us if we would like to join them. Before I had time to utter a word, Claire had already nodded 'yes' with sparkling eyes.

We found a crowd gathered around a fire, its flickering flames throwing shadows which seemed to be alive with the fleeting faces of men and women. As we sat down on logs, fascinated by the movements of the dancers who were stamping to the intoxicating rhythm of drums, a low, haunting chant arose while bodies began swaying sensuously. Suddenly a voluminous woman enveloped in a length of printed cotton came towards me, her shoulders rolling to the provocative rhythm of the drums.

'Yes, yes, you dance, too,' she said boldly and in a flash she snatched me up and began teaching me how to dance from the feet up to the knees, then to the swinging hips, while I felt another woman taking hold of my shoulders from behind, saying, 'You shake your shoulders like this.'

The drummers now began to beat out a fast rhythm of increasing intensity in the darkness of the night and I was scarcely able to keep pace with the women. Then, as the magic of Africa took hold of me, I was gripped by a strong feeling of excitement and expectancy which enfolded me in its bewitching power. So strange was the sensation of unreality as I was carried along by elemental instincts that, had the ghosts of ancestors materialised, it wouldn't have surprised me.

The next day we visited a plantation of pyrethrum, a white flower resembling an ordinary field daisy which, when grown at high altitude, can be turned into a toxic powder that is one of the best natural insecticides in the world. The scenery was magnificent. Wide-sweeping views stretched towards distant plains under a blinding sun, a few cumulus clouds hung immobile in an immense blue sky, and in the distance we could see the snow-capped mountain range of Mount Kenya.

A smell of earth and cow-dung hung over the little village of the people who cultivated the pyrethrum, while the shrill sounds of crickets and the tinkle of bells were all around us. One of the women was sitting in front of a calabash preparing a greenish dough made from millet flour and mashed plantain flavoured with a kind of spinach. Two young women were pounding millet for the evening meal with heavy wooden pestles in a hollowed-out log; they carried their children on their backs and were pounding in unison, one lifting up her pestle while the other woman's came down, the monotonous rhythm serving as the babies' lullaby. This muffled 'thump, thump' was as much part of the sound background as the cooing of doves or the tinkle of goat-bells.

We ended the day in the Aberdare Mountains, 7,000-feet high. It had been warm but the moment the sun disappeared the temperature dropped rapidly, although we were on the equator. The mist rolled in and a piercing wind started blowing by the time we were ready to creep into our Land Rover.

We dug out our heavy camelhair blanket, folded it double and snuggled up together underneath it, thankful for the warmth it gave us.

Back in Nairobi, we went to visit N'djeru who worked in the EEC office and lived in a residential area of the town. He was proud to receive us and paraded his four well-dressed children in front of us; he wanted them all to study. His living room, which sported a fake-leather sofa and a TV, was an example of how African society was being sucked into the maelstrom of modernisation. Those who could afford it would equip their houses with metal chairs, plastic furniture and any imported paraphernalia they could pay for. Africa was getting rid of the symbols of its past at a fast pace.

The change had begun so many decades earlier that in most places the old ways had been wiped out almost completely. Today you no longer saw any Kikuyu men wrapped in blankets with ear lobes elongated by heavy earrings. All the Kikuyu men, not only those in towns but also the ones working the thousands of mini-plots that covered the central highlands like a mosaic, now wore shirts and long trousers, and thick woollen jerseys and balaclavas in the (for them) cold season. And instead of going barefooted as they had in the past, they walked about in flip-flops or shoes (or in rubber boots in the countryside). Middle-aged Kikuyu women, too, in their nondescript flowery gowns, were no longer even a faint imitation of the traditional splendour of their grandmothers. With the dowdy type of clothes the older women now wore, they would certainly not make the front pages of fashion magazines. But girls in upper secondary schools were often elegantly dressed, wearing their school uniforms as if they were smart models. Young Africa was connecting with the rest of the world. An unstoppable wave of modernisation seemed to be sweeping over the continent.

To Turkanaland

A day later, I was told to get ready early next morning to fly to Lodwar in the far northwest of the country. The EEC had hired a small, single-engine propeller plane, luggage had to be kept to the minimum and I wasn't allowed to take more than my camera and a small bag. To keep costs down, Uwe Werblow, a German aid specialist working at the EEC office, was going to pilot the plane; he had just gained his flying permit after sixty hours of training and this was his first solo flight. Uwe and Jesse were to occupy the two front seats, whilst I would be squashed in the back with a French woman who had to visit an aid project up north. So, unfortunately, I had to leave Claire behind.

Had I not been so excited about going up in a small plane, I might have felt worried when Uwe began to read the instruction booklet as soon as we were all strapped in our seats and the doors had been locked. He was glancing from the booklet to the dashboard, repeating aloud: push this button, turn that switch, press the starter. 'Hurrah!' he exclaimed when the engine started. 'It works!' Slowly he moved the plane to the take-off strip, revved up and as we gathered speed, the plane took off.

We turned westward, following the road leading out of Nairobi towards Nakuru.

'Look out carefully,' urged Jesse. 'You must all help to find Lake Nakuru ... you know ... the one with the pink flamingos.'

We found the lake and turned north over the Rift Valley. Soon Lake Bogoria came into view and then Lake Baringo but after that, volcanic desert stretched below us as far as the eye could see.

'We must find Lake Turkana!' shouted Jesse over the noise of the engine. 'It's somewhere down there!' But however much we looked, there was no lake to be seen, only jagged hills rearing up in the hot air; we seemed utterly lost.

For endless moments everyone was gazing in all directions when suddenly Uwe let out a loud shout. 'The lake!' He immediately headed for it and soon we were flying over Mount Teleki, a volcano at the southern end of Lake Turkana. Everything was easy now; Uwe just had to follow the long, narrow lake up north and less than an hour later, Lodwar, capital of Turkanaland, loomed up on the horizon.

'Phew!' said Uwe, wiping his brow, 'no more worries. We've reached our destination!' He pressed a lever to put the small plane down on the landing strip, but when its wheels touched the ground it began to bounce wildly as if it had been a kangaroo. The rising hot air was pushing the plane upwards as our pilot tried to land it, whilst a strong lateral wind was blowing it off course and Uwe had to pull on the joystick with all his might to keep the plane straight. Before we knew it, we were at the end of the landing strip and Uwe just managed to pull the plane off the ground before it crashed.

'I can't land!' he yelled in a panicky voice. He turned to Jesse. 'Isn't there somewhere else we can fly to?' but Jesse cut him short.

'There's nowhere else. And the petrol gauge's showing zero. You've got to land!'

'OK,' said Uwe with resignation in his voice and he turned the plane full circle, just avoiding the hill behind Lodwar. He approached the landing strip once more and resolutely pushed the lever down. The wheels touched the ground, the small plane made a few wild leaps shaking terribly and then we were up in the air again.

'I've got to land!' yelled Uwe, sweat dripping off his face as he veered around the hill a second time while the French woman and I started retching into the plastic bags we were holding ready. And the third time he did manage to land. When the plane came to a standstill Uwe swung round. We were looking slightly green by then, but he gave us a wide grin and said proudly, 'See, I did it. There was really nothing to worry about!'

In Lodwar, we dumped the little luggage we'd brought in an African version of a motel run by the local bishop, an Irishman. The rooms were next to each other along an open veranda. They were small and contained just a bed and cupboard; and there was a common toilet and shower at the end of the passage. But the bishop's hospitality more than made up for the lack of comfort: he treated us to cool drinks in the mission – just what we needed after the emotions of the journey. Refreshed, we set off in a four-wheel drive to see some projects close to the small town.

That evening during supper with the bishop, I gathered a lot of information about the Turkana. They belonged to the Nilotic group of nomadic tribes along with the Samburu, the Maasai and a number of others, notably in southern Sudan, and they moved their livestock and families over a large area, following the scanty rainfall and available grazing.

Despite their contact with civilization, the Turkana had remained fiercely independent and hostile to any intruders. This manifested itself in contempt for authority and indifference to all that came from the foreigner. And they caused problems, too: they raided their neighbours' cattle. Raiding had always been the central theme of the men's lives.

Then, two years before our visit, there had been a long drought and the subsequent famine had been so severe that the nomads had become destitute and dependent on food-aid, finally allowing the Kenyan government to intervene. Some Turkana had been resettled around towns or on the shores of the lake where they had been trained to become fishermen. Others had been incorporated into aid programmes.

'Nomads despise manual labour and have few mechanical skills,' said Jesse, 'but we're working on it, as you may have noticed. Tomorrow you'll see how much the EEC has done and how we are contributing to changing the Turkana.'

Early the next morning, I heard someone bang on my door. As I stuck my head out, half asleep, there stood Jesse urging me to get up.

'We're going to have a quick breakfast,' he said, 'and then we must be off. The car is already waiting.' It was the only time in my life I've ever seen an ambassador in his underpants!

We rushed from project to project – to a workshop, schools, a modern windmill for pumping water, fishing activities at the lakeside … and I filmed everything as well as time permitted.

The Turkana were cattle herders. They lived mainly off their cattle's blood and milk, which they kept in long-necked gourds, but they had always gone in for some subsistence farming when the rains were good. We visited fields planted with sorghum. Several women were busy cutting the ripe plants, while a man was sitting on a platform made of sticks, watching out for unwanted intruders; he was assisted by a boy and two women, ready to scare away any animals that might approach to eat the sorghum.

In spite of this, the area still wasn't producing enough food for all the inhabitants and food-aid had to be continued. We drove to one of the distribution centres. Bags of maize, part of an international aid programme, had been brought in on lorries and people were lining up with any receptacle they had at hand to receive their allocated rations. What struck me most was the sight of young children and women crawling about on the stony ground when the food distribution was over, searching every square inch for grains of maize that had been dropped. It brought home to me how precious food really is – something we seem to have completely forgotten in the West.

Our visit was short, but I thought the Turkana wonderful. They were very different from the people we had seen before: there was a suggestion of ancient Egypt about them and some men carried wooden neck-rests similar to those of ancient Egypt, too, beautifully carved and polished. Many young women were bare to the waist, they had shapely breasts and wore triangular, leather aprons in front and behind; they also wore beads and brass bangles, and ornaments were dangling from their ears. Claire would so have liked this, I thought sadly. What a pity she couldn't come. Then I made up my mind. She must see this, I decided. I'll find a way to come back.

It was late afternoon by the time we were ready to leave Lodwar and Jesse, who thought of everything, had planned a stopover at the oasis of Loiyangalani. 'That way we can land in Nairobi tomorrow in full daylight,' he explained. 'It'll be a lot safer.' He looked sternly at Uwe who in vain tried to make himself invisible. 'I want to make sure there are no more problems with the plane.'

At Loiyangalani we had gone to bed early after a refreshing dip in the pool and a copious supper and I was fast asleep when I was woken up by loud knocking on my door. As I opened it I saw Uwe Werblow in a state of great agitation. 'Come quickly!' he urged.

'But ... but ... it's the middle of the night. What's the matter?'

'Just come!'

'But I'm not even dressed!'

'No time for that.' And without further ado he pulled me outside where a strong wind was blowing. Jesse was standing there too and we all rushed to where the plane was parked. The howling wind was tearing at it and it was shaking violently. We caught the wings just in time to stop a sudden gust of wind from sending the plane flying and kept hanging on. Finally some of the Africans working in the hotel arrived and after several hours of hard effort, we managed to secure the plane with lengths of rope pegged into the stony ground.

'I should have known,' grumbled Jesse as we returned to our rooms. 'This sometimes happens at the lakeside.' And indeed, the contrast in temperature between the lake and the surrounding land can become so great over the course of the night that it causes violent air movements.

It was 3.00 a.m. by the time we turned in again and the next morning found us all bleary-eyed.

'At least there won't be any more unpleasant surprises,' said Jesse grandiloquently as the plane took off. 'Everything will go smoothly now.'

We managed to find the Nakuru-Nairobi road and got as far as the capital, but then Uwe couldn't find the airport! As we cruised around the town at low altitude gazing left and right, suddenly high-voltage cables loomed up straight ahead of us.

'Watch out!' screamed Jesse.

Uwe jerked up the joystick and cleared the high-voltage line with only feet to spare, saving our lives in the last split second, while Jesse bent over and I heard him retching helplessly in front of his seat.

I felt very lonely after Peter had left for Turkanaland, but worse was to come: I had a violent bout of malaria. We had taken our anti-malaria pills unfailingly until we reached Dar es Salaam where we had run out. The town was a mosquito-infested place and we had spent a few days in a small African hotel where the anopheles mosquitoes must have injected their poison into my blood.

As the fever gripped me there was a vile roaring in my ears, as if express trains were passing through my head. Then, at length, the room started to sway and delirium came sweeping over me. I had a feeling that I was slipping away and lost awareness of time and reality.

Hours later, I awoke to a queer sensation of cold; I lay in bed sweating and shivering. I half raised myself, weak and trembling, and tried to get up to see if I could find some help but I had only just reached the door of my room when my strength gave way and I had to crawl back into my bed.

When I returned to the guesthouse, I found Claire in a very weakened condition. It upset me terribly but she reassured me, 'I've had malaria, but don't worry. A doctor has come and the worst is over.'

I told her about Turkanaland and said I wanted to take her after she had recovered. She listened with sparkling eyes and then declared, 'I'm feeling better already. I'll go with you now if you like.' I thought it safer to let her rest a few more days but she wouldn't hear of it. So the next day I went into town to get an introduction to the governor of the Turkana district from Jesse, and two days later we set off in our old Land Rover.

On our way north we turned into the Rift Valley to visit a Belgian project near Lake Baringo; I had heard such a lot about it at the Belgian Embassy that I thought it worth the detour. It was a prestigious project that had already cost well over £1 million, but if it lived up to expectation it would turn Kenya into an important energy producer. It was all based on a daring idea: to grow euphorbias in unproductive semi-deserts. The East African euphorbia variety is a drought-resistant, cactus-like plant, which contains latex, a highly-irritating milky sap, and it was hoped that this could be converted into petrol. The rest of the plant, after drying, would supply firewood for the local populations, thus combating deforestation at the same time.

The project leader was on holiday but Grégoire, the Belgian chemist who ran the sophisticated chemical laboratory that had been built to analyse the extracted sap and transform it into petrol, was there. He was happy to be able to speak French, we were soon on the best of terms and he kindly invited us to stay with him.

A large area nearby had been cleared of its bush cover and planted with euphorbias over the previous few years, and they were still planting more to find out which were the fastest-growing varieties. As I was filming the area, a few children from the nearby Pokot tribe appeared out of nowhere, intrigued by what I was doing. The boys, young as they were, already carried spears, bows and arrows as their ancestors had for millennia, and the girls were wearing the colourful ornaments of their tribe.

That evening, while we were having supper with Grégoire, I said, 'Just think what this region will become once it starts producing energy.'

My host didn't seem enthusiastic. 'Don't bet on it,' he replied.

His reaction surprised me. 'Why not? Otherwise, what's the point of this million-pound project?'

Grégoire hesitated for a while, but finally decided to speak. 'Do you want the official version or my personal opinion?'

'Your opinion of course.'

'Well …' he sighed, 'I've just finished my chemical analysis. I've been trying hard,' he said, almost excusing himself, 'but the foul poisonous liquid inside euphorbia plants can't be transformed into petrol!'

'Hell!' I exclaimed. 'They're not going to be pleased when they hear that. But at least,' I remarked, trying to look on the bright side, 'you'll be able to use the plants for firewood?'

'It's not as simple as that.' Grégoire sighed again. 'You see … euphorbias don't dry out easily, which is how they manage to survive in semi-desert areas. In order to dry those awful plants you have to heat them, and I'm sorry to say that this consumes more energy than you get out of the firewood afterwards. So the whole thing doesn't make sense.'

'But then … what's going to happen to those thousands of acres they've planted out there with euphorbias?'

Grégoire shrugged his shoulders. 'I don't really know. Before this project came along to disrupt the environment we had a varied ecosystem where the local Pokot took their camels to browse. And now we have a euphorbia monoculture. The camels don't like the toxic euphorbia plants, but fortunately they're not averse to eating the young shoots, otherwise it would be a complete disaster.'

Early the next day, we continued northwards. Stark grey boulders jutted out between high hills as we drove on and on, the wheels turning monotonously over a dirt road that seemed to continue forever through the nudity of the landscape. Would this ever end?

Peter was looking at the map with an expression of exasperation on his face. 'This stupid road,' he muttered. 'It just keeps going west. It'll be at least two hours before we join the northbound road that leads to Lodwar. We'll never get there before nightfall.' Then he brightened up. 'There's a shortcut!' he exclaimed, pushing the map under my nose. 'Look here.'

'Peter, please, I can't look. I'm driving.'

'Well, anyway … we're going to take that shortcut. I'll watch out for it.'

A quarter of an hour later, we came to a point where a wide dirt road split off towards the northwest. 'This must be the shortcut,' concluded Peter. 'Take it!'

For a few miles the dirt road was in reasonable condition, but then it narrowed and soon the Land Rover was crawling forward over a rutted track between rocky hills. I didn't like the look of it. 'Shall we turn back?' I proposed hesitantly.

Peter was adamant. 'Don't worry!' He sounded firm. 'The road can't get any worse than this. Just carry on. This'll save us miles and miles.' So on I went.

The dirt road was now climbing steeply and we reached a wide plateau dotted with scattered bushes. The track was becoming really bad as it led through a clump of trees, and I was concentrating on the patch ahead of the wheels when suddenly we found ourselves surrounded by armed soldiers in camouflage outfits. I stepped on the brake in fright. We had driven straight into an army camp!

The soldiers were very agitated and pointed their rifles at Peter as he got out, their eyes bulging. They were going to shoot him! I sat there, paralysed with fear, waiting for the inevitable when abruptly an officer thrust his way forward, yelling, 'What are you doing here? This is military territory!'

'Doesn't this track lead on to the road to Lodwar?' asked Peter, surprisingly calm. 'We have to drive there. I've got a letter for the governor.'

'Oh!' exclaimed the officer, and he made a sign to his soldiers to put their rifles down. Then he turned again to Peter, drawing himself up. 'You shouldn't be using this track,' he said sternly, 'but yes … if you keep following it you will eventually join up with the main road to Lodwar.'

'Thank you very much, Captain,' replied Peter. And without any further ado he climbed into the passenger's seat and I set off again.

We carried on, but the going was rough. Our route was strewn with boulders and every now and then we came to a sandy patch in which we might easily have got bogged down. Then, as we descended into a dry riverbed, I was suddenly overcome with fatigue. I still felt weak after my bout of malaria and the encounter with the soldiers had shaken me thoroughly. I found it difficult to concentrate on driving and completely forgot to switch to high gear, four-wheel drive mode before going up the steep slope on the other side.

As the Land Rover started climbing, it struggled ever more and I just hoped we would make it to the top. We had nearly got there when suddenly the engine stalled and then, slowly but surely, we began to slide backwards. I pushed the brake pedal, but in vain; I couldn't stop the heavy vehicle. It was terrifying and as we gathered speed while skidding uncontrollably back into the riverbed, I panicked and screamed, 'We're going to turn over!'

Then I felt Peter's hand near mine on the steering wheel, jerking it slightly to the left or right to control our descent, while he kept looking over his shoulder. Every time the Land Rover swerved dangerously I held my breath, but time and again Peter managed to restore the balance while we continued sliding down backwards between big boulders. After what seemed endless moments, we somehow came to the bottom and ended up in the loose sand of the riverbed. I leant on the steering wheel, my heart racing away, trembling but so thankful that we had escaped.

After this, Peter took over. He managed to start up the engine again and then turned back the way we had come. 'This shortcut is too risky,' he said disapprovingly. 'We shouldn't have taken it.'

'What about the army camp?' I ventured timidly.

'That'll be all right,' he replied with an even face. 'I'll just drive through.'

And that's what he did. The soldiers were preparing their evening meal and were completely taken by surprise; we heard them shout as we whizzed by waving goodbye.

Night was falling, we were tired out after the day's events and our only wish was to get into bed as quickly as possible. We decided to stop in the first good spot we found and after a frugal meal in the open air, we settled down and were soon fast asleep beneath the star-speckled dome of the African sky.

Above: Digging a trench at Tawa

Below: Tawa: a personalised decoration made from beer-bottle tops

Above: Peter made warrior of the Meru tribe

Below: Filming with the ostrich-feather mask

Above: Claire receiving a woven bag

Below: Children at a water hole

Above: Samburu women

Right: Women of the Samburu choir

The Samburu choir: a feast for the eyes and the ears

Above: A Rendille girl

Below: Two young Rendille girls. Note the thorns of the acacia tree

Above: The bull's song, Marsabit

Below: Boran mothers, Marsabit

Above: School girls, Marsabit

Below: Young boys herding cattle

Above: Claire talking to a young woman

Below: The 'beast of burden'

Above: Dancing with the women, central Kenya

Below: Growing pyrethrum in central Kenya

Above: Turkana women

Below: The platform from which to watch animals

Top: The euphorbia project, Lake Baringo. Pokot children watching

Above: Pokot children

Right: A Pokot woman: still young but her beauty is already ruined by breast-feeding her children

CHAPTER 12
In Brightest Africa

The Turkana

We had been driving for hours under the scorching sun through a monotonous dry landscape speckled with thorn bush and clusters of flat-topped thorn trees and were already close to Lodwar when we noticed a few Turkana with their camels. Claire immediately stopped the Land Rover and went over to them.

> An older man with a short white beard was sitting on the sandy bank of a dry gully with some of his children, while a young woman, probably the man's latest wife, was crouching in the riverbed. She was lovely but she kept her eyes lowered, however much I tried to make her smile; she just continued dipping a tin into a waterhole and when it was full, emptying it into a calabash from which the camels came to drink. I felt sad. The man looked proud and probably owned many animals, including the camels standing around, but he seemed so old next to the beauty of the woman's youth.
>
> Then the silence was disrupted by the shrieking cries of a few boys driving a herd of goats down into the bottom of the wide gully. Suddenly we were caught in a whirlwind of moving animals; we stood there among the haughty camels while goats ran around us sending the dust flying. It was a wonderful first contact with Turkanaland and its harsh but pure and captivating environment in which the Turkana had learned to survive.

We reached Lodwar by late afternoon, drove straight to the mission and found the Irish bishop at home. He recognised me and kindly allowed us to sleep not in his 'motel', for which we would have had to pay, but in a partly covered space at the side of the mission where a warm breeze flowed through the open-stone construction. We took the mattress out of our Land Rover, laid it on the cement floor and fixed our mosquito net to the ceiling. As the shadows lengthened, the air grew cool and balmy, night fell and we were ready to turn in when the sound of singing floated up to us. It came from the large *manyatta*, the village of straw huts below Lodwar where many Turkana, displaced two years before by the great famine, were still living.

'Let's go outside,' Claire whispered.

As we sat down on the stony ground, darkness enveloped us and we remained there for a long time, listening to the enchanting singing under the deep blue of the African sky full of stars sparkling like brilliant tears.

We woke up refreshed, delighted to be alive and to be here, and dressed slowly, enjoying the exhilarating scent of early morning. When we went into the mission, the bishop had already gone. He was always engaged in one thing or another, but that week he was particularly busy. He got up every day at the crack of dawn and after saying mass and having a quick breakfast, he drove off in his pickup truck loaded with materials for a school they were building. Dressed in shorts, he helped to lay the bricks with his own hands. Here at last was a bishop I could admire.

He had told us that we should feel free to come to the mission to have breakfast, so we made tea and toast, had a lazy breakfast and then went to the governor's office. The man wasn't in but we handed the letter of introduction to his secretary, hoping the governor would react favourably to it and allow us to visit and film the district.

Afterwards we strolled through the town. It consisted of little more than a cluster of bungalows, a few shops and sheds whose tin roofs shone like mirrors in the sun, a small hospital, some government buildings and a prison. A plaque proudly commemorated that Jomo Kenyatta, first president of independent Kenya in 1964, had been detained here between 1959 and 1961 by the colonial authorities.

The liveliest part of the town was the open-air market where we wandered among brightly coloured goods spread out over straw mats, laid on the ground in the shade of acacia trees. Throngs of people from the manyatta were strolling about, women were discussing prices in excited voices and there was laughter everywhere. Claire seemed to be enjoying everything tremendously; then, as I turned around to point something out to her, she was no longer there! I couldn't think what had happened and was looking around, perplexed, when she reappeared carrying a few tightly woven baskets.

'Aren't the colours beautiful?' she said, holding her acquisitions up to me with an expression of pure delight on her face.

The market closed at sunset and the area, which had been an animated scene all day long, loud with talk and spontaneous merriment, suddenly became silent and deserted. Night fell and once again, the singing would begin in the manyatta below.

I was asked to go to the governor's office with my camera the next morning, and to my surprise found everything ready for a filmed interview. The double doors to the office were wide open, the desk had been moved almost into the entrance, allowing the sunlight to shine on it and the governor was sitting behind the desk while a smartly dressed woman – the secretary – was standing proudly behind him. They were waiting for the cameraman!

It was not what I had expected but I duly filmed the governor while he read a long rambling speech in English from a few sheets of paper lying in front of him. The 'interview' pleased him no end and resulted in us being allowed to go wherever we liked in the Turkana district to film projects. Furthermore he instructed one of his interpreters – a pleasant young man called Gregory – to accompany us for the duration of our stay without specifying how long that was going to be. That was lucky because two weeks later there was a *coup d'état* in Nairobi. While the government was trying to regain control of the situation, no one was allowed to travel through the country and this provided a welcome excuse to stay much longer in Turkanaland.

I was relieved that the governor had given me permission to film any projects I fancied. More than that, however, I wanted to film the daily life of the Turkana and I hoped that the governor's support would open up possibilities that otherwise would have remained closed.

There was one important development project I had to film, though, before setting off towards the interior: a Norwegian fish factory at the western edge of Lake Turkana. I had heard a lot about it before coming. The project was part of a modern, quasi-industrial approach to jump-start development in remote African areas. Norway was very keen on giving aid and knew all about fishing – so, what could be better than building a factory to exploit the abundance of great Nile perch and tilapia in the lake?

Leo, an Irish brother who lived at the mission, didn't have much to do that day and he was happy to guide us. As we were driving towards the lake he told us about the project. A modern factory had been constructed at the edge of the lake a number of years ago, motor launches had been brought over to constitute a fishing fleet and a jetty had been built to offload the fish. Until the factory had been built, the local fishermen had just dried their catch in the sun to preserve it, but this was going to be a thing of the past now that modern methods were available. The grand idea had been to deep-freeze the fish captured in the lake and send the frozen fish in lorries to Nairobi and maybe as far as Rwanda. Everything was going to be done on an industrial scale from now onwards. However, problems soon surfaced. Here, just north of the equator, it was significantly hotter than in Norway; also, the lake was slightly brackish and the result was that they had been unable to turn the lake water into ice and deep-freeze the fish! To top it all, the edge of the lake was now a full 100 yards away from the factory. As the region was drying out, Lake Turkana had been shrinking slowly for centuries but those who had conceived the project had not bothered to inquire about this beforehand!

When we entered the factory, I noticed some activity. A few men were packing dried fish in a corner of the huge inside space. Transporting the fish on men's backs from the launches to areas where it was left to dry in the sun, and carrying it inside to pack it into bales once it had dried, had nothing much in common with the modern industrial activities that were supposed to have taken place here. It was all very different from the project's blueprint, but at least it functioned.

'What do they plan to do with the factory?' I asked.

'Maybe they'll use it as a church?' proffered Brother Leo with a twinkle in his eye. 'Or transform it into a hotel? They could easily turn the flat area between the factory and the lake into a golf course. Now that really would attract the tourists!'

On the way back, Claire broached the subject of the Turkana singing at night in the manyatta near Lodwar. We found it enchanting, but Brother Leo didn't share our enthusiasm.

'That's all those young men and unmarried girls ever do,' he sighed, barely able to hide his disapproval. 'Sing and dance!'

'But don't young people dance the world over?' I said.

'You call that dancing?' he objected disparagingly. 'The men do nothing but jump as high as possible. And all that to impress the girls!'

'What else do you expect?' I replied, laughing.

'But it's just a preliminary to the same old thing!' His voice rose. 'And here it's the girls who choose, imagine! And then they disappear into the bushes!'

'Well … that's all quite innocent, no?'

'Innocent!' Brother Leo exclaimed. 'You call this innocent? Premarital relations!'

'But they need some fun every now and then, don't they?'

'Every now and then? That's all the men here have got on their minds the moment night falls!' He snorted contemptuously. 'Either they're going towards it, or they're coming from it, or they're *at* it!'

All the same, we loved the untamed abandon with which the Turkana threw themselves into their dances. Some of the young men were extremely tall; for the most part they were bare to the waist, but wore lengthy measures of cloth wound around their hips. They jumped up and down in the centre with the girls swaying around them, holding hands, while the strong smell of rancid fat with which they all smeared their bodies wafted around the dancers.

> The sun was setting over the plains, lighting up the infinity in stretches of gold and flames of fire, and igniting pure joy in my heart as we went to see the dances. Below in the manyatta the air was filled with laughter, shouts and songs, and dust flew up as the men jumped towards the sky to show their strength. The girls danced facing them, moving slowly around them until one of the girls would stop in front of the man she fancied, sway her hips and spring up to let him know that he was her choice for the night. How extraordinary that the young Turkana women were free to love each night before they married and could even choose their lovers!
>
> The night seemed alive with excitement as couples slipped into the darkness, fading away like shadows. As we wound our way back up the hill under a blaze of brilliant stars, I thought how simple and natural life was among the Turkana. Later the warm night air embraced us and my head nestled into the dip of Peter's shoulder where it knew it had always belonged. Stretching my fingers, I felt I could touch eternity.

The following morning, we awoke to the delicious smell of fried eggs and toasted bread, and the aroma of freshly made coffee drew us to the mission. As we went into town after breakfast, we found an old man waiting for us. When he saw Claire his face lit up and he began to talk excitedly while pointing at his hat. I had got used by now to the amazing variety of hairdos of the Turkana men, but this was something totally different. The old man was wearing a lady's straw hat entwined with red silk from which feathers stuck out! It looked worn, but was still recognisable as the sort of hat English ladies of the better classes might have worn maybe thirty years before. We had no idea what this was all about, so I went to fetch Gregory to translate.

The old man just stood there, looking at me almost with veneration mingled with great pride until Peter returned with Gregory.

'Can you ask him what he wants to tell us and what we can do for him?' I asked Gregory.

He did and then said to me, 'He has come to show you the hat.'

'Oh!' I was astonished. 'How nice, but why?'

'The man says,' explained Gregory, 'that when he heard that the young woman with hair the colour of the sun had arrived, he set off early in the morning from his manyatta.'

'Is that far from here?'

'Some fifteen miles.'

'And he walked all that way just to show me his hat?'

'Yes. He has come to show you that he has still got it. He says he's been waiting a long, long time … His story sounds a bit confused … and when you go home he also wants you to tell the lady that she mustn't worry; that the hat is still safe with him.'

I felt my head spin. 'Which lady?'

'The one who gave him the hat many, many rainy seasons ago, asking him to keep it till she returned.'

I suddenly understood! 'But still,' I asked Gregory, 'why would he think that I could possibly know that lady?'

'He says he was sure you belonged to the same tribe of golden-haired people as the lady the moment he heard about you; and today, when he saw you, he was overcome with relief. There is no doubt, he says, you look just like her. So, obviously, you know the lady and must have heard about the hat.'

I closed my eyes, my throat tightened, and I just went to the old man who had been looking at me all the time with eyes full of expectation, took both his hands into mine and nodded, saying, 'Yes, your great wish will be fulfilled.' After this he wanted a photograph of him with his hat, which I was to show to the lady in the faraway land so that she would feel reassured.

My heart was deeply touched by the dignity of this dear old man and I thanked him for faithfully keeping the precious hat during all those years.

Filming the daily life of the Turkana was not a straightforward matter. I had been told that not very long ago some Turkana men had thrown stones at a tourist when he got out his camera and attempted to take a photo – and that in Lodwar market! But we came with the official permission of the governor and our arrival in the manyattas was announced beforehand; we had an interpreter who helped greatly in establishing contacts and the Turkana somehow associated us with the foreign donors who gave them food. They received us with singing and dancing wherever we arrived and so I was indeed lucky enough to be able to film the life of these amazing people.

This was not as easy as one might think. If possible I filmed them with the sun in their faces and, to compensate for their dark skins, I systematically opened the diaphragm half an aperture more than my light meter indicated, but they were not the kind of people you could arrange. They danced whenever and wherever *they* wanted, irrespective of light and contrast, or the shadows thrown by trees and they took very little account of the man with the camera as long as he kept out of their way. Filming conditions were often chaotic; the dancing stirred up a great amount of dust; the smell of rancid fat, so typical of the Turkana, was very strong as they danced; it was stiflingly hot; sweat was flowing into my eyes as I peered into the viewfinder; and I had neither operators nor technical advisers to help me. My only assistant was Claire and she was unable to lend me a hand because she had enough to do on her own, recording the sound and trying to stop the dancers from stepping on the tape recorder or the microphone. And she, too, was difficult to control. Sometimes she let herself be carried away by the fiery ambience, almost behaving like a Turkana girl.

> Peter was filming raiding dances and all was frenetic movement and rising excitement. As the men rushed towards us, Gregory stood guard near the tape recorder while I tried to capture the wild atmosphere and wonderful voices, the raiding songs ringing out strong and guttural, and growing in intensity as the men stampeded past us raising their sticks. The women followed, their ululating cries rising up like birds into the sky as they moved towards the camera. Then I saw two of the women advance towards Peter and they started dancing for him, swinging their hips and jumping up, their bracelets making a swishing sound. They both seemed to have chosen him for their man! And I fell under the spell of the exhilarating excitement and felt an irresistible urge to join in.

I had just stopped filming, feeling tired after running about with my heavy camera trying to keep out of the way of all those stampeding people, and returned to where Claire had set up her tape recorder near an acacia tree, but she was nowhere to be seen. I found Gregory, watching over the recorder on his own.

'Is everything all right?' I asked, worried.

'Yes, yes,' he nodded, smiling. 'The tape is still turning.'

Then I looked at the recorder and nearly had a fit. The reel on which the sound was supposed to have been taped had finished and the loose end was making a tchic-tchic sound as it spun around idly! The sound of the last minutes of the dances I had filmed had not been recorded!

'Where's the missus?' I asked, upset.

Gregory didn't know, so I set off between the thorn trees and eventually found Claire: she was dancing amongst the women!

The women were eye-catching, especially the younger ones. They wore leather goatskin skirts around their loins and nothing above the waist but a massive load of bead necklaces, earrings, shells and other ornaments. As they moved, bracelets tinkled on their wrists and their skirts swayed gracefully with every step.

The men, if possible, were even more extraordinary. Although they never wore more than a blanket or a length of cloth draped loosely from one shoulder, leaving the other one bare, they were immensely proud, strutting about arrogantly, and they could be very fierce; they wore round wrist knives with which they would deal devastating blows in duels. The lobes of their ears were pierced and distended, and they had metal lip-plugs. Most striking were the caps made of clay that were plastered and woven into their hair where they remained permanently. The men preferred to sleep in a most uncomfortable position, their wooden neck-rests stuck under their necks to keep their heads from touching the ground rather than risk disturbing their headdresses!

Turkana men couldn't see the point in doing any manual work, yet their stamina was impressive. They would set off early in the morning, walk the most incredible distances with their camels under a blazing sun and upon arrival in a manyatta in the evening, they would dance as if they had lazed about all day.

Cattle-raiding was the central theme of the men's lives and if in the course of such raids they died, so be it. There was an extraordinary indifference to dying. There might be a short outburst of emotion, and then life would carry on. Death was considered a normal happening in the life of any man; the Turkana just accepted their fate.

We were grateful to be able to film these amazing people. Feeling that we were taking so much from them, we wanted to give something in return, but knew there wasn't much they coveted.

'What can we give them?' I asked Brother Leo when we were back in Lodwar.

'There's one thing they are very keen on,' he replied. 'Tobacco.'

'But I've never seen anyone smoke,' I objected.

'Oh, they don't smoke. They chew their tobacco.'

Then I remembered having seen pouches knotted in the hems of the men's blankets. That was where they kept their tobacco!

We went into one of the small shops in Lodwar. On the counter was a display of goods such as cheap plastic jewellery and sunglasses, laid out to tempt the local inhabitants. An assortment of hurricane lamps, pots and pans hung from nails in the walls and the floor was stacked with canned foods, drums of paraffin and palm oil, and sacks of salt and sugar. They also sold matches, soap and crude tobacco, besides the enticing strings of beads the Turkana women used for embroidery on their goat-leather skirts. We bought a large bag of tobacco, enough to satisfy at least twenty men and I entrusted it to Claire.

The next day we set off to a manyatta where we filmed raiding dances. I was fully concentrating on my camera work as usual when suddenly there was a great commotion. To my utter surprise, I saw Claire being seized by ululating women; she was hoisted shoulder-high and then the mad crowd ran off with her in a jogging sort of way and disappeared amongst the umbrella trees. I had no idea what was going on. Maybe Claire had done something wrong and the women were furious with her. I was about to run after them to rescue Claire when the procession reappeared and I learned what had happened: Claire had given the whole bag of tobacco to the women and they were letting out great yells of joy and carrying her around in triumph.

'But … but the tobacco was supposed to be for the men!' I cried out over the noise. 'Why did you give everything to the women?'

'Why shouldn't I? They never get anything and they have a right to it, too,' she called back and waved quickly before the women headed off once again towards the trees with Claire bumping about, falling backwards and lying flat on their shoulders.

Most manyattas were difficult to reach, but eventually we would arrive at our destination – a group of yellow beehive huts nestling lazily around a few umbrella trees. As we walked inside the thorn-bush barricades that encircled some of the manyattas, we would be welcomed by skinny dogs and naked children. Women of all ages, ranging from toothless grandmothers to girls plump with youth, would peer at us from the shade in which they were sitting or from their huts. All wore leather aprons and often a long piece of brown or ochre cloth around their waists or shoulders, heavy coils of beads and pendants in their ears. After having satisfied their curiosity, they would carry on with what they were doing.

Inside the huts, furnishing was minimal; there were some carved, wooden head-rests, which also served as low seats, and a number of cauldron-shaped calabashes and long-necked gourds were hanging from the straw walls.

On our way to the manyattas we would sometimes run into animals. Camels often strayed off on their own, and we encountered one standing across the track we were following. When we got closer it panicked and started running just in front of the wheels. It raced our Land Rover for a full 100 yards, desperately trying to keep ahead, before it finally swerved off the track.

But the cutest animals were the donkeys. Claire was very keen on them and made me stop whenever we saw some. They were free to roam around and were as independent as any Turkana; they had even learned to find water and to dig for it on their own in the sandy riverbeds. But they were wily animals.

The first time we noticed a group of donkeys while driving through the open landscape, Claire made me swerve towards them and as I stopped quite close, I couldn't help thinking how attractive they looked against a background of low thorn trees. As I got out my camera and walked towards the donkeys, they eyed me with curiosity and didn't even move. This was going to be an easy shot! Then, just when I had set up everything and looked through the viewfinder, I saw them turn, run away and hide behind a clump of low bush. I ran around the bush with the cine camera and tripod on my shoulder until I faced them again, but the moment I bent down to film them they turned and retreated once more! However, now that I had got this far I was determined to film them. I followed them into a dry, tangled mass of bush, but every time I got close enough and installed the camera they would scamper off; then, when they were out of range, they would stop and turn expectantly towards me. I was sure they did it on purpose, the damned animals! I could have sworn they had a smirk on their faces as they looked at me, trying to lure me on.

Finally I gave up. The heat hung over the land like a heavy cloak, the pale, opaque sky was the colour of lead and pressed down upon me as I walked back a quarter of a mile through prickly bush. The tripod seemed to find a heathen pleasure in getting caught in the vegetation whenever possible, and the camera and battery were becoming heavier and heavier as I trudged along, sweating profusely.

In one of the outlying manyattas where we stayed for a couple of days, Peter had a faithful young admirer who followed him wherever he went. Her features were delicate and charming, and her long slim arms and legs lent grace to her nimble figure as she walked with Peter, hand in hand. She was captivated by his cine camera and all he was doing, but he had just been filming some long grasses waving in the breeze and she seemed at a loss to understand why he wanted to do that. What was so special about grass?

Suddenly she made a sign and pulled Peter along to her hut; she wanted to show him something that was really worth filming. Inside she crouched down, began rubbing some sticks, blew on the embers and after a while flames shot up: she had lit a fire and now looked up at him with pride! Yet in all the time we stayed there, never did a smile light up her lovely face. It intrigued me because she was a beauty among the Turkana children, and I asked Gregory to find out why.

'Because she hates her teeth,' he said. 'They stick out.'

So young and she was already self-conscious!

We drove many miles through the Turkana district, a harsh, arid land made up of thorn and shrub. After the abundant last rains all the bushes and trees had sprung into new life and the landscape had turned a lush green, but now, barely two months after the end of the rains, the semi-desert was taking its own back. The grass was sheer gold, swaying in the soft wind; another month and it would begin to wither and disappear, following the eternal cycle of nature.

The light shone on a great expanse of long waving grass, bush and anthills – an arid land come to life where everything, every tree, bush and blade of grass, was really precious. The bright golden plains speckled with thorn shrub seemed to go on forever, all the way to the heat-blurred horizon and beyond. I was pervaded by an exhilarating sensation that the world was infinite.

As we looked out over this incredibly beautiful landscape where time had stood still, we seemed to have left the inhabited world far behind. Before us stretched sunburnt plains, a vision of eternal splendour that was burnt into my eyes, my mind and heart. All was light; all was silence but for the rustling of a slight breeze.

When the soft wind of Turkanaland blows low the golden grasses and lifts the hair from your cheeks, you know that it was worth wandering through the thorns to reach this golden life on earth; that this moment makes it worth having lived.

We were heading westward towards the Ugandan border where, far away, we could see a suggestion of the Karamoja escarpment – just a hint of the mauve-blue outline of the mountains. Here, in an area that remained covered by vegetation during the dry season, there was a great concentration of cattle, which were confined in thorn-scrub barricades every night to prevent raiding. In the daytime the animals were led to riverbeds to drink.

As we emerged from dense vegetation, the sandy bed of a wide river opened before us and a scene of great beauty unfolded before our eyes. Tall trees spread their branches like umbrellas over herds and men gathered together in the shade, and the mingled sounds of lowing cattle, bleating goats and tinkling camel bells greeted us as we descended into the dry riverbed.

Men were fetching water from deep enormous holes, scooping it up from the bottom and passing the calabashes, filled to the brim, to others standing on narrow ridges above them, up and up, from hand to hand, untiringly, empty calabashes going down as full ones came up. Then, when the water reached the top, it would be carried to the cattle waiting patiently for their turn to quench their thirst. No hurry here; time was immaterial among the patches of light and shadow where little donkeys trotted lightly.

The scene filled me with an immense sense of serenity and I sunk onto the warm sand, wishing this moment would last forever; there was such peace in my heart as only perfect harmony can create.

We were returning to Lodwar when the Land Rover began making an ominous rattling noise. Driving over the uneven tracks of Turkanaland had taken its toll! I discovered that we had broken the top leaf of one of the sets of springs. Fortunately we carried a spare leaf with us on the roof rack, but doing this kind of repair was way beyond my capabilities. We managed to limp into the mission where the bishop welcomed us cheerfully and invited us to his table as he always did whenever we reappeared.

When I mentioned our problem, Brother Leo suggested, 'There's a Dutch project in Lodwar; they've got a workshop and some Land Rovers. Maybe they'll be willing to repair your springs.'

As Dutch is my mother tongue, I got on very well with the project leader, but repairing the broken leaf wasn't easy. They would need to adapt the spare I carried, drill holes in the right places, take the old set of springs apart and fix everything properly again. 'That's a full day's work,' sighed the project leader, hesitating. Then he eyed the spare parts and jerry cans we were carrying on our roof rack. 'OK,' he said, 'we'll do it. But would you agree to part with what you've got up there? You see …' he looked at me hopefully, 'spare parts are extremely hard to find around here. And I could do with some jerry cans, too. I'll pay you a good price for anything you're willing to sell.'

I didn't need time to think. I had just counted our remaining money and realised it wouldn't cover more than the cost of the fuel we needed to drive back to Europe – if we could buy it cheaply. So I was happy to sell almost anything, including our main jack, and kept only one spare wheel and two jerry cans. I just prayed that we wouldn't break down during our return trip.

Weeks had passed without us thinking of time, but we could no longer put off our return to civilisation. As we drove away to face once more the realities of our journey, we were well aware of the incredible luck that had befallen us. More so than anywhere else in Africa, Turkanaland had been a timeless experience, a radiance of light and warmth. We had loved Goundam and the people there, and had thought that we would never experience anything like it again, but now we had been allowed to share the life of a truly exceptional tribe. I felt as if I had been on another planet – a better one, perhaps, than the one we were returning to.

The nomadic way of life was very different from anything we were used to in the West. Survival in the harsh and unadulterated environment where the Turkana lived was precarious, even at the best of times, but in this semi-desert an extraordinary sense of freedom permeated you – a full awareness of what it was to be alive.

Yet all this was changing before our very eyes: modern life was progressing inexorably. The people here still went about with majestic grace of bearing, in harmony with their environment, their movements slow, their arms swinging lightly, their backs upright, their heads held high. How intense the feeling of freedom among these nomadic people! They were not overloaded with worldly goods or tied up with ambitions but simply lived with what nature had given them.

But how much longer would their men stand chatting when they met, leaning against a tree or on their sticks as if they hadn't got a care in the world while a blanket, hanging casually from their shoulders, barely covering their lean, muscular bodies, was their only piece of clothing? How much longer would their young women walk about gracefully, their magnificent velvet-skinned bodies dressed only in goatskin skirts, which swayed with every step, baring their supple thighs? How long before all this would disappear forever?

> We were following a winding track, our hearts heavy, when glancing up we suddenly saw them on a crest above, looking at us, immobile, etched against the twilight of a darkening blue sky: the silhouettes of a few Turkana. It was a farewell of eternal beauty we shall never forget. We left with sadness in our hearts. (See back cover photo.)

Out of Africa

It took us two days of hard driving to return to Nairobi. Night was falling by the time we were climbing out of the Rift Valley on the second day but we carried on, tempted by a comfortable bed in town. I was extremely tired by now but couldn't afford to relax; the failure of a reflex when rounding a corner of the winding road, a clumsy pull on the steering wheel, a moment's lapse of attention might send the vehicle over the edge and plunge us into the ravine so close to our wheels.

Suddenly two pairs of headlights appeared next to each other, taking up the whole width of the road: a car was overtaking another on a bend and coming straight towards us! I avoided a head-on collision by wrenching the steering wheel round, but our tyres literally scraped the edge of the ravine and we escaped hurling ourselves into the abyss by only a couple of inches.

After this, the Land Rover started behaving strangely. At times the steering wheel began to vibrate in my hands and I found it hard to control the vehicle; it seemed to be pulling towards the side of the road. I stopped once to inspect the wheels by the light of a torch but couldn't see anything, and we kept crawling along, trying to follow the bends in the pitch dark. We were immensely thankful to reach Nairobi; I felt utterly exhausted by the time we drove into the courtyard of the guesthouse of the American Missionary Society and I was able to cut the engine.

The next day I set out in the busy morning traffic of Nairobi and got as far as the EEC office. I was looking around for a place to park and had just turned into a narrow, single-lane street with cars parked on either side, when the Land Rover suddenly refused to budge. I jumped out, flustered, and when I looked at the front I simply couldn't believe what I saw: the left front wheel was pointing outwards to the left while the right one was pointing outwards to the right! I climbed inside again and turned the steering wheel; the right wheel followed, but the left one didn't. As I got out and slid underneath on my back, I finally understood. The tie bar connecting the two front wheels had come undone; the system that held it together had broken.

With a shock I realised how lucky we had been. Remembering last night's constant fight to keep the Land Rover from swerving towards the edge of the road, it dawned on me how our lives just hang by a thin thread. Had the tie bar snapped on the pitch dark escarpment while curving around one of the hundreds of bends, we would have plunged into the abyss! A great wave of relief surged through me when I thought that Claire had been unaware of the danger we had been in, or had she? She had kept unusually silent throughout the long drive.

In the meantime, the morning traffic was piling up in the narrow street behind me and several drivers began to hoot. I had no idea what I could possibly do when a car moved out of a parking space ahead on my left, the direction in which the left wheel pointed. I carefully turned the steering wheel and just managed to drive into the space that had been freed! Lucky again, Claire would have said.

After this I rushed into the EEC office to explain what had happened and they sent their mechanic to see what could be done.

'Oh,' he said after looking at the tie bar, 'it's come apart. Very unusual! If I can find spare, all right.' He gave me a wide grin. 'Otherwise, big problem.'

The man immediately drove to the Land Rover garage on the other side of the town in one of the EEC cars and I waited nervously for his return. He reappeared within an hour and got out, triumphantly holding up a brand new tie bar. He set to work and after half an hour he had reconnected the two wheels.

Afterwards, in the EEC office, I was kept abreast of the latest news. Jesse had gone to Europe for his annual holiday, so no more safaris for the time being. Something urgent had cropped up, though: a fire had broken out in Lamu, a town on the Indian Ocean south of the Somalian border, devastating a large number of houses. Two of the EEC delegates were to fly out there the next day to report on the extent of the disaster and they had been desperately looking for a cameraman. They were extremely pleased when I turned up in the nick of time.

'Seeing the devastation on film will make it much easier for our specialists in the EEC headquarters in Brussels to decide on the reconstruction aid budget,' explained the English delegate who was temporarily replacing Jesse. 'Would you mind accompanying us to film the damage?'

I hesitated. I was thinking of the flight to Turkanaland with Uwe Werblow and wasn't very keen on repeating that experience.

'Oh no,' countered the delegate, 'there's nothing to worry about. This time there will be nothing untoward. We have hired a plane with a professional pilot.'

'What about my wife?' I asked.

The man assured me that there was room for Claire, too, so I said yes. Then he glanced at my jeans and T-shirt. 'Could you please put on a suit tomorrow?' he suggested stiffly. When I shook my head saying I hadn't got a suit, he sighed. 'Well … anyway … try to dress as smartly as possible. You see … we're going to be received by local government officials in Lamu and we want to look our very best.' He gazed at me with disapproval. 'It's important to make a good impression, and clothes are a vital part of a man's appearance!'

We were driven to the airport the next morning, got into the plane, took off and cruised over northeast

Kenya without any problems, as the English delegate had promised; the pilot knew his job. Then, as we approached Lamu, we ran into a tropical storm. Suddenly the plane began to shake violently, torrents of rain reduced visibility to nil and as the pilot put the plane down on an island off the coast, it skidded through the mud on the short landing strip and came to a standstill with only yards to spare before plunging into the Indian Ocean!

We rushed towards a hangar, lashed by wind and rain, and jumped into a motor launch that was waiting to take us to Lamu. As we set off, waves were slamming into the hull; a howling wind tore at the tarpaulin awning under which we were desperately trying to shelter; huge raindrops were thudding on the deck and there was a tremendous creaking and groaning as the launch rocked wildly. Then, just as we entered Lamu harbour, a particularly large wave struck us sideways, flooding the stern where we were all crowding under the awning and soaking us to the bone.

We had barely got out, our legs trembling, when the storm abated as suddenly as it had started. We found some men waiting for us; they took us to the nearby town hall and as we went in, dripping wet, our shoes making a squelching sound, servants rushed forward. They seemed horrified at the state we were in, divested the EEC delegates and me of jackets and shirts, shoes and socks, and gave us towels to rub ourselves down. Then they vanished with our shoes and the bundles of clothes, which they intended to dry and iron. But as this was a Muslim area, Claire, being a woman, had to remain completely covered – and wet.

Unfortunately there was no time for our clothes to dry. We were already very late and were ushered without delay into a large dining room where a number of men, all in flamboyant outfits, were waiting to receive us. They looked surprised when we came in barefooted with just our trousers on, but politely refrained from commenting.

After we were seated at a table laden with an assortment of tropical fruit and local sweets, the bedraggled-looking Europeans on one side, the well-dressed men from Lamu on the other, the most important local dignitaries stood up one after the other to wish us welcome and good health, and the EEC delegates had to get up in their turn to answer.

The introductions over, we were served tea while delicacies were pressed on us. It was a bizarre sight. There we were, the important European delegation, our bare tops sticking out above the table as if we were completely naked and, facing us in rich silk robes and coloured turbans, the local men trying hard not to look shocked. Claire thought it extremely funny. This was colonial times turned on its head: stylish Africans and naked Europeans! She was just about to get up and take a photograph, but one look at the face of the English delegate who had insisted on 'proper' clothes put her off.

'Don't you dare!' he hissed under his breath.

After lunch, Claire and I set off into town; fortunately my clothes were dry and ironed by now. We filmed the damage done by the fire, which appeared to have started when someone had inadvertently knocked over a cooking pot; the straw roof had caught fire and the flames had jumped from roof to roof in a very short time.

The filming over, we ventured into the narrow streets where children crowded around us. Centuries of Arab presence had left deep marks here; it was just as evident in the faces, language and culture of the people as in the shape of the ships at sea. As we walked along the waterfront, we noticed many colourful dhows lying at anchor. Most were old and looked creaky, and some stood out for the number and variety of patches on their mainsails. Lamu had been a trading hub for centuries and although there was no longer any bargaining for spices as in the old days, it had remained an oriental town, very different from the rest of Africa.

Back in Nairobi, we were told that a large group was due to arrive in the guesthouse where we stayed, so could we please vacate our room within two days? We had liked the guesthouse and its friendly atmosphere and were loath to leave, but this forced us to take action.

For a long time now we had been living with an African mindset, surviving from day to day, coping with situations as they came along and going where fate pushed us. Time had been flying by, but somehow I had pushed all thoughts about our future to the back of my mind. Having to move out brought them fully to my attention. We were approaching the end of August; I had to start work again at the University of Brussels within a month; we were still deep in Africa and our funds were very low. How was I going to solve this intractable problem?

With the additional money obtained from selling most of our spare parts and jerry cans we might just be able to get back to Europe via the Sudan and Egypt, but this was very risky. Problems were bound to arise and if ever the Land Rover broke down we wouldn't be able to repair it and would be stuck in some Godforsaken place without a penny. Still, I couldn't see any other solution. But first we had to find affordable lodgings in town and after driving around and enquiring at a number of places, we finally managed to book a room in a small African hotel.

The next day, Claire drove me to the Sudanese Embassy where I hoped to get transit visas. It was a total fiasco. They simply refused to issue me a permit to enter the Sudan! I returned to the Land Rover at a loss as to what to do when I saw Claire, still sitting behind the steering wheel, talking to a European.

While I was waiting for Peter, a tall, suntanned man came strolling along on the opposite pavement; he looked like one of those intrepid travellers you sometimes meet in Africa and to my surprise he began staring at our dusty Land Rover. Then he walked across, smiled and said, 'Hello,' leaning on the open window.

In Africa you can easily strike up a friendship; you need neither preliminary enquiries nor introductions; you just talk and find out what you have in common. And we had a lot in common. Ditmar, a German in his mid-thirties, had sold the small firm he had founded, bought a motorbike and started travelling. Then he met Ann, a British girl of West Indian origin, and together they decided to set off for Africa because she had always wanted to see it. They had crossed the Sahara on motorbikes, sold these in Nigeria where they bought a second-hand Land Rover instead, and had just reached Nairobi.

It was an amazing story and I spontaneously invited Ditmar and Ann to share a meal with us. I had hardly spoken when Peter, who had returned by now, murmured in my ear, 'We can't afford to go to a restaurant.'

'All right,' I whispered back and turning to Ditmar, I frantically thought of what I could do. There was only one way out. 'We'll have the meal in our hotel room instead of in a restaurant,' I said, 'but don't expect too much. It'll be spaghetti with tomato sauce.' I smiled at him. 'I'm sure you won't mind.'

'Sounds fun,' laughed Ditmar. 'I'll go and get Ann.'

'It'll be ready in an hour. See you.'

'You shouldn't have said that,' I protested on the way back. 'Don't you know the hotel rules forbid preparing meals in the rooms?'

'Well, you said "no restaurant", so what else was I to do?' countered Claire. 'But don't you worry. It'll be all right. We'll just smuggle the gas stove and the food inside. And we'll be very quiet and clean.'

I kept talking to the receptionist, trying to distract him while Claire sauntered by, carrying a few bundles, and she managed to smuggle it all inside. I wedged the gas stove between two chairs, hoping it wouldn't topple over and set fire to the fitted carpet. Then I looked doubtfully at the large tin of tomato sauce, which Claire pressed into my hands. 'Do you think this is still all right? It's travelled all the way from Brussels.'

'Don't dilly-dally,' urged Claire. 'Just open it. They're going to be here any minute now.'

'All right.' I picked up the tin opener and punched a big hole in the lid, but I wasn't ready for what happened next: a jet of red gluey liquid spouted out of the hole like a geyser and hit the ceiling where it made a large red stain. The heat of many months had thoroughly fermented the tomato sauce! Then the foul stuff started dripping from the ceiling, staining the carpet, my hair and shirt, and the bedspread.

We rushed for a basin and towels and started mopping up the mess. Perched on a chair placed on a table I just about managed to reach the ceiling, and I was stretching my arms upwards when there was a knock on the door: Ditmar and Ann had arrived. When they saw Claire appear in the doorway, her face disfigured by red smears, and then spotted me looking totally bewildered, balanced precariously on a chair standing on a table, their mouths fell open. I saw them make huge efforts not to burst out laughing, but when Claire explained what had happened Ditmar was unable to control himself any longer. 'An exploding tin … ha ha ha … This I have never heard of before … ha ha ha … This is not tomato sauce … ha ha ha … This is dynamite sauce!' And he laughed his head off.

'Shhht …' motioned Claire, putting a finger on her lips. 'Don't make so much noise and close the door. Nobody must find out. It's forbidden to cook in the rooms.'

'Ha ha ha …' Ditmar kept on, roaring away, 'you have committed a very messy crime … ha ha ha.'

It took him minutes to quieten down but then we all got busy and, sponging and wiping, and emptying basins full of red-stained water into the toilet, we finally managed to clear up the traces of our 'crime'.

We ended up in a cheap local restaurant and for the next two days I had terrible diarrhoea. Still, it was lucky we had met Ditmar. He suggested that we all drive to Mombasa. He wanted to go there because he had always dreamed of swimming in the Indian Ocean, and convinced us to accompany him. He was sure we would find a cheap shipping company that would take the Land Rover and us back to Europe.

As we set off for Mombasa I was thrilled by the thought of all the animals we were going to see. I had read so much about them. In the past, barely sixty or seventy years ago, the savannah had been teeming with wildlife. To those arriving in Kenya for the first time (in those days via Mombasa by boat), seeing thousands upon thousands of animals from the train as it steamed slowly towards Nairobi, had been a marvel to behold. The wonders of this train journey have been described many times. There was a sense of travelling through a gigantic game park: there were enormous herds of zebra and gnu; elephants and buffalos were roaming in great numbers; everywhere giraffes were arching their necks to nibble treetops; rhinos stood about glaring in surprise as the train passed by; there were graceful gazelles, impalas, elands, little reedbucks, ostriches and guinea-fowl; and the predators – cheetahs, silver-backed jackals, ungainly hyenas and fearsome lions. This was how East Africa had been for thousands of years.

As we drove along, the same savannah stretched far away on either side of the road, but only here and there in the distance did we glimpse a few scattered animals. Where had all the wildlife gone? It made me wonder what this land would look like in another sixty or seventy years.

We reached Mombasa, turned south along the Indian Ocean towards Diani Beach, the famous tourist resort, drove past all the hotels, found an empty beach and parked within yards of the ocean under the shade of palm trees. It was a beautiful, quiet spot and I would have liked to relax there without thinking of anything, but I could no longer ignore the problem of our return. It had to be solved urgently and so, early next morning, we were back in town doing the round of the shipping agencies. We soon found out that Ditmar had been far too optimistic. They were willing to ship the Land Rover to Europe and would even take us, but the lowest price they could do it for was $3,000, an amount of money we no longer possessed!

By late afternoon we were getting tired and I had almost given up hope when, going into the office of an obscure shipping company and explaining our situation, they said that, yes, they might have something for us. They had a containership sailing to Barcelona within less than a week and it still had lots of empty space. After some bargaining they brought their price down to $1,000! There was, however, one major drawback: the ship didn't take passengers. It was nevertheless a great relief to have found a solution for the Land Rover and I decided on the spot to accept the offer, signed and paid. They would complete all the paperwork within the next few days and accompany me to the port before closing time on Friday.

As we had supper on the beach that night our lives seemed idyllic. A small circle of light surrounded us in the darkness under a star-spangled sky; a soft breeze was rustling in the palm leaves and we could hear the surf breaking on the coral reef a few hundred yards away. Life was good and after our luck with the shipping company, everything seemed possible, even if we only had £500 left. Ditmar too was optimistic.

'Tomorrow we'll go to Mombasa and look around together,' he said. 'Five hundred pounds is a lot of money. I'm sure that'll be enough to get you back to Europe.'

The next day, we went into town and started looking for travel agencies. Ditmar had been certain that we would be able to fly back to Europe on the little money we had left, but as we began doing the round of the agencies, our illusions faded rapidly. The agents were willing to sell us tickets, but when we mentioned the amount of cash we could pay them, they shook their heads in commiseration. All we could buy for that, they said, were tickets on an Air Ethiopia flight that would get us as far as Addis Ababa, Ethiopia.

'It doesn't matter,' said Claire, trying to buck me up as I sank down on the pavement, my back against a wall. 'If we can't fly back we'll stay and work until we've earned enough to pay for our return. We'll manage somehow.'

Ditmar was determined to carry on, though, and went off on his own. He reappeared half an hour later, looking very excited. 'I've found something,' he said jubilantly. 'There's a man and a woman who arrived on a charter flight from Frankfurt a week ago. They want to stay in Kenya and are trying to sell their return tickets!' And he rushed me along to the agency where the couple had left their tickets that same morning, hoping to sell them.

'How much do they want?' I asked the travel agent, holding my breath.

'Four hundred pounds?' The man looked at me expectantly.

'All I can offer is two hundred and fifty …'

'OK,' he replied. 'It's a deal.'

As we drove home, I wondered whether we would be able to get on board that charter flight to Frankfurt the following Monday with names that didn't match those on the tickets, but it was that or nothing.

In the meantime, one of the biggest hotels on Diani Beach was organising a tennis tournament and Ditmar had decided to participate. Ann decked him out in impeccable white shorts, shirt and socks to comply with dress regulations, he borrowed tennis shoes and a racket, strolled over to the organisers pretending he was staying in one of the hotels and managed to enrol!

Early every morning, Ditmar would dive into the ocean, swim as far as the reef and return in record time.

'You seem to like swimming in the ocean,' I commented one morning.

'I do it mainly to keep fit,' he corrected, 'but yes, I like the ocean. And to think that I nearly didn't see it.' He sat there for a while, reliving events in his mind's eye. Then he asked unexpectedly, 'Do you know the Kilimanjaro?'

'Yes. We've been there.'

'You've climbed it?' He looked at me incredulously.

'No. Don't overestimate my capacities.'

'Well, *I* have.' He stuck out his chest. 'I was determined to get to the top. It's the highest mountain in Africa, you know.'

'And you climbed it without mountaineering equipment?'

'Of course.'

'That's incredible!'

He looked pleased with himself. Then, almost unwillingly, he admitted, 'Well … actually, it's not really difficult,' before correcting himself, 'but it's a long stiff climb that requires a lot of stamina; and it's very cold up there.'

'You went up with Ann?'

He laughed. 'That's not the sort of thing you could make her do. I went up with Ian.'

'Who's Ian?'

'An Englishman. He and his wife travelled through Uganda and into Tanzania with us.'

'So who got to the top first?' I asked jokingly.

'*He* did, the bastard!' Ditmar looked quite upset.

'Well … I suppose someone had to get there first,' I said soothingly.

'That wasn't it! I helped him all the way up the mountain because he said he was tired, but when the summit came into view he suddenly rushed ahead singing, "Rule Britannia, Britannia rules the waves!" And then he stood there on the top, looking triumphantly at me.'

'I see …'

'After that our ways parted. They went on to the coast while we drove back to Uganda. But the moment we'd got there I regretted not having seen the Indian Ocean and decided to head towards Kenya instead of the Sudan. That's how we met in Nairobi … and now I'm at the ocean.' He looked with great satisfaction at the surf pounding the coral reef. Then he turned towards me muttering, 'Rule Britannia!' with undisguised disgust. 'But I'm getting my own back. You know the tennis tournament? I've already eliminated two English players.' And he smiled with evident satisfaction.

Diani Beach was one of the world's top tourist resorts and it supplied the exotic entertainment Western tourists expected. Every night there were 'traditional' dance groups performing in one or another hotel, but once the show was over the dancers changed back to modern clothes and returned to

Mombasa. There were also many young African women who supplied another type of entertainment to lone male tourists, and they had to put in much longer hours.

One of Ditmar's tennis matches took place in the evening and while he was playing, Ann sat waiting in a bar when the police abruptly stormed in and rounded up all the young women. Ann protested vividly that she was a British subject but as she couldn't show her passport, which she had left in their Land Rover, she was pushed into an armoured vehicle with the other young black women and driven to a police post in Mombasa for interrogation. They were speaking Swahili, Ann couldn't understand a word of what they asked her and the police began treating her very rudely, claiming she was just pretending to be British. They were about to throw her into prison when Ditmar, who had finished his tennis match and heard what had happened, arrived with her passport and saved her in the nick of time!

The next afternoon, I was cleaning our Land Rover for the return journey when Ditmar came strolling along and began inspecting it, an expression on his face as if he were a trained mechanic.

'Everything seems all right,' he remarked, 'except for this tyre. It looks rather worn. You'd better change the wheel.'

'Oh … I'm not sure. I've only got a very small jack left and it's difficult to use. I think I'll leave that tyre alone until I get home.'

'No, no,' insisted Ditmar. 'You must never put off problems. Always tackle them straightaway, otherwise they'll hit you when you least expect it. Look here, I've got a super-sized jack – the best model there is. You can use it if you like.' And without further ado he climbed up on his roof rack and, jumping down, shoved a yard-long, heavy metal thing into my hands. There was nothing for it now but to change the wheel, so I unwillingly left the others and drove some hundred yards further till I found a level space where I parked. As I stuck the jack underneath the Land Rover I had to admire it. This was a super model indeed: it had a long lever which you moved up and down to jack up the vehicle and when you stopped, the lever stayed in the position in which you left it. What a wonder of technology!

I had just finished jacking up the Land Rover, got out a wrench and bent down towards the wheel, when unexpectedly the long lever shot up instead of staying in position as it was supposed to do, and hit me on the chin, knocking me out flat. When I came to I was sprawled out on my back and my chin was hurting terribly. I began fingering it, quite sure I had broken my jaw, but the bone seemed intact. I heaved myself up and began to stumble back towards the beach. By the time I got there my cheek was the size of an inflated balloon and when Claire saw me she was so upset that she became cross.

'How can you do such a stupid thing just changing a wheel!' she exclaimed, exasperated, while pressing a wet cloth on my cheek. 'From now on you just stay sitting here in the shade. And don't you touch anything! I'll do all the rest. Then, at least, I know you'll be safe,' she added as she set off towards our Land Rover.

Claire managed to take away the jack, drove the Land Rover back and then began cleaning it out, dumping things on the grass, when she came upon one of the Little Bee stoves. As soon as Ditmar saw it his eyes opened wide with interest. 'What's that?' he asked.

'Oh,' replied Claire, doing her best to look innocent. 'This is my special oil stove.' She held it up enticingly. 'The copper looks a bit dull right now but wait.' She got out a piece of cloth and began rubbing a small patch, making it shine. 'Isn't it attractive?'

I saw Ditmar's eyes grow wider. 'That must be a very expensive stove?'

'Yes, it is. It came from an exclusive shop in Brussels.'

A gleam appeared in his eyes. 'What are you going to do with it?'

'I don't really know. I won't be needing it now.' Then, as if moved by a sudden inspiration, she held out the Little Bee with both hands. 'If you really want it, it's yours. It's a present.'

'Oh yes, I want it!' Ditmar's face lit up with excitement. 'Thank you, thank you!' he exclaimed, bending down towards Claire and kissing her on both cheeks. 'This is most wonderful!'

'Wait,' said Claire, repressing a grin and diving inside our Land Rover's back compartment. 'I've even got a second one.'

'Two exclusive oil stoves!' Ditmar seemed hardly able to believe his luck. He pressed the Little Bees to his chest, then put them on the ground, dug some cleaning materials out of his vehicle and spent the next hour rubbing the stoves till they shone like mirrors in the sun. Then he asked, 'How do they work?'

'You'll need unrefined oil and alcohol,' explained Claire. 'Luckily we've still got plenty of both. Here, take this.' And she handed him two half-full cans. 'And once the stoves burn you just keep pumping,' she added gleefully.

'That sounds very easy,' replied Ditmar. And he declared magnanimously, 'I'm going to make breakfast for all of us tomorrow morning on *my* Little Bees.'

The day was only just dawning when we were woken up by activities around Ditmar's Land Rover. We heard rummaging and clanging, and finally a prolonged pshh, pshh as if someone was pumping; then there was a long silence. After a while we again heard an energetic pshh, pshh, followed by an irritated, '*Das ist nicht möglich!*'

I nudged Claire, whispering, 'Ditmar is up against the Little Bees …' trying hard not to laugh.

There was a renewed pshh, pshh suddenly interrupted by a loud, '*Scheisse!*'

As I stuck my head out I saw Ditmar sitting on the grass in front of a Little Bee stove, red-faced and very agitated, attempting to keep the flame going against the little breeze that was blowing. Claire now got up and strolling towards him she asked innocently, 'Do you need any help?'

'No!' he retorted. 'I shall make this work on my own!'

'Well … I'll leave you to get on with your Little Bee stove then,' said Claire with a twinkle in her eyes. 'In the meantime, I think I'll make tea and perhaps start our breakfast.'

We had reached the end of Africa – the end of our journey. As I gazed up, Peter and Ditmar stood on our empty-looking roof rack etched against the cloudy sky above the Indian Ocean. Gone our heavy load of jerry cans, wheels and spare parts; gone also the boxes full of medicine and hope, and the pencils, pens, exercise books and games for the schoolchildren of Africa.

The two Land Rovers stood close together, stained by the many miles of African earth through which they had struggled, looking worn-out, their backs to the sea but still facing Africa, as though they were unable to forget – as I couldn't forget this land where all the wonders of creation come to life in a glory of colour under the flaming sun; where stars shine brilliantly in the velvet sky at night and the moonlit shadows of the silent desert bewitch the lonely traveller.

As I sat listlessly under the waving fronds of the palm trees, a sense of loss pervaded me and the sight of our brave old Land Rover, our home that had carried us safely through so many known and unknown dangers and adventures, brought tears to my eyes. Soon Peter was going to take it to Mombasa.

I had an appointment with the shipping agency that Friday and got there well before 1.00 p.m., but the employee who was handling my papers wasn't in. 'He's just gone out,' they told me, 'but he'll be back soon. Maybe you could go and have a drink somewhere while waiting?'

I went to a nearby restaurant, shaking my head. I had been told to be there in good time because we still needed to get clearance from customs before putting the Land Rover in a container, and the port closed at 4.00 p.m. on Fridays. I ordered a passion fruit iced drink, swallowed it quickly and rushed back to the agency. Half an hour later the employee turned up with a big smile; he picked up the documents, jumped in next to me and we set off.

'Got everything?' he asked as we drove towards the port area.

'Yes.'

'Got money to pay the export taxes?'

'Export taxes?' I enquired incredulously. 'That's ridiculous! Why should I have to pay export taxes? With my vehicle carnet I don't have to pay import or export taxes.'

'That is correct if you enter or leave the country by road,' stated the agency man, 'but as your vehicle is leaving by ship you'll have to pay taxes. It's the law.'

This was an unforeseen last-minute complication. 'But I have no money left to pay any taxes,' I objected.

The man thought for a while and then said, 'I think it can be arranged. Have you got fifty pounds?'

We went into the customs office and as we sat down in front of the officer, he asked me what the value of the Land Rover was, to allow him to calculate the export tax I would have to pay.

'It gives the value here,' I said, opening the vehicle carnet and pointing at the stated value.

The officer stared at the carnet and then at me. 'It says 100,000 Belgian francs here. That doesn't mean anything to me. How much is that in Kenyan shillings or in pounds sterling if you like?'

I made a quick mental calculation, divided the amount I had reached by ten and replied, 'A hundred and forty pounds.'

The officer's eyes nearly popped out of his head. 'That cannot be!' he exclaimed. 'That's far too little!'

Was it the tension or the heat? I was suddenly beginning to feel quite unwell. I didn't know what to do, but at that very moment I saw the man from the shipping agency bend forward. He stuck his arm under the table and touching the officer's knee, he proffered the fifty pounds I had given him! The officer looked down in surprise, pocketed the money with a quick gesture and then turned to me. 'If your carnet states that the value is one hundred and forty pounds,' he said affably, 'it must be right. We shall calculate taxes on that.' I paid the now very reasonable export taxes and the officer stamped the vehicle carnet and port documents with a great show of energy.

As we left the office I had violent stomach cramps, but there was no time to lose. It was 3.30 p.m. already and we drove hastily towards an area of the docks where rows of containers were standing. The man from the agency began searching for the container carrying the number he had on his papers until he found it, and immediately called out to several men who were hanging around. They opened the doors, I positioned the Land Rover straight in front of the container, revved up and then, as I attempted to drive into the big iron box, I heard a loud bang and my head hit the windscreen; the roof rack stuck up 3 inches above the container's doorframe!

I've got to do something, I thought feverishly. If I can't get the Land Rover inside this container, the ship will leave without it! I was feeling really ill by now and I could no longer reason clearly. I hoisted myself onto the roof rack, got a small metal saw out of the nearly empty toolbox and began to attack the steel sides of the roof rack, attempting to saw off three inches. It was ridiculous! After a lot of effort, I hadn't even made a dent in the steel and the minutes were ticking away inexorably: it was nearly 4.00 p.m.

The Africans below were shaking their heads. Some began to laugh and one of them finally suggested, 'Shall we deflate the tyres?'

'Do anything you like!' I shouted in a state of collapse and they all set to it with gusto. It was over in no time and I crawled behind the steering wheel and moved forward again. This was my last chance! The roof rack made a horrible sound as it scraped against the top of the doorframe, but the Land Rover shot in, the Africans rushed to secure it with straps, slammed the doors of the container shut and sealed them. As I stumbled out of the port I was violently ill and had to stagger into a corner to vomit. The iced drink had done me in! It took me an hour to walk in the sweltering heat to the ferry connecting the island of Mombasa to the coastal road running south towards Diani Beach. The ferry was just about to leave when I jumped on board and slumped down on a bench, feeling whacked out.

'You don't look well,' came a voice next to me.

Gazing up in surprise, I stared into the face of a fair-haired European. We started talking and he seemed very interested in my story and plied me with questions. 'But that's incredible!' he exclaimed. 'And you're camping out next to Diani Beach?'

'If I can get there tonight,' I said despondently. 'I don't even know whether there are any buses going that way.'

'You will get there for sure,' he replied. 'I'll drive you.'

'Would you really?'

'Yes.' He held out a hand. 'I'm Peter Hutchensee. I run a small boat company with my wife not far from where you're camping.' Then, to my utter delight, he added, 'Why don't you and your wife come and stay with us. I've got a spare bungalow on the beach. It'll be much more comfortable than sleeping in a tent and you'll be quite independent there.'

By the time I got back, Ditmar had pitched a tiny tent on the beach and I found Claire huddled inside. I explained what had happened and Ditmar immediately said, 'Of course you must go.'

'But we can't leave you after all you've done,' protested Claire. 'That would be ungrateful.'

'Don't worry,' he replied magnanimously. 'If I were you I wouldn't hesitate a second.'

And that's how we came to spend a few wonderful last days in Africa.

That evening we enjoyed a delicious meal and afterwards the two Peters found great pleasure in talking of their many experiences and discussing books, their mutual passion. Later I was lying in a soft bed while reading a book from our host's library – things I hadn't been able to indulge in for a long, long time.

The next morning Peter Hutchinsee took us out in one of his glass-bottomed boats to admire the coral reef and the dazzling beauty of the undersea world of fish, an unending fascination of life's creation. I spent the afternoon in the garden, the lawn sloping down to the beach, our host's horse free to graze wherever the grass was greenest, his much loved, friendly dogs running around me and the sound of the surf on the shore … All this made me feel in paradise.

Days of quiet friendship, days of rest under the shade of the palm trees, the leaves rustling in the soft ocean breeze … I shall always remember our host's unstinting kindness and care, letting us spend a few last carefree days before having to resurface among the bustle of modern society.

The bungalow in which we stayed felt light and spacious. There was no ceiling, just wooden beams rising up to support the roof, creaking like the timber of an old wooden ship. We slept peacefully, protected in its fold.

When we opened the doors in the morning, the cool sea breeze wound its way inside as if it belonged there. We had breakfast on the veranda in the shade of palm trees, the coast – hot and lazy – only yards away. Then, as we walked to the shore, the beach of fine white sand stretched warm and soft under our feet while the Indian Ocean pounded the coral reef just out to sea.

One of my greatest joys was rummaging in Peter Hutchensee's extensive library, and I found a book that caught my attention: *Eyelids of Morning*, by Peter Beard. It related many events that had happened in and around Lake Turkana and one tale, which struck me particularly as being 'so Turkana', was the story of the first airplane arriving in Turkanaland. It had landed close to a group of surprised men and the pilot decided to take one of the elders up in the air, believing he would be duly impressed. After he returned and the man had got out and sat down in the shade under one of the wings, the pilot asked him what he thought about it. 'Wasn't this a fantastic invention?' The elder nodded wisely. 'This thing is very useful,' he replied. 'You can take it anywhere to make shade.'

The book took me back to everything that had endeared me about Turkanaland. So many images unrolled before my eyes as I lay on my bed looking at the wooden beams that supported the high roof. Thoughts kept coming, strange ideas appearing out of nowhere. I seemed to be living in a world without time, here and yet somewhere else. It was a warm, peaceful and pleasant close to our year of freedom.

Early on Monday morning, Ditmar and Ann drove us to the airport and as we said goodbye we felt very apprehensive for them. He had decided to drive into the Sudan; it was extremely brave but also very foolish since he had no permit. We hoped with all our hearts that they would get through.

We proceeded towards the airline desk amongst a throng of German tourists returning to Frankfurt, trying to look very self-assured, holding up our tickets. Claire's carried the name of a certain Mrs Hubke, whilst mine had belonged to a Mr Singh. Claire didn't exactly look like a hefty German Brunhilde, but she put on a good show, saying, '*Guten Tag! Ich bin Frau Hubke*,' while shoving her ticket forward. I followed close behind, a turban around my head, bending low and speaking with a strong Indian accent, 'Good morning, sir. I am Mister Singh.' Then we waited, holding our breaths …

It would no longer be possible today, but those were the early 1980s, we were in Africa, everything was done by hand and there was great confusion all around. People were queuing up behind us to board, the airline employee was under great pressure and she just took our tickets without checking our identities, asked where we would like to sit, gave us boarding passes and let the fake Mr Singh and Mrs Hubke proceed towards emigration.

We heaved a sigh of relief and quickly moved on to border control several yards further on. 'We've got our boarding passes,' we said and without further ado, they put an exit stamp into our passports! We followed the throng of German tourists to the plane, found our seats and sat down, waiting in tense silence until they closed the door. Then, after what seemed ages, the plane taxied slowly towards the runway. Seconds later we were airborne.

Above: The old man, some of his children and his latest wife

Below: At Lodwar market

Above: At Lodwar market

Below: The old man and his hat

Above: A proud Turkana. Note the bump on his neck made by sleeping on his neck-rest

Below: A man asleep on his neck-rest

Above: Turkana dancing

Below: Turkana getting ready for raiding dances

Above: Claire installing her sound-recording equipment.
Gregory (with jacket and papers) is watching

Below: Peter filming women dancing

Left: A man in his blanket. Note the pouch where he keeps his tobacco

Right: Turkana girl returning from her foraging trip: she carries a gourd full of water, nuts of the doum palm on her head for making a fire, and she has got a long stick to keep wild animals at bay

Above: Turkana women and Claire: a meeting of Africa and Europe, different in style, one in heart

Below: Highly pregnant or not, the work has to be done. Note the small boy already holding on to a neck-rest

Above: Inside a manyatta

Below: Pounding maize with a round pebble, one grain at a time

Above: In one of the manyattas

Below: Peter and his little girlfriend

Above: Showing how to light a fire

Below: Filming the 'golden' grass

In the riverbed

Above: Nairobi Airport: the plane to Lamu. Claire looking her 'very best'

Below: A street scene in Lamu

Above: Ditmar and Peter on Diani Beach

Below: Claire in Peter Hutchinsee's garden

Interlude: Ten Golden Rules for Those Foolish Enough to Drive on Their Own Through Africa

1. Try to be lucky, not once but all the time.

2. If you really have to break down, do it in front of a repair garage (not that there are many of these in Africa). Otherwise, make sure you can diagnose the cause, have the spare part with you and be capable of installing it yourself.

3. Never ever drive at night on African roads unless you want to commit suicide.

4. Be wary at all times of what you eat and drink. Take the greatest care of your own health. Nobody else is going to do it for you and if you fall ill there is very little chance of finding a doctor.

5. Never take anything for granted. Things are often not what they seem. Always expect the worst and hope for the best.

6. Don't plan anything for next week. You can be sure that tomorrow will be full of unforeseen events. When these are sprung upon you, be ready to adapt and change course.

7. Never leave things about or display the money you've got with you: there are many hands around and they move quickly, but if you get robbed, don't make a drama out of it. Remember that you have only lost material things and that Africans need them more than you do!

8. Don't talk down to Africans and never, under any circumstances, lose your temper. It may relieve your feelings for the time being, but chances are that you will bitterly regret your outburst afterwards.

9. Show the utmost deference for authority. Never oppose the police or army people, or even contradict them. They are always right, even when they are wrong. Remember that they are the ones who have the guns.

10. Death may be lurking just around the corner. Avoid that corner at all costs!

PART 5

Return to Europe
A Very Different World

CHAPTER 13
Is This Where We Live?

Coming Home

We were flying back to Europe and as the plane was cruising over the Sahara at an altitude of 33,000 feet, my nose was glued to the porthole. I didn't want to miss any detail; I wanted to see the Sahara one last time. Far below I could make out rapidly changing landscapes, brightly coloured patches and folds of what must have been mountains, and yet it didn't touch me. I was sitting at a remote distance in an air-conditioned cabin and what I saw might have been a projection. It was virtual reality, not reality; it had nothing to do with anything I remembered. If this was the desert, it certainly wasn't the one I had known. Too many dimensions were lacking for it to be *that* desert. Where was the heat, the dust, the sweat and fatigue? Where was the loneliness, the feeling of infinity? And above all, where was the freedom, the awareness that you were truly alive?

> Africa! Images kept flashing through my mind ... red earth, smiling people, light and golden grasses ... Suddenly I saw our Land Rover disappearing into a tight container, sucked away from us – our home imprisoned! Then my brain went numb; I could no longer focus, Africa was dwindling into oblivion before my desolate gaze. We were returning ... to what?

In just eight hours the thread, which had unwound slowly, month after month, was rewound and suddenly our journey was over. Gone were the thousands of miles that had taken us almost a year of struggle and effort to cover. But not only did we move in space; we also travelled in time, from a way of living that was deeply human to a modern way of living; from a society where values were eternal and changes almost imperceptible to a world where people have little time and fashions change constantly.

When we disembarked at Frankfurt Airport, the shock was complete. We stood there, unable to take it all in, looking aghast at the people rushing by as if they didn't have a second to lose. And their faces! Closed to the outside world, focused on their own business, a fixed expression in their eyes. No one was smiling; there was no one to welcome us and shake hands. In what kind of world had we landed? Where had all the warmth gone? The empathy? We felt totally lost among these anonymous hurrying crowds. It was like hitting a wall of cold indifference; it was frightening. Was this where we belonged?

Home … I wanted to be out of all this, get back to Brussels and hide for a while in a place of our own until the effect of the first shock had worn off. And once again, we were in luck. Our remaining cash was just sufficient to buy two second-class train tickets to Brussels. We were relieved to get on the train, but found that nobody took any notice of us. The passengers all kept themselves to themselves.

I glanced at Claire who was sitting very quietly opposite me, appearing strangely out of place in her long, blue-patterned African dress and sandals. She was staring out of the window but soon she closed her eyes, looking very forlorn as she fingered her cowry necklace. This was all too different from the sun and warmth of Africa.

There was worse to come. Within hours, we were beginning to get very hungry and thirsty, and we hadn't got a penny left to buy food or drinks on the train. In Africa, local people, poor as they were, would have offered us food, but here no one offered us anything. We had forgotten that nothing comes for free in Western society.

When we finally reached Brussels South Station around 8.00 p.m., another problem loomed. We couldn't pay for a bus, let alone for a taxi. I already saw myself dragging our bags and my heavy cine camera along the streets of Brussels for an hour or two when, before my astounded eyes, Claire performed a conjuring trick: from the depths of one of her pockets she produced a 5-franc coin which she had kept all through the journey! It was just enough to make one call from a public phone box, but the only number we could remember was our home number and surely, there wouldn't be anyone in. But yes, there was; Claire's son, Philippe, was home and half an hour later he turned up with a friend in an old car!

For months we had been facing the discomforts of the journey, having to search for a secure place where we could stay for the night and then sleeping within the narrow confines of our home on wheels. We had got used to it but still, I had sometimes dreamed of being back in our own house where we had all the security we could wish for and a comfortable bed in which we could stretch in all directions. But strangely enough, now that we were home, we missed our Land Rover and even the hardships we had been through.

Suddenly we were back in our urbanised Western world and within no time we learned that things were bad. 'The economy isn't going well,' our neighbours and friends told us. 'Didn't you know?'

'No …'

'But didn't you watch TV in Africa?'

When we replied that we'd had very little news for nearly a year, they stared at us with disapproval, as if we were uncivilised, nay, primitive people. How could anyone survive without watching TV? Without staying constantly connected and discussing the latest news bulletins?

'So you really don't know anything?' they repeated as if wanting confirmation of such a shocking fact. 'You haven't followed all the important events that have been going on in the world?'

'No …'

They shook their heads and didn't think it worth pressing the point any further.

So there was a severe recession! We expected the worst: that people had hardly any money left, just like ourselves; and yet we found that everyone was giving parties, boozing and wasting. Or we imagined that, at the very least, the shops would have little to sell. The first time we went to the nearby supermarket and came to the bread shelves, we found dozens of different kinds of breads all neatly stacked up. It was almost shocking. In Africa, when you reach a town and discover a shop that has a loaf of bread for sale, you immediately buy it because you may not find another one for a week! As we stood there, overwhelmed by such incredible abundance, a well-dressed couple approached the bread section. The woman looked at the shelves with a discontented face; then she tilted her head back and I heard her say to her husband, 'Darling, there isn't much choice today. Let's go somewhere else.'

As they left I stood there, speechless, wondering whether I'd heard correctly. Are we really living on the same planet? I thought, or have I stepped into a kind of parallel world?

We heard nothing but complaints about how difficult life was and how dissatisfying. The cost of living had soared, goods were expensive and everyone was becoming poorer by the day. Apparently people could no longer afford to buy everything they wanted. If this continued they would be unable to keep up their way of life! How trivial people's preoccupations suddenly seemed. Listening to them you would have thought that survival was much more difficult here than in the African wilds.

So all these well-dressed, well-fed people believed they were badly off! They found reason to grumble amidst all this opulence! Nobody seemed to be pleased, let alone overjoyed at having enough to eat, at having a place to themselves, a bed to sleep in and not having to worry about their security or health. Do they really know what they're talking about? I couldn't help thinking. Don't they realise how privileged they are?

Getting the Land Rover Back

In order to secure the vehicle carnet before setting off, we had to leave 100,000 Belgian francs (about £1,400) in a bank account. To release the money upon our return, I had to show the Land Rover and vehicle carnet to an inspector of the Belgian Touring Club who would then sign a discharge for my bank. We needed the money badly, but the Land Rover was still in a container on a ship sailing from Mombasa to Barcelona via the Red Sea, the Suez Canal and the Mediterranean. Then, suddenly, things looked up. We got a message from the shipping company telling us that their ship with our Land Rover had arrived in Barcelona. I immediately rushed to my bank to ask for some money but the manager was uncooperative. My account was not only deep in the red, but I was well over my limit.

'I'll pay you the moment I get the vehicle carnet guarantee back,' I promised, 'but I can't do that until you advance me some money to fetch the vehicle.' It sounded logical to me, but the bank manager wasn't impressed. It took me a while to persuade him to part with what I hoped was enough cash to see me through to Barcelona and back.

I arrived in Barcelona on Sunday afternoon, dog tired after sitting upright on a hard bench in a second-class compartment for a day and a night, found an affordable room in a *hostal* in the old quarter of the town, had a snack and collapsed on my bed. I had foolishly believed that I would be able to pick up the Land Rover on Monday morning and drive away, but that wasn't how things worked.

'You'll need to go to a shipping agency for clearance,' they told me in the port area. 'They're the only ones authorised to issue these documents.'

Finally, two days later – because making up documents was obviously a time-consuming business – I followed a customs officer into the port to where a container was standing on one of the docks. The man broke the seal and there, inside, was our Land Rover, looking lost and miserable. I handed the officer the clearance document, he checked everything carefully and told me I could take possession of the vehicle. It was only then that I noticed the four flat tyres. I'd forgotten all about them!

'Is there any possibility of inflating the tyres in the port?' I asked hopefully.

'You have to go to a petrol station in town for that,' said the customs officer, unconcerned.

'But I can't drive all the way into town with flat tyres!'

The man just shrugged his shoulders and replied, 'That's not my problem.' Then he turned and left.

There was nothing to do but move off extremely slowly. Driving on flat tyres made a horrible scrunching noise but I managed to get out of the port, praying they would hold out. Finding replacements would take days and even if I found them, I wouldn't be able to pay for them. I drove on and on until three miles further I found a petrol station where I could inflate them. And miraculously, they were OK!

Crossing France took me two whole days. I spent the night sleeping in my Land Rover parked in a motorway layby, but it didn't have the same charm as camping out in the African bush. All through the night I heard the roar of heavy lorries and I was glad when daylight came and I could move on.

Given the frequency with which I had to pull in to petrol stations to fill up, it was obvious that the engine was in a pitiful condition. Fuel consumption was double what it had been at the outset of the expedition and the engine was also dripping oil.

French motorways are toll roads and they are quite expensive to boot, so I decided to move over to the *routes nationales* to save my remaining cash for diesel fuel and oil; and I just hoped that it would be sufficient to get me home.

I was passing through a small town halfway between Lyon and Dijon when two uniformed men, whom I took to be policemen, overtook me on their motorbikes and signalled to me to stop. I was just about to enquire if anything was wrong, when they asked sharply, 'Where are you going?'

'Belgium,' I replied, surprised.

'Then, why aren't you on the motorway?'

'I didn't know there was a law against driving on the *routes nationales*,' I retorted with barely hidden sarcasm.

They didn't seem to like my reply and began to circle the Land Rover with suspicion; then one of them asked, 'Where have you come from?'

'From Spain.'

They pointed at the roof rack and the winch. 'Then, why do you have all this equipment?'

'Well … I've been travelling through Africa.'

When they heard the word 'Africa' the men's faces hardened. 'We're going to check everything,' they barked.

'But we're in the middle of France! They've already checked me at the border.'

One of the men cut me short. 'We're mobile customs. We have the right to operate all over France.' He moved towards the back of the Land Rover with a determined step. 'Open up!' he commanded.

This is going to be fun, I suddenly thought. Every time a customs officer in Africa had asked me to open the back I had excused myself profusely, saying, 'I'm willing, but you see …' pointing at the missing handle, 'look what thieves have done to this in Mali! The back flap can no longer be opened.' I would then take the officer to the front, open the door and point at the narrow passage in the plywood panel between the cabin and the back compartment, saying encouragingly, 'but if you really want to check everything, you are welcome to climb through there.'

It had worked all over Africa but here, no joking! The French officer just replied rudely, 'Even if the handle is missing you can still open the back flap from the inside. Climb in there yourself and open up!'

The moment I did so the customs officers shot into action. They began to unload everything, the mattress, the wooden board underneath, the kitchen equipment and water filter, maps and documents … dumping the whole caboodle on the pavement. I stood there, not believing that such a thing could happen in 'civilised' Europe, but on they went, searching every little nook and cranny methodically in spite of the red dust that covered the inside. Suddenly one of the men let out a yell of satisfaction. He had dug up a plastic bag filled with what looked like white powder! He showed it triumphantly to his colleague and brought some of the powder to his lips to taste it. Then he spat it out in disgust. It was fine white sand from Diani Beach on the Indian Ocean, which Claire had collected! Meanwhile his colleague had discovered another bag. He eagerly stuck his hand inside but immediately pulled it out screaming and began to suck his finger. It contained the acacia thorns Claire had kept since Mali, and the man had stuck his finger straight into one of them! Serves him right, I thought, feeling great satisfaction.

An hour later, the men gave up, dusted off their trousers with an expression of disgust on their faces and without so much as a goodbye, they jumped on their motorbikes and drove away, leaving me to stuff everything back into the Land Rover. And this was the EEC (now the European Union)!

I had never come across anything like it in the whole of Africa.

The customs people had delayed me considerably and it was well past midnight by the time I crossed the Belgian border. I had just enough money left to buy ten litres of diesel fuel and I prayed that this would get me home. It was past 2.00 a.m. by the time the lights of Brussels came into view; the fuel gauge indicated zero, but the engine kept going and after what seemed endless, anxious minutes, I entered the suburb of Uccle through empty streets. The Land Rover crawled up the slope to our avenue in first gear and suddenly there was our house. I drove into the garage entrance, switched off the engine and headlights, and nearly collapsed. It was 2.30 a.m. but I was home!

The following day, I went to show the Land Rover and vehicle carnet to an inspector of the Belgian Touring Club. He signed a discharge and I immediately drove to my bank where they released the 100,000 francs guarantee, which allowed me to pay off our debts. Then, as I got home, the engine gave out a low plaintive sigh as if to tell me, 'I've done what I could but now I need a well-deserved, long rest,' and broke down in front of our garage.

The Beginning of a New Life

It was the morning of 1 October, we had no car and were not likely to get one very soon, so I caught the shuttle train that took me from the suburb of Uccle, where we lived, to Brussels University. The commuters in the train seemed numbed by the monotony of routine; there wasn't a smile to be seen on anyone's face. I got out at Etterbeek Station, joined the throng of students and employees shuffling towards the exit, and after a few minutes, the grey, concrete buildings of the university loomed up. They looked dirty and lifeless against the low, dull sky – no bright African colours here, no sense of space, no uplifting feeling. It was probably going to rain later in the day or, more accurately, going to drizzle – you couldn't call this proper rain.

When I saw the university buildings I automatically began to hurry because I was sure I was going to be late. Suddenly time was important again and I still had no wristwatch. For months there had been no need to know the exact time. I just looked at the position of the sun in the sky if I wanted an approximate idea. But how could I have any idea of the time in a country where the sun rarely shone?

So, here I was again. I pushed open the door that led to my department and emerged into what was a long corridor with offices and workshops on either side. After a few, 'Hey, you're back!' exclamations from people who had left their doors open, I reached my office and sank down in my chair. I automatically started rummaging in my desk, but soon found I lacked the courage to begin anything and just sat there, staring out of the window at the grey building opposite.

As I left my department for lunch in the cafeteria, I saw that the bottom part of the wall was covered in graffiti. One of these read, 'IS THERE LIFE *BEFORE* DEATH?'

I wondered.

In the weeks that followed, I was taken aback by the reaction of my colleagues at the university, or rather by their almost total indifference. My life had changed – theirs hadn't. After listening politely for a minute or two to my African experiences, they would indicate that they had to get on with whatever their occupation of the moment was. Or if I bumped into people in the cafeteria during lunch, they would change the topic to something 'more interesting' at the first opportunity: to gossip about a colleague or the minutes of the last faculty meeting. Africa was too far removed for them; they just weren't interested.

I assumed I would have more success with people involved in African development. During our travels we had visited a large number of projects, some huge, others at micro-level, and upon our return I had expected to be able to talk about my impressions to those working in that field.

Before starting the journey, I had hoped, no, I had been convinced that I would be able to bring back some answers, but the further we had penetrated into Africa, the more I found the reality to be very different from what I had imagined. Somehow, though, I felt that whatever outsiders wanted, Africans would do things in their own way, at their own speed and rhythm, or else wouldn't do them at all.

When I tried to convey this, and my doubts about the usefulness of many large projects, to development specialists, they suddenly seemed very busy and didn't have much time to listen. Maybe what I had to say wasn't what they wanted to hear? The West had been doing its best since colonial times to intervene in order to show Africans what it thought they needed and as I left the office of one of those 'specialists', I had the feeling that this attitude was not about to change.

Every now and then, some of the people we had met during our journey came along, bringing us warmth and sunshine. Even Ditmar and Ann called on us to tell us they had made it through the Sudan! Our house had always been open to friends and this became all the more so after Africa. It was a joy to see some of those who had shown us hospitality when we were in need and at last to be able to return the generosity we had experienced.

In the meantime, I kept working on my films whenever I had any free time. After months of editing, cutting, pasting everything together and synchronising sound and music, I managed to produce two documentaries, one for the Belgian Ministry for Cooperation and Development and the other one for the European Commission. And to my delight and relief, they bought them! It paid back all the costs of our African journey!

Still, I was again caught up in the maelstrom of working life and there seemed nothing for me to do but to continue to function within the neatly ordered schedule at the university. I attempted to make the best of it and to convince myself that it was better to carry on just like everyone else, but however much I tried I was unable to do so; I no longer found total satisfaction in my work as my colleagues did. Once you've tasted freedom, it is hard to put on the harness and blinkers again and pull along as usual. I just couldn't see myself going on like this until retirement. Did the life I was leading, comfortable as it might be, correspond to my deeper aspirations? Is this the great adventure of life, I thought, having to force my body and mind to do what I wouldn't dream of doing if I had the freedom to choose?

The contrast between the self-centred materialistic world in which we found ourselves and Africa couldn't have been greater. Here you rushed off to work in the morning with millions of others – not a minute to lose – and when you returned home in the evening you no longer had the drive to do anything constructive. In Africa, as we set off in the morning on our own, the world seemed infinite – it stretched all the way to the horizon and beyond, a world of serendipitous meetings, of welcomes in villages, of cordiality and discovery. Each moment was lived so intensely that there was no need for more. And we had time, a luxury that made days seem long and made us look forward to whatever came our way, to meeting others – and in Africa people are genuine, and we too were treated as real human beings.

And the evenings: cooking supper in the bush, camping out under a vast starry expanse with only a small circle of light in the darkness of the endless space around us. Then, months later, thousands of miles further on, at the end of this immense continent, the ocean … but reaching the ocean wasn't the aim. There was no aim; each day was sufficient unto itself. This was real life, timeless, eternal; a dream of youth where life was beating in all its strength; a world truer than anything we had known in Western civilization.

After travelling to remote places far out in the bush there was one thing I was absolutely certain about: despite its poverty and deprivations, Africa was a truly happy continent. I had heard more laughter in its harsh, hard deserts than in our civilised cities; I had seen more smiles and happy faces in less than a year there than I had in all the years before in the West.

Deep in my heart lies a space overflowing with the warmth of the sun, from which images spring up, images of gold-tanned faces, smiling yet shy; of Leila; of young Maasai girls…

Butterflies often fill this space with a whirlwind of colour, making my senses come alive with their ethereal beauty. Or sometimes at night thunder resounds, great streaks of lightning flash down to the muddy earth into which our feet have sunk and around us the red eyes of fiery warriors burn like flames until the chief raises his hand and we are led to his village – to safety – in the darkest of nights.

Then, at other times, a soft little hand slips into mine; or Leila's small son is sitting on my lap, in his eyes the trust of a young life; or a light bundle is pressed into my arms – a baby – a gift of trust from one woman to another.

There are fleeting images of proud men who have found a way of living in harmony with their harsh environment, of Turkana women moving gracefully over the golden sand, of laughter, dance and song, and of children running free …

Africa will always stay alive in my heart.

Africa is humanity's cradle, the continent we've all come from, and maybe we are still nomads at heart. Returning to the way humans had lived as they had wandered over the Earth for thousands of years – being able to go wherever we liked without fixed schedules and to live as we liked, asking permission neither from man nor God – had felt good. We had been responsible for our own fate and enjoyed the feeling of freedom and independence this had brought. It was in Africa that I felt in harmony with life.

Africa! Once it has caught you, its magic never lets you go. Like a loved one who is calling you, you long to go back to her. For months afterwards I dreamt of Africa. I wanted to return to its vastness, its light and freedom. At times I was gripped by such a longing for Africa that anyone who hasn't been there will find this difficult to understand. Africa! The glory of the mornings in the tropics, the luscious vegetation, the profusion of flowers, the cleansing feeling of the wind on your face, this sense of immense space, which no longer exists in overcrowded Europe. Western society appeared tame and grey in comparison. Where had the colour gone? Where were the smiles? Where was the warmth of human contact? The fun? The carefree living we all long for deep down?

I now saw Western consumer society in all its stark, naked selfishness and its futility struck me fully. Is there nothing more to our existence than making money and buying goods? I thought. Is this how we squander the incredible luck and privilege of having been given life? How we let our talents atrophy? How all our dreams and expectations are ground down into one long, dreary passage from birth to death?

I longed for a life worthy of the name, but how was this going to come about? If I waited for the modern world to adopt living conditions more in keeping with human nature, I would have to wait forever! I finally realised that if I wanted a different life, I would have to create it myself. So I swore that I would do whatever I could to break the ties that kept me enslaved, however much toil it would take.

Everything became easier after I had made this decision. I found that the uncertainty – not knowing what to do after our return to Europe – had been much worse than the hard work and struggle in the years afterwards. After all, life is what you make of it. You set yourself a goal, decide on your priorities and then go ahead. When your own capacities are your yardstick, when you aim to find out what these are and then see how far you can get, everything is within your power. The art is not to look around and make comparisons with what others do or have, not to let yourself be taken in by what modern society wants us to be: unthinking consumers who work to buy what they don't really need. And after Africa this was easy; we had learned to whittle down what we needed and to carry on whatever. I also fully realised how lucky we had been: before setting off on our mad, thrilling journey I would never have thought that this incredible adventure would ever happen to us, but it had! After this, how could I grumble about society or blame my condition on external forces?

Somehow I felt cheerful again. The smiles, the lightness, the happiness, the sunshine and bright colours of Africa had penetrated my heart and blown away the dark shadows that had begun to oppress me. Africa's carefreeness had rubbed off on me. Nothing seemed to matter any longer.

When I was young, I had sometimes wondered whether it wouldn't be best to die at forty. The novelty of life, the discoveries, the excitement, wouldn't they all be gone by then? Will there remain anything to learn after forty? I had asked myself. Surely, by that time, I'll know it all; I'll have seen it all; there will be nothing left of interest.

I was forty when we set off for Africa and the journey opened the door to wisdom, to looking upon our existence so differently from the way I had done before that it was like a revelation. Many years have passed since and life has been so full and varied that I wouldn't have believed it possible beforehand. I know now that it would have been a great shame to die at forty. Life doesn't end at forty. Maybe it begins at forty. If you want it to begin. If you really want it …